MAJOR POLITICAL EVENTS
IN SOUTH AFRICA
1948–1990

MAJOR POLITICAL EVENTS IN
SOUTH AFRICA
1948–1990

Eileen Riley

Facts On File
Oxford • New York

MAJOR POLITICAL EVENTS IN
SOUTH AFRICA 1948–1990
Series editor: Thomas S. Arms
Copyright © 1991 by Eileen Riley

Facts On File Limited   or
Collins Street
Oxford OX4 1XJ
UK

Facts On File, Inc.
460 Park Avenue South
New York NY10016
USA

A British CIP catalogue record for this book is available
from the British Library

Library of Congress Cataloging-in-Publication Data.

Riley, Eileen.
    Major political events in South Africa, 1948–1990 / Eileen Riley.
        p. cm. – (Major Political events series)
    Includes bibliographical references and index.
    ISBN 0–8160–2310–7
    1. South Africa – Politics and government – 1948- I. Title.
II. Series.
DT1945.R54 1991
968.05–dc20   90–22490
                                                           CIP

ISBN 0–8160–2310–7
Australian CIP data available on request from Facts On File

Facts On File books are available at special discounts when
purchased in bulk quantities for businesses, associations,
institutions or sales promotions. Please contact the
Special Sales Department of our Oxford office on
0865 728399 or our New York office on 212/683–2244
(dial 800/322–8755 except in NY, Ak or HI).

Jacket design by Richard Garratt
Typeset by Selectmove Ltd, London
Printed and bound in Great Britain by
Biddles Ltd, Guildford and King's Lynn

10 9 8 7 6 5 4 3 2 1

This book is printed on acid-free paper.

C O N T E N T S

For my Father
JAMES J. RILEY

INTRODUCTION

The First Europeans

The Portuguese explorer Bartholomew Diaz was the first European to discover the Cape of Good Hope as part of his search for a route to the riches of the East. Diaz landed on the shores of South Africa on 3 February 1488 and called the southernmost point of his explorations the Cape of Storms because of the terrible weather he encountered. But Portugal's King John II, with a keen sense of public relations, renamed it the Cape of Good Hope. Nine years later, Vasco da Gama made history when he rounded the Cape and carried on northwards eventually to reach India and return.

From then on, the Portuguese ignored the Cape, preferring to establish their South African settlements on the eastern and western coasts of the African continent in the areas that later became known as Angola and Mozambique. Slavery quickly became the economic staple of these settlements and it has been estimated that 100,000 African slaves were shipped out of the Angolan port of Luanda by the end of the sixteenth century.

The British were the next to arrive. The East India Company from 1601 began using the area now known as Table Bay as a regular half-way stop for provisions. In 1614 a group of British convicts was sent to Robben Island (later a prison for Black prisoners, including Nelson Mandela) to establish a provisioning station for the ships of the East India Company. But the half-hearted attempt at settlement soon ended in failure with the British convicts either dying of disease or fleeing to the mainland.

The first successful attempt at settlement was made by the rival Dutch East India Company. On 6 April 1652 a group of 125 men and four women landed at Table Bay and established the first permanent European settlement in South Africa. The Dutch and German settlers were led by Jan van Riebeeck and their purpose, like that of the British before them, was to provide supplies for the ships plying between Europe and the East Indies.

When van Riebeeck arrived he found the Cape area inhabited by the Khoi-Khoins (dubbed Hottentots) and, to a lesser extent, the Bushmen. The natives at first greeted them warmly. But within two years the warmth had evaporated and been replaced by open hostility. The root causes of this hostility were cattle and the land needed for grazing them.

Nomadic grazing and cattle stealing were a way of life for the Hottentots. But the early Cape settlers were determined to introduce a European order with neatly demarcated boundaries and laws against theft. Within five years, van Riebeeck was writing back to Amsterdam arguing that the only way to end the conflict between the Hottentots and settlers was to launch a full-scale attack against the Hottentots with the avowed aim of wiping them out and seizing their land and cattle. Eventually war did break out in May 1659 and it ended the following year in victory for van Riebeeck. As a result of the First Hottentot War, the settlers and natives signed a treaty drawing the first boundary between the European and African settlements.

At about the same time, the European settlement began to import slaves. Van Riebeeck had tried to force the Bushmen into either slavery or indentured labour, but they had refused to submit and found it easy to escape back to their tribal lands. So slaves were brought from Madagascar, Angola, India, Ceylon (now Sri Lanka) and Malaya. The Malays in particular came in great numbers and formed the core of the Cape Malay and Coloured communities. More Coloureds came as a result of mixed marriages between the Dutch and German settlers and the Hottentots. In the seventeenth century these links were encouraged by the Dutch East India Company.

The next major change in South Africa came in 1688 with the revocation of the Edict of Nantes by France's King Louis XIV. This led to the flight of thousands of French Hugenots, 300 of whom accepted an offer of free passage to the Cape settlement and a land grant by the Dutch East India Company. These French settlers were encouraged to intermingle with the existing Dutch and German colonists. The three groups eventually formed the ethnic and cultural base of the Afrikaners and their spoken languages merged into Afrikaner, although it did not replace High Dutch as the written language of the Afrikaners until the twentieth century.

Trouble with the Hottentots continued as the White settlement expanded beyond the borders negotiated by van Riebeeck. But a series of smallpox epidemics in the first half of the eighteenth century almost completely wiped out the Hottentots and destroyed their power to resist European expansion. The settlers were then faced with the Bushmen who continued the Hottentots' practice of cattle stealing. The colonial government responded with a reward for every Bushman captured or killed, thus making the eradication of the Bushmen official policy. The government were encouraged in this policy by the preachings of the local Dutch Reformed Church who branded the Bushmen as the 'children of Ham'. The church has ever since been in the forefront of the White supremacists and the protection of Afrikaner culture.

Up until the end of the seventeenth century the Cape settlement had been confined by the natural border of inland mountain ranges. But when these ranges were breached in the early eighteenth century, the settlers spread rapidly across the rolling grazing lands of the African veldt. These early frontiersmen were the first of the Afrikaner trekkers who pushed increasingly northwards, escaping the authority of the Cape settlement and leading the successive wars against Bushmen, Xhosa, Zulus, Matabeles and others. These hardy, independently minded, deeply religious and, at times, ruthless men and women became the cultural ancestors of the National Party.

The trekkers had little contact with the government in Cape Town and no relations at all with the powers in Amsterdam who were becoming critical of the Cape settlement's policies towards the African natives and the imported slaves. To protect their position, the settlers began to press for an increased say in the running of the colony's affairs. In 1795, the farmers of Graaff Reinet and Swellendam rebelled against the Dutch East India Company and established their own independent republics. In their independence declarations, they declared: 'Every Bushman and Hottentot . . . shall be lawful property of such burghers as may possess them and serve in bondage from generation to generation.'

But before the Dutch East India Company could put down the revolt, the British in 1795 landed at Cape Town. Thus began the history of the British presence in South Africa.

2

INTRODUCTION

The Start of British Colonial Rule

Early British colonial rule towards the non-White community was neither the enlightened liberalism spoken of by the current English-speaking South Africans or the blatant hypocrisy and repression of which the Afrikaners often accuse the British. Certainly, it is true that the British laid down some of the basic precepts of apartheid and, like the Afrikaners, were driven by the goal of maintaining White political supremacy. But the British efforts were directed mainly towards negotiation and compromise with the non-White community and were imbued with a spirit of British liberalism which conflicted with the Afrikaners' belief in their God-given right to govern South Africa and all of its inhabitants.

One of the first British proclamations was decidedly racist. It came in 1809 when the first British governor, the Earl of Caledon, decreed that the Hottentots and Bushmen had to work for White employers and introduced the first passbooks which prevented them from moving about without official permission. The British also allowed the continuing practice of raids on native settlements for the collection of 'apprentices'. These apprentices were effectively no more than slaves, or, at best, forced labourers. In 1812, it was decreed that Hottentot children born to apprentices were to remain with their White masters until they were eighteen.

These laws, however, were increasingly criticized in London and by English missionaries in South Africa, especially those belonging to the London Missionary society. The Anglican Church thus became an early supporter of African rights. At the church's urging, additional laws were passed prohibiting the ill-treatment of Hottentot servants. These were largely ignored by the Afrikaners and in 1815 a group of Hottentot policemen were sent to arrest one Afrikaner farmer charged with abusing a servant. He fired on the police and was killed. This led to a rebellion throughout the district and the public hanging of five more Afrikaner farmers at Slachter's Nek. The chain of events became an early and major cause of the conflict between the British and Boer communities.

The next major source of conflict was the British emancipation of the slaves in 1836. This was the final straw for many Afrikaners who resented the British attempts at trying to dictate the structure of their society. In 1837 whole families packed their belongings into covered wagons and trekked out of the Cape colony on the Great Trek into the northern interior, fleeing what they regarded as British oppression. These pioneers became the revered Voortrekkers.

The Voortrekkers established two republics, one in the Transvaal and the other in the Orange Free State. But the Boers fled into territories which at that time were being conquered by Xhosa and Zulus. On 16 December 1838, the Boers won a great victory over the Zulus at the Battle of Blood River when 3,000 Zulu warriors were killed and only three Boers wounded. Before the battle, the Boers had made a sacred covenant to commemorate the day every year if God granted them victory. The event is now a public holiday known as the Day of the Covenant and helps to strengthen the link between the Dutch Reformed Church and Afrikaner nationalism.

The Battle of Blood River led to the establishment of the Boer Republic of Natalia in what is now known as Natal. But the area had already been claimed by Britain and a small British trading post had been established at Durban. This led to an inevitable clash, and within a few years the Republic of Natalia ended as the Boers trekked back into the Transvaal. Britain at first continued to claim sovereignty over the two remaining Boer republics, but by 1854 had accepted their existence, thus dividing contemporary South Africa between the two British colonies of Natal and the Cape colony and the loosely linked Boer republics of the Transvaal and Orange Free State.

At the same time, the British, who continued to fight against the Xhosa on the edge of the Cape colony and the warlike Zulus in Natal, offered military protection to natives who were being threatened by continued Afrikaner expansion. This protection resulted in the establishment of the British protectorates of Swaziland, Basutoland (later Lesotho) and Bechuanaland (later Botswana). This further fuelled Afrikaner resentment and remained a bone of contention until the middle of the twentieth century.

The British versus the Boers

The nineteenth-century division of what is now South Africa might have continued to the present day if not for the discovery first of diamonds and then of gold. The diamonds were discovered in 1867 at Kimberley in Griqualand West and led to a dispute over ownership among the Boer republics, the British, and numerous Griqua and Tswana tribes. The dispute was ended in 1871 with the British annexation of Griqualand West.

In 1872, gold was discovered in the Lydenburg district of the Transvaal. The discovery brought great wealth to the Boer republic but it also brought a rush of gold miners from around the world. In 1877, the British unilaterally annexed the Transvaal, using the excuse of economic and political mismanagement and the failure of the Boer forces to control raiding Zulus. The Boer republic was indeed politically divided and badly managed and in no position to resist the British annexation, but by 1881, the forces of Afrikaner nationalism had united to launch a rebellion which ejected British colonial government.

In the subsequent treaty, however, the British retained an ill-defined sovereignty over the Transvaal while the Boers were allowed full internal government. This agreement satisfied neither the British imperialists nor the expansionist Boers and in the 1880s two men came to power who typified the extremes of both camps and pushed the two sides towards war.

Cecil Rhodes had left England for his health in 1870 and within a few years emerged as the diamond king of the world. He was a staunch British imperialist who dreamed of a British-controlled Cape-to-Cairo railway and a benign British imperial rule over the world. The Boer republics stood between Rhodes and his dreams of British territorial expansion.

S.J.P. Kruger was a devoutly religious Afrikaner who had participated in the Great Trek as a boy. After the British annexation of the Transvaal he led a delegation to London in a vain attempt to persuade the British government to reverse the move. In 1881 he led the Afrikaners in their rebellion against British rule and in 1882 was elected president and remained in that post until the end of the Boer republic in 1902.

In 1886, a second, and much larger, deposit of gold was struck in the Transvaal at Witwatersrand near the present site of Johannesburg. The result was a gold rush which dwarfed the earlier one of the 1870s. Prospectors from around the world, but mainly Britain, swarmed onto the gold reefs and by 1890 they comprised 70 per cent of the non-Black population of the Transvaal. Kruger had nothing but contempt for these miners and dubbed them 'uitlanders', or foreigners. He also refused to extend the political franchise to them, justifiably fearing that this would lead to a second British annexation.

In 1890, Rhodes was elected prime minister of the Cape colony and set about trying to extend British rule to the Transvaal. He and the British government repeatedly, but unsuccessfully, insisted that the uitlanders be allowed to vote. When Kruger remained obstinate, Rhodes offered him financial inducements out of his seemingly bottomless pocket. Kruger was invulnerable to such blandishments.

Rhodes decided that the only logical course still open was a rebellion by the uitlanders against Boer rule. With the support of the British colonial secretary Joseph Chamberlain he sent a 500-strong expeditionary force into the Transvaal under the command of his trusted lieutenant Leander Starr Jameson. The plan was that when the force reached the Transvaal, the uitlanders would rise up in rebellion and Kruger would be overthrown.

The Jameson Raid was launched on 29 December 1895 and ended in a fiasco for Rhodes. The uitlanders failed to rebel as planned; Jameson's force was quickly defeated and Jameson himself imprisoned. Official inquiries were held in Cape Town and London, and Rhodes was forced to resign not only from all of his public offices but from his corporate positions as well.

More important, however, was the ill-feeling that the secret plot engendered between the Afrikaner and British communities. Rhodes had carefully cultivated good relations with the Afrikaner community in the Cape colony, but after the Jameson Raid they turned their backs on Rhodes's vision of a benign British imperialism to associate themselves with the Afrikaner nationalism of Kruger.

The raid also hardened Afrikaner attitudes towards the uitlanders, and Kruger became more resolute in his refusal to extend them the vote. In April 1899 a mass petition signed by the uitlanders was sent to the British government asking for protection. Britain sent 10,000 troops from India and Egypt and on 11 October 1899 war was declared.

The following two and a half years of the Anglo-Boer War was one of the most unsavoury chapters in the history of British imperialism. Using guerrilla tactics, the small Boer fighting force of 35,000 men repeatedly defeated the superior numbers of the British empire. The British retaliated by burning farms, shipping prisoners of war to Ceylon and elsewhere and rounding up Boer women and children and herding them into concentration camps where 26,000 of them died of disease and starvation. In the end it took a British force of 500,000 men to defeat the Boers.

Colonial Whites versus the Blacks

The differences between the two White communities largely overshadowed the conflicts with the Black Africans, but they continued until after the Anglo-Boer War. In Natal, throughout the latter half of the nineteenth century, the British were engaged in fighting the Zulus, who battled not only against the British but also embarked on a campaign of conquest against the Boers and other African tribes. The first major Zulu chief was Dinigiswayo. He was followed by Shaka who united the Zulus under his banner and invented the brutal assegai spear. Shaka was succeeded by Dingaan who was defeated by the Boers at Blood River.

INTRODUCTION

The Battle of Blood River largely halted Zulu expansionism and allowed the British development of Natal while an independent Zululand was allowed to continue until 1877 when it was annexed by the British. The new Zulu chief, Cetawayo, was ordered to disband his army. He refused and in 1879 he marched on a British encampment at Isandlwana, killing 1,000 British troops. Flushed with success, 3,000 Zulus set out to drive the British from Natal but were held in check by a small garrison at the mission station of Rorke's Rift. Reinforcements were rushed from Cape Town, defeating the main Zulu force of 20,000 at Ulundi. This was the last major Zulu uprising. In 1906, there was a final uprising in response to the imposition of a poll tax. British troops were again called in from Cape Town and the uprising was swiftly and ruthlessly suppressed.

The other major South African tribe was the Xhosa. Their conflicts with the British stemmed mainly from the traditional and complementary sources of cattle and grazing land. In 1850 war broke out between the Xhosa and the British which eventually cost the British taxpayer £2 million and led to a 20-year lull in British expansionism in Southern Africa.

The Xhosa eventually destroyed their own power with an incredible act of religious self-destruction which stemmed from a dream by the chief witch doctor. In his dream, he saw the great Xhosa warriors of the past rising from the dead to drive the Whites out of Africa. To achieve this act, the counsellor called on the Xhosa to perform tremendous acts of self-sacrifice. They accordingly slaughtered all their cattle and destroyed their crops. The resultant famine led to the starvation of 30,000 Xhosa; the remainder were forced into the White settlements to seek food and work, transforming them overnight into the servant class of the White community. The Xhosa made one final stab at independence in an 1877 rebellion, but their power had already been broken; they were easily defeated and their remaining tribal lands were confiscated.

Another continuous source of conflict between the natives and both the Boer and British authorities was the Whites' determination to exploit the Blacks as a servant class, even against their will. The early nineteenth-century laws introducing passbooks and *de facto* forced labour were built upon and refined with a series of bills known as the Master and Servants Acts. These laid out the relationship between White employers and Black servants and allowed, among other things, flogging for 'disobedience', 'impertinence' or 'neglect of duty'. These acts remain in force to the present day.

In the seventeenth century, the Black determination to avoid forced labour led the Afrikaners to import Malay slaves. In the nineteenth century, it led the British to import indentured servants from India to work as farm labourers on the sugar plantations of Natal. By the end of the nineteenth century there were 100,000 Indians in the Natal province. They provided the core of yet another South African ethnic group.

The Union of South Africa

The Anglo-Boer War was followed by an eight-year period of reconstruction in the two Boer republics. The British were generous in providing aid to rebuild the Boer farms and the national infrastructure. This won the support of some of the Boer generals, most notably Louis Botha and Jan Christiaan Smuts, who became enthusiastic disciples of British imperialism. Self-government was also granted to the two republics, but this time it was under a carefully defined British suzerainty which suppressed the Afrikaner language and culture.

By the end of the first decade, it had become clear to all the constituent parts of the British empire in southern Africa that their future lay as a single political unit. Starting in 1908, the republics of the Transvaal and the Orange Free State and the colonies of Natal and the Cape held a series of meetings to discuss political union. Also attending as observers were representatives of the British protectorates of Bechuanaland, Basutoland and Swaziland and the colony of Rhodesia. The result was the South Africa Act of 1910 which brought together the two Boer republics and Natal and the Cape colony into the self-governing Union of South Africa. The act also allowed for the later extension of the Union to include Rhodesia and the three British protectorates. In 1922 the White voters of Rhodesia narrowly voted to stay out of the Union of South Africa. The British respected the wishes of the ruling African governments in the three protectorates and refused to allow them to be absorbed into the Union after apartheid was formally introduced in 1948. In the 1960s they were granted independence as separate sovereign African states.

The main discussion points at the constitutional assemblies that led to the 1910 South Africa Act were the Union's relationship with Britain, the language and racial issues. The majority of White South Africans, English and Boer alike, had accepted British dominance and favoured a continuing link with the British Crown and dominion status within the British Commonwealth. A vocal Afrikaner minority, however, continued to fight for the establishment of a republic completely independent of Britain. This group became the central core of the future National Party and the struggle for a republic remained a central feature of Afrikaner nationalism until it was finally achieved in 1961.

Language was expected to be a major issue as the British high commissioner after the Anglo-Boer War, Lord Milner, had outlawed the speaking of Afrikaans in the hope that this would dampen Afrikaner nationalism. But by 1908 this had been accepted as a retroactive policy and English and Afrikaans were accepted as the two official spoken languages. High Dutch and English were the two official written languages as there was no Afrikaans dictionary until 1930.

The most divisive issue of the conferences was race. This was because each of the four constituent states had widely differing policies and race laws. The most restrictive laws were found in the Boer republics where there was simply no question of any political rights for the Black majority or any non-White racial group. But in both the Cape colony and Natal there had been a long-standing limited franchise for Africans, Indians and Coloureds, although the property and educational restrictions placed on Africans meant that virtually none qualified in Natal and only 6,637 (a mere 4.7 per cent of the electorate) in the more liberal Cape colony.

However, the Cape colony prided itself on its relatively liberal race policies and its delegates to the constitutional assembly were determined to extend the qualified franchise to Africans, Indians and Coloureds throughout the Union. The Boers, and the Natal delegates, were as determined to keep non-Whites off their voting register. The result was a compromise which allowed the Cape to keep its voting arrangements but for only Whites to be elected to Parliament. There was a further proviso that the voting laws could be altered with the support of two-thirds of the parliament. The result was that the Africans lost the right to vote in 1936 and the Coloureds were struck off the common voters' roll in 1956.

INTRODUCTION

It would be wrong to say that the English-speaking community wanted to hand over political power to the native Africans while the Boers waged a ruthless war of antediluvian racial discrimination. Both groups and all major political parties pursued a policy of White supremacy but they both did so from the perspective of their own historical experience. The tiny Afrikaner community had fought a long rearguard action against the overwhelming British presence and feared that further dilution of their political power would result in the complete disappearance of Afrikanerdom. The British culture, on the other hand, was in the ascendant around the world and it developed a policy of expansion through the assimilation of native cultures into the British system. It confidently expected to do the same with the native communities of South Africa. The issue then was not *whether* to maintain White supremacy, but *how* this was to be achieved and maintained.

The native Africans took little or no part in the debate over their country and their political rights. They were either consciously excluded by the Boers or deemed educationally inferior for the time being by the Cape Whites. In 1912 the African National Congress (ANC) was founded by the Union's handful of well-educated middle-class Blacks to press for nonradical change. The ANC's moderate programme had little impact until a Youth League was founded by the activist-minded Nelson Mandela, Walter Sisulu and Oliver Tambo. They gained complete control of the ANC in 1949 and launched a campaign of massive civil disobedience which eventually led to the banning of the ANC in 1960. Driven underground, the ANC formed a military wing, Umkhonto we Sizwe (Spear of the Nation) which launched a series of terrorist attacks.

The years after 1910 (when the South Africa Act was passed) set the political scene for the establishment of the National Party by the government in 1948. The first election, held in 1911, was won by a generally pro-British alliance led by Louis Botha and Jan Christian Smuts. But a controversial note was struck by ascending Afrikaner J.B. Hertzog who insisted that the English and Afrikaner groups retain their separate identities in a 'two-stream' policy. Hertzog's ideas – which were later extended to include (or rather exclude) the native African community, Coloureds and Indians – became the intellectual base for apartheid. Hertzog was taken into the first cabinet of Prime Minister Botha, but his Afrikaner nationalist views forced Botha to drop him in 1912. Two years later, Hertzog formed the National Party. Botha's coalition, had, in the meantime, formed itself into the South Africa Party.

During the First World War, the British asked the South African government to occupy German South West Africa (later Namibia). Despite the objections of a large section of the Afrikaner community, an expeditionary force was sent to South West Africa under Smuts. It was successful, and after the war the League of Nations awarded South Africa the mandate to govern South West Africa.

Botha died in 1919 and was succeeded by Smuts, who had been accepted by the British establishment as a leading figure in the British Empire and Commonwealth. To many Afrikaners, he was a traitor to the cause of Afrikanerdom, and he just barely managed to hold on to power in the elections of 1920 and 1921. In April 1924 he lost power to a coalition headed by Hertzog. The result was a renewed upsurge in Afrikaner nationalism. A South African flag was adopted and 'Die Stem van Suid-Afrika' was placed on equal footing with 'God Save the King' as South Africa's national anthem. Hertzog also successfully pressed the British to accept the equality of the dominions and the right of countries to secede from the Commonwealth, but he disappointed his more radical supporters when he refused to press for the immediate establishment of a republic.

Economic problems forced Hertzog into a national government with Smuts in February 1933, but the Afrikaner nationalist retained the position of prime minister. In protest, the right-wing Dr Daniel Malan left the National Party to form the Purified National Party which later replaced Hertzog's creation and won the historic election of 1948.

The 1930s also saw a revival of Afrikaner culture which reached its peak with a re-enactment of the Great Trek in 1938 and the centenary celebrations to mark the victory of the Battle of Blood River. The twentieth-century trekkers set out from around the country and merged on a hill outside Pretoria where a monument to the Voortrekkers was dedicated in a festival of Afrikaner nationalism.

Hertzog and Smuts split over the issue of supporting Britain during the Second World War. Smuts continued to pursue a determined pro-British policy while Hertzog, mindful of the continuing anti-British sentiments of his Afrikaner political base, refused to enter the war unless South Africa's national interests were directly threatened. Smuts forced the issue on to the floor of Parliament where the House of Assembly voted in favour of war by a narrow majority of 80 to 67.

Smuts emerged from the war covered in international laurels. During the war, he went to London where he was made a field marshal and became a trusted adviser to Winston Churchill. South African forces also served with distinction in battles around the world. But within South Africa, there was a large Afrikaner minority who not only opposed South African involvement but admired Nazi Germany's racial policies and launched terrorist attacks against British targets. Most of these Afrikaners gathered under the banner of the Ossewabrandwag (Ox-wagon Guard). One of its leaders was John Vorster, who later became prime minister. His activities led the authorities to intern him during the war.

During the war Smuts had participated in the international discussions for the postwar world order. The discussions on human rights that surrounded the 1941 Atlantic Charter, and the 1945 San Francisco conference which founded the UN, convinced Smuts that a political formula had to be found to accommodate the political ambitions of South Africa's non-Whites. Between 1943 and 1948 he made a series of tentative steps in that direction when he extended indirect parliamentary representation to Indians and unemployment insurance to native Africans and advocated recognition of Black trade unions.

These moves only served to frighten the White Afrikaner community into believing that their cultural identity would be swallowed up by the even more alien Black society. In November 1942, Hertzog died, leaving Malan and the Purified National Party as his *de facto* political heirs. Using the fear of the 'Black Menace', Malan managed to win the support of the Afrikaner Party, led by Nicolaas Havenga, and he defeated Smuts in the elections of 26 May 1948.

This book details chronologically the major political events during the critical period of South Africa's history from 1948 until the release of Nelson Mandela on 11 February 1990.

16 January In his reply to the King's Speech, leader of the Opposition Daniel F. Malan introduces a motion to have the representation of Indians in Parliament and the Native Representative Councils abolished and replaced with tribally based local executive bodies. Malan was defeated by 87 votes to 44, but the debate did have an important side effect in that it led to the virtual collapse of the South African Party, formerly the Dominion Party.

6 February The South African parliament votes to loan $320 million in gold to Britain. Britain had announced on 2 February that it had sold another $106 million worth of gold in January in order to obtain dollars.

On 11 February, the South African Reserve Bank announced that facilities for the forward sale of foreign exchange to cover the purchase of consumer goods by South African importers would be available only in special cases. This was the first official sign of the financial crisis that was to come in the later part of the year.

1 March The Fagan Commission reports that it is impossible entirely to separate Whites and Blacks since the country needs both groups. The Commission concluded that the Black housing problem was national not municipal. It was the national government's responsibility to house all Blacks with a legitimate right to live in the cities and should do so.

The report was endorsed in principle by Prime Minister Jan Christiaan Smuts's United Party while rejected by the National Party of Daniel Malan.

26 May The Reunited National Party and Afrikaner Party coalition win a surprise victory over the United Party of Smuts. The 1948 electoral victory provided National Party leader Malan with the mandate he needed to introduce South Africa's apartheid policies.

The main election issue was the question of White supremacy in South Africa, a position that the Nationalists pledged to uphold. The National Party argued that any racial integration would result in the loss of White domination and pledged to introduce their system of apartheid, which literally means separateness and calls for the strict separation of the races. Many White South Africans feared that their dominant position in South Africa was being eroded by Smuts's United Party; as evidence the Nationalists pointed to such government legislation as the indirect parliamentary representation for the Indian community, the extension of unemployment benefits to Blacks and the *de facto* recognition given to Black trade unions.

As a result of the election, the National Party won 70 seats, its coalition partner the Afrikaner Party nine seats, the United Party 65 seats and its Labour Party partners six seats. The National Party–Afrikaner Party coalition, therefore, obtained a total of 79 parliamentary seats as opposed to the United Party–Labour Party coalition's 71 seats but polled a minority of the total number of votes cast. The vote represented an unprecedented swing of 25 seats but left the National Party with only a meagre majority.

Smuts lost his own seat in Standerton, Transvaal. It was a bitter blow for a man who had been in power continually since 1910. He resigned as prime minister on 28 May and announced his retirement from public life. He reconsidered his decision and on 1 June agreed to contest the Pretoria East by-election which came about when a United Party Member of Parliament, C.W. Clark, vacated his safe seat for him. He returned to Parliament as leader of the Opposition.

4 June Daniel François Malan is sworn in as prime minister by the governor general. He took an oath of allegiance to King George VI, but made it clear that South Africa would not tolerate any 'external' interference 'in our domestic affairs'.

Under its apartheid philosophy, the new government envisaged South Africa as being strictly divided into White and Black areas. It would allow into the White areas only those Blacks needed as labourers. All other Blacks would be returned to reserves set aside for them. The government said that in these areas Blacks would be encouraged to develop along their own lines and would be able to participate fully in the political and economic life of the reserves. The government described apartheid as a policy of 'separate but equal' and said it was needed to ensure that the White race remained pure. It would enforce this separation by enacting laws to regulate the interaction of the races.

4 June South Africa tells the UN Trusteeship Council that it feels under no obligation to account to the UN for its administration of South West Africa.

10 June As one of the first acts in the implementation of its apartheid policy, the Nationalist government repeals the not-yet-proclaimed Chapter 2 of the Asiatic Land Tenure and Indian Representation Act of 1946. The act had granted Transvaal and Natal Indians the right to elect Whites to represent them in Parliament and for Natal Indians to represent themselves in the National Provincial Council.

14 June Minister of Labour Barend J. Shoeman announces, as 'one of the first official acts', that the training of Blacks as artisans is to stop immediately. The former government's bill to recognize native trade unions would be dropped but he said that 'steps would be taken to protect native workers from exploitation and to ensure that any genuine grievances on their part would be brought to the attention of the authorities'.

18 June In another important decision that showed the new government's orientation, the ban on civil servants becoming members of the Ossewabrandwag and Broederbond was lifted. The Ossewabrandwag (literally, 'Ox-wagon Guard') was founded in 1939 as a society to protect and foster the cultural, religious and material needs of the Afrikaners, but it soon took on military overtones. The Broederbond (Band of Brothers) is a secret Afrikaner society that was formed in 1918 to promote Afrikanerdom. In banning public servants from belonging to it in 1944, Smuts described the Broederbond as a secret Fascist organization.

9 July The administrator of South West Africa announces that he will convene a conference of National Party and Union Party supporters in South West Africa to prepare parliamentary proposals on the question of South West African representation in the Union parliament.

Prime Minister Malan announced on 21 October an agreement on the administration of South West Africa as an 'integral part of the Union'. The main points of the agreement were: South West Africa would be represented in South Africa's House of Assembly by six members elected by Europeans and in the Senate by one senator elected by the South West African Legislature and South West African senators in the same way that the South African Senate was elected, and would have one senator appointed by the governor general to represent non-Whites; the governor general would appoint as chief executive an administrator for South West Africa who would have a five-year term of office; and South West Africa would have a Legislative Assembly with 18 members elected by the European electorate and six appointed for a five-year term of office by the governor general. Malan said that there was 'absolutely no question of extending the franchise to non-Europeans'.

29 July Elections are held for the upper house of Parliament, the Senate. The opposition wins a one-seat majority. The Senate on its own had minimal political power, but a two-thirds majority of both houses of Parliament was needed to change or abolish entrenched constitutional clauses such as the vote for the Indian and Coloured communities.

9 August Finance Minister Nicolaas Havenga unveils the new government's first budget, which includes a 300 per cent spending increase over the next ten years. Havenga also stressed that the government intended to remain inside the sterling area.

19 August Defence Minister François C. Erasmus announces a ban on all military training for non-Whites. The members of the Cape Corps and the Native Military Corps were invited to join the Essential Services Protection Corps but would not be allowed to wear any military insignia, carry weapons or receive military training.

16 September Interior Minister Theophilus E. Donges announces government plans to appoint a commission to study Indian occupation and ownership of property in the Cape. Any laws which came into effect as a result of the commission's findings were to be retrospective.

In a meeting with representatives from the South African Indian Organization on 26 November, Donges reiterated the government's view that the South African Indian population should be reduced to an 'irreducible minimum'. He said that repatriation would be conducted in a 'friendly way with the assistance of the governments concerned' and that those repatriated would be fully compensated for the move. Indian leaders said that all Indians in South Africa were South African nationals and that any government attempts to remove them to another country would be 'against all legal and moral ethics of a civilized country'.

17 September Prime Minister Malan introduces the Asiatic Laws Amendment Bill into Parliament. The bill repealed Chapter 2 of the Asiatic Land Tenure and Indian Representation Act, passed by the Smuts government in 1946 in the face of fierce Nationalist opposition to allow the representation of Transvaal and Natal Indians in Parliament and Natal Indians in the Natal Provincial Council.

During the bill's second reading on 22 September, Malan said that the representation of some 250,000 Indians as allowed in the original act would result in increased demands by the other non-White groups for representation themselves. He maintained that the Indians in South Africa were not permanent residents and not entitled to participate in the country's political affairs.

2 November The National Party federal council meets and adopts a resolution calling for the unification of the Reunited National and Afrikaner Parties into the 'National Party'. It called the merger 'essential in view of the difficult task ahead of the Government'.

Afrikaner Party leader Nicolaas Havenga stated on 9 November that he felt it would 'be unwise and undesirable to force the matter because the necessary good feeling and faith obviously do not yet exist'. National Party leader and prime minister Malan replied on 12 November that he agreed with 'deep disappointment and a measure of anxiety' with Havenga's statement and that a merger was not on the agenda for the present, but added that he hoped it could be attained within a 'measurable space of time'.

5 November The government issues regulations limiting the amount of money which can be spent on importing goods from both the sterling and dollar areas. The importation of certain classes of goods was completely banned.

17 November Prime Minister Malan, speaking at the Transvaal National Party Congress, calls for the speedy incorporation of the British protectorates of Basutoland (now Lesotho), Bechuanaland (now Botswana) and Swaziland into the Union of South Africa. He reminded the meeting that provision for the incorporation of the protectorates had been made under the South Africa Act but that movement towards this end had not been made since 1910.

Malan said that the British government now contended that the protectorates could not be incorporated into South Africa without the approval of their native populations. Malan maintained that the consent of the native peoples was not a condition of the South Africa Act and that the only thing needed for incorporation was the consent of the British government.

19 November The UN Trusteeship Committee urges the General Assembly to insist that South Africa submit a trusteeship plan for South West Africa. On 8 November, South Africa once again told the Trusteeship Council that it would not abide by a 1947 UN General Assembly decision to place South West Africa under the Council's control.

The General Assembly voted on 26 November to adopt a compromise resolution expressing 'regret' that South Africa had failed to present a trusteeship plan for South West Africa and asking South Africa to continue reporting on its administration of the area while the Trusteeship Council continued its effort to promote an agreement on South West Africa's future. The Assembly also passed a resolution that South West Africa be placed under the trusteeship of the UN.

3 December John Hendrick Hofmeyr, the former deputy prime minister and successor-designate to Jan Christiaan Smuts as leader of the United Party, dies after a short illness. Hofmeyr had led the movement for greater tolerance towards and sympathy with black aspirations. He came under heavy attack during the May general election from Nationalist supporters who thought he was too liberal on the race issue. His death at the age of 54 left the United Party without a clear successor to the elderly General Smuts.

17 December The governor of the South African Reserve Bank, M.H. de Kock, announces that he has asked commercial banks to cut back on issuing credit facilities. He also said that the government did not feel that unilateral devaluation of the currency would offer any real solution to the country's monetary problems.

South Africa was facing a financial crisis because, like many other nations, it was running short of the dollars needed to finance its importation of many goods and services. Gold was the main export by which South Africa could obtain dollars. The problem was that the International Monetary Fund had set a strict limit on the price at which gold could be sold but the cost of producing the gold kept rising steadily. The result was that South Africa would have to sell more and more gold in order to make the same number of dollars, thus depleting its gold reserves. By the end of 1948, South Africans were spending more money in a week on foreign imports than its gold mines were producing in a month.

15 January Prime Minister Daniel F. Malan announces that his government has decided not to proceed that year with plans to disenfranchise the Cape Coloureds.

Malan and his National Party held that it was possible to amend the constitution and disenfranchise the Cape Coloureds by a simple majority vote in Parliament. Afrikaner Party leader Nicolaas C. Havenga, Malan's colleague in the coalition government, disagreed and maintained that two-thirds of both houses of Parliament were required to make such a change. He refused to change his position and forced Malan to postpone the legislation.

16 January Four days of race riots between Zulus and Indians end in Durban. Race riots also took place in the Rand mining area of the Transvaal. The rioting, described as one of the most horrific racial incidents in South African history, resulted in 142 people dead and 1,087 injured. A factory, 58 stores and 247 homes were also destroyed. A commission of inquiry blamed the riots on slum conditions, tension and foreign criticism of South Africa's racial laws.

The riots began on 13 January after rumours began to circulate that an Indian merchant had killed a Black boy during an incident in the Indian market. The Zulus began to 'revolt' against the alleged mistreatment of Blacks by Indians and small-scale sporadic rioting began. Peace was restored in Durban on 16 January but rioting then broke out in the Transvaal.

7 February Finance Minister Havenga announces a proposed government experiment to sell a set amount of semi-processed gold bullion to a London firm for resale to a restricted market. On 8 February, the International Monetary Fund announced that it had approved the sale of 100,000 ounces of 22 carat gold at $38.20 an ounce, equivalent to a $3.20 premium, by South Africa in London on the strict condition that it be used only for industrial or professional purposes. Havenga said that the sale was needed because of 'pressing foreign exchange difficulties' and to encourage gold production.

24 February Prime Minister Malan announces that South Africa will stop sending the UN reports on South West Africa. In July, the government reiterated its position, saying that the submission of reports had provided the Trusteeship Council and Commission with 'a forum for criticism and censure of South Africa'.

4 March Economic Minister Eric Louw announces that imports from the sterling area will be severely curtailed. The measure was necessary because the drain on South Africa's sterling reserves had become acute in addition to its lack of dollars. Louw did not expect the consumer to be immediately affected since there was a large stockpile of sterling goods. He released a list of goods banned as non-essential and said the government would ensure that prices of goods in stock would be controlled. The South African commercial world opposed the measures but South African manufacturers saw it as a great opportunity to expand their industries.

Further import restrictions on sterling goods were announced on 23 May by Acting Minister of Economic Affairs Theophilus E. Donges. These restrictions took effect from 1 July and resulted in a 'beat the ban' campaign as British manufacturers and carriers madly rushed to fill South African orders before the restrictions came into effect.

9 March Elections are held for the four provincial councils and result in the National Party winning 86 seats to the United Party's 78 seats.

The elections were the first test of government strength since the 1948 general election. They also had a national importance because, in the South African system, a proportion of senators are elected by the provincial councils. The government, therefore, saw these elections as an important opportunity to increase their power in the Senate, in which the Opposition held a small majority.

The government obtained a small majority of seats but had an overall minority of votes, while the United Party, which ran candidates unopposed in a large number of constituencies, again emerged as the single strongest party. Malan, however, announced that he considered the election results a mandate for apartheid.

16 March Finance Minister Havenga introduces the budget amidst worsening economic conditions. Although the actual budgetary measures were fairly mild, he warned that difficult days were ahead and that the task confronting South Africa would not be easy. He announced that government spending would be slashed and that strict economies would also have to be made in the industrial and commercial spheres.

11 April The South West Africa Affairs (Amendment) Bill passes Parliament. It closely followed an October 1948 agreement between Prime Minister Malan and representatives of the National and United parties in South West Africa. It provided the territory with direct representation in the South African parliament and was seen as a step towards incorporating the area into the Union.

The amendment called for six elected representatives in the House of Assembly and for four senators. Two of the senators were to be elected and two nominated, one of them on the basis of his special knowledge of native affairs. South West Africa was to retain its autonomy in financial affairs.

The measure was opposed inside and outside South Africa. Opposition leaders protested that the bill would result in an over-representation of South West African voters in Parliament. The UN rejected Malan's claims that the bill was designed to associate the territory more closely with rather than incorporate it into South Africa.

21 April The conference of Commonwealth prime ministers opens in London and ends with the issuance on 27 April of the London Declaration, by which India was allowed to continue as a full member of the Commonwealth of Nations as an independent sovereign nation.

India's request to remain in the Commonwealth after becoming a republic had posed a difficult constitutional problem for the Commonwealth. It was solved by India accepting the British king as 'the symbol of the free association of its independent member nations, and as such the Head of the Commonwealth'.

Prime Minister Malan welcomed the settlement and said that South Africa's continuing membership in the Commonwealth was now assured either as a republic or on the existing basis. His National Party had been committed to the principle of a republican South Africa since 1941. In an interview after the conference closed Malan said: 'These sister nations are sovereign independent States freely associated with one another, and so long as there is no infringement of her rights – even her right to become a republic – South Africa has no intention of leaving the Commonwealth.'

14 May The UN passes a resolution calling for a round table discussion of South Africa's treatment of its Indian population. South Africa, in opposing the measure, contended that the problem was an internal matter and not the UN's concern.

29 June The Nationalist government introduces one of its first major pieces of apartheid legislation – the Prohibition of Mixed Marriages Act. The act imposed a ban on marriages between Whites and non-Whites and nullified mixed marriages entered into by South Africans abroad.

The law imposed a ban on all mixed marriages, although there were probably less than one hundred a year throughout the country. It was seen as an important part of the government's policy of enforcing a separation of the races in all areas of life, and as part of the government's attempt to obtain its stated aim of eliminating 'points of friction between the races'.

13 July The first ever meeting of Commonwealth finance ministers discusses the recent fall in the level of dollars and gold in the sterling area, and agree on recommendations for immediate measures to be taken to check the continuing heavy drain on the sterling area's central reserves.

The ministers believed that emergency measures to stem the drain would be counterproductive and instead proposed the establishment of a pattern of world trade in which both dollar and non-dollar nations could coexist within a single multilateral system. They agreed to work towards that goal and to meet representatives from the US to consider ways of creating such a trade pattern. The British chancellor of the exchequer, Sir Stafford Cripps, called the meeting 'one of the most successful Commonwealth conferences ever held'.

2 September The controversial and divisive South African Citizenship Act takes effect. Under the terms of the act, South Africa renounced common citizenship arrangements existing among members of the Commonwealth and suspended the automatic granting of citizenship to immigrants from the member nations.

Citizenship by registration caused the greatest controversy as it affected recent immigrants. The interior minister reserved the right to grant or withhold citizenship without recourse to the courts. A certificate of citizenship would be granted to a person who had passed a still undefined test on the rights and responsibilities of citizenship.

The Opposition bitterly attacked the bill and organized a nationwide campaign against it. In spite of this, the bill was passed with only minor changes.

15 September The US agrees to a South African proposal that the International Monetary Fund study problems related to the price of gold. But, US Treasury Secretary John Snyder said there was no possibility that the US would raise its $35-an-ounce price for gold and let gold-selling countries earn more dollars in that manner. South African Finance Minister Havenga had put forward a plan that called for half of the world's newly mined gold to be sold at $35 an ounce and the rest to sell for whatever it could on the 'free market'.

18 September South Africa, along with 22 other countries, follows Britain's example and devalues its currency. The new value of the pound was $2.80 as opposed to the previous price of $4.03.

Theophilus E. Donges, acting minister of finance during Nicolaas Havenga's visit to the US, explained the government's reasoning the following day. He said that South Africa faced serious balance of payments difficulties because the cost of imported goods had doubled while the price of its main export, gold, had remained the same. The country, he said, had been buying foreign consumer goods at an extravagant rate in addition to the capital goods needed for industry. The full extent of the problem had been hidden by a much larger than usual influx of capital from Britain in 1947. A drop in foreign investment in South Africa had finally resulted in a balance of payments deficit of such proportions that South Africa might have had to devalue its pound unilaterally.

The immediate result of the devaluation was a rise in the price of gold from £8 12s 3d to £12 10s. Mines that were faced with closure had a new lease of life and profits rose. Salaried workers, however, found that the cost of living had also risen and did not benefit from the devaluation.

29 November The UN Trusteeship Committee passes a resolution to seek advice from the International Court of Justice on whether South Africa can absorb South West Africa in defiance of a UN decision to place it under a trusteeship.

On 6 December, the UN General Assembly voted to ask the International Court of Justice for an advisory opinion on whether the UN, South Africa or some third party had legal sovereignty over South West Africa. The resolution was opposed by South Africa, the Soviet bloc (who were against involving the International Court of Justice in the matter) and Liberia (who was opposed to conceding any question of the UN's right to assume trusteeship over South West Africa). The General Assembly asked for the fourth consecutive year that South Africa submit a trusteeship plan for the territory. It also requested South Africa report to the UN on current South West African affairs.

16 December The Voortrekker Monument, the Afrikaners' most important shrine, is opened with great fanfare and national rejoicing on the anniversary of their greatest national holiday, the Day of the Covenant. The holiday commemorates the Battle of Blood River at which the Afrikaners defeated the Zulu army under Chief Dingaan in 1838 and vowed that if God granted them victory, they and their descendants would commemorate the day every year.

The monument is a massive memorial standing on a hill outside Pretoria and was designed as a testimonial to the Afrikaner pioneers, called Voortrekkers, who rejected British rule in the Cape and journeyed into the unknown to form their own two republics in 1838.

The Voortrekker monument was opened by Prime Minister Malan in 1949 before the largest crowd ever assembled in South Africa. Thousands of people came from all over the country to participate in the four-day Afrikaner cultural festival that preceded the opening ceremonies. There were fears that the festival would exacerbate racial unrest but they turned out to be unfounded and the opening ceremony was described as one of the happiest events in South African history.

---

1 9 5 0

---

31 January Interior Minister Theophilus E. Donges announces the establishment of a commission of inquiry into the South African press. The move followed strong criticisms of the South African English-language press and foreign correspondents by Minister of Defence François C. Erasmus.

Erasmus had said that although the conditions of Blacks in South Africa were better than anywhere else in the world, the country had come under a ferocious attack by the press and that a slanderous campaign was under way which was misleading people abroad and at home about South Africa. The Opposition, while not opposing an inquiry, felt that the establishment of a commission would create the impression that the government was trying to 'muzzle' the press. It suggested instead setting up a meeting with the leading English-speaking editors.

6 February A 12-day exploratory meeting between South Africa, India and Pakistan on the treatment of South African Indians opens in Cape Town. A final communiqué described the meeting as having been held 'in a cordial and sympathetic atmosphere' and 'animated by a sincere desire to restore and develop friendly relations between the three countries'. It was agreed to convene a round table conference 'to explore all possible ways and means of settling the Indian question in South Africa'. The time and place of the round table meeting was later set for 6 June but it never took place after South Africa and India fell out over the introduction of the Group Areas Act (see 7 July).

India referred the matter to the UN General Assembly which, after a long and bitter debate in November and December, passed a resolution calling for a round table meeting between South Africa, India and Pakistan. They requested South Africa to rescind the Group Areas Act until after the meeting, but South Africa responded by condemning the UN's 'interference in the domestic affairs of a member state'.

3 April The South African Treasury announces that all future exports of rough or cut diamonds, except to Britain, will have to be paid for in US dollars. Any non-dollar sale would contravene the exchange control regulations and would make the exporter liable for a substantial penalty. The measure was directed against middlemen who had been paying for the diamonds in 'cheap sterling' or other soft currencies and then reselling them to markets in the US. This practice deprived South Africa of considerable amounts of much-needed dollars.

13 April Prime Minister Malan announces in Parliament that his government proposes to resume negotiations with Britain on the future of the British protectorates of Basutoland (now Lesotho), Bechuanaland (now Botswana) and Swaziland. Negotiations had been broken off by the outbreak of the Second World War but Malan had told his 1948 National Party Congress that he was 'just waiting for the appropriate moment to make representations to the British authorities for the incorporation into the Union of the British Protectorates'.

While speaking to the Senate on 4 May, Malan reiterated his determination to have the protectorates incorporated into the Union and said that if movement towards that end was not forthcoming, South Africa would have to regard the areas as 'foreign territories administered by an outside Power'.

25 April Prime Minister Malan announces that the bill abolishing the right of appeal from the South African Appeal Court to the Judicial Committee of the British Privy Council has been signed into law by King George VI. The government had held that appealing to the British tribunal, whose members were appointed exclusively by the British government, was not in keeping with South Africa's sovereign, independent status. Severing the link with the Privy Council was seen as removing one of the last remnants of the imperial relationship.

The South Africa Act of 1909, which served as the country's constitution until it became a republic in 1961, established a South African Supreme Court, made up of an appellate division and four provincial divisions. It allowed appeals from the appellate division to the Privy Council, the British monarch's private council, and made the Privy Council South Africa's highest court of appeal. Although there had been numerous leaves to appeal to the Privy Council since 1909, only ten appeals were actually referred to London and only one had been successful.

3 May The International Monetary Fund rejects a South African proposal that half of all the world's newly mined gold be sold to the highest bidder instead of at the present $35-an-ounce ceiling price.

Finance Minister Havenga had submitted the plan during his September 1948 visit to the US. On 5 May, the government announced that it would not be bound by the International Monetary Fund's $35-an-ounce price limit for gold.

12 May The Immorality Amendment Act becomes law. The Act, making sexual relations between Whites and Cape Coloureds illegal, amended a 1927 Immorality Act prohibiting intercourse between Whites and Blacks. It meant that relations between Whites and all non-Whites were imprisonable offences and was considered one of the cornerstones of the apartheid legislation.

In introducing the bill into Parliament on 1 March, Justice Minister Charles R. Swart said that the purpose of the bill was to end the further mixing of blood between Whites and non-Whites so that the dimensions of the race problem would not be any more serious in the future than it was at present. The Opposition described the bill as 'evil' and compared it to Nazi race laws.

16 May The House of Assembly passes the Population Registration Act, considered to be one of the cornerstones of apartheid legislation. It enabled the government to classify the entire population according to racial origin and was the first step in the separation of the races.

Interior Minister Donges introduced the act in the House of Assembly on 20 February. It required all adults to be entered on a central register and to provide information on their name, sex, date and place of birth, population group, address, electoral division and polling district, date of registration or naturalization as a citizen, date of arrival in South Africa if not born there, marital status, occupation, language group and, for the deceased, the date and place of death. Blacks were also required to provide information on their tribal group. Every person would then be classified as either White, native or Coloured.

White was defined as anyone 'who in appearance obviously is, or is generally accepted as a White person, but does not include a person who, although in appearance a White person, is generally accepted as a Coloured person'. Whites were subdivided into citizens, permanent resident aliens and temporary residents.

Natives were anyone who 'is in fact or is generally accepted as, a member of any aboriginal race or tribe of Africa'. Natives were subdivided into tribal groups such as Xhosa and Zulu.

Coloureds were anyone who 'is not a White person or a Native'. Coloureds were subdivided into ethnic groups such as Cape Malay, Chinese, Indian, Griqua, other Asiatic and other Coloured.

Anyone who contested their classification could appeal in the first instance to a special board set up for that purpose and headed by a judge or magistrate, present or former, and then to the law courts.

20 June Parliament passes the Suppression of Communism Act on the same day that the Communist Party of South Africa announces its decision to dissolve itself. The act gave the government broad powers to outlaw any activity it considered hostile to its policies.

The government claimed that the act was necessary to prevent Communists and other subversives from causing unrest among non-White groups. It made the Communist Party illegal and empowered the governor general to outlaw any other organization, publication or individual which he considered to be either communistic or Communist-inspired.

The act gave a broad definition to the term Communism and defined it as 'any doctrine or scheme which aims at bringing about any political, economic, social or industrial changes in South Africa by the promotion of disorder or disturbances or which aims at encouraging feelings of hostility between the White community and non-White community'.

The minister of justice was given arbitrary power to declare any organization Communist, to ban anyone named as a Communist from attending gatherings, in particular political meetings, and to stipulate where Communists could live. The minister could also outlaw meetings and close down publications. His power was total and his decisions could not be appealed in court. The result was that the government could prevent any group or individual from carrying out its activities by naming it Communist and declaring it illegal under the act. Trade unions were among the first groups to be affected by the new law.

The South African Communist Party, anticipating the passage of the act, dissolved itself earlier in the day. Public protests against the new law were held throughout the country. One such demonstration in Cape Town on 14 June turned into a riot.

7 July The Group Areas Act, one of the most far-reaching pieces of the early apartheid legislation, becomes law. The act provided the government with the legal framework effectively to segregate the country by assigning 'separate areas to the different races' and by allowing forced removals and resettlements, government expropriation of property and the establishment of racial reserves.

The act was introduced to the House of Assembly on 29 May by Interior Minister Donges. It empowered the governor general, with the advice and consent of Parliament, to designate any section of the country as a 'group area' where only members of the designated racial group could live, own property and carry on business. The areas could be declared a designated area for ownership and/or occupation. If the governor general set aside an area as an occupation area, only people from the permitted group could live there but people from other groups could continue to own property in the area. If an area was also zoned for ownership, people of different racial groups could continue to own their property for their lifetimes but could not pass it on to anyone outside the designated group. Others outside the group could not buy new property.

The bill resulted in entire communities being uprooted when their section was re-zoned for a different group. Blacks were the most frequently dislocated group. They often found themselves living in townships on the edges of the cities when their original neighbourhoods were re-zoned for the Whites.

11 July The International Court of Justice rules that South Africa is still bound by its League of Nations mandate for South West Africa and that the Union cannot change the mandated area's international status without the consent of the UN. The court ruled that South Africa must transmit petitions from the inhabitants of South West Africa to the UN but that it has no obligation to place the territory under trusteeship. Although the UN asked only for an 'advisory opinion', the

Court held that South Africa must accept its 'compulsory jurisdiction'. South African Economic Affairs Minister Eric Louw rejected the ruling and said that South Africa still intended to absorb South West Africa.

28 August The government announces that the UN and the US had accepted its offer of a South African Air Force (SAAF) fighter squadron for use in Korea. The SAAF had begun recruiting an air squadron to serve with the UN forces on 4 August and the planes went into action on 26 November. The government had originally decided against committing any of its forces to the Korean war effort, but widespread protests forced them to reverse that decision.

30 August South West Africa's first elections to the South African parliament are held and result in a sweep for the National Party. The Nationalists won all six South West Africa parliamentary seats and 16 of 18 local legislature seats.

The campaign was fiercely fought by both sides because of the effect the outcome would have on the parties' strength in the South African parliament itself. The Nationalists fought the election on their policy of apartheid and on their position as regards South West Africa with the UN. The United Party fought the campaign on economic issues and on the government's decision not to submit the reports to the UN.

Prime Minister Malan greeted the National Party's success by telling the South West African voters that they had made history. They had given South Africa a stable government, had shown the UN the path that South West Africa wanted to follow, and given the Nationalists a mandate to continue their apartheid and anti-Communist policies.

The elections resulted in a government majority of 13 in the House of Assembly. The number of seats each party had were: Reunited National Party 77, Afrikaner Party nine, giving the government 86 seats; the United Party 64, Labour Party 6, Native Representatives three, giving the Opposition a total of 73 seats. In the Senate the Nationalists had a majority of six seats, including the president and two seats filled by government-appointed senators and two others elected by the South West African electoral college.

11 September Field Marshal Jan Christiaan Smuts, former Prime Minister and one of the country's leading statesmen, dies at his home near Pretoria at the age of 80. He had been suffering from pneumonia since May. His illness caused him to resign as the leader of the United Party and leader of the Opposition on 14 June and his death was seen as depriving the party of its most influential figure at a time when it was still recovering from the sudden death of its deputy leader, Jan Hofmeyr, in December 1949.

Smuts was replaced as leader of the United Party by his new deputy, Jacobus Gideon Nel Strauss. Many observers felt that the party would disintegrate without Smuts and Hofmeyr, but Strauss established a 'new leadership group' of bright young men. His leadership was not universally popular and he encountered some difficulty in holding the party together. However, by the end of the year, many observers believed the party was more united than at any time since the Nationalists came to power in 1948.

13 October Prime Minister Malan and Afrikaner leader Havenga agree that Cape Coloured citizens will cast special ballots separately from White voters.

The agreement removed the last obstacle to the merger of the two parties.

In a speech to the Afrikaner Party Congress on 25 July, Havenga had said that he would help Malan get the Coloureds placed on a separate voting roll if Malan strongly wanted that, but that he would not cooperate with him in any proposals which meant a diminution of the political rights that the Coloureds had at the time.

In October, they agreed that: it was in the best interests of both the Coloureds and Whites if the Coloureds were to exercise their political rights separately; this would be brought about by having all registered Coloured voters placed into separate constituencies; the legislation to enable the government to accomplish this would be introduced in the following session of Parliament; the quota of registered voters per constituency would be as near equal as possible between White and Coloured voters; Coloureds would be able to elect four White Members of Parliament and one White senator to represent them.

2 December The UN General Assembly passes a resolution criticizing South Africa's treatment of its Indian minority under the Group Areas Act and other discriminatory measures. It asks South Africa to hold a round table conference with India and Pakistan on the problem before 1 April 1951 or accept the mediation of a three-member UN commission to be set up then. South Africa's argument that the resolution was the 'most naked form of intervention' by the UN in the domestic affairs of a member country persuaded 21 countries to abstain.

5 December The UN General Assembly passes a resolution requesting South Africa to accept and comply with an International Court of Justice opinion on the status of South West Africa. The court, responding to a request by the UN Trusteeship Committee to study the situation, had decided that the international trusteeship established after the First World War was still in effect.

14 December The Atomic Energy Commission announces an agreement under which the US and Britain will purchase the entire amount of uranium obtained from South Africa's gold mines. The uranium was to be extracted from the Witwatersrand gold reef near Pretoria and Johannesburg.

South African gold ores did not contain a large percentage of uranium but the quantity of ore mined was so vast that a 'relatively large' amount of uranium could be obtained from it. It was an economically viable proposition because the uranium-containing ore was a waste product after the gold had been mined.

16 December The two main Black political groups, the militant All African Convention and the more moderate Native African Congress meet in Bloemfontein. It became obvious during the course of the meetings that more Blacks favoured the adoption of radical means to obtain their political and other rights.

The Bloemfontein meetings closely followed a stormy session of the government's advisory body, the Natives' Representative Council, which ended in a deadlock. The council, established in 1936, was intended to act as the main vehicle for Black political expression, but, in fact, it had no actual power or influence. In protest, the council voted to adjourn itself indefinitely and did not meet again until the newly appointed minister of native affairs, Hendrik Verwoerd, convened this meeting to present the government's statement on its apartheid policies. The council's demands to debate the statement were denied and it again adjourned amid much bitterness to seek clarification from the courts about its rights and powers.

1 January Ernest G. Jansen succeeds Gideon Brand van Zyl as governor general of South Africa. Jansen, a life-long advocate of a republic, was the National Party's first minister of native affairs and a former speaker of the House of Assembly. He had served as chairman of the group that inaugurated the Voortrekker monument, and wrote several books on the Voortrekkers. At the time of his appointment, he was the leader of the National Party in Natal.

10 January Minister of Native Affairs Hendrik Verwoerd announces that all future appointments to the Native Affairs Commission will be made from among the government's pro-apartheid supporters in Parliament.

The all-White commission was an advisory body comprising a maximum of five members. In outlining the role he envisaged the commission to play under his directorship, Verwoerd said that one of the commissioners would specialize in the administration of native reserves, another in special areas and a third in matters relating to Blacks living on White farms.

19 January The new parliamentary session opens with a fight over the appointment of the speaker of the House of Assembly.

The National Party nominated one of its members, J.H. Conradie, as the new speaker. The nomination is usually a formality but, for the first time in the history of the South African parliament, the nomination was opposed. The opposition United Party said that, as speaker, Conradie would be called upon to rule on the compatibility of the entrenched clauses and the proposed Separate Representation of Voters Bill. They argued that he had already given his opinion on the issue while a private Member of Parliament and had, therefore, compromised his position on one of the most vital questions that was likely to come before him. Conradie was eventually elected by a vote of 82–59.

1 February The British secretary of state for Commonwealth affairs, Patrick Gordon-Walker, arrives in Bechuanaland on the first stop of a month-long tour of Bechuanaland, Basutoland, Swaziland, Southern Rhodesia and South Africa.

In a meeting with the tribal leaders in Basutoland on 5 February, Gordon-Walker reiterated the British government's promise that none of the protectorates would be incorporated into the Union of South Africa without prior consultations with both the local people and the British parliament.

9 February Prime Minister Daniel F. Malan uses the occasion of a state banquet given in honour of British Secretary of State for Commonwealth Affairs Patrick

Gordon-Walker to demand that the British protectorates be incorporated into the Union without further delay and to attack other Commonwealth countries for meddling in South Africa's domestic affairs.

23 February Prime Minister Malan attacks Britain's Commonwealth policies. He told a press conference that when the Commonwealth had consisted only of Britain, Australia, Canada, New Zealand and South Africa, the 'conditions for solidarity were present – namely common interests and the necessary homogeneity'. But he maintained that this homogeneity and common bond was being destroyed by the inclusion of non-White states.

British Secretary of State for Commonwealth Affairs Patrick Gordon-Walker replied on 23 February that the Commonwealth should form a bridge between the established Western countries and the new nations coming into being in Africa and Asia.

8 March The Separate Representation of Voters Bill is introduced to the House of Assembly by Interior Minister Theophilus E. Donges. The government's attempts to get the bill enacted into law led to a six-year constitutional crisis that was described as one of the most bitterly fought and prolonged parliamentary battles in the history of the country.

The leader of the Opposition, Jacobus G.N. Strauss, attacked the bill on moral and legal grounds maintaining that the Coloured franchise was protected under the entrenched clauses of the South Africa Act of 1909 and required a two-thirds majority of both houses of Parliament sitting together. Opposition to the bill also centred on the fact that English language rights were also protected under an entrenched clause of the South Africa Act and English speakers feared setting a precedent that could later be turned against them. It was also noted that the majority of Coloured voters cast their ballots against the National Party, which increased the government's desire to have them removed from the electoral rolls. Meanwhile, the Nationalists, while promising to respect the entrenched clause on language rights, maintained that the Coloured franchise had to be changed. It insisted that, since the Statute of Westminster was passed in 1931 guaranteeing the complete sovereignty of Parliament, the entrenched clauses of the earlier 1909 act could be amended or repealed by a simple majority.

The bill provided for: the removal of all Cape Coloureds from the present electoral roll; the drawing up of a new electoral roll for Coloured males able to meet the exisiting literacy and property qualifications; the holding of separate elections for those on the Coloured roll to select four Whites to represent them in the House of Assembly, one in the Senate and two in the Cape Provincial Council; the establishment of a Board of Coloured Affairs to advise the government on Coloured matters and to act as an intermediary between the Coloured community and the government. The 11-member board would be under the direction of a White commissioner and would be made up of eight Coloureds elected in the Cape, and three nominated by the government to represent Natal, the Orange Free State and the Transvaal.

The bill was formally signed into law by the governor general on 18 June.

23 April Minister of Native Affairs Hendrik Verwoerd announces in a speech to the Senate that the Natives' Representative Council was concerning itself too much with political interests and not spending enough time on the real Black interests of housing, training and employment. He said that the government 'would waste no more time or money' on it in its present form.

4 May The South African War Veterans' Torch Commando holds a major demonstration in Johannesburg against the Separate Representation of Voters Bill. A resolution calling the bill a violation of the constitution's spirit was adopted. The participants pledged to take all the legal steps possible to force an early general election.

The organization held mass torchlight demonstrations throughout South Africa. It pledged itself to ousting the ruling Reunited National Party from power and to 'undying opposition to those who would bind the free spirit of men with the chains of bigotry and ignorance and who would prostitute the spirit of democratic government in South Africa'. The demonstrations often ended in clashes with the police.

The organization, which first came to the public's attention in May 1951, was originally called the War Veterans' Action Committee but changed its name when it became a national movement on 30 June. Group-Captain A.G. 'Sailor' Malan, a distant cousin of the prime minister, was elected president. It held its first national executive meeting in July.

8 May The results of a national census are released. For the first time in history, Asians outnumbered Whites in Durban by some 143,750 to 129,633. The total population of South Africa was recorded at 12,437,227. The population was broken down as follows: Whites 2,588,933; Blacks 8,410,935; Coloureds 1,078,621 and Asians 358,738. Although numerically the smallest group, Asians, with a 25.8 per cent rise over the 1940 census, were the fastest-growing segment of the population. The results of the census confirmed the government's fears that the Asian community was growing and strengthened their resolve to follow through on their plans for Asian immigration control and repatriation.

16 May The Separate Representation of Voters Bill is introduced to the Senate. The Opposition challenged the Senate's competence to consider the bill without the House of Assembly. A report from the parliamentary draftsman was introduced on 18 May which argued that: any legislation seeking to change the Coloured franchise had to be considered by a joint session under the conditions of the entrenched clauses; any attempt to do otherwise went against a fundamental part of the constitution; the courts should decide if a bill passed unicamerally was a valid Act of Parliament; Parliament was no longer subject to external restrictions or restrictions 'from outside or from our courts, in order to survive as a Parliament and make effective laws it must be constituted and function according to the law from which it derives its authority – the South Africa Act'. The president of the Senate, C.A. van Niekerkj, ruled on 24 May that the Senate could consider the bill. It was subsequently passed with minor amendments after a series of acrimonious debates.

28 May Police and a crowd of some 50,000 people demonstrating against the Separate Representation of Voters Act clash outside the Houses of Parliament. It was described at the time as the worst riot in Cape Town's history.

Violence erupted when some Coloured demonstrators threw lighted torches on a Dutch Reformed Church. In the subsequent clashes with the police, some 28 persons were seriously injured and several were arrested.

A judicial inquiry reported on 16 June that the crowd had intended to storm the Houses of Parliament and that the police did not act until they had come under attack. Justice Minister Charles R. Swart claimed that the Opposition's supporters and the Torch Commandos had been responsible for the trouble. Both the judicial report and Swart's statement were disputed by the Opposition which called for a full official inquiry.

21 June The Bantu Authorities Act is passed. The legislation abolished the Natives' Representative Council and established in its place Bantu tribal, regional and territorial authorities with executive, administrative and judicial functions. The act was unpopular with Blacks, who resented the abolition of the Natives' Representative Council and resisted its implementation.

The Bantu Authorities Act gave the government the base for pursuing its policy of retribalizing the Blacks and installing government-supported chiefs. In explaining this policy in 1950, Minister of Native Affairs E.G. Jansen had said:

> The natives of this country do not all belong to the same tribe or race. They have different languages and customs. We are of the opinion that the solidarity of the tribes should be preserved and that they should develop along the lines of their own national character and tradition. For that purpose we want to rehabilitate the deserving tribal chiefs as far as possible and we would like to see their authority maintained over the members of their tribes. Suitable steps will be taken in that direction.

23 July The 1951 Suppression of Communism Act is amended to make it clear that the provisions of the act applied to past as well as present members of the Communist Party or to anyone who was a member of any organization outside South Africa that 'professed by its name or otherwise to be an organisation for propagating the principles or promoting the spread of Communism'.

21 August The Nairobi Defence Conference of African Powers opens under the auspices of the British and South African governments. The conference was attended by representatives from Belgium, Britain, South Africa. Ethiopia, France, Portugal and Southern Rhodesia to a 'defence facilities conference'. A communiqué, released at the end of the conference on 31 August, said that the participants had unanimously agreed on ways to ensure the rapid movement of supplies and troops to central and eastern Africa.

29 August Applications asking for the Separate Representation of Voters Act to be declared invalid are filed with the Cape Supreme Court on behalf of four Coloured voters. The applications also called on the court to issue a declaration that the four voters should remain on the common electoral rolls and be eligible to participate in any elections for the House of Assembly. The court heard arguments from 9 to 16 October and dismissed the applications with costs on 26 October. The judges ruled that the court did not have the authority to test the validity of parliamentary legislation but added that only the appellate division of the Supreme Court could make a final ruling on the meaning of the word 'parliament' and on the true scope of parliamentary powers. The four applicants were given permission to appeal the decision to the appellate division of the Supreme Court.

28 September The International Monetary Fund announces it will give up its four-year effort to limit the price of gold to $35 an ounce. It added that it still opposed gold transactions at premium prices, over $35, but will leave the policing up to individual fund countries. South Africa admitted it had been selling 40 per cent of its gold output at premium prices, now about $40 an ounce, for non-monetary commercial and artistic uses.

3 October The Johannesburg city council agrees in principle to accept responsibility for the removal of some 15,000 Blacks to a new township. The removals were legal under the terms of the Group Areas Act, which came into effect on 30 March. On 25 November, the plan for the residential subdivision of Durban along racial lines as set out in the act was published by the Durban city council.

22 October The Reunited National and Afrikaner parties formally merge, forming the National Party. The new party listed its basic aims as 'furthering the welfare of South Africa and its people, and the development of an effective sense of national self-sufficiency and independence based on undivided loyalty to South Africa and the acknowledgement of the equal rights of Afrikaans- and English-speaking South Africans'.

A party spokesman said that it was basing itself on 'the unambiguous acknowledgment that South Africa is a sovereign independent State, possessing all the rights to carry out all State functions in the fullest international sense'. It stipulated that the only people who could become members of the party were those who were 'prepared to place the interests of South Africa above those of race, country, or people of his origin and above those of any other country' and went on to say that it was 'convinced that a Republican form of Government, separated from the British Crown, is most suited to the traditions, circumstances and aspirations of the South African people, and is the only effective guarantee that South Africa shall never again be involved in Britain's wars'.

On race relations, it said that it was in favour of apartheid, felt that the Coloured and native communities were 'a permanent part of the population under the Christian guardianship of the European races' but was fervently opposed to any mingling of the races. It promised to protect all the races from the immigration and competition of Asians by means of a plan for the repatriation and segregation of Asians.

The final obstacle to the merger was removed when Afrikaner Party leader Nicolaas Havenga announced during the debate on the Coloured Franchise Bill that he was finally satisfied that the passage of the bill would not result in any diminution of the Coloured people's political rights. Havenga had opposed the merger until the question of Coloured franchise could be solved to his satisfaction.

Observers believed that the National Party was destined to have some stormy times ahead since members of the old Afrikaner Party were considerably more liberal than their National Party counterparts, particularly on the question of native representation in Parliament.

10 November South Africa announces an agreement with the US under which the US will supply South Africa with military equipment. South Africa had previously declared that in the event of the outbreak of war, it would defend

Africa from Communism and fight alongside the anti-Communist powers. Earlier in 1951, it had been deemed eligible under the Mutual Defence Assistance Act to receive reimbursable US military aid.

2 December The South African government refuses to issue travel documents to the Herero chiefs who had been invited to testify before the UN Trusteeship Committee meeting in Paris on conditions in South West Africa. The committee approved a resolution on 5 December allowing the Reverend Michael Scott to represent the chiefs at the meeting 'without prejudice to any further hearing of the South West African chiefs'. Scott appeared before the committee on 9 December and gave evidence of South Africa's discrimination against the native peoples of the territory.

12 December The UN Trusteeship Committee adopts, as at previous sessions, two resolutions calling on South Africa to: put South West Africa into the UN trusteeship system; submit reports on its administration of the territory; and resume negotiations with the UN for an agreement leading to the implementation of a July 1950 International Court of Justice opinion, which found that South Africa was still bound by its League of Nations mandate for South West Africa and that the Union could not change the mandated area's international status without the consent of the UN.

Prime Minister Malan announced on the same day that South Africa would be temporarily withdrawing from the General Assembly. He accused the Reverend Michael Scott, who had testified before the Trusteeship Committee on behalf of the leaders of the principal tribe in South West Africa, of being 'a hostile and fanatical foreigner and agitator' and the UN of having 'defamed and insulted' South Africa. Interior Minister Donges, South Africa's chief UN General Assembly delegate, was called home for consultations on 12 December. The entire South African delegation withdrew from assembly sessions the following day.

4 January The South African government announces that the Reverend Michael Scott has been barred from returning to his mission in South West Africa. The Anglican missionary had been declared a prohibited immigrant under the 1913 Immigration Act, which empowered the government to deny entry into the country to those people deemed to be 'unsuited to Union requirement'.

18 January Interior Minister Theophilus E. Donges, in an address to the UN General Assembly, reiterates South Africa's position that the Trusteeship Committee had not been empowered by the UN Charter to allow Reverend Scott to address it because he was 'an individual not representing any of the population of South West Africa'. Donges concluded that the committee's actions were unconstitutional, unwise and unjust and that for those reasons South Africa would not participate in the committee's vote on the resolutions concerning South West Africa.

6 February Elizabeth II is proclaimed Queen upon the death of her father, King George VI. The proclamation, signed by the governor general and prime minister after being unanimously passed by Parliament, describes Elizabeth as 'by the grace of God of Great Britain, Ireland, and the other Dominions beyond the Seas, Queen, Defender of the Faith, Sovereign in and over the Union of South Africa'.

20 March The South African Supreme Court Appellate Division in Bloemfontein, hearing the appeal of four Coloured voters who were removed from the common electoral role under the provisions of the Separate Representation of Voters Act, rules that the act was unconstitutional and invalid because it had not been passed by the necessary two-thirds majority of a joint sitting as was required under the South Africa Act. Prime Minister Daniel F. Malan told Parliament that his government rejected the decision as intolerable and said steps would be taken to ensure voter segregation. He held that the 1936 Statute of Westminster had confirmed the complete sovereignty of South Africa's parliament and that the entrenched clauses were, therefore, no longer binding.

6 April The African National Congress (ANC) and South African Indian Congress hold a nationwide series of meetings to launch a campaign of 'defiance of unjust laws'. The day was chosen because it was the culmination of a three-month celebration to mark the founding at the Cape in 1652 of the country's first White settlement by Jan van Riebeeck and some 90 men from the Dutch East India Company.

The leaders of the ANC, the Black political movement established in 1912, had written to Prime Minister Malan in December 1951 asking for the repeal of the apartheid legislation and direct parliamentary representation for Blacks in Parliament. When the prime minister refused, they and the South African Indian Congress leaders decided to launch the Defiance Campaign. By the end of the year more than 8,000 protestors had been arrested.

16 April The formation of the United Front is announced at a Cape Town meeting by Opposition leader Jacobus G.N. Strauss. The United Party, Labour Party and War Veterans' Torch Commando formed the Front in response to the constitutional crisis brought about by the government's decision to pass the High Court of Parliament Act and to 'act as one until the fears that now beset the people are removed by the restoration of a democratic Government'.

28 April The Natives (Abolition of Passes and Co-ordination of Documents) Act is published. Under the act, all Blacks over the age of 16 were required to carry a reference book and to present it upon demand to the police or other designated officials. The book, commonly called the passbook, replaced the various forms and papers Blacks were previously obligated to carry. It contained the individual's photograph and personal particulars as well as blank pages for employers' signatures, and labour bureaux, poll tax and influx control information. Blacks were fingerprinted when they received their books and their fingerprints registered with the Central Native Affairs Bureau, established under the act.

The government claimed the act would both give Blacks freedom of movement and enable the police to carry out their duties more effectively. The bill passed the senate on 10 June and the House of Assembly on 25 June.

2 June The government begins to crack down on the leaders of the defiance campaign. ANC executive committee member and former general secretary of the Communist Party Moses Kotane is arrested for addressing a political meeting in defiance of the orders served on him under the Suppression of Communism Act. He was sentenced on 15 July to four months in prison. South African Indian Congress President Y.M. Dadoo and the secretary of the ANC's Transvaal branch, David Bopape, were both arrested on 5 June for the same offence. Dadoo was sentenced to six months' imprisonment while Bopape received a four-month sentence. All three men were released on bail pending appeals.

Kotane's appeal was upheld and his sentence quashed on 25 September. The appeal succeeded because the Transvaal Provincial Division of the South African Supreme Court found that the prosecutors had not proved that the meeting he attended was not a bona fide recreational, social or religious gathering.

3 June The High Court of Parliament Act is signed by the governor general and passes into law. The act made Parliament the country's highest court and enabled it to set aside, by a simple majority vote in both houses, any appeal court judgment that invalidated an act of Parliament.

Opponents of the bill strongly protested its passage. Opposition leader Strauss said he would test the validity of new law 'almost immediately' before the Supreme Court. Meanwhile, the War Veterans' Torch Commando, which had been charged by Malan on 2 May with plotting dangerous and illegal actions against his government, marched silently through the streets of Cape Town on 4 June to protest the new government measure giving supremacy to Parliament over the judiciary. The government of Prime Minister Malan was, however, determined to 'go ahead with our plans to protect the sovereignty of Parliament, no matter what happens'.

16 June The Electoral Laws Amendment Bill is passed by the Senate. The bill, which had first been introduced in Parliament in April, provided for: the delimitation of electoral constituencies based on the total number of registered White voters in the country, rather than on the basis of Whites over the age of 21 at the last census as was laid down in law by the 1909 South Africa Act; the general registration of voters throughout South West Africa and the Union; supplementary registrations of two- to three-year intervals; the convening of delimitation commissions every 10 years rather than five as at present; and the reduction of the interval between nomination day and election day from 28 to 35 days. The bill was passed by the House of Assembly on 2 June and the Senate on 16 June.

19 June The Native Laws Amendment Act is passed. The act, introduced in February, extended influx controls to all urban areas and to Black women who had previously not been affected. It provided that: any Black who wanted to move to another area had to register at a labour bureau; Blacks should be prohibited from moving to any area where it was unlikely they would find employment; Blacks could remain in a town for up to 72 hours without requiring a permit but that the burden of proof over how long they had been there rested with the Blacks; and 'agitators' could be deported from any trouble area without recourse to the courts.

26 June Justice Minister Charles R. Swart issues orders under the Suppression of Communism Act on former Member of Parliament Sam Kahn and former Cape Provincial Councillor Fred Carneson requiring their resignations from the Cape Town city council within 30 days.

26 June The defiance campaign officially begins. The purpose of the non-violent action was to defy the government's 'unjust' legislation on racial segregation and to prove the apartheid laws unworkable. The police made some 132 arrests on the first day of demonstrations.

The first actions of the campaign were held in Johannesburg, Boksburg and Port Elizabeth, where non-White groups deliberately broke apartheid laws by having, among other things: Indians enter locations designated for Blacks only; Blacks enter prohibited locations without passes; Blacks refuse to carry the special passes they were required to have with them at all times; non-Whites use White entrances to railway stations and post offices; and Blacks break curfew by being on the streets after 11pm.

ANC President James S. Moroka emphasized the peaceful nature of the demonstrations and announced that 'my people will ... give the Whites, particularly the police, no opportunity to use arms', and would submit to 'anything that will be done to them without restraint'.

After the first month, a total of 1,452 non-Whites were arrested on charges of violating the apartheid laws. The campaign spread to smaller cities and large towns by end of June and to smaller towns in September.

Justice Minister Swart announced on 4 August that the government would introduce new legislation to deal with people who violate the laws if it was found that the current legislation was not effective in combating the passive resistance campaign.

15 July The government crackdown on opponents using the Suppression of Communism Act continues as the former general secretary of the multiracial Garment Workers' Union E.S. 'Solly' Sachs is convicted of contravening it. He was found guilty by the Johannesburg magistrates court and sentenced to two concurrent terms of six months with hard labour for addressing public meetings in violation of an order served on him under the act. His appeal was denied but his sentence was suspended for three years.

Sachs antagonized the Nationalists by being a Jew, a former Communist and a trade unionist in charge of the country's largest multiracial union. He was named a Communist under the new law in spite of the fact that he had been thrown out of the Communist Party in 1931. He was ordered to resign as a union official, banned from attending any political meetings and restricted to remaining in an area of the Transvaal for two years. He defied the order by twice addressing crowds of his supporters outside the Johannesburg city hall and was arrested, tried and convicted. Although Sachs was never imprisoned, his career was ruined and he was forced to resign from the elected position he had held for 24 years.

22 August Leader of the Opposition Strauss condemns the defiance campaign and asks for it to end. Speaking at Brits in the Transvaal, he said it was 'neither in the interests of the non-Europeans nor the country as a whole', and that the laws which the 'resisters' were violating were constitutionally adopted and would have to be changed according to the constitution. He added that the government was as responsible for the present circumstances as were those who had started the campaign.

27 August The new High Court of Parliament, created by the High Court of Parliament Act on 3 June, holds its first meeting at which it reverses a Supreme Court decision and declares the Separate Representation of Voters Act valid. The Opposition boycotted the meeting.

29 August The Cape Supreme Court votes unanimously that the act creating the High Court of Parliament was 'invalid, null and void, and of no legal force and effect'. The government announced that day that it would appeal against the decision.

Prime Minister Malan said on 15 September that the government would win this battle with the judiciary because 'with all the implications of this matter we, as a Government, cannot allow ourselves to lose' and added that, historically speaking, the legislature had always won in countries that had had such a disagreement.

18 October Serious rioting breaks out in the Port Elizabeth area in which four Whites and seven non-Whites are killed. The riots started when some 3000 Blacks attacked the railway station and tried to set it alight after rumours circulated about the arrest of two Blacks. Police fired into the crowd in an effort to disperse it and rioting then spread to other areas.

Justice Minister Swart claimed the riots were a direct result of the Defiance Campaign. He warned that the Government would take 'very stern and drastic measures against this form of lawlessness' and that he would introduce new legislation if necessary to deal with the civil disobedience campaign. The ANC condemned the riots as 'an unfortunate, reckless, ill-considered return to jungle law' and denied that the ANC had been involved.

7 November The government bans all meetings at East London, Port Elizabeth, and some smaller Cape province towns for one month and names 52 ANC members as ineligible to attend political meetings for six months under the Suppression of Communism Act.

10 November At least 22 persons are reported killed and 105 injured at the end of three days of race riots. On 8 November, police in Kimberley killed 13 Blacks and injured 34 when they fired on diamond mine workers who were stoning them and burning mining camp buildings. Two Whites, including a Catholic medical nun, and seven Blacks were killed in fighting that broke out in East London on 9–10 November, and 30 others were injured when fighting erupted as police tried to disperse a Defiance Campaign meeting. A Roman Catholic church was burned on 9 November and an Anglican mission was fired on on 13 November in East London. A riot in Port Elizabeth on 10 November followed a 24-hour strike called by the ANC to protest the curfew rules. The local council responded by dismissing striking Blacks in its employ and indefinitely suspending the construction of new Black houses.

11 November Left-wing newspaper editor Brian Bunting is overwhelmingly elected a Member of Parliament in the Cape Western by-election. The election was necessary because the incumbent, Sam Kahn, had been removed from the seat in May under the Suppression of Communism Act.

Bunting was served an order by Justice Minister Swart naming him a Communist under the same act and prohibiting him from becoming a Member of Parliament, a provincial council or the South West African Legislative Assembly. By that time, however, he had already been nominated to contest the Cape Western by-election and the order could not prevent his name appearing on the ballot paper. In compliance with the order, he did not campaign but still won the seat by a massive majority.

On 18 December, Bunting was acquitted of contravening the Suppression of Communism Act by becoming a Member of Parliament.

13 November The South African appellate court rules that the High Court of Parliament, as established under the High Court of Parliament Act, is illegal. In making the ruling, the chief justice said: 'The so-called High Court of Parliament is not a court of law but simply Parliament functioning under another name . . . Parliament cannot, by passing an act giving itself the name of a court of law, come to any decision which will have the effect of destroying the entrenched provisions of the constitution.' The ruling ended, at least temporarily, the most serious constitutional crisis in South Africa's history.

Prime Minister Malan announced on the following day that the government would accept the appeal court ruling and that the Cape Coloureds would be on the electoral register for the 1953 general election. He added that the issue would be 'taken to a higher appeal' when the electorate was asked at that election to give the government a mandate to take whatever steps were needed to put the sovereignty of Parliament beyond doubt.

26 November The trial opens in Johannesburg of 20 Black and Indian leaders of the Defiance Campaign charged with encouraging Communism and contravening the Suppression of Communism Act. They were accused of being part of a plan to obtain full equality between Whites and non-Whites.

The accused included ANC President James S. Moroka, South African Indian Congress President Y.M. Dadoo, ANC leader Walter Sisulu, and former Communist Party General Secretary Moses Kotane. All of the defendants were found guilty on 2 December and sentenced to nine months' imprisonment with hard labour. Their sentences were conditionally suspended for two years provided they were not convicted of further offences against the act within that period. In giving his sentence, the judge said that they had been found guilty of 'statutory Communism' which had 'nothing to do with Communism as is generally known'.

28 November In an effort to deal with the Defiance Campaign, Native Affairs Minister Hendrik F. Verwoerd issues a proclamation designed to curtail Black political meetings. The order prohibited anyone except a senator, Member of Parliament, or member of a provincial council from presiding at, addressing or holding any meeting of more than ten Blacks in a Black area without the chief or headman's permission and only with the written approval of the local magistrate or local native commissioner.

12 December The British government announces that the Commonwealth countries had agreed to changes in the royal title. Each country would in future use a separate form of the title but all would retain the phrase 'Head of the Commonwealth'. South Africa had agreed that the monarch's title would be 'Elizabeth the Second, Queen of South Africa and of her other Realms and Territories, Head of the Commonwealth'.

5 January Native Affairs Secretary W.M. Eiselen outlines a proposed government programme to improve the living conditions of urban Blacks. The plan covered the elimination of shanty towns, influx control, the provision of adequate areas for Black occupation, the establishment of large-scale site and service projects in these areas and loans to help Blacks buy their own homes. The announcement indicated an abandonment of the government's previously announced plan for the establishment of separate Black and White states as set out in the Group Areas Act.

27 January The government introduces the Public Safety Act into Parliament and asks for the power to suspend the laws and govern by decree. It was one of the two bills, the other being the Criminal Law Amendment Act, which the government introduced in order to deal with the Defiance Campaign. The United Party, facing a general election, believing that the majority of the White voters wanted action, voted for the bills. Their election partners, the Labour Party, voted against them.

Under the Public Safety Act, the governor general could declare a state of emergency for twelve months renewable in any or all parts of South Africa and South West Africa if he felt that: any actual or planned action by any person or organization constituted a threat to public safety or maintenance of public order; circumstances had arisen which threatened public order or safety; or ordinary law was inadequate to maintain public safety or order. During the state of emergency the governor general could make whatever regulations he deemed 'necessary or expedient' and make contravention of them a punishable offence which could result in the confiscation of property. The laws could be made retrospective for four days to cover any emergency action taken by the police. The emergency regulations could suspend any act of Parliament, with a few exceptions. If the justice minister or administrator of South West Africa deemed it necessary, they could declare a state of emergency but the governor general had to approve their action within ten days. The bill was passed by the House of Assembly on 16 February and passed the Senate on 19 February.

2 February The Criminal Law Amendment Act, known as the 'whipping post' bill, is introduced into the House of Assembly. The bill makes passive resistance against any law illegal and punishable by severe penalties. These included fines, imprisonment, confiscation of property and lashings. It also made it illegal to raise money to assist the families of anyone resisting the law.

The Criminal Law Amendment Bill spelled out the following penalties: anyone protesting a law by breaking it or by supporting the Defiance Campaign would be subject to a £300 fine, three years' imprisonment and/or ten lashes of the whip, with whipping and imprisonment imposed for second and subsequent offences; anyone encouraging or inciting the protest of a law by breaking it would receive a £500 fine, five-year jail sentence and/or 15 lashes of the whip. Imprisonment and whipping were to be automatically imposed for second and subsequent offences. If fines were not paid within 48 hours, property could be seized. The post could be opened if the police felt that it contained money or other items to assist in the Defiance Campaign.

The United Party did not oppose the bill because, it said, there existed 'a very real danger of an unexpected transition from passive to violent resistance taking place at any moment'. The bill was passed by the House of Assembly on 23 February.

23 March The South African appellate court finds that racial segregation is invalid unless the facilities provided for non-Whites are equal to those offered for Whites. Prime Minister Daniel F. Malan said on 24 March that the court's judgment would 'shock the whole country' and promised that if his National Party was re-elected, they would write the principle of racial discrimination into the law to 'leave no court in doubt about the wish and intention of Parliament and the people'.

15 April The National Party of Prime Minister Malan wins the general elections with an increased majority in the House of Assembly. The election had been fought on the issue of apartheid, in particular the government's attempts to remove the Cape Coloureds from the common electoral roll. The Nationalists interpreted their victory as a mandate for their segregationist legislature. One of the features of the election was the continuing decline in the United Party's strength in the countryside and the National Party's increased strength in urban areas. The results were a major disappointment for the English-speaking section of the United Party, as the government's post-election speeches indicated that many Nationalists regarded the election as a victory over 'British imperialism' and increased their calls for the formation of a republic.

The final returns, published on 17 April, gave the National Party 94 seats, up eight from 1948, for a majority of 30 over the combined opposition. The United Party polled about 50 per cent of the vote but won only 57 seats. The Labour Party won five. Four other seats went to native representatives.

The Cape Coloureds remained on the roll for this election as Prime Minister Malan had promised following the Supreme Court's judgment that the Separate Representation of Voters and the High Court of Parliament Acts were invalid, but he was determined that it would be the last election in which they participated along with Whites.

9 May The South African Liberal Party is launched. The new party announced that membership would be open to anyone who agreed with its principles, regardless of colour or creed, and vowed to campaign for equal rights for all races. The leader of the seven White native representatives in Parliament, Mrs Margaret Ballinger, was elected president. Author Alan Paton was named vice president.

10 May The Union Federal Party is formed by prominent members of the War Veterans' Torch Commando, among them former United Party leader of the Senate G. Heaton Nicolls. The founders of the new party, largely pro-British and living in Natal, opposed what they saw as the ruling National Party's efforts to convert South Africa into an Afrikaner republic instead of a British dominion.

The Federal Unionists claimed that the country needed 'a new movement, pledged to a realistic and courageous approach to South Africa's problems, appealing to no narrow sectionalism or prejudices and devoted to principle rather than expediency'. As part of its political platform, the party pledged itself to create opportunities for people of all races.

12 May United Party leader Jacobus Strauss says that the two new political groups, the Liberal Party and the Union Federal Party, have been launched 'by people who have had no real experience of the nature of the battle which the United Party is waging against the forces of extreme nationalism in South Africa'.

On 13 May, Prime Minister Malan said South Africa would benefit by the formation of the two new parties because 'party divisions have now become sounder and also much more honest'.

30 May The President of the African National Congress (ANC), Albert Luthuli, is prohibited by the government from attending public meetings in South Africa for one year. His presence in 21 districts, mostly suburban areas, was also banned.

13 June The Torch Commando ends its national congress with a 420–394 vote not to disband the organization. The vote was called because of a dispute that broke out after the Federal Union Party was formed by high-level members of the movement. Despite the insistence of Commando leader Group Captain A.G. Malan that the Federal Unionists had acted as individuals rather than as members of the Commando, several leading Commandos resigned over the issue. The congress decided that anyone of any party who agreed with the Commando's principles could join the organization but that no one could hold a high office in both the movement and a political party.

10 July The provisions of the Native Labour (Settlement of Disputes) Act are published. The act was designed to control the massive pool of cheap Black labour which was essential to the economic development of South Africa. The main provisions of the act were that: participating in or instigating strikes by Black workers was prohibited and violators could face a three-year jail sentence and/or a £300 fine; Black labour disputes would be referred to a regional native labour committee made up of a White chairman and Blacks appointed by the minister of labour to represent the workers' interests; an all-White central native labour board would be appointed by the minister of labour to resolve any dispute that the regional committee referred to it; and all disputes still unsettled would be referred to the minister of labour who, after consultation with the wage board, would issue the conditions of settlement, binding for up to three years.

The bill was given its third reading in the House of Assembly on 27 August with the United Party supporting the government; it passed the Senate on 30 September.

27 July The Korean War ends after three years and 32 days with the signing of the armistice in Panmunjom. South Africa had assisted the UN operations against the Communist forces of North Korea by deploying a South African Air Force squadron of fighter airplanes. The South African airmen carried out more than 12,000 missions and suffered some 41 casualties, including 12 dead.

5 August The Reservation of Separate Amenities Act is published. The act strengthened the apartheid regulations in vehicles and public places and followed from the Cape Supreme Court's 23 March decision that separate facilities for Whites and non-Whites on railways must be equal.

The act enabled the railway and other authorities to provide separate facilities for Whites and non-Whites in all public places and vehicles and stipulated that the separation of the races was legal whether the facilities were equal or not. Justice Minister Swart said that the separation of the races had always been provided for in South Africa and that this was 'a sound and natural policy'. The bill passed its third reading in the House of Assembly on 4 September and passed the Senate on 1 October.

4 September The United Party holds a caucus at which a motion of confidence in the leader, Jacobus Strauss, is passed, but only after a long and bitter debate. His leadership had been under attack for some time by a group of right-wing Members of Parliament, led by the party's Transvaal leader Bailey Bekker, who objected to the formation of an electoral alliance with the more liberal Labour Party and Torch Commando and demanded a greater accommodation with the ruling National Party. Another faction, known as the liberal group, also existed within the party that wanted a stronger opposition to the Nationalist government. Strauss, faced with this situation, was forced to act in order to maintain party unity and, after a series of stormy caucus meetings, decided to rid the party of its more conservative elements. Bekker and the other dissidents were either expelled from the party or forced to resign.

8 September Interior Minister Theophilus E. Donges introduces the Immigrants Regulation Amendment Bill aimed at ending free entry into the country by the foreign-born wives and children of Indians resident in South Africa.

The act provided that: no foreign-born Indian woman married to an Indian resident in South Africa after the date of Donges's announcement would be allowed entrance into South Africa nor would the children of a marriage made after that date; foreign-born wives of resident Indians married before 10 February 1953 and the children of such marriages could freely enter South Africa until 10

February 1956 but not after that date; foreign-born Indian women and children who were resident in South Africa would not be permitted reentry if they left the country for more than three years.

9 September United and Labour Party Members of Parliament challenge Justice Minister Swart over his 'abuse' of the Suppression of Communism Act and accuse the National Party of using the act to gain control over the trade union movement. The move comes after two trade union leaders, Fred Carneson and Piet Huyser, were named under the act and ordered to resign as the general secretaries of their unions.

16 September The South Africa Amendment Act fails to pass by the required two-thirds majority of a joint sitting of Parliament. The government failed to win approval for the constitutional amendment permitting the removal of Coloured voters from the common electoral roll.

The government had published the South Africa Amendment Act on 2 July. It was designed to end the constitutional deadlock caused by the Supreme Court's findings that the Separate Representation of Voters Act and the High Court of Parliament Act were both invalid. The bill was introduced as soon as Parliament reconvened after the National Party's election victory. Dr Malan announced on 3 July that there would be a joint sitting of Parliament on 13 July to consider the bill. The final vote was 122–78 in favour of the bill, which was 16 votes short of the two-thirds majority required.

28 September Finance Minister Nicolaas C. Havenga announces that the government will drop, at least temporarily, the Appellate Court Bill that it had introduced on 18 September. The bill was designed to reorganize the appellate court so as to enable the governor general to name judges to a new Court of Constitutional Appeal. The court would be the only one authorized to hear appeals concerning acts of Parliament and its decisions would be final. The Opposition had strongly criticized it saying that it enabled the government to 'pack' the court with judges known to be sympathetic to its views. Many observers believed that the government itself had had some reservations about possible future implications of the bill's provisions and had changed its mind on introducing it.

29 September One of the four native representatives in Parliament, Brian Bunting, is convicted under the Suppression of Communism Act of being a Communist and is ousted from Parliament. Bunting had been overwhelmingly elected to the Cape Western constituency in a by-election held on 11 November 1952 because the incumbent, Sam Kahn, had been expelled from Parliament under the same act.

1 October The Bantu Education Act is passed by the Senate. The purpose of the act was to restructure the Black educational system so that it would conform to the requirements of separate development and provide Black children with sufficient knowledge and skills to enable them to participate in society at the level accessible to them. Minister of Native Affairs Hendrik Verwoerd explained the new system created by the act. He said that the old system was based on church or mission schools so that 'by blindly producing pupils on a European model, vain hope was created among natives that they could occupy posts within the European community despite the country's policy of apartheid'.

The act prohibited the establishment, running or maintaining of a school for Blacks without the minister of native affairs' authority. The minister was given discretionary power to decide whether to withdraw grants to mission schools in preference to government or community schools and whether to allow Black schools to continue to function.

2 October A joint session of Parliament approves a motion enabling the government to introduce the Separate Representation of Voters Act Validation and Amendment Bill. The new bill would validate the Separate Representation of Voters Act, which removed Coloureds from the common electoral roll and give them separate representation in Parliament. Prime Minister Malan said that the bill would be referred to a joint select committee for consideration before a final vote was taken on it. Observers believed the delay was calculated to allow time for tensions between the United Party leadership and some of its dissident right-wing members to ferment.

26 October The head of the Anglican Church in South Africa, after an Episcopal synod in Pretoria, states that: 'We believe that the only national policy which is morally defensible must be that which gives the fullest opportunity of development to the members of all racial groups.'

On 29 October, the Methodist Church of South Africa unanimously approved a similar condemnation of apartheid. It said that the 'mass differentiation on the ground of colour alone' made great injustice inevitable because it ignored 'the sacredness of personality and the potentiality of men and women as individuals'.

28 October The three-man commission of inquiry into South Africa's racial problems submitted its report to the UN General Assembly. The commission, established by the 60-member Special Political Committee said that the UN Charter permitted the General Assembly to investigate the internal affairs of a member country and found South Africa's racial situation was 'a most important political and human problem which overshadows the political, economic and social life of this young and promising nation'. These problems, said the commission, had significant impact far beyond the borders of South Africa or even Africa itself.

On 29 November, the General Assembly adopted two resolutions on South West Africa. The first established a seven-man commission to study and report to the Assembly on the situation in South West Africa in terms of the League of Nations mandate system. The second reiterated past UN resolutions on the issue and reasserted that the trusteeship of the territory should be handed over to the UN.

26 November The South African appeal court unanimously decides that anyone named as a Communist under the Suppression of Communism Act and subsequently banned from attending meetings of a political or other nature was not bound by the ban if he had not first been given the opportunity of a hearing.

The government protested that an investigation into any banned person's case would delay the implementation of the law which had been designed to show quick and decisive action. On 26 November, Justice Minister Swart announced that the appeal court's decision could not be allowed to stand and that the loophole the court had used to reach its decision would be closed.

The court's decision made the restriction notices served on some 100 named people invalid. A further five convictions for contravening the act were set aside on 7 December.

11 December Prime Minister Malan, addressing a graduation ceremony at the Afrikaans-speaking Stellenbosh University, announces that the government had decided to end the *gemengheid* (intermingling) of Whites and non-Whites at the English-speaking Universities of Cape Town and Witwatersrand. He said: 'This crying anomaly in our education system obviously cannot continue without having the most harmful results. The Government has therefore decided to end it as speedily as possible.'

The two universities under dispute, Cape Town and Witwatersrand, were required under their charters to admit any student, regardless of race, who had the necessary qualifications. The charter could be changed only by an act of Parliament.

The National Union of Students protested that the principle of *gemengheid* had long been entrenched in both universities and had never been criticized until 1948 when 'politicians started to attack it for political ends'.

---

1 9 5 4

1 January The Bantu Education Act, which restructured the Black educational system to conform to the needs of apartheid, comes into effect. (See 1 October 1953.) It was the first of three bills to become law during the year that greatly increased the importance of the Department of Native Affairs and its minister, Hendrik Verwoerd. One of the other two bills transferred control of native affairs in the territory of South West Africa to Verwoerd's department, while the Native Resettlement Bill gave the department the power to forcibly relocate Black residents. (See 1 March 1954.)

21 January Ray Alexander, former general secretary of the Food and Canning Workers' Union, is chosen to contest the Cape Western by-election for Natives' Representative. The selection was controversial as Miss Alexander had been named under the Suppression of Communism Act and forced to resign her union position in September 1953. The seat had been declared vacant twice in less than two years because of the elections and subsequent expulsions of named Communists Sam Kahn and Brian Bunting.

28 January The five right-wing Members of Parliament who had been expelled from the United Party in late 1953 for challenging the leadership of Jacobus Strauss, with two others who had resigned in sympathy, form an 'Independent

United Party'. The group's leader, Bailey Bekker, emphasized that the group was not a new political party and said it would abide by the United Party's constitution. By the end of the year, however, it had transformed itself into the Conservative Party.

3 February The Riotous Assemblies and Suppression of Communism Amendment Act is published. The bill enabled the justice minister to prohibit public gatherings on either a specific or general basis and, without disclosing a reason, ban anyone from attending public meetings who was either named under the Suppression of Communism Act or thought to be disseminating Communist propaganda. Named Communists could also be prohibited from visiting certain areas, becoming members of trade unions or accepting the nomination to run for a seat in a national, provincial or territorial assembly. The minister was further empowered to prevent all public meetings, including religious ones, from being held on specific days and recordings of speeches from banned persons being played at meetings.

The new act was in direct response to the 26 November 1953 ruling in which the Supreme Court found that anyone named as a Communist and subsequently banned from attending public meetings was not bound by the ban if he had not first be given a hearing.

1 March The Natives Resettlement Act is introduced into the House of Assembly by Native Affairs Minister Hendrik Verwoerd. The bill provided for the forced removal of Blacks from the western districts of Johannesburg and for their relocation ten miles away at a new site called Meadowlands. It also created a native resettlement board to administer the movements in association with local authorities. Under the bill, Blacks would be permitted to own their own homes but could only lease the land for a period of 30 years. The government said that its motivation for the bill was slum clearance, while the Opposition contended that it was to remove Blacks from an area that was close to White sections and in which they could own the freehold on land. The bill passed the House on 27 April and the Senate on 24 May.

12 April Prime Minister Malan introduces a motion to the House of Assembly that the British protectorates of Basutoland, Bechuanaland and Swaziland should be transferred to South Africa as soon as possible and that negotiations towards that end should be resumed with Britain. The pro-British United Party agreed on the principle of incorporation but said that the government should have reached an agreement with Britain on restarting talks before it presented the motion to Parliament. The motion passed the House of Assembly on 13 April and the Senate on 14 April.

British Prime Minister Winston Churchill reacted on 13 April by saying: 'There can be no question of Her Majesty's Government agreeing at the present time to the transfer of Basutoland, Bechuanaland and Swaziland to the Union Government', and promising that the protectorates would not be transferred until both the local inhabitants and the British parliament had been consulted. His statement was applauded by both sides of the British House of Commons.

12 April The parliamentary select committee established on 2 October 1953 to study the Separate Representation of Voters Validation and Amendment Bill publishes its report. The committee stated that opinion among the Coloured community on the bill was split but that the two largest Coloured bodies, the South African Coloured People's Organization and the Coloured People's National Union, both strongly opposed the principle of separate representation. The Nationalist members of the committee recommended that the bill go ahead while the Opposition members opposed it.

27 April Miss Ray Alexander wins a decisive victory in the Cape Western by-election. She was prevented from entering the Houses of Parliament and was told by Justice Minister Charles Swart that she was 'incapable' of taking her seat. The Speaker of the House informed Parliament that Alexander, a named Communist, was unable to take up her seat under the terms of the Suppression of Communism Amendment Act and that the seat was therefore vacant.

17 May A joint sitting of Parliament meets to consider the Separate Representation of Voters Validation and Amendment Bill. In order to obtain the support of the Independent United Party faction led by Bailey Bekker, Prime Minister Malan introduced an amendment that would allow Coloureds currently on the common electoral roll to remain on it but would require all new Coloured voters to be registered on the separate roll. When Parliament voted on the bill on 14 June, the government was nine votes short of the two-thirds majority needed for passage and the Speaker was forced to rule that it had failed to pass.

25 May Opposition leader Strauss introduces a motion calling Speaker of the House J.H. Conradie 'temperamentally unfit for the office' and said he was unable to disassociate himself from his previous National Party allegiances. Strauss had tabled the censure motion, the first against a Speaker in South African history, because he felt that Conradie had not acted impartially during the debate on the Separate Representation of Voters Validation and Amendment Bill. The resolution failed to pass.

1 July India accedes to South Africa's request and closes its high commission in Cape Town. The two countries agreed that all future contact would be conducted either directly or through their high commissions in London. South Africa reportedly made the request because India had broken off trade relations in July 1946 and recalled its last high commissioner for consultations in August 1947. The government said that it could 'no longer accept this anomalous position' of allowing an Indian diplomatic presence in South Africa, without a high commissioner, while India was maintaining a trade embargo against the country. India contended that it had withdrawn its high commissioner and instituted the trading ban to protest South Africa's adoption of the Asiatic Land Tenure and Indian Representation Bill. The Indian government had hoped the position of South African Indians would improve so it could return the high commissioner but this had not happened.

22 August The National Party claims South West Africa as part of the Union of South Africa, rejecting the UN position that the League of Nations mandate over the territory was still in force and that South Africa must report on its stewardship to the UN.

26 August The Cape provincial council, controlled by the Nationalists as a result of the 18 August provincial elections, passes a motion for the general extension of compulsory apartheid in the province. The motion particularly applied to buses, which had until then been integrated. On 2 September, it also passed an ordinance amending the province's education law and extending compulsory home language instruction to all primary schools and the first three years of secondary school. The Nationalists had already introduced the policy in the Transvaal and Orange Free State, where they had long had majorities. The home language was to be determined by a school inspector and not by the parents. The United Party-controlled Natal council rejected on 9 November for the fourth time in five years a National Party motion calling for compulsory home language instruction.

6 September US President Dwight D. Eisenhower announces that the US, South Africa, Britain, Canada, France and Australia were proceeding with plans to form an international atomic resources and development pool. The six allies had agreed to establish an agency to develop 'new atomic technology for peaceful use' and expected other 'friendly nations' to join.

12 September Defence Minister François C. Erasmus returns to South Africa after discussions with defence chiefs in London and Amsterdam. He announced that while in Britain he had proposed the formation of an African defence organization which would provide mutual assistance against Communist aggression. It would involve all those countries with African interests, particularly sub-Saharan. He had previously said that the greatest danger to that part of Africa was 'the advent of the "quit Africa" policy of anti-colonialism – a policy which not only plays into the hands of the Communists but may, in fact, be inspired by them'. He had also discussed the future of the strategic Simonstown naval base near Cape Town but no decision on that had been reached.

5 October A two-day 'unity conference' of trade unions ends in Durban after delegates decide to establish the South African Trade Union Council (SATUC), which was expected to become the largest trade union organization in the country. The resolution to form the SATUC was supported by most of the major trade unions and said that, although the new body recognized that true trade unionism meant the unity of all workers, in the South African context the inclusion of non-registered unions or Black unions would make effective and broad union impossible. Black unions were, therefore, excluded from the new organization although Indian, Coloured and Mixed unions were allowed to join. The delegates decided that SATUC would come into existence on 1 December 1954 and that liaison be established and maintained between it and the Council of Non-European Trade Unions.

24 November The National Conservative Party is formed in Bloemfontein by the seven right-wing Members of Parliament who had left the United Party in 1953 and set up the Independent United Party. Bailey Bekker, who was named party leader, had announced in August the group's intention to turn itself into a new political party. He said that the pro-apartheid Conservative Party would be an exclusively Afrikaner party but that he hoped it would become 'a political home for reasonable people of both sides'.

30 November Daniel Malan resigns as prime minister and retires from public life. The 80-year-old Malan had announced his 'irrevocable' decision to step down at a special Cabinet meeting on 11 October. He later said that a leader should know when to 'hand over the reins' and not wait until he was compelled to do so for health or other reasons.

Although it was widely believed that Finance Minister Nicolaas Havenga was Malan's personal choice as his successor, Havenga appeared to have lost the power struggle. He withdrew his name from consideration 'in the interests of party unity' and announced 'the end of a long public career'. Lands and Irrigation Minister Johannes Gerhardus Strydom was then elected without opposition as leader of the National Party and, consequently, as prime minister. Strydom was the National Party's leader in the Transvaal. His election, in place of Havenga, was seen by political observers as a sign that the long-anticipated shift of power from the Cape to the Transvaal had occurred.

The new prime minister, an ardent supporter of apartheid, announced that he would continue the party policy of 'justice and fairness towards all sections of the population' and promised that he would do whatever was necessary to turn South Africa into a republic. Strydom announced his new cabinet on 2 December.

1 December Elections are held for the three Native Representatives in the House of Assembly. An independent, L.B. Lee-Warden, won the Cape Western seat left vacant by the election and subsequent expulsion of three named Communists. Lee-Warden, while not named under the Suppression of Communism Act like his predecessors Sam Kahn, Brian Bunting and Ray Alexander, had been banned from attending any public gatherings for two years and had not participated in any electoral meetings.

8 February The first forced resettlement of Blacks into segregated townships in the Cape Western province begins. Some 150 families were moved into government-sponsored housing outside city limits while the government banned all public gatherings in Johannesburg and Roodepoort for 20 days to prevent violence. A total of some 178,000 Blacks were scheduled to be moved.

Minister of Native Affairs Hendrik Verwoerd had informed the House of Assembly on 28 January that the Cape Western province would be one of the places where the government would apply the first phase of apartheid, the movement of people according to race. He contended that the Whites in that region were in great danger of being overwhelmed by a massive Black influx. He emphasized that although the Black presence in the province was not permanent, some Blacks would still be needed in the labour force and, for that reason, not all Blacks would be immediately removed from the area. He added that the migration of whole families would be severely restricted and that hostels for workers only would be built. When Blacks were no longer required as workers, they would be moved to Black areas and the hostels could be converted into housing for Coloured families.

21 February The Departure from the Union Regulation Bill is published. The bill tightened passport regulations and made it illegal to either personally leave South Africa without the proper travel documents or to assist someone else in doing so. The government contended that the bill, which prescribed heavy penalties for anyone convicted of violating it, was required to close a loophole by which South Africans could travel to Communist countries, undergo training and return to South Africa to disseminate Communist propaganda.

Under questioning by the Opposition, the government conceded that the bill would also enable it to prevent the travel of anyone who disagreed with its policies. Interior Minister Theophilus E. Donges said that while the main aim of the bill was to curb Communism, it 'would have a much wider impact than that', since the country was not only under threat from Communism.

21 February Finance Minister Eric Louw announces the introduction of new exchange controls and says that, in future, South Africans would have to declare their holdings in sterling as well as in other currencies. The announcement followed South Africa's decision not to raise the bank rate as the British had done. It was seen as a means of preventing the flight of South African investment money to Britain in search of higher interest rates.

6 March Delegates from 35 national and regional trade unions agree to form the multiracial South African Trade Union Congress after a two-day meeting in Johannesburg. The unions, representing some 42,000 members, had opposed the disbanding of the old South African Trades and Labour Council in October 1954 and had refused to join the new South African Trade Union Council because of its ban on the membership of Black unions.

25 March The Appeal Court Quorum Bill is introduced in the House of Assembly by Justice Minister Charles Swart. The bill raised the total number of appeal court judges from six to 11 and stipulated that a quorum of five judges would be required to hear final appeals in cases other than those concerning the validity of acts of Parliament, which would be heard by a quorum of the full 11 judges.

The justice minister said that the government wanted a strong court to decide on the validity of 'other steps' it intended to introduce and that it would not rest until 'Parliament is supreme and the courts have no right to test its legislation'. The Opposition attacked the bill as another government attempt to have the Cape Coloureds removed from the common electoral roll.

The bill was passed by Parliament on 5 May, after which the new judges were named and directed to assume their duties on 1 October.

5 April External Affairs Minister Louw announces that South Africa had decided to withdraw from the UN Educational, Scientific and Cultural Organization (UNESCO) because of that organization's 'interference in South Africa's racial problems'. He added that the $72,800 which South Africa contributed annually to UNESCO would be spent that year by the State Information Office to distribute information about South Africa abroad.

South Africa also announced that it would not participate in International Court of Justice hearings on its administration of South West Africa which had been scheduled for May.

24 April Proposed talks between South Africa, India and Pakistan on the treatment of people of Indian origin in South Africa break down. External Affairs Minister Louw said the talks had to be abandoned as a result of a recent public attack on South Africa's racial policies by Indian Prime Minister Jawaharlal Nehru.

The talks had been recommended in a 1954 UN resolution which asked the three countries to try to resolve their differences by direct negotiations. South Africa, while maintaining that the issue was strictly a domestic affair, had indicated its willingness to attend the talks 'on the clear understanding that such a discussion will not affect South Africa's legal position'. India denied responsibility for the failure of the talks to take place, saying it had always openly criticized South Africa's apartheid policies and that it was 'unreasonable' for South Africa to expect them to be silent during the run up to the talks when South Africa had not stopped applying its 'oppressive measures'. India said the only conclusion possible was that South Africa did not want to cooperate in implementing the UN resolution.

11 May The Senate Act, which increases the size of the Senate from 48 to 89 members, is published. The bill prepared the way for the government to finally remove the Cape Coloureds from the common electoral roll by constitutional means. By 'packing' the enlarged chamber with its supporters, the government was confident it could obtain the two-thirds vote of a joint session of Parliament needed to alter the entrenched clauses of the 1909 South Africa Act that protected the Coloured franchise.

The bill changed the manner in which senators were elected. There had previously been eight senators elected from each province, eight nominated by the government, two elected and two nominated from South West Africa and four Native Representatives. Under the new act, the number of senators from each province was based on its number of registered White voters, while the number of appointed senators doubled to 16. The system of proportional representation was ended and the majority party in each province now gained all of the seats for that province.

Protests against the adoption of the bill were staged throughout South Africa by a wide variety of organizations and individuals. The Opposition branded the two bills as 'political fraud' and even some of the National Party supporters in the academic community protested against them on constitutional and moral grounds.

The National Party admitted that the Senate and Quorum Acts were 'distasteful measures' for the government to use in order to obtain the removal of the Coloured voters but blamed the Opposition, saying that its intransigence in the issue had rendered such acts necessary.

27 June A two-day Congress of the People is ended by police in Kliptown, near Johannesburg. It was attended by some 3,000 multiracial delegates who had been gathered by the African National Congress, the South African Indian Congress, the South African Coloured People's Congress, the South African Congress of Democrats and the South African Congress of Trade Unions.

The purpose of the Congress was to adopt a 'Freedom Charter' based on the UN Universal Declaration of Human Rights. The charter declared that 'South Africa belongs to all who live in it, Black and White, and no Government can justly claim authority unless it is based on the will of all the people.' It went on to say that 'our people have been robbed of their birthright to land, liberty and peace by a form of Government founded on injustice and inequality'. The delegates demanded equal treatment for all under the law and said that 'the mineral wealth beneath the soil, the banks and monopoly industry shall be transferred to the ownership of the people as a whole'. The government recognized the strength of the non-Whites acting together and kept the Congress and its leaders under close surveillance. In December 1956, some 156 people were arrested on treason charges for having attended the Congress and signed the Freedom Charter. The mass trial lasted until the beginning of 1959.

4 July British Prime Minister Sir Anthony Eden announces that the control of the royal naval base at Simonstown will be transferred to South Africa. Simonstown had been the main British naval base in South Africa since 1814, but a 1930 agreement had given South Africa the freehold to the base.

Under the new agreement Simonstown would become the headquarters for an enlarged South African navy; South Africa would purchase some £18 million worth of new warships from Britain; and a naval command structure would be established to strengthen the defences of the Cape's sea routes.

9 November South Africa refuses to participate in any further work of the UN General Assembly or any of its committees for the rest of the session after the Assembly's Special Political Committee adopted a resolution expressing 'concern' that South Africa had maintained its policies of racial segregation after previous requests from the Assembly to abandon apartheid.

The resolution also noted with 'regret' that South Africa had refused to cooperate with the special three-man committee on the racial situation in South Africa, established in 1952 but never recognized by South Africa, and extended the committee's mandate for a further year. That committee had reported on 12 October that South Africa's apartheid policy had basically remained unaltered, although efforts to put it into practice in the past year were 'if not almost at a standstill, at least very slow'.

South Africa's chief delegate to the UN, Wentzel C. du Plessis, announced the boycott immediately after the resolution was passed. He argued that it interfered with the domestic affairs of a member state and was, therefore, a 'flagrant' breach of the UN Charter. The leader of the Opposition, Jacobus Strauss, issued a statement in which he endorsed the government's action.

25 November The four provincial electoral colleges elect a new, enlarged Senate according to the regulations adopted by Parliament on 16 June. The old 48-member Senate had been dissolved on 4 November.

The elections for the 67 new members of the enlarged Senate were a formality as the Senate Act, passed in June, stipulated that all the seats in each province would go to whatever party was in the majority. As a result of the elections, the National Party won 77 of the total 89 seats.

The government was now in a position to call a joint session of Parliament, knowing that it was assured of the two-thirds majority needed to change the entrenched laws and that the appeals court was unlikely to intervene to prevent the disenfranchisement of the Coloured voters.

Meetings were held throughout South Africa to protest the election of the new Senate. Members of the Women's Defence of the Constitution wore black sashes to show their mourning for the 'death' of the country's constitution. The organization, known as the Black Sash, had become increasingly more active since the Senate Act was passed in June and went on to become one of the leading anti-apartheid organizations in South Africa.

3 December The UN General Assembly adopts a resolution calling for further investigation into the situation in South West Africa. On the following day, the Trusteeship Committee approved three resolutions that criticized South Africa for failing in its obligations as trustee nation in South West Africa, calling on it to place the territory under the trusteeship of the UN and requesting it to make annual reports on its administration of the area.

6 December The UN General Assembly adopts a resolution expressing 'concern' over South Africa's racial policies and calling for it to meet its obligations under the UN Charter. At the same time, however, a resolution to continue for another year the work of the three-man special committee that had already been studying the apartheid situation in South Africa for three years failed by a single vote to obtain the required two-thirds majority needed to pass. Another resolution, which would ensure that South Africa's racial situation was on the agenda at the Assembly's next session, also failed to obtain the necessary two-thirds vote. The two votes reversed the decision reached by the Assembly's *ad hoc* committee on South Africa that the commission should continue its work and that the issue should be reviewed at the next session.

South African Foreign Minister Louw said on 7 December that the decision to leave the discussion of South Africa off the agenda 'opens the door' for South Africa's return to the UN in 1956.

---

1 9 5 6

---

1 February South Africa orders the Soviet Union to close its two consulates and 'any other Soviet agencies that may exist in South Africa' by 1 March. External Affairs Minister Louw told the House of Assembly that the Soviets had been informed by diplomatic note that their consular representation 'was not in the interest of peace and the well-being of South Africa'. The government accused the Soviets of cultivating and maintaining contacts with 'subversive elements in South Africa, particularly among the Bantu and Indian population' and of using their consulates in Pretoria and Cape Town 'for the diffusion of Communistic propaganda directed particularly at the Bantu population.'

Louw pointed out that South Africa had not broken off diplomatic, trade or other relations with the Soviet Union and said that all future contact would be through the two country's diplomatic missions in London.

27 February The South Africa Amendment Act is approved by more than a two-thirds majority of a joint session of Parliament. The passage of the act meant that the government had won its five-year battle to remove some 45,000 Cape Coloured voters from the common electoral roll and established the supremacy of Parliament over the judiciary.

The Amendment Act reinstated the Separate Representation of Voters Act, removed the entrenched clauses in the 1909 Act which protected Coloured franchise rights, retained the entrenched clauses protecting language rights, and stipulated that no court could rule on any act of Parliament other than one affecting language rights.

The Opposition strongly opposed the South Africa Amendment Act, which they described as another attempt to subvert the entrenched clauses protecting the Coloured franchise. The Labour Party, calling the joint session 'a packed Parliament and a fraud' refused to participate in the debate on the bill and walked out. The United Party made an application against the validity of the South Africa Act Amendment with the Supreme Court on 2 March claiming: the enlarged Senate was not one of the Houses of Parliament; the joint session to consider the bill was not properly constituted; and legislation passed by the joint session with the help of the enlarged Senate was invalid.

The South Africa Amendment Act received the governor general's assent on 2 March and passed into law.

21 March The Separate Representation of Voters Amendment Bill is published. The bill regulated the status of Coloured voters after they had been removed from the common electoral roll, and provided for the establishment of a 27-member Union Council for Coloured Affairs to advise the government, 'at its request', on matters relating to the educational, economic, political and social interests of the Coloured community. Some 15 of the Council's members were appointed by the government while 12 were elected. The bill stipulated that Coloured could elect four White members to the House of Assembly and two White Cape provincial councillors.

The Amendment Bill was considerably different from the original 1951 Act. One of the major alterations was that the 1951 version allowed Coloureds to be elected to the Cape provincial council, while the 1956 version called for Whites to represent Coloureds on the council.

The Opposition strongly opposed the bill, saying that the Union Council for Coloured Affairs would make 'a mockery of democratic representation' as most of its members would be appointed by the government. It also claimed that the bill breached the National Party's agreement with the then Afrikaner Party leader, Nicolaas Havenga, that Coloureds could be represented by Coloured members in the Cape provincial council. The government denied both accusations.

The bill passed the House of Assembly on 27 April and the Senate the following week.

27 March The ten-member Commission on the Socio-Economic Development of the Bantu Areas presents its report to Parliament. It recommended a plan to restrict the majority of South Africa's Black population to seven native reserves or Bantustans while allowing some Blacks to enter White areas as migratory workers.

The group, under the chairmanship of Frederick Tomlinson and better known as the Tomlinson Commission, was established by the Nationalist government in 1951 to 'devise a scheme for the rehabilitation of the native areas with a view to developing within them a social structure in keeping with the culture of the native based on effective socio-economic planning'.

The commission contended that there 'could be no middle way between complete integration of Black and White and complete separation, and a clear-cut choice was now inevitable between the two alternatives'. It rejected the idea of racial integration and concluded that the only hope for the peaceful development of all the races would be the 'establishment of the separate communities in their own separate territories, where each will have the fullest opportunity for self-expression and development'. The commission recommended separate development and said for it to work the Bantu areas would have to be fully developed and more land had to be delegated to them. The land would be consolidated into seven main sections, called Bantustans, which would also eventually include the British protectorates of Bechuanaland, Basutoland and Swaziland.

Because of the poor quality of the land and the uneconomic farming practices in the Bantustans, the commission found that the government would have to help develop alternative farming methods, set up new jobs and develop industries both in the Bantustans and on the borders. It suggested £104 million be spent developing the areas over the next ten years.

The commission concluded that total apartheid would never be a possibility but that if the Bantustans were fully developed they could, by 1981, support some nine million Blacks, while six million Blacks would be available to work in the rest of South Africa.

16 April Apartheid is introduced on Cape Town's buses and trams. The African National Congress, South African Coloured People's Organization and a White group, the South African Congress of Democrats, called a boycott of those lines affected to protest 'bus apartheid'. The Government-backed National Transport Commission, acting upon the recommendations of a 1952 inquiry into segregation on public vehicles, ordered that particular seats on certain routes be reserved for Whites despite the city council's opposition to the move.

24 April The government publishes its views on the Tomlinson Commission's plan for the establishment of Bantustans.

While welcoming the commission's conclusion that separate development was the only course to be pursued and accepting the principle of Bantustans, the government would not commit itself to any of the commission's specific recommendations. It rejected the commission's suggestion that some £104 million be allocated over a ten-year period to develop the Black areas by saying that that no government could set budgets that far in advance and that it would have to examine the situation and determine the budget for the development of the Bantustans each year. It assured the nation, however, that the funds were available to develop the Black areas without cutting White services. The government also rejected the suggestion that Whites be allowed to invest private capital in the areas because it argued that inexperienced Blacks could not compete with White entrepreneurs.

Parliamentary debate on the Tomlinson Commission's report was held on 14–16 May. Prime Minister Johannes Strydom announced that the government would spend some £3.5 million on developing the Bantustans during the current fiscal year, while the opposition United Party said it would support the principle of Bantustans if the government did not insist that it also accept 'the ideological trappings of the word apartheid'. Whites in general, including church groups, supported the Tomlinson Commission's proposals for separate development and the establishment of Bantustans and observers believed that government's response to them disappointed many people, including Nationalist supporters. Blacks were united in their opposition to the Tomlinson plan.

26 April Minister of External Affairs Eric Louw announces the end of South Africa's boycott of the UN and says that the country will participate in that year's (1956) session of the General Assembly.

9 May The Industrial Coalition Act, which permits the minister of labour to restrict certain skilled jobs to White workers, completes its passage through Parliament.

The bill had originally been introduced in the House of Assembly in May 1954 but was sent to a select committee for minor changes. It prohibited the formation of new mixed trade unions, required existing mixed unions to divide their members into single race sections, prohibited mixed trade union meetings, restricted the membership of union executive committees to Whites, forbade unions from affiliating with political parties and enabled the minister of labour to reserve certain kinds of work on a racial basis. The minister could also declare any occupation or industry an essential service and prohibit workers engaged in it from striking.

9 May The Bantu Education Amendment Act is passed by Parliament and brings private schools under the provisions of the original act. The amendment enabled the minister of native affairs to: cancel or refuse the registration of a private school regardless of the recommendations of the Native Affairs Commission; stipulate conditions for the registration of private schools, such as qualifications of staff and level of fees; and approve subsidies to schools. By empowering the minister to set fees and determine subsidies, the act could ensure that private schools which accepted Black children were economically unviable and would have to close down.

18 May The Cape Supreme Court unanimously upholds the validity of both the Senate Act and the South Africa Amendment Act. The court had dismissed the petitions of two Cape Coloureds that a 'packed' Senate, as obtained by the Senate Act, did not constitute a House of Parliament and could not, therefore, vote to amend the entrenched clauses. The petitioners were given leave to appeal, and, on 9 November, the appellate division of the Supreme Court upheld the lower court's decision and refused to declare the Supreme Court Act of 1955 and the South Africa Act Amendment Act of 1956 invalid.

14 June The Natives (Urban Areas) Amendment Act 1956 is passed by both the

House of Assembly and the Senate. It enabled municipalities to expel without trial any Black who was considered a threat 'to the maintenance of peace and order' and made failure to obey the ejection order a punishable offence. The chief native commissioner could confine to particular areas the movements of any person who received two such orders within five years. Failure to comply with that order could result in the person being sentenced to a work colony. The act was part of a series of laws by which Whites tried to restrict the influx of Blacks to urban areas while still ensuring an adequate supply of Black labour.

28 June The Commonwealth Prime Ministers Conference opens in London. While in Britain, Prime Minister Johannes Strydom unsuccessfully restated South Africa's demand that the protectorates of Basutoland, Bechuanaland and Swaziland be transferred to its control without delay. He also proposed that the Commonwealth and other European countries with colonies south of the Sahara (France, Belgium and Portugal) form a defence alliance against any Soviet thrust into Africa.

4 October Black leaders from all over South Africa meet in Bloemfontein to discuss the Tomlinson Report. The meeting rejected the report in its entirety and said that implementing it would 'mean a continuation of the status quo' and would deny Blacks 'the inalienable basic human rights'. The delegates welcomed the principle of developing the Black areas but warned that separate development based on apartheid as laid out in the report was 'totally unacceptable'.

21 November A special United Party Congress meets in Bloemfontein to elect Sir de Villiers Graaff as party leader. He succeeded Jacobus Strauss, who had been in ill health for some months. Sir de Villiers was previously the chairman of the Cape province branch of the United Party.

27 November Foreign Minister Louw informs the UN that South Africa is 'not prepared to be even an unwilling party to the continual interference in its domestic policies' and will maintain 'only a token or nominal' delegation at the UN to protest against that organization's interference in South Africa's 'essentially domestic' racial affairs.

5 December A series of dawn raids is carried out throughout South Africa by the Special Branch of the South African police. Some 140 leading opponents of apartheid were arrested on treason charges; their homes and offices of political organizations with which they were affiliated were searched and documents were confiscated. Sixteen others were later arrested on the same charges.

Of the total 156 detained, 23 were White, 22 Indian, eight Coloured and 103 Black. Among the defendants were L.B. Lee-Warden, the Native Representative in Parliament for the Cape Western district, ANC President-General Albert J. Luthuli, General Secretary Oliver Tambo, former Secretary Walter Sisulu and numerous other professional and business people. Two of the lawyers retained to defend the accused were arrested on 13 December.

19 December The preliminary hearing in the trial of 156 anti-apartheid activists opens in Johannesburg. The defendants were charged with a treasonable plot to set up a Communist-type regime that would break with the principle of apartheid and violate the Suppression of Communism Act. They were all granted bail as the long trial got under way on the provision that they did not attend any public meetings and reported to the police on a weekly basis.

The formal charges were never actually read out until the prosecution concluded its case 14 months later on 21 January 1958. The accused were charged with committing hostile acts against the Union of South Africa, including: organizing or participating in campaigns against the apartheid legislation; conspiring to overthrow the government by violent, illegal, unconstitutional or extra-parliamentary means; convening a 'People's Congress' in June 1955 and adopting a 'Freedom Charter'; advocating the establishment of a Communist state; inciting the public to commit violent acts against both the police and Whites; spreading hostile feelings among Whites and non-Whites; distributing documents and making speeches to stir discontent with the aim of changing the government; and recruiting 'freedom volunteers' to participate in the 'Freedom Charter'.

7 January Black leaders call for a boycott of buses between the Black township of Alexandria and Johannesburg to protest a fare rise of one penny. The increase represented a major hardship to the Black users of the bus service, while the bus company argued that the increase was needed to make the service viable. The boycott, which started off as an economic issue, soon took on political significance with liberal Whites offering their support to the boycott while the government brought in strict measures to break it. In spite of the government's attempts, the boycott was 100 per cent successful.

The boycott ended on 1 April after unofficial negotiations between Black leaders, city councillors and church officials. They agreed that fares would remain the same and that the extra money the bus company would have earned from the increase would instead come from a fund set up by the Blacks' employers.

9 January The preliminary hearing in the treason trial of 156 anti-apartheid activists resumes in Johannesburg. The opening of the mass trial in December 1956 was marked by violent demonstrations outside the courthouse by supporters of the multiracial defendants. Over 500 policemen were brought in when the trial reopened to prevent a repetition of those stormy clashes.

In a statement to the court, the lawyer for the defence contended that the defendants, who represented a wide cross-section of the population from Members of Parliament to priests, students, clerical workers and labourers, were the victims of 'political kite-flying' and said that the prosecution was 'testing the political breezes to ascertain how far the originators can go in their endeavors to stifle free speech and criticism of the policies of the Government'.

The prosecution opened its case against the defendants, accusing them of attempting to overthrow the state and set up a Communist regime. The preliminary hearing continued until 11 May, when the case was adjourned until

13 January 1958. On 17 December, the Crown withdrew its case against 61 of the accused, including African National Congress (ANC) President-General Albert Luthuli, for lack of evidence.

23 January The leader of the Conservative Party, Bailey Bekker, announces to the House of Assembly that the party has been disbanded. He said that the election of Sir de Villiers Graaff as leader of the United Party in place of Jacobus Strauss had vindicated the actions taken by the six United Party members in forming the Conservative Party. He said that although 'certain friendly differences' still remained between the two parties, every Conservative Party member would from now on be free to act and speak for himself and 'decide about his own political destiny'.

30 January The UN General Assembly adopts two resolutions, previously approved by the UN Special Political Committee, which are highly critical of South Africa.

The first asked the South African government to 'reconsider' its policies of racial segregation in the light of its obligations and responsibilities under the Charter and of the principles subscribed to . . . in other multi-racial societies' and asked it to 'cooperate in a constructive approach to this question'. The second resolution noted 'with regret' that South Africa still had not agreed to negotiate with India and Pakistan on conditions for people of Indian and Pakistani origin living in South Africa and asked it to 'cooperate' on this issue. The resolutions were similar to ones voted in at other sessions.

30 January A presidential ordinance comes into effect in India empowering the government to control the movement of all Commonwealth citizens in India and allowing it to exempt from restrictions the citizens of any Commonwealth country it wished. The Indian government immediately exempted the nationals of every Commonwealth country except South Africa and Pakistan making them, in effect, the only Commonwealth citizens to be treated as foreigners. South Africans in future had to report their movements to the Indian police and were subject to deportation for overstaying their visas. The move was part of India's ongoing protest against South Africa's apartheid policies as applied to South Africans of Indian origin.

19 February The Natives Law Amendment Bill is introduced into the House of Assembly. The highly controversial bill stipulated, among other things, that Blacks could not attend churches outside the Black areas without the minister of native affairs' permission and was vigorously opposed by the various churches throughout South Africa.

11 March The Separate University Education Bill is introduced into the House of Assembly by Education Minister Johannes H. Viljoen. The bill would have effectively extended apartheid to all South African universities and ended non-Whites' right of admission to the 'open' universities of Cape Town and Witwatersrand.

Under the bill, non-White students would not only be separated from White students, but they would also be separated from each other along strict racial and tribal lines. Five new 'ethnic' universities would be established, one each for

Indians near Durban, Coloureds in Cape Town, Zulus in Zululand and Sothos in the northern Transvaal. Fort Hare College, which had an international student body, would become a Xhosa tribal college. Minister Viljoen said that separate institutions were necessary because a future leader had to be 'in close touch with the habits, ways of life and views of his population group'.

Whites who tried to register in non-White institutions or non-Whites who sought enrolment into White establishments could be sentenced to six months' imprisonment or a fine of £100. Non-Whites who were already enrolled in White schools would be allowed to remain but no new enrolments would be permitted. Viljoen added that as the new ethnic institutions became more established and added more courses to their curriculum, the ban on students attending courses at facilities other than those for their own ethnic group would be strengthened.

The Opposition parties and academia protested against the bill, calling it 'a serious interference with traditional academic freedom'. Staff and students of the English-speaking universities demonstrated outside Parliament. The University of Witwatersrand pledged 'to uphold the principle that a university is a place where men and women, without regard to race and colour, are welcome to join in the acquisition and advancement of knowledge'. The government's reaction to the demonstrations was summed up by Viljoen, who told Parliament that 'the only possible inference is that this agitation is taking place under the influence of a leftist movement in our country'.

The government announced on 17 May that a select committee would be established to study the Separate University Education Bill. The decision effectively postponed further action on the matter for at least one year.

26 March The Flag Amendment Act is signed into law by the governor general and establishes the Union flag as the only national flag of South Africa. The new act amended the 1927 Flag Act, which had represented a compromise in a bitter dispute between those who wanted the British Union Jack as South Africa's flag and those who wanted to completely abolish its use. The 1927 Act created a Union flag and stipulated that both it and the Union Jack should be flown together on all official occasions and on all government buildings.

The Opposition strongly opposed the bill on the grounds that dropping the Union Jack would weaken South Africa's ties with the Commonwealth and deprive the country of a strong symbol of its association with that organization. Many observers saw the act as part of the government's plan to eventually declare South Africa a republic.

2 May Prime Minister Johannes Strydom announces that 'Die Stem van Suid Afrika' ('The Call of South Africa') will in future be the country's only national anthem and will be played on all official occasions, including those at which the Queen or her representative, the governor general, is present. Until this announcement, Britain's 'God Save the Queen' had been given equal status in South Africa. The two anthems had both been played at all official events since 1938.

In explaining his decision, Prime Minister Strydom said that as the country would in future have only one flag, it followed that it should have only one national anthem.

15 September Fierce rioting breaks out between Zulus and Basutos in a Black township outside Johannesburg. More than 40 people were killed in the disturbances, including women and children. When the government refused to hold an inquiry into the riots, the Johannesburg city council established one itself to examine not only the riot but also the general Black living conditions that might result in similar violent outbreaks. Welfare workers, church organizations, the media and city councillors had for years attempted to show that Black living conditions had deteriorated to such an extent that lawlessness was rife, police were powerless and a generation of young Blacks were growing up to accept crime, violence and contempt for authority as the norm.

18 September South Africa announces that recent defence talks in London, held to review 'the threat to Africa from external aggression', had resulted in South Africa being granted the right to overfly the British protectorates of Basutoland, Bechuanaland and Swaziland. The British government emphasized that, although South Africa could overfly the protectorates and have access to certain facilities located there, the defence of the territories remained an exclusively British responsibility.

Reports from the meeting, at which the countries also agreed to cooperate more on defence issues, suggested a difference of opinion between South Africa and Britain on how South Africa could best be protected. South Africa advocated an anti-Communist defence organization, consisting of countries with sub-Saharan colonies, while Britain felt the best method would be to heavily defend the Middle Eastern gateway to Africa.

15 November The South African Garment Workers' Union stages a temporary work-stoppage to prove that the government's plans to reserve certain skilled jobs for Whites would not work in the garment industry because there were not enough Whites to do the work. The government had passed the Industrial Conciliation Act in May 1956, enabling the minister of labour to declare that certain occupations and skilled work could be performed only by Whites. The union called for all of its non-White members to perform only those non-skilled jobs which would be left open to them. Within two days work ground to a halt as non-Whites waited for the few skilled Whites employed in the industry to process the work and send it on. Most factories in the Transvaal had to close until the chaos was straightened out.

13 January The preliminary hearing in the treason trial of 95 anti-apartheid activists reopens in Johannesburg, after an adjournment of eight months. Treason charges against a further 61 people had been withdrawn over the course of the past year.

The prosecution concluded its case against the accused on 29 January, more than a year after it had given its opening statements. The recorded evidence ran to almost 2.5 million words and included some 10,000 documents and police reports on statements allegedly made by the defendants. The defence, who had announced on 21 January that it would not be calling any witnesses, called for all the charges against the defendants to be dropped on the grounds that the Crown had failed to prove that any offence had actually been committed. The defendants' lawyer contended that the prosecution's witnesses all admitted that the defendants had called for racial harmony and had consistently pleaded for the avoidance of violence. He argued that the June 1955 Congress of the People at which the Freedom Charter had been adopted had been a peaceful occasion and that delegates from the National Party, as well as from all other recognized political parties, had been invited to attend. The defence concluded that: 'If that which the Crown has established be evidence of treason, subversion or Communism as defined in our law, then there is an end in this country to all that is implicit in the term democracy'. The prosecutor maintained that the Freedom Charter had treasonably advocated racial equality and Communistic principles, such as the public ownership of banks and basic industries.

On 30 January, the court found that the accused had a case to answer and ordered the 17 Whites, 18 Indians, 58 Blacks and two Coloureds to stand trial on charges of high treason. All charges were subsequently dropped, without explanation, against the White Native Representative L.B. Lee-Warden and two of his Indian co-defendants.

16 March The African National Congress (ANC) holds a mass meeting near Johannesburg in defiance of a 14 March proclamation by Native Affairs Minister Hendrik Verwoerd that the government had the power to ban the Congress. Black leaders at the meeting demanded representation in the government, the end of apartheid and the establishment of a Black minimum wage.

17 March Governor General Ernest Jansen issues a proclamation banning the ANC from several Black reserves. The proclamation empowered the minister of native affairs to extend the ban to other areas or organizations as necessary and to order ANC possessions to be disposed of or destroyed. ANC members in the banned reserves who did not resign from the organization, or anyone who subsequently joined the ANC or participated in its activities, faced fines of up to £300 and/or three years' imprisonment.

3 April Cape Coloured voters go to the polls for the first time since the Separate Representation of Voters Act removed them from the common electoral roll in 1956. Under the provisions of the act, between 29,000 and 30,000 Coloured males were eligible to elect four Whites to represent them in the House of Assembly. The 51.6 per cent of the electorate who participated in the election chose three United Party-supported independents and one United Party candidate as their representatives. The National Party fared extremely badly with all of its candidates losing their deposits.

14 April ANC leader Oliver Tambo cancels a planned election day strike after Prime Minister Strydom announces that his government would 'act drastically' to curb Black unrest during the current election campaign.

The ANC's plans to stage a strike and demonstrations to demand a $2.80

minimum daily wage and the repeal of the pass laws were abandoned when the government stated that harsh measures would be taken to deal with potential demonstrations and that full protection would be given to all those who decided to defy the strike call.

On 12 April, the government prohibited meetings of more than 10 Blacks in parts of the Transvaal, the Orange Free State and the Cape to prevent 'irresponsible elements' from causing unrest among the workers. The Johannesburg offices of the ANC and the Transvaal Indian Congress were raided by the police, who seized pamphlets and documents urging Blacks to participate in the strike.

15 April The first-ever conference of independent African states opens in the Ghanaian capital of Accra. The week-long meeting, aimed at 'forging closer links of friendship, brotherhood, cooperation and solidarity', was attended by representatives from Ethiopia, Ghana, Liberia, Libya, Morocco, Sudan, Tunisia and the United Arab Republic. Political observers in South Africa believed that the importance of the meeting lay not in the anti-colonial resolutions that were passed but in the fact that it was the first time high-ranking African politicians established personal contacts with each other on such a scale. The eight states went on to form a new political bloc in the UN 'to assert a distinctive African personality', and left many South Africans with an increased sense of isolation.

16 April Prime Minister Strydom and his National Party are returned to power with an increased majority as a result of South Africa's first all-White elections. Opposition leader Sir de Villiers Graaff was defeated in his own constituency. The National Party won 103 of the House of Assembly's 163 seats while the United Party won 53 seats. The 43-seat majority was 10 seats greater than in the last election and resulted from a nine-seat gain by the National Party and a one-seat loss by the United Party. The Labour Party lost all of the four seats it had held in the previous House, making it the first time in South African history that the party was unrepresented in the House of Assembly. The Liberal Party and independents also failed to gain a seat. The four Cape Coloured representatives, elected under the provisions of the Separate Representation of Voters Act on 3 April, supported the United Party. This brought the United Party's total strength in the House up to 57 and made the indirectly elected two Liberal and one independent Native Representatives the only third force in the lower House of Parliament.

9 July The government publishes its Special Criminal Courts Amendment Act. Under the provisions of the act, the justice minister ordered special courts to be constituted to hear cases involving treason charges or violations of the Suppression of Communism Act, whenever it was 'in the interests of the administration of justice'. He was further empowered to appoint two or three judges to conduct such a court.

The new act was introduced after the 1 July announcement that a special criminal court would be appointed to hear the case against the anti-apartheid activists currently charged with treason in Johannesburg. The Opposition opposed the bill on the grounds that it had been introduced specifically to 'validate the decision that the government had already taken on how that trial would be conducted and that it would give the minister of justice too much discretionary power in cases involving treason or Communism.

15 July External Affairs Minister Eric Louw announces that South Africa will resume full participation in the UN after having had only token representation at the organization since November 1956. He added that South Africa would be represented at the next session of the UN General Assembly at the ambassadorial level.

17 July South Africa and Britain announce the details of defence-planning facilities which will be granted to South Africa in the British protectorates of Swaziland, Basutoland and Bechuanaland. These facilities included reciprocal overflying rights; inspection of possible emergency airstrips in Bechuanaland for use by South African aircraft; access through Basutoland for proposed South African radar sites; and permission for the South African Defence Force to reconnoitre south-western Bechuanaland for potential emergency routes to South West Africa. The details were worked out in talks in Pretoria between the South African defence minister and the British high commissioner for the protectorates and followed meetings in Britain on the same subject.

24 August Prime Minister Strydom dies in Cape Town, aged 65. He had been suffering for the past two years from heart disease.

Strydom, a strong proponent of apartheid, was the country's fifth prime minister and had held the premiership since November 1954. He was returned to power with an increased majority in general elections held earlier this year. In view of his serious illness, however, the governor general had appointed Justice Minister Charles R. Swart as acting prime minister on 21 August.

Parliament adjourned on 24 August after paying tribute to Strydom in order to give the National Party time to select his successor as leader of the party and, automatically, prime minister.

2 September Native Affairs Minister Hendrik Verwoerd is elected leader of the National Party in succession to the late Johannes Strydom and automatically becomes South Africa's new prime minister. He was chosen on the second ballot over Justice Minister Charles Swart and Interior Minister Theophilus E. Donges by the National Party's parliamentary caucus, meeting in Cape Town. Political commentators observed that the party, in selecting Verwoerd, had chosen one of the most determined proponents of racial discrimination available to it. Both the parliamentary opposition and the liberal press reacted cautiously to his election, describing him as a committed republican and the government's 'most rigid and forceful practitioner of apartheid'.

Prime Minister Verwoerd announced shortly after his election that he would direct all his efforts to establishing a republic in South Africa 'in such a way and at such a time that it will be lasting'. He went on to say that apartheid did not oppress any part of the population but was rather designed to ensure 'happiness, security and stability for both the Bantu and the Whites by having their own home, language and administration'.

23 October Some 900 Black women are arrested in three days of demonstrations against new Native Pass Office rules that required Black women to carry identity books for the first time. The women were later freed on bail of £1 but another 900 women were arrested for illegally demonstrating on 27 October and refused to accept being released on bail.

A Johannesburg court withdrew the charges against the women, while police outside the courthouse used tear gas and clubs to disperse a further 500 Blacks demonstrating against the pass system. Some 128 of the women were fined £3 each on 6 November for taking part in the demonstrations.

30 October The UN General Assembly passes resolutions expressing 'regret and concern' that South Africa had ignored UN calls for an end to apartheid and reiterates its requests that South West Africa be placed 'under the International Trusteeship System'.

22 November Some 30 of the 91 defendants in the long-running treason trial are reindicted in Johannesburg for treasonable conspiracy. They were charged with conspiracy to endanger the security or existence of the state by actively preparing to subvert or overthrow it by violence and to then substitute a Communist or other form of state. The government announced that the accused would be reindicted in two groups.

19 January A special court convenes in Pretoria to hear the case against some 30 anti-apartheid activists accused of conspiring to overthrow the government and replace it with a 'Communist State'. A total of 91 people, who had been tried without result in 1958, were facing treason charges but it was decided to retry the defendants in two groups. A defence motion to have the indictment against the 28 Blacks and two Whites quashed as 'bad in law and defective on the face of it' was rejected on 2 March, but the defence was given leave to appeal and the case was adjourned while awaiting the appellate court's decision.

23 January Prime Minister Hendrik Verwoerd unveils his government's new policy to create separate independent Black African states, or Bantustans, in which Blacks could exercise their political rights. The policy was the government's solution to the problem of how to give Blacks the self-determination they would eventually demand, without abandoning its philosophy of strict racial segregation.

Verwoerd left unclear his government's timetable for creating the homelands, saying the speed of implementing the plan depended on the Blacks themselves and could take 50 to 100 years or more. The new Bantustans were to be geographically based on the old tribal boundaries and eight were suggested: North and South Sotho, Swazi, Tsonga, Tswana, Venda, Xhosa and Zulu. As the first steps towards establishing the independent homelands, Bantu tribal authorities with some limited powers were to be set up and commissioners appointed to liaise between the government and the Bantustans.

Verwoerd's proposals, presented by the Nationalists as their 'new vision' and the 'positive' side of apartheid, were the government's reaction to the criticism that apartheid was a one-way street in which Blacks lost rights but never gained them. As a result of the introduction of the plan, most people predisposed towards apartheid saw the racial policy in a new moral light, which it had previously lacked. The new call for 'parallel development' was taken up by many Nationalists who had been uneasy about the ethics of some of the discriminatory legislation that Blacks had had to suffer.

The opposition United Party, thrown into a confusion exacerbated by the internal rift it had been subjected to between its right and left wings, merely objected to the scheme on the grounds that it was not only economically suspect but also impractical. It also objected that the six million Blacks not living in homelands would be unaccounted for under the new proposals. The reactions of the Blacks themselves ranged from unease to hostility.

26 February Two bills designed to establish apartheid in South African universities are introduced into the House of Assembly. The Extension of University Education Bill called for the gradual expulsion of all non-White students from the 'open' universities of Witwatersrand and Cape Town and the concurrent opening of five 'ethnic' universities: three for Blacks on a tribal basis and one each for Indians and Coloureds. The bill passed the House of Assembly on 30 April and the Senate on 8 June. The University College of Fort Hare Transfer Bill reserved the college, which had previously had an international student body, for the exclusive use of members of the Xhosa tribe and transferred control of the institution from Rhodes University to the Department of Native Affairs. The bill was passed by the House of Assembly on 26 June and the Senate on 27 June. The bills replaced the Separate University Education Bill, which was introduced in 1957 to cover both issues but subsequently withdrawn and reintroduced in the amended form.

5 March Finance Minister Donges announces that the new monetary unit to be introduced when South Africa's currency is decimalized will be called the rand. The name, originally suggested by the late Finance Minister Nicolaas Havenga, was chosen because it was bilingual in English and Afrikaans and had 'the ring of gold about it' which would make it 'recognized as South African in the money markets of the world'.

24 March The Promotion of Bantu Self-Government Bill is introduced in the House of Assembly by the minister for native affairs, Daan de Wet Nel. It provided for the establishment of eight Black 'national units' with limited legislative authority but, at the same time, abolished Black representation in the South African parliament.

The bill was seen as the second stage of the government's 'positive' apartheid that would transform the Black reserves into self-governing Bantustans, where non-Whites would be encouraged to develop separately. The first stage had been the 1951 Bantu Authorities Act that established tribal, regional and territorial authorities throughout South Africa. The government's purpose in establishing the Bantustans was to advance the basic principles of apartheid by first providing Blacks with their own areas and then ensuring that they only enter 'White' areas as migrant workers.

Under the bill, five White commissioners-general would be appointed to guide and advise Blacks on constitutional, social and economic matters and to act as a link between the government and the Bantustan. One of the main problems with the plan was that the eight Bantustans were not eight distinct areas that could become eight self-governing units. Each unit was, in fact, made up of widely scattered pieces of land separated from each other by White areas.

The Opposition contended that the bill sought 'to embark South Africa on a course which will lead to the destruction of the Union and prove disastrous to the future of our people', and that it would create a state where non-Whites had no voice.

6 April Dissident African National Congress (ANC) members announce the formation of a new non-White political group, the Pan-Africanist Congress (PAC). The PAC was founded by some 300 Blacks who had rejected the ANC's policy of forming alliances with liberal White and Indian organizations and as a result either resigned or were expelled from that organization. At its inaugural meeting, the PAC elected Robert Sobukwe as its leader and defined its aims as 'Africa for the Africans'. Sobukewe denied that his group was anti-White as such and said it would accept as an African 'anyone who owes his only loyalty to Africa and is prepared to accept the democratic rule of an African majority'.

20 April The treason trial for the second group of anti-apartheid activists opens in Pretoria. The mass treason indictment against the 61 Black, Indian and Coloured defendants was dismissed when the three judges ruled that it cited insufficient evidence of their alleged conspiracy to overthrow the South African government. All charges against the accused were dismissed.

22 May The president-general of the ANC, Albert Luthuli, is banned from attending or addressing any meetings for a five-year period and is banished to his home district in Lower Tugela, Natal province, by Justice Minister Swart. Swart made the orders under the Riotous Assemblies and Suppression of Communism Acts. Political observers condemned the move calling Luthuli 'the strongest influence within the Congress movement in favour of moderation and race cooperation'.

26 May The first all-Black local authority to be created under the Bantu Territorial Authority Act, which aimed to divide South Africa into separate White and Black areas, is inaugurated by Minister of Bantu Development Daan de Wet Nel. The Transkei Territorial Authority replaced the White-ruled Transkei General Council and was to be given local government powers under the pending Bantu Self-Government Act.

19 June A series of violent clashes between Blacks and police begins in Durban. Police opened fire on crowds in the Cato Manor slum area after some 4,000 Black women burned three municipal beer halls and attacked buildings, buses and the police. Four Black men were killed while 24 Black men and women and one White policeman were injured.

Blacks were prohibited by law from buying any kind of alcohol, except 'Kaffir beer' which is sold in municipal beer halls. Many Black women, however, brew illicit alcohol to augment their incomes. The rioting began after the Durban city council, trying to cope with a typhoid epidemic, ordered the illegal stills destroyed because they encouraged the breeding of flies. The women, however, believed the real motive was to increase the sales at the municipal beer halls. The destruction of the stills came at a particularly bad time since slum clearance plans for the area meant that some of the Blacks were being moved to the new township of Kwa Mashu 11 miles away, where rents and transport costs were higher. Some 41 people, including 38 women, were arrested on public order charges after the disturbances.

Sporadic incidents occurred throughout the summer. A demonstration by Kwa Mashu women protesting installation of water meters was dispersed on 22 June by police using tear gas, while some 15,000 Blacks at Clermont township, near Durban, began a bus boycott on 22 June to protest expropriation of African land to build a bus station. Some 20 Black women were arrested on 7 July for an attack on a beer hall in Verulem, a Durban suburb, while police fired on Black demonstrators protesting liquor curbs on 13 July in Lamont, another Black suburb of Durban.

26 June Blacks observe 'Freedom Day' by beginning a boycott of businesses supporting the Nationalist government. The action had been called by ANC President-General Luthuli at an April rally in Cape Town and supported by the South African Coloured People's Organization. The ANC appealed for foreign support for the action and the boycott of South African goods spread to Ghana, the West Indies, British East Africa and Britain. By the following year several other African and Asian countries had joined the movement.

13 August The United Party ends a three-day national congress in Bloemfontein with the resignation of 12 of its 53 Members of Parliament. The split came over the adoption of a resolution by the congress that opposed the acquisition of more land for the consolidation of the Bantustans. The liberal wing strongly opposed the resolution saying they felt it was a 'clear breach of the promise given by the United Party in 1936' that native reserves would remain an integral part of South Africa. The resolution was passed after a long and acrimonious debate and was seen as the immediate catalyst for a revolt that had been brewing for some time, as liberals in the party had long been frustrated by the United Party's racial policies.

The 12 Members of Parliament and their supporters formed the new Progressive Group. They adopted a four-point statement of principle in which they declared their belief that the United Party had reneged on its promises to non-Whites in order to obtain the support of moderate Nationalists.

16 August The clashes which have been taking place between Black demonstrators and the police since June spread out from Durban into other parts of Natal. Blacks protesting against the government's Bantustan policy in a village near Pietermaritzburg set fire to government buildings and schools. Police shoot dead two of the rioters. The following day, some 1,000 spear-carrying Black women marched on a church mission near Harding where White women and children were sheltering under the protection of armed vigilantes. On 18 August, 118 Black women were sentenced to two months' hard labour in Natal after their arrest for building road-blocks and exhorting Black men to strike for farm wages of £1 daily. Some 39 women and one man were arrested on 20 August after clashing with police outside a courthouse in Escourt, while 186 women were arrested in the Port Shepstone area on 21 August for armed attacks on government cattle-dipping stations. Another 200 women were dispersed by armed police in Camperdown on 24 August after they had walked 35 miles from Durban to present grievances to their native affairs commissioner. By 24 August, some 1,100 Black women were in jail.

Women played the major role in many of the disturbances that took place in the countryside because the men from these areas were generally away at jobs in the mines or in the cities. The demonstrators had four main grievances: a new government decree which ordered women to help with the fortnightly cattle dipping under penalty of a £5 fine but without pay; a recent rise in the poll tax which in turn led to demands for wage rises; and government measures to control the movement of Blacks into cities that they saw as a way of ensuring cheap farm labour and of preventing Blacks from earning enough money to pay the increased tax.

23 August The minister for Bantu development, Daan de Wet Nel, discloses a revised government plan to establish an all-Black Bantustan in the Transkei African reserve. The plan was designed to enable the full segregation of the neighbouring Ciskei area of Cape province. The minister reassured White merchants that apartheid would not force them out of Black areas because Blacks would not be capable of handling trade there themselves 'for many generations'. Indian traders would be removed from the Black areas to prevent 'racial friction'.

6 September More than 1,000 Blacks meet in Durban to plan a campaign of passive resistance against the government's apartheid policies. The meeting was called by ANC leader Albert Luthuli, who had been banished in May to his home district north of Durban, and attended by representatives of the ANC, Natal Indian Congress, the multiracial South African Congress of Democrats and the South African Trades Union Congress. Delegates discussed Luthuli's appeal for using Black 'buying power and labour power' to 'induce South Africa to mend its ways'.

15 October Provincial elections are held throughout South Africa and result in National Party candidates capturing at least 110 of the 170 seats in the provincial legislatures. The National Party retained control of the Cape province, Transvaal and Orange Free State while the United Party remained in control in Natal.

26 October Mrs Elizabeth Mafeking, president of the African Food and Canning Workers' Union and vice president of the Women's League of the ANC, is banished to a remote farm 700 miles from her home on the grounds that her presence in the Cape province town of Paarl was 'injurious to peace, order and good administration of the Natives in the area'. The decision to exile her was taken after reports from the police and officials of the Bantu Administration Department showed she had attended a 1955 world food canning workers' conference in Bulgaria, visited Communist China and Poland, and addressed an anti-passbook rally in Cape Town.

Rather than accept banishment, Mrs Mafeking secretly crossed into Basutoland on 10 November. Her treatment by the government was greatly criticized both in

South Africa and abroad. It also lead to a series of violent disturbances in her home town of Paarl in which thousands of non-Whites participated and one man was killed.

14 November The Progressive Party of South Africa is formally constituted after a two-day congress in Johannesburg. The new party, founded by 12 liberal United Party Members of Parliament and their supporters, elected Jan Steytler as party leader. Observers saw the Progressive Party's political programme as a clear alternative to the policies of the National Party. The party did not initially win enough support to change the two-party system of politics in South Africa but it did play an important role as a catalyst for political realignments in the 1960s and 1970s.

25 November South Africa's first Nationalist governor general, Ernest Jansen, dies in Pretoria at the age of 78. Jansen, a former Speaker of the House of Assembly and minister of native affairs, had held the post since 1951. He had been suffering from leukaemia for several years.

On 6 December, Justice Minister Charles Swart was appointed governor general by Queen Elizabeth II, effective 12 January 1960. Swart, the leader of the National Party in the Orange Free State, was a former lawyer, teacher, journalist and Hollywood film actor.

14 December The Union Council for Coloured Affairs, established under the provisions of the 1956 Separate Representation of Voters Act to advise the government on matters of interest to the Coloured community, holds its first meeting. The 12 elected members of the 27-member Council were all independents as all the organized Coloured groups in Cape province had boycotted the elections.

20 January Prime Minister Hendrik F. Verwoerd unexpectedly informs Parliament that a referendum will be held later in the year on the question of whether South Africa should become a republic. The Whites-only referendum was to be decided by a simple majority. Verwoerd warned that any decision on the republic's membership of the Commonwealth would be taken based on the country's interests and the attitude of British political groups towards South Africa. A bill providing for the referendum was introduced in Parliament on 23 April and passed by a voice vote of the House of Assembly on 2 May.

21 January The worst mining disaster in South African history takes place at the Clydesdale Colliery in Coalbrook, near Vereeniging. Some 426 Black and six White miners were trapped more than 500 feet underground when an entire section of the mine collapsed. New slides, flooding and the accumulation of deadly methane and carbon monoxide gases forced an end to rescue operations on 23 January, and the bodies were never recovered.

3 February British Prime Minister Harold Macmillan delivers his famous 'Winds of Change' speech to a joint sitting of both houses of the South African parliament. In a speech that the South African government interpreted as an abandonment of White South Africans, Macmillan announced that Britain was no longer prepared to tolerate apartheid.

Macmillan spoke of the emerging African nationalism and said:

> *The most striking of all the impressions I have formed since I left London a month ago is the strength of this African National consciousness. In different places it may take different forms, but it is happening everywhere. The wind of change is blowing through the continent. Whether we like it or not, this growth of political consciousness is a political fact. We must all accept it as a fact. Our national policies must take account of it.*

He warned that this 'political fact' must be accepted and dealt with so as not to 'imperil the precarious balance of East and West' on which peace depended.

He went on to say that Britain could not support South African apartheid because 'there are some aspects of your policies which make it impossible for us to do this without being false to our own deep convictions about the political destinies of free men, to which in our territories we are trying to give effect.'

The speech created a sensation in both South Africa and Britain. South Africans, English- as well as Afrikaans-speaking, were incensed that Britain appeared to believe that the White man had no place in Africa.

Prime Minister Verwoerd, in his reply to Macmillan's speech, declared that South Africa was a 'true White state' prepared to grant the 'fullest rights' to Blacks in areas that 'their forefathers had settled'. White South Africans, he said, had 'made it possible, by bringing benefits to Africa, for African nationalism to develop'. He added, 'We have nowhere else to go.'

External Affairs Minister Eric Louw accused Britain on 8 February of sacrificing White South Africa and said that Macmillian's premise was that 'for the sake of Britain's foreign policy ... the permanent White population of South Africa must be handed over to Black domination' and that because of Britain's foreign policy and prominent position in the North Atlantic Treaty Organization, the 'White man who developed and built up' South Africa 'must be prepared to abdicate'.

15 February The Senate Bill, to reduce the number of senators from 90 to 54 and reestablish the system of electing senators by means of proportional representation, is introduced into the House of Assembly. The Senate had been enlarged and the means of electing senators changed as a result of the 1955 Senate Act, which the government had passed as part of its plan to remove the Cape Coloureds from the common electoral roll.

21 March Answering a call from the Pan-Africanist Congress (PAC), Blacks throughout South Africa protested against the pass laws by leaving their passbooks at home and presenting themselves at police stations for arrest. In most areas, the police were able to disperse the crowds without incident, but in an infamous incident in the Transvaal township of Sharpeville police opened fire on the estimated 20,000-strong crowd of rock-throwing protestors, killing 67 and wounding 178. Three more Blacks died when police fired on crowds at the Langa location near Cape Town. Many of the victims had been shot in the back. The government reacted by banning all meetings in the main centres and by passing the Unlawful Organizations Act, which authorized the banning of the PAC, the ANC and any similar Black nationalist organizations. Blacks protested the killings by staging strikes in Cape Town and Durban, while violent disturbances broke out throughout South Africa. A state of emergency was declared on 30 March which lasted until 31 August. During it, some 12,000 non-Whites were arrested under the emergency regulations.

The Sharpeville shootings and the government's reactions to it scandalized the rest of the world. South Africa's opposition Liberal, United and Progressive Parties blamed the government's apartheid policies for the violence; mass demonstrations were held in London and outside the South African consulate to the UN in New York; while the UN Security Council called for an end to apartheid. Foreign capital fled the country and the price of gold slumped.

24 March Justice Minister François Erasmus bans all public meetings of more than 12 people, either Black or White, in 24 major cities and towns. The ban, which was imposed under provisions of the 1956 Riotous Assembly Act, was effective until 30 June. It was extended on 26 March to cover an additional 49 magisterial districts but did not apply to church services and funerals.

26 March The government temporarily suspends the pass laws in an effort to calm the tense situation in the country, but says the laws will be reinstated as soon as conditions return to normal. Police were ordered to refrain from arresting Blacks who were found without their passes on the grounds that many Blacks were being intimidated into burning their passbooks. The leaders of both the ANC and the PAC rejected the temporary pass-law suspension and called on their followers to continue to burn their books. A few public pass-burnings were staged by African leaders before police warned on 30 March that they would be prosecuted.

28 March The ANC and PAC stage a 'day of mourning' for the victims of the Sharpeville and Langa shootings. Highly successful strikes were held in Johannesburg, Cape Town and Port Elizabeth while moderately successful strikes took place in Durban.

Most Blacks returned to work the following day according to the ANC's instructions. Strike action, however, continued in other areas of the country. Some 50,000 of Cape Town's 60,000 Black workers were on strike by 30 March and similar walkouts were reported to have paralysed services and industries in many other cities. The strikes and mass demonstrations had mostly died out by 6 April under forceful police action to contain Black communities and force Blacks back to work.

30 March The government proclaims a state of emergency in selected areas throughout South Africa in the face of mass Black strikes, unrest and demonstrations against the passbook system and other apartheid legislation. The emergency laws were put in force in 117 of the country's 300 magisterial districts, including all major urban areas. The regulations, which were later extended to more districts, gave the government, military and police sweeping powers and enabled them to: detain people secretly and without warrants; make it an offence to remain away from work or incite others to strike; order curfews, control public services, close any place, business or industry and ban the public from any area; ban the production or circulation of subversive statements; and authorize fines of up to $1,400 and/or five years' imprisonment for violations.

The proclamation of the state of emergency had been preceded by the mobilization of 18 regiments of territorial (reserve) troops to help police and armed forces put down the disorders, and by the predawn arrests of some 234 Black, White and Asian anti-apartheid leaders. The government used its emergency detention powers to arrest ANC President Albert Luthuli, National Chairman of the Liberal Party Peter Brown and other high-ranking members of the ANC, the Indian National Congress, the South African Federation of Women, the Congess of Democrats and several trade unions. The leaders of the PAC, who had been responsible for the initial protests, had been arrested on 21–22 March.

31 March Some 30,000 Blacks from Langa and other nearby townships marched on Cape Town despite the military cordon that had been placed around Langa to seal off the area. The procession was turned away from the parliament building by machinegun-carrying troops and police after being promised that a delegation would be permitted to meet Justice Minister Erasmus. The promise was not kept but the crowd still dispersed after demonstrating briefly. A similar march in Durban, however, ended in bloodshed when troops fired on the crowd.

1 April The UN Security Council unanimously passes a resolution urging South Africa to abandon its apartheid policies and end the political repression of non-Whites. The resolution regretted the fact 'that the recent disturbances in ... South Africa should have led to the loss of life of so many Africans', deplored 'the policies and actions of the ... Union of South Africa which have given rise to the present situation' and extended the council's 'deepest sympathies' to 'the families of the victims'.

5 April The Unlawful Organizations Act is passed after being rushed through both houses of Parliament. The act, only introduced on 28 March, enabled the government to ban by proclamation the ANC, the PAC and any other organization which either directly or indirectly carried on their activities. The measure had been supported by most members of the Opposition. The governor general quickly signed a proclamation banning the groups until 6 April 1961.

In introducing the bill, Justice Minister Erasmus warned that the aims of both the ANC and PAC were a virtual 'revolution in South Africa' and said that the bill would halt the two groups' 'reign of terror' over other Blacks.

6 April Justice Minister Erasmus orders the pass laws, which had been temporarily suspended at the height of the recent unrest, to be reimposed. He said that Blacks who were no longer in possession of their books could obtain temporary replacements and warned Whites that it was illegal to either employ or retain the services of Blacks who did not have their reference books.

9 April In the midst of great political turmoil, an assassination attempt is made on the life of Prime Minister Hendrik Verwoerd. The prime minister was shot twice in the head and seriously wounded as he attended a special exhibition being held in Johannesburg to mark the Union of South Africa's fiftieth anniversary. The attack was made by a wealthy British-born farmer, David Pratt, who was known to be vehemently opposed to the government's apartheid policies. Pratt, who said he shot at 'the epitome of apartheid rather than Dr Verwoerd', was judged mentally unfit to stand trial on 26 September. The prime minister did not appear in public again until 31 May.

10 April The Cabinet, in an emergency meeting, appoints Minister of Public Works Paul O. Sauer as temporary leader of the government while Prime Minister Verwoerd is unable to perform his duties. Sauer, known as a moderate, assured the House of Assembly the following day that Verwoerd's racial policies would be carried out, saying 'as far as Parliament is concerned, there will not be any deviations from existing programmes as a result of what has happened'.

12 April Interior Minister Thomas Naude announces a new programme designed to increase White immigration to South Africa while decreasing the country's dependence on Black labour. He said that immigration was of 'the highest importance' and that the government no longer considered it necessary to screen immigrants as drastically as it did in the past. The new programme would encourage White immigrants particularly from Germany, the Netherlands and Belgium. Erasmus told Parliament that thousands of Black 'idlers' would be removed from the cities and returned to native reserves while their places would be taken by the new immigrants. He warned farmers that they would also have to manage without foreign Black labour imported from neighbouring countries.

14 April The underground leadership of the ANC and the PAC issue a joint strike call to protest against 'the savage attack the Government has made on us and our leaders'. The strike never materialized after the government issued warnings of the harsh penalties that would be imposed on anyone who obeyed the call and announced that police would be mobilized 'to protect Natives who ignore . . . stay-at-home week'.

20 April Acting government leader Paul O. Sauer causes a split in the National Party when he publicly calls for a 'new approach' to the Black problem, higher wages for urban Blacks and an easing of the passbook and liquor restrictions. He said that the events in Sharpeville had closed the 'old book' of White–Black relations and contended that apartheid legislation should be changed to give Blacks 'a hope for a happy existence'. Foreign Minister Louw openly rebuked Sauer and his moderate supporters when he told Parliament the same day that 'basically, the Government's policy remains unchanged'.

4 May The president of the PAC, Robert M. Sobukwe, is convicted of planning the recent campaign against South Africa's pass laws and sentenced to three years' imprisonment. His 18 Congress co-defendants were sentenced to prison terms ranging from 18 months to two years.

Sobukwe had told the Johannesburg court on 14 April that the aim of the PAC was to create a 'non-racial democracy in South Africa . . . [and] throughout the whole of Africa'. He said, 'We stand for government of the African, by the African, for the African, with everybody owing his allegiance to Africa and prepared also to accept the rule of the African majority.' Sobukwe said the PAC hoped to achieve 'complete freedom' for Africans in South Africa by 1963 and to 'contribute toward a United States of Africa'.

13 May A Commonwealth conference of prime ministers meeting in London ends with a communiqué saying that the conference, while adhering to the traditional practice of not discussing member nations' domestic affairs, had expressed their views on apartheid and had 'emphasized' in 'informal discussions' with South African representative Eric Louw 'that the Commonwealth itself is a multi-racial association'.

Louw had informed the prime ministers on 10 May that South Africa intended to become a republic and was told that, because it made no pledge to retain Queen Elizabeth as the Commonwealth's 'symbol of the free association of its independent member nations', it would have to obtain the other members' consent for it to remain in the organization.

16 May Justice Minister Erasmus releases the names of some 1,900 people who had been detained since the emergency regulations went into effect in March. Most of the leaders of the ANC and PAC were among those under detention, as were prominent members of the Liberal Party and other Whites with leftist political views. Erasmus accused 175 of the detainees of being Communists.

20 May A motion to adjourn Parliament for eight months, until 20 January 1961, is passed by the House of Assembly against bitter opposition from the United Party. The Opposition charged that the government wanted the adjournment so that it would not be subject to any Parliamentary restraint in the use of its emergency powers.

31 August Justice Minister Erasmus announces the lifting of the state of emergency throughout South Africa. The emergency regulations had been imposed in 123 of the country's 300 magisterial districts after the outbreak of racial unrest in March. In lifting the regulations, Erasmus said there were no indications that any individuals or organizations would instigate trouble if the emergency was completely lifted but warned that the government would immediately reimpose regulations if necessary. All those detained under the regulations were automatically released when the regulations were lifted.

The regulations had already been lifted in 20 magisterial districts on 11 May, in another 34 on 23 June and in a further 23 on 12 July but had remained in force in all the main urban centres.

5 October Whites in South Africa and South West Africa go to the polls in a national referendum to decide if South Africa should become a republic. The proposal to end South African allegiance to the British monarchy and replace Queen Elizabeth II as head of state by a president was approved by a vote of 850,458 to 775,878. The proposal, which only needed a simple majority to pass, was primarily supported by Afrikaners and opposed by English-speaking Whites as well as by the United, Progressive and Liberal Parties. It did not result in any material changes to the constitution and gave no indication as to whether South Africa would remain in the Commonwealth. The prime minister later announced that the Republic of South Africa would come into existence on 31 May 1961.

The government's slogan in the final run-up to the referendum of 'Vote republican and keep South Africa White' was seen as reflecting their belief that the bloody civil war that had broken out in the Congo since it attained its independence on 30 June and the unprecedented levels of Black unrest and violence taking place in neighbouring southern Rhodesia were major issues that Whites were taking into consideration when voting on the referendum issue. Political observers believed that it was difficult to determine just how much those outside events influenced South African political thought, but felt that the impact on the vote was considerable.

30 November The government declares a partial state of emergency in five districts of the remote Pondoland African reserve in southeast Cape province. The move followed violent clashes between the police and rebel Black tribesmen opposed to tribal chiefs, appointed by the government under the Bantu Authorities Act to run tribal authorities. The violence had begun on 7 June when 25 Black tribesmen and five Black policemen were killed as police fired into a crowd of more than 400 demonstrators protesting the appointment of unpopular chiefs and subchiefs to rule the reserve. Sporadic killings occurred in rebel attacks since then. The Minister for Bantu Affairs, Daan de Wet Nel, blamed the violence on Communist agitators and closed Pondoland on 1 December to all private travellers. Journalists had previously been barred from entering the area.

7 December Prime Minister Verwoerd announces government plans to extend its apartheid policies to the country's 1.5 million Coloured people. He said that Coloureds would be given autonomy in their own local districts and would be encouraged to live, work and play separately from both Whites and Blacks. A ministry of Coloured affairs would also be established that would be responsible to the government, but Coloureds would have no direct representation in Parliament.

9 December The Republic of South Africa Act is published. It contained the draft constitution which would come into effect when the country became a republic and would replace the Union of South Africa's 1909 South Africa Act. It was largely based on the 1909 Act but substituted the word 'State' whenever 'King', 'Queen' or 'Crown' appeared. The act called for the country to become a republic on 31 May 1961 and stipulated that the president should be elected before that date.

17 December The results of the 1960 census are published. It showed that the population of South Africa consisted of nearly 11 million Blacks, three million Whites, 1.5 million Coloureds and half a million Asians. The non-White population was growing at almost twice the rate as Whites, while the number of Blacks living in urban areas was rising, despite the government's policies on controlling their influx to the city.

1 9 6 1

5 January The government officially announces that peace has been restored in Pondoland. The area had been the scene of unrest throughout 1960 as tribesmen, under the leadership of a group calling themselves 'The Men of the Hills', demonstrated against the authority of unpopular tribal leaders.

6 January UN Secretary General Dag Hammarskjöld begins a week-long visit to South Africa to examine the country's racial policies, as instructed by a UN Security Council resolution adopted after the 1960 Sharpeville shootings. He toured the country and held several private sessions with Prime Minister Hendrik Verwoerd and met representatives of the African National Congress (ANC) and the church. Hammarskjöld issued a communiqué on 12 January describing his talks with Verwoerd as 'frank, constructive and helpful'. On 23 January, he reported to the Security Council that he had been unable to reach an agreement with Verwoerd 'on arrangements that would provide for appropriate safeguards of human rights' in South Africa but said that he did not regard the lack of such an agreement as conclusive. He reported that both sides were willing to continue talks at an 'appropriate time'.

15 March Prime Minister Verwoerd, addressing the Commonwealth heads of government meeting in London, announces that South Africa is withdrawing its request to remain in the Commonwealth after becoming a republic on 31 May. Verwoerd had previously said that South Africa wished to stay in the Commonwealth but would not tolerate any interference in its domestic affairs. The decision to withdraw came after South Africa's apartheid policies were strongly attacked by Canada and the Afro-Asian Commonwealth states, and a compromise solution proposed by British Prime Minister Harold Macmillian proved unacceptable to the South Africans.

In his statement, Verwoerd said that South Africa had made the request to remain in the Commonwealth as a republic 'in the expectation that it would be willingly granted without reservations' and that he was 'amazed at, and shocked by, the spirit of hostility and . . . of vindictiveness shown towards South Africa'. He said that the question of a republic was not the problem but 'the peg on which to hang the attack' and added that 'it was clear that something similar would have developed soon, perhaps in the form of a motion for expulsion'. He said, 'I wish to assure the friendly-disposed Prime Ministers of the Commonwealth that . . . we hope and shall endeavor to cooperate in all possible ways with all those members of the Commonwealth who are willing to maintain their former good relations with us.'

On his return to South Africa on 20 March, Prime Minister Verwoerd was greeted at the airport in Johannesburg by thousands of supporters who hailed him as 'the leader of the White man in Africa'. Verwoerd told them that South Africa's withdrawal from the Commonwealth was 'not a defeat but a victory' and said, 'We have not triumphed over Britain, we have released ourselves from the pressure of the Afro-Asians who were taking over the Commonwealth' and contended that

South Africa would not have been 'at home in the Commonwealth' as it became increasingly non-White.

South Africa's withdrawal from the Commonwealth left the country extremely isolated from the rest of the international community. It came at a time when South Africa had diplomatic relations with no other independent African country, in the middle of a bitter dispute with the UN over the future administration of South West Africa and while facing international economic boycotts.

20 March The minister of Bantu administration and development, Daan de Wet Nel, announces the creation of the post of director of Bantu development and says that, since White housing problems had satisfactorily been dealt with, the government would now be addressing the problems of Black housing. He said that a five-year plan had been drawn up for the development of eight Bantu areas 'at an increased tempo and in an energetic manner'.

29 March The longest trial in South African history ends when a special three-judge court in Pretoria unanimously acquits 28 anti-apartheid activists of plotting to overthrow the government. The presiding judge ruled that the banned ANC, to which many of the defendants belonged, had neither 'adopted a policy to overthrow the state by violence' nor was Communist-infiltrated. The 22 Black, two White, three Indian and one Coloured defendants were among a group of 156 people who had been arrested during a government crackdown, on 6 December 1956, on opponents of its racial policies. A total of 92 were indicted for treason, while the charges against the other 64 were dropped soon after the four-year trial started on 1 August 1958. One of the accused died during the trial and another fled the country. Among the accused had been ANC leaders Nelson Mandela and Walter Sisulu.

13 April The UN General Assembly adopts a resolution condemning South Africa's apartheid policies as 'reprehensible and repugnant to human dignity' and urging 'all states to consider taking such separate and collective action as is open to them [under the UN Charter] . . . to bring about the abandonment of the policies'.

21 April Members of the Transkei territorial authority demand that Transkei be declared an independent, self-governing Black state. It claimed that the proposal was in keeping with the South African government's stated policy of separate development. The authority as a whole rejected the call for independence but agreed to pursue the call for self-government. The minister for Bantu administration and development announced that the Transkei might become self-governing within a few years, once the necessary administrative structure was in place.

3 May Police begin the most widespread and intensive raids ever conducted in peacetime against non-Whites threatening to strike as a protest against the republican constitution. The raids, which lasted until the end of the month, took place throughout the country as police searched strike organizers' homes, seized documents and arrested thousands. Some 8,000–10,000 people were arrested as a result of the raids.

The strike, scheduled for 29–31 May, had been planned at an 'all-African' conference that was held in Pietermaritzburg on 25–26 March and attended by more than 1,000 members of the banned ANC and the Pan-Africanist Congress (PAC). The conference condemned the new constitution as 'fradulent', as it had been voted on by only 20 per cent of the population, and claimed that it would result in the even greater oppression of non-Whites. The main speaker at the meeting, ANC leader Nelson Mandela, avoided arrest in the crackdown by going into hiding.

The strike had minimal response, except in Johannesburg where roughly 50 per cent of the Black workforce remained at home.

4 May The General Law Amendment Act is introduced in Parliament. It gave the minister of justice and attorney general far-reaching powers to refuse bail to anyone for 12 days after their arrest and to dispense with trial by jury for those accused of attempting or committing arson or murder.

31 May South Africa celebrates Republic Day as the country officially becomes a republic and severs all ties with the British Commonwealth. Charles Swart, South Africa's last governor general, was sworn in as the first president of the Republic of South Africa in Pretoria. He had resigned as governor general on 30 April and was elected president on 10 May.

The Republic of South Africa came into being under the provisions of the renamed Republic of South Africa Constitution Bill, which had been introduced into Parliament in December 1960 as the Republic of South Africa Bill. It was passed by the House of Assembly on 12 April and the Senate on 23 April, and was immediately signed into law by the governor general. The new republican constitution that came into effect was largely based on the 1909 South Africa Act but substituted the word 'State' whenever 'King', 'Queen' or 'Crown' appeared. The Queen was replaced as head of state by a state president, who was elected by an electoral college comprising the joint houses of Parliament. The president was to be elected for a period of seven years and did not have executive powers.

Opposition leader Sir de Villiers Graaff said that Republic Day would be 'a day of deep sorrow' for those many South Africans who had been 'bluffed into believing that the Republic would be inside the Commonwealth'.

18 October South Africa goes to the polls in the first general election held since the country became a republic. The National Party of Prime Minister Verwoerd was returned to power with an increased majority of both seats and total votes. The results were as follows: the National Party 105 seats, up from 102 in the previous election; the opposition United Party 49 seats, up from 42; its coalition partner the National Union one seat, no change; the Progressive Party one seat, down from 11 in the previous house, where they had all been elected as members of the United Party but subsequently split from that party and founded the liberal Progressive Party. It was the Progressives' first test in the polls. Although they won only one seat, they captured a significant percentage of the total opposition votes, especially considering their radical multiracial policies. Separate elections for the four representatives of the Cape Coloureds were held on 4 October, with the four incumbent United Party-supported independents all being returned.

Verwoerd claimed that the National Party's electoral success after 13½ years in power was a reaffirmation of the South African government's 'tremendous stability' and said that the growing majority of votes it obtained showed that the party was widening its base among Afrikaans- and English-speakers alike.

He promised that the government would maintain both its racial policies and its determination 'not to compromise'.

28 November The UN General Assembly passes a resolution condemning the South African government for its apartheid policies after provisions calling for the expulsion of South Africa from the UN and for the placing of economic sanctions against it had been removed. The revised resolution deplored South Africa's refusal to abide by earlier UN resolutions to 'revise its racial policies' and condemned those policies as 'reprehensible and repugnant to human dignity'.

10 December The belated 1960 Nobel Peace Prize is awarded to ANC leader Albert Luthuli as a 'democratic declaration of solidarity' with South African Blacks. In his acceptance speech, Luthuli denounced South Africa as a country where 'the cult of race supremacy and of White superiority is worshipped like a god' and 'the ghost of slavery lingers on to this day in the form of forced labour'. The award was seen as being politically important in South Africa, where the government objected to Luthuli's win saying that his receipt of it 'must necessarily rob the Nobel Peace Prize of all its high esteem in the judgment of objectively minded people'. There was some doubt as to whether Luthuli would be allowed to receive the award in person, but the government eventually issued him with a special passport valid for 10 days.

16 December Five bombs explode in Johannesburg and another five in Port Elizabeth as Blacks begin a campaign of sabotage, in resistance to apartheid. Over the next several months, post offices and government buildings were bombed, telephone lines were cut and electricity pylons were blown up. Several people died or were injured in the attacks and hundreds were arrested.

The military wing of the banned ANC, the Spear of the Nation, had distributed leaflets in December warning that 'new methods' were being adopted in 'the struggle for freedom and democracy'. The government adopted the General Law Amendment Act, more commonly called the Sabotage Act, in June 1962 to deal with the campaign.

19 December The UN General Assembly passes a resolution proclaiming 'the inalienable right of the people of South West Africa to independence' and establishing a seven-member special committee to study how this could be brought about. The Assembly noted South Africa's persistent failure to observe the terms of its 1920 League of Nations mandate over South West Africa and ordered the special committee to visit the region by 1 May 1962. The committee was charged with obtaining: the release and repatriation of all political detainees; the withdrawal of the South African armed forces; the repeal of apartheid legislation; and making preparations for UN-supervised general elections in South West Africa. The General Assembly also dissolved the Committee on South West Africa that had been studying the issue, in light of the establishment of the new special committee.

Tensions within the UN had been rising since an eight-member UN committee investigating conditions in the area was refused permission to visit South West Africa in July. The committee's chairman informed the Security Council that South African policies in the territory were 'endangering peace'. From that time onwards, the South African government appeared aware that the Afro-Asian bloc in the UN was determined to terminate South Africa's mandate. The South African delegation to the General Assembly met unprecedented levels of hostility and it appeared at times likely that South Africa would suffer sanctions or even expulsion.

23 January Prime Minister Hendrik Verwoerd informs Parliament of his intention to grant home rule to the 'Xhosa nation' by mid-1963 as part of his plan for 'separate development'. The announcement was the first step towards implementing his 'positive apartheid' programme, which attempted to give the government's racial policies a moral justification.

Verwoerd said that the two million Blacks, belonging to nine tribes and living in the 16,000 square miles of the Transkei African reserve south of Durban, would get a 'wholly Black Parliament and Cabinet' that would have jurisdiction over local matters such as health, education, roads and agriculture. The South African government would retain control of defence, foreign affairs and 'certain aspects of the administration of justice . . . for the time being'. Non-Blacks living in the Transkei would have 'no political rights there' and would be subject to the local laws. Verwoerd promised a 'five-year replacement programme of as many White civil servants as possible by Blacks'.

The Transkei 'experiment' in self-rule was seen by many political commentators in South Africa as a turning point in the country's history. They felt that if the government's 'separate development' policy did not work in a region as relatively homogeneous, ethnically and geographically, as the Transkei, it would not work anywhere else.

The leader of the Opposition, Sir de Villiers Graaff, called the separate development programme 'a political propaganda stunt', while Transvaal Progressive Party leader Bernard Friedman said the proposal was 'window dressing' to deflect foreign criticism of South Africa's racial policies.

9 February The Pan African Freedom Movement of East and Central Africa ends a week-long conference in Addis Ababa, Ethiopia. The organization adopted a resolution charging South Africa with using North Atlantic Treaty Organization weapons to oppress its non-White population and accepted the banned African National Congress (ANC) as a member. ANC leader Nelson Mandela, who was being sought by South African police for his anti-government activities, represented the South African group at the meeting.

12 March Defence Minister J.J. Fouche, in an address to Parliament, outlines the basic principles of South Africa's defence policy. Fouche announced that the defence forces were being strengthened in order to meet the threat posed by several Afro-Asian countries, which were secretly planning military action against the country. He said that although South Africa's military policy was to cooperate with the West, it could not depend on Western forces. He argued that such dependence could lead to having policies forced upon South Africa that could not be reconciled with her own.

The speech came as a surprise to most South Africans. The government presented it as a call for Whites to unite against Communist-backed Black Africa, while the Opposition condemned it as scare-mongering. It was followed by Budget Day on 21 March, on which the government put forward a 'budget of national security' and increased the defence budget by 67 per cent over 1961 figures. Observers saw the development as further proof of South Africa's growing sense of political isolation from the rest of the international community.

19 March Prime Minister Hendrik Verwoerd meets a 27-member committee from the Transkei territorial authority to discuss some of the more controversial proposals of his plan for Transkei self-government. The committee, comprising headmen and chiefs, had been appointed by the authority in April 1961 to press its demands for greater autonomy. Under discussion were clauses in the proposed constitution that called for a large proportion of the members of the legislative assembly to be nominated and a clause requiring the Transkei state president's approval of any law passed by the assembly. In the end, the government agreed to lower the proportion of nominated to elected Assembly members, and said that the legislative assembly would comprise 65 appointed chiefs and 45 elected members as opposed to the original proposal of 94 appointed and 35 elected members. The committee, for its part, reluctantly agreed to grant the state president the right of assent over its laws.

The 123-member territorial authority held its annual session in Umtata on 1 May to discuss the proposals and approved the proposed constitution on 4 May. The main constitutional provisions adopted were: the central governing body would be a legislative assembly composed of 65 appointed chiefs and 45 elected representatives; assembly members would be required to take an oath of allegiance both to the Transkei and South African governments; laws passed by the assembly would be submitted to the Transkei state president for approval; all Transkeians over 21 within and outside the territory would have the right to vote.

4 June The government discloses its plans for a new immigration programme designed to attract White settlers to South Africa. The aim of the plan, which would cost at least $4.2 million annually, was to achieve an 'approximate equalization' of the country's White and non-White populations. The government hoped to attract some 40,000–50,000 White Europeans each year and wanted to increase the current White population of just over three million to 10 million by the year 2000. The current non-White population was nearly 13 million.

The plans were outlined in letters sent to over 10,000 South African industrial companies and businessmen asking them for details of their employment needs. Under the new programme, each immigrant would be offered free passage, a grant of $84 and an interest-free loan of $84, repayable over two years. The government pledged to help the settlers find housing and jobs and to assist them towards 'full adaptation in the White community and its customs'.

20 June The International Commission of Jurists denounces South Africa's Sabotage Bill. In a statement from its Geneva headquarters, the commission said that the bill was 'the culmination of a determined and ruthless attempt to enforce the doctrine of apartheid', and that it would curtail liberty 'to a degree not surpassed by the most extreme dictatorship of the Left or the Right'.

27 June The General Law Amendment (Sabotage) Bill is enacted into law and gives the government the strongest police powers in South Africa's peacetime history. The bill was the government's response to a Black campaign of sabotage that had begun in December 1961 as a protest against apartheid.

The bill, which authorized the death penalty for those convicted under its provisions, defined the crime of sabotage for the first time. It was any act that endangered law and order, public safety, health or the free movement of traffic; which jeopardized the supply of fuel, food, water, light and power; or which hindered medical and municipal services. Anyone who trespassed on any land or building or who destroyed private and public property could also be penalized under the act.

A Supreme Court judge, acting without a jury or pre-trial examination, was authorized to try any person accused under the act, and there was no right of appeal. Those convicted could be sentenced to 'civil death' penalties, which confined them to their homes, possibly for life, and prohibited them from seeing anyone but members of their immediate families.

The opposition United Party objected to the bill on the grounds that it would: deprive South Africans of court protection and put them at the mercy of Justice Minister John Vorster, who would administer the bill; create a new crime of political opposition; and give further extensive powers to the government, which was empowered by current laws to deal with sabotage or crises. Some opponents of the bill regarded it as a government pretext to crack down on opponents of its racial policies. Opposition leader Sir de Villiers Graaff charged that Vorster, interned during the Second World War as a Nazi sympathizer, would become 'the main inquisitor, lord chief justice and lord high executioner if the Bill became law'.

Cape Town police had to use tear gas to break up a crowd of 6,000 demonstrators opposing the bill, while 5,000 protestors marched in Johannesburg. Meanwhile, the sabotage campaign continued throughout the year. Government buildings were bombed, telephone lines were cut and electricity pylons were blown up. Some 500,000 tons of sugar cane were destroyed as a result of at least 75 acts of widespread arson. Police raids discovered secret radio transmitters and seized quantities of detonators, dynamite, time bomb kits and photographs of military and civilian establishments.

The police used the new law in October to make a series of 'house arrests', which confined a person to his home for all or large parts of the day and severely limited his ability to communicate with others. These bannings caused an international outcry that South Africa was moving towards becoming a police state.

30 August The government publishes the names of those opponents of its racial policies who had been barred from making public statements under the terms of the new anti-sabotage law. Among those named were Nobel Peace Prize winner and former leader of the banned ANC Albert Luthuli, Black nationalist leaders Walter Sisulu and Oliver Tambo and several prominent Whites.

31 August The UN Special Committee on South West Africa unanimously adopts a report stating that it was 'imperative' that the UN 'take firm and resolute action' in establishing its presence in the territory to prevent 'a serious political disaster' there.

The committee had studied a report submitted to it on 27 July by the special two-man commission that had been sent to study South Africa's racial policies in South West Africa. That report said it was the 'overwhelming desire' of Africans there that the UN take over the territory. The Special Committee did not, however, refer to a controversial joint statement issued on 26 May by the South African government and the two members of the commission, Victorio Carpio and Salvador Martinez de Alva. The statement said that the commission had found no evidence of a military build-up in the territory, of plans to exterminate the population, of the detention of political leaders or to support a UN resolution that apartheid was threatening world peace. They had been informed that some people had been 'repatriated' to other parts of South West Africa and Prime Minister Verwoerd promised to investigate those charges.

On 8 June, Carpio disassociated himself from the joint statement saying that it had been drafted while he was sick and that the commission had not seen enough of the territory to enable it to reach any conclusions. The Special Committee passed a resolution on 3 August that 'the alleged communiqué' was not an official act of either the committee or its chairman and was not binding on the UN.

4 September Prime Minister Verwoerd unexpectedly announces that the incorporation of the British protectorates of Basutoland, Bechuanaland and Swaziland was 'neither possible nor wise'. Successive South African governments had fought for the eventual inclusion of the three high commission territories since the possibility was outlined in the 1909 South Africa Act. Verwoerd, however, now declared that under the principles of apartheid, the territories would more properly find their future political association with the Bantustans.

6 November South Africa's relations with the UN markedly deteriorates when the General Assembly adopts a long-anticipated resolution calling for diplomatic and economic sanctions against South Africa. It also voted to urge the Security Council to consider expelling South Africa from the UN unless it abandoned apartheid and to encourage UN member states to sever diplomatic relations with South Africa.

7 November Nelson Mandela, former secretary general of the banned ANC and a leader of the underground National Action Council, is sentenced in Pretoria to five years in prison. He received three years for inciting a national strike to protest the republican constitution and two years for travelling abroad without a passport.

Mandela, who had been in hiding from the police for the previous two years, was arrested on 5 August. He was well known as a Black activist and was one of the organizers of the 1952 defiance campaign. He was banned in November 1952 under the Riotous Assemblies Act and ordered to resign from his position as secretary general of the ANC. He first appeared in court on 16 August, but his actual trial did not get under way until October. Large demonstrations of supporters demanding his freedom were held around the country and outside the courthouse until they were banned. Mandela, a lawyer, conducted his own case to indicate 'that his trial was a reflection of the aspiration of the African people'. He said, 'I consider myself neither legally nor morally bound to obey laws made by a Parliament in which I have no representation.' He offered no defence to the charges and called no witnesses, contending that his conscience made it imperative that he oppose laws that were 'unjust, immoral and intolerable'.

17 December Some 200 members of the Poqo ('Ourselves Alone') terrorist organization are arrested in a police round-up in the Qamata district of the Transkei. Poqo was a new group formed by ex-members of the PAC who had found the PAC leadership too moderate. Unlike the ANC, Poqo was a militantly Blacks-only organization and favoured the use of violence. The group was linked with several violent incidents, including an attack on a police station in Paarl on 22 November that resulted in two young Whites being hacked to death by rampaging Blacks and six Blacks shot dead by police and armed civilians. Poqo members were also involved in an attempt on 12 December to burn down the house of Transkei territorial authority chairman Chief Kaizer Matanzima. Poqo had branded Matanzima a 'Government stooge' for cooperating with South African plans to grant the Transkei partial home-rule.

---

1 9 6 3

---

11 February Defence Minister J.J. Fouche announces a further expansion of the South African armed forces. He told Parliament that the strength of the country's permanent army would be increased by 50 per cent. He also stated that South Africa had obtained a weapon 'of exceptional value' from a country that had said it would not sell weapons to South Africa.

28 February The Economic Commission for Africa (ECA), a regional offshoot of the UN Economic and Social Council (Ecosoc), meets in the Congo. The group tabled a resolution requesting the council to: rescind South Africa's membership until it had 'set a term to its policy of racial discrimination'; reconsider its earlier decision to uphold South African membership despite the ECA's previous requests; and 'transmit the recommendations of the Commission to the General Assembly'.

12 March A government inquiry into the Paarl riots of November 1962 concludes. A new terrorist organization, Poqo, was thought to be responsible for the violence, although the commissioner heard evidence that Poqo was merely a new name for the banned Pan-Africanist Congress (PAC). Poqo, Xhosa for 'Ourselves Alone', limited its membership to Black males, who were charged with infiltrating all spheres of life 'from the sports field to the graveside'. The members, organized into cells, were reportedly waiting for instructions from their national committees before acting to 'achieve freedom in 1963 for the African people'. The group planned to accomplish this by overthrowing the government and killing all the Whites as well as those Black chiefs and headmen who supported the government. During the course of the investigation, witnesses warned that extremist organizations like Poqo were steadily growing in popularity because many Blacks were beginning to feel that the African National Congress (ANC) 'was too moderate in making its demands for Africans'. They said Blacks were becoming increasingly frustrated and, with no legal avenues available to them to express their frustrations, 'the temperature of the people rises daily'.

2 May The General Law (Amendment) Act is approved by President Charles Swart and becomes law. The act, aimed at suppressing Black nationalists, gave Prime Minister Hendrik Verwoerd and his Cabinet the widest-ranging powers ever conferred upon a South African government in peacetime. It strengthened the 1962 Act of the same name by further defining political crimes, and gave the government the power to: authorize police to arrest suspects without warrants and repeatedly imprison them for up to 90 days without access to legal advice or visitors and without the courts being able to interfere; and impose sentences ranging from a minimum of five years' imprisonment to death for anyone leaving the country to learn sabotage techniques, for advocating the forcible overthrow of the government or for urging the forcible intervention in domestic South African affairs by an outside power, including the UN. The government was also given wider scope for declaring a state of emergency.

One of the act's most controversial provisions empowered the government to detain for an indefinite period anyone serving a sentence for sabotage or a similar crime after the expiration of their sentence. The government admitted that that provision, known as the 'Sobukwe Clause', was aimed at PAC leader Robert Sobukwe, due to be released from prison in May after serving time on incitement charges. The clause was, in fact, used to detain him further.

4 May The former secretary general of the banned ANC, Walter Sisulu, is sentenced in Johannesburg to six years in prison for having incited Black workers to strike in May 1961 in protest against the South African Constitution Act. Sisulu was also found guilty of contravening the Unlawful Organizations Act by promoting the ANC's activities in 1961, a year after the organization had been banned. He was released pending appeal.

10 May Two Black nationalist organizations, Poqo (Ourselves Alone) and Umkhonto We Sizwe (Spear of the Nation), are accused of organizing terrorist campaigns and formally outlawed by President Charles Swart.

24 May The Transkei Self-Government Bill, which set out the draft constitution and established rules under which the Transkei would obtain self-government, is enacted into law. The bill gave Blacks limited self-government within a defined area for the first time in South African history. The minister for Bantu administration, Daan de Wet Nel, described the introduction of the bill as 'an historic occasion' and said that every South African prime minister had promised Blacks in the Transkei what they were now receiving. The Opposition said it would oppose the bill throughout its passage through Parliament because: it threatened to 'undermine South Africa at its very being'; it was 'part of a pattern of the reshaping of South Africa which must offer a breeding ground for Communism and Pan-Africanism'; and because the Transkei chiefs were not consulted. The bill passed the House of Assembly on 10 May and the Senate on 13 May.

25 May The representatives of some 31 African countries, including 29 heads of state, meet in Addis Ababa, Ethiopia to establish the Organization of African Unity (OAU). The OAU's charter bound the nations together in a loose federation aimed at cooperation in politics, defence, economics and education and called for the elimination from Africa of all forms of racial oppression and colonialism. South Africa was one of the only two independent African states excluded from the conference, Togo being the other. Among the OAU's first resolutions were those: demanding the immediate release of ANC leader Nelson Mandela and PAC leader Robert Sobukwe; approving a joint approach by African foreign ministers to the UN secretary general to discuss the 'explosive' situation in South Africa caused by apartheid; and appealing to all governments to immediately break off diplomatic relations with South Africa. Following the adoption of the last resolution, those African countries that had commercial or diplomatic relations took steps over the next several months to sever them.

1 July New passport controls come into effect between South Africa and the British protectorates of Basutoland, Bechuanaland and Swaziland. From this date, valid travel permits or passports were required between South Africa and the British territories and border control posts were set up by South African authorities.

The move came at South Africa's request. Prime Minister Verwoerd had announced in Parliament on 23 April that the British government must differentiate between 'ordinary political refugees' and people who fled to the protectorates in order to organize revolutionary activities against South Africa. He warned that if such political refugees were allowed to 'organize revolution' in the protectorates, then those territories must 'expect retaliation'.

11 July ANC leaders Walter Sisulu and Nelson Mandela, along with 15 other anti-apartheid activists, are arrested in a police raid on a private house in the Johannesburg suburb of Rivonia. Police believed that seven of the detainees made up the high command of the Spear of the Nation, and announced that they had smashed the ANC's underground headquarters. All 17 were arrested under the General Law (Amendment) Act aimed at suppressing Black nationalists. Sisulu had been sentenced to a six-year prison term in May but had jumped bail while free pending an appeal.

15 July Prime Minister Verwoerd announces that South Africa would withdraw from the ECA, a regional offshoot of the UN Ecosoc, because of the hostility shown to it by the other African member states. In a later clarification, South Africa's delegate to the commission said that South Africa would not participate in the ECA's work but was not giving up its membership of the body.

Verwoerd's announcement came as the Ecosoc met in Geneva to discuss ECA's recommendation that South Africa be expelled from the organization because of its apartheid policies. The council rejected a resolution based on that recommendation but passed another one suspending South Africa from taking part in the ECA's activities until 'the Economic and Social Council, on the recommendation of the Economic Commission for Africa, finds that conditions for constructive cooperation have been restored by a change of its racial policy'.

7 August The UN Security Council, after a long and acrimonious debate, passes a resolution calling for a complete embargo on arms shipments to South Africa. The resolution 'solemnly' called on 'all states to cease forthwith the sale and shipment of arms, ammunition of all types and military vehicles to South Africa'. A second resolution, calling for a boycott on trade with South Africa, failed by two to get the necessary seven votes to pass.

22 August Libya announces that it intends to close its airspace to all South African aeroplanes. The move, after similar ones by Algeria and Egypt, effectively made it impossible for South Africa aircraft to overfly North Africa. This forced South African Airways to reroute its European services via the much longer western African route, overflying the Canary Islands, Cape Verde, the Congo and Angola.

3 September Prime Minister Verwoerd offers the British protectorates of Swaziland, Basutoland and Bechuanaland South Africa's help to 'develop to independence' and says that South Africa would be willing to administer them as self-governing Bantustans. Verwoerd insisted that he had no territorial ambitions over the areas, since annexing them would be against his policy of separate development. He contended that South Africa could bring the territories to independence faster and more efficiently than Britain as their economies were tied into South Africa's, but warned that if the people of the territories refused the offer, it would be 'the end of the matter' and they could 'go their own way in ever increasing isolation from the Republic'. The British government took no official notice of the proposal, but public opinion was strongly against it.

11 September South Africa's intensified immigration efforts are reported to have resulted in a marked increase in the number of White settlers. There was a net gain of some 11,972 Whites for the first six months of 1963, which exceeded the figure for the whole of 1962 and was almost ten times the 1961 total. The immigration programme's immediate goal was to attract professional men and skilled workers to South Africa, while its long-term aim was to achieve a White population of 10 million by the year 2000.

9 October Eleven leading opponents of the government's racial policies, arrested in Rivonia on 11 July, were indicted in Pretoria on charges of planning a revolt. The six Blacks, four Whites and one Indian were charged with attempting to start a guerrilla war inside South Africa while organizing an armed invasion by outside forces. They were also accused of planning, ordering or carrying out 221 acts of sabotage over a 20-month period. The defendants included ANC leaders Walter Sisulu and Nelson Mandela and Secretary General of the Transvaal Indian Congress Ahmed Kathrada.

The 'Rivonia trial', one of the most important of its kind in South African history, opened in Pretoria on 29 October. The following day, however, a Supreme Court judge dismissed the indictment against 10 anti-apartheid activists accused of sabotage and conspiring to overthrow the government on the grounds that the prosecutor's charges during the trial were too vague. The eleventh defendant had been released after agreeing to testify for the prosecution.

The 10 defendants were immediately rearrested and the government announced on 31 October that it would retry the men on the same charges.

11 October The UN General Assembly passes a resolution condemning South Africa for its 'repression of persons opposing apartheid' and calling on it to 'abandon forthwith the arbitrary trial now in progress and forthwith to grant unconditional release to all political prisoners and to all persons imprisoned, interned or subjected to other restrictions for having opposed the policy of apartheid'.

20 November Voters in the Xhosa Bantustan of the Transkei go to the polls for the first time to fill the 45 elected seats in the new legislative assembly, which had been established by the Transkei Self-Government Bill in May. Some 180 candidates stood for the seats in nine constituencies. There were no political parties and voters chose between candidates who supported either the pro-apartheid Chief Kaiser Matanzima, the former chairman of the Transkei territorial authority, or Paramount Chief Victor Poto Ndamase, who was believed to favour multiracialism. South African Minister for Bantu Administration Daan de Wet Nel let it be known that the 'idea of multi-racialism is completely against the Government's policy' and stressed that 'no multi-racial Parliament will be allowed in the Transkei, no matter what happens.' Even so, the government had to concede on 4 December that the majority of those elected supported Chief Poto's multiracial policies. Voter turnout was high, with an estimated 800,000 of the eligible 880,425 voters living in the homeland casting their ballots. Members of the Xhosa tribe living outside the Transkei were also entitled to vote under the provisions of the 'separate development' policy that gave Blacks the right to political expression only in their own homelands, but they largely ignored the election.

The newly elected members and the 64 appointed members of the legislative assembly met in Umtata on 6 December and narrowly elected Chief Matanzima as chief minister of Transkei over Chief Poto. Poto blamed his defeat on the nominated members and said he would go on to form an opposition party. The assembly was formally opened on 11 December by Minister de Wet Nel, thus becoming the first Bantustan officially to become semi-autonomous.

18 December South Africa withdraws from the UN Food and Agriculture Organization (FAO) after being barred on 5 December from attending African regional meetings. The FAO's African members had passed a resolution the previous year calling for South Africa's expulsion from the organization because of its apartheid policies. The FAO's secretary general, however, had informed them that he could not comply with their wishes since, under FAO rules, all regional members were entitled to the rights and privileges of membership and suggested the resolution be put before the FAO's 1963 annual meeting.

South Africa also withdrew from the ECA and its continued membership of the World Health Organization and the International Labour Organization was also in doubt after delegates from the Afro-Asian bloc refused to attend any conferences at which the South Africans were present.

By the end of the year, South Africa had voluntarily withdrawn or been forced to leave some nine international bodies since 1954 because of its apartheid policies.

31 December The Federation of Rhodesia and Nyasaland is formally dissolved at midnight. Almost all the links formed between the British colony of Southern Rhodesia and the territories of Northern Rhodesia and Nyasaland during the ten years of federation were severed.

The federation had been formed in 1953 after years of intense lobbying by White settlers, who wanted to band together against the overwhelming Black majority, despite the Blacks' strong opposition to the proposal. Their fears that the federation would be dominated by the Whites in Southern Rhodesia were well founded and largely borne out. Their resentment finally erupted in 1959, when widespread violence broke out in Nyasaland, and the British government became convinced that it would have to yield to Black majority rule. Nyasaland thus became the independent state of Malawi under the leadership of Hastings Banda on 6 July 1964, and Northern Rhodesia won its independence as Zambia on 24 October 1964 under President Kenneth Kaunda.

The dissolution of the federation caused the Whites in Southern Rhodesia to intensify their efforts at preventing the colony's independence under Black majority rule and eventually led to their illegal unilateral declaration of independence in November 1965.

---

1 9 6 4

---

27 January The Odendaal Commission publishes its report in Cape Town. The Commission had been appointed by Prime Minister Hendrik Verwoerd in September 1962 to devise a five-year plan to 'accelerate the development of non-Whites in South West Africa' and to determine 'the best form of participation by the Natives in the administration and management of their own interests'.

The commission concluded that since the population of South West Africa was made up of groups that differed from each other 'both physically and spiritually and harbour strong feelings against each other', it would be unwise to attempt to administer the area as one unit. It recommended that the principles of apartheid be applied and that ten non-White homelands be established 'for each population group in which it alone will have residential, political, and language rights and where it can develop towards self-determination'. Most of the homelands would have their own legislative assemblies while the White area, which would include the major mining areas, would remain under the jurisdiction of the present legislative assembly. All legislation passed by the assemblies would be subject to the approval of the South African president. The report also proposed a five-year development plan in which the South African government would spend more than £78 million developing the area over the first five years and a further £45.5 million over the next five years.

The prime minister announced on 29 April that he would not take any steps to implement the plan until after the International Court of Justice had concluded the hearings it was conducting on South West Africa.

1 March The foreign ministers of the Organization of African Unity (OAU) end their week-long meeting in Addis Ababa, Ethiopia, after disclosing the existence of the OAU 'Freedom Fighters Fund'. The fund was established to provide financial assistance to African liberation movements in South Africa, South West Africa and the Portuguese colonies.

5 May The Transkei's all-Black legislative assembly is opened for the first time by South African President Charles Swart. The chief minister of the newly self-governing Bantustan, Chief Kaiser Matanzima, called on 18 May for the 'gradual' departure of the 17,630 Whites living in the Transkei. He labelled multiracialism a 'mess of pottage' and advocated apartheid as the only policy by which different races in South Africa could 'live side by side in peace and harmony'.

In an apparent contradiction to Chief Matanzima's call, the South African government's chief administrator for the Transkei, Commissioner General Hans Abraham, reassured Whites on 20 May that they could remain in the Transkei as long as they wished.

11 May The South African Press Commission presents a report to Parliament in which it condemns foreign press coverage of South African events and advocates the establishment of a government press council to censor all news reports. The commission, which had been working on its 4,262-page report for some 14 years, alleged that the foreign press had a 'preponderance of bad and very bad reporting of political and racial matters' in South Africa. It also strongly criticized the South African press for its inaccurate and biased reports. Prime Minister Verwoerd had himself told Parliament in April that South Africa's English-language opposition newspapers were 'approaching treason' in their coverage.

23 May Nobel Peace Prize winner and former leader of the banned African National Congress (ANC) Albert Luthuli is placed under a further five-year ban by the South African government. Under the banning order, Luthuli was prohibited from making public statements either in print or verbally, was restricted to the Groutville native reserve and was denied any visitors unless they had first obtained the permission of the government.

12 June One of the most spectacular of South Africa's political trials ends with eight of the ANC's leaders sentenced to life imprisonment. The Rivonia trial, named after the suburb of Johannesburg where the men were arrested, had originally begun in October 1963 but the defence counsel had applied for the indictment against the accused to be quashed because the prosecution had failed to provide sufficient details of the charges to enable the preparation of a defence; this application had been granted on 30 October 1963. The defendants were, however, immediately rearrested and charged with sabotage on 31 October 1963 and the new trial began on 26 November 1963.

Eleven men in all (six Blacks, four Whites and one Indian) went into the dock charged under the General Law Amendment (Sabotage) Act and the Suppression of Communism Act with some 221 acts of sabotage designed to ferment 'violent revolution'. One defendant, Bob Hepple, was released in exchange for testifying for the prosecution soon after the trial was started. Eight of the remaining men –

ANC Deputy President Nelson Mandela, ANC Secretary General Walter Sisulu, Elias Matoaledi, Govan Mbeki, Raymond Mhlaba, Andrew Mlangeni (Blacks), Denis Goldberg (White) and Ahmed Kathrada (Indian) – were convicted, while another White, Lionel Berstein, was acquitted but later rearrested on charges of furthering Communist aims.

In what was later described as a 'spellbinding' five hours of testimony, Mandela took the stand on 20 April and admitted that he had planned sabotage, but not terrorism, 'as a result of a calm and sober assessment of the situation and tyranny of my people by the Whites'. He said that 'all other means of opposing' White supremacy 'were closed by legislation. We either had to accept inferiority or fight against it with violence. We chose the latter.' Mandela said that the ANC leadership had concluded in June 1961 that since violence was inevitable, they would be both wrong and unrealistic to pursue their policy of non-violence when the government 'met our demands with violence'. They, therefore, decided that the ANC would 'no longer disapprove of properly controlled sabotage'. He explained that they had decided on sabotage instead of terrorism because they did not want to kill people. Instead, their aim was to drive away foreign investment and to attract international attention to the plight of South Africa's non-Whites. The trial ended on 2 June after Mandela and Sisulu admitted that they had recruited people for training in the 'preparation, manufacture and use of explosives in both South Africa and abroad for a campaign of sabotage against the South African Government'.

The sentences were strongly condemned by the UN. The Security Council had passed a resolution on 9 June asking South Africa to stop executing and trying anti-apartheid opponents and noting 'with great concern' that the imminent verdict (in the Rivonia trial) would be delivered 'under arbitrary laws prescribing long terms of imprisonment and the death sentence' and might have 'very serious consequences'. After the life sentences were announced, the chairman of the Afro-Asian bloc in the UN issued a statement charging that the sentences were 'a provocation and a challenge flung by the racist rulers of South Africa against all the people of Africa' and 'a direct challenge' to the UN.

18 June The UN Security Council adopts a resolution condemning South Africa's racial policies and establishing a UN special committee on apartheid to examine possible economic sanctions that could be imposed against it. The committee was charged with undertaking 'a technical and practical study' and was to report to the Security Council by 30 November on 'the feasibility, effectiveness and implications of measures which could, as appropriate, be taken by the Security Council under the UN Charter'. The final report was to be completed by February 1965. The South African government was requested to inform the committee by 30 November about whether it would cooperate with the committee.

26 June The International Olympic Committee announces that it will bar South Africa from the 1964 Olympic Games unless its racial apartheid policies are modified by 16 August. The South African minister of the interior, Senator Johannes de Klerk, replied on 26 June that his country would not allow a mixed team to represent it at the Olympics. South Africa was subsequently banned from participating in the Games.

21 July The OAU concludes a four-day meeting in Cairo after adopting a resolution urging its 34 member states to sever trade relations with South Africa and Portugal in protest at their racial policies and to ban their aeroplanes and ships from African airports and harbours. The resolution also called on the oil-rich African countries to prohibit the shipment of petroleum to the two countries.

24 July A time bomb explodes in the main Johannesburg railway station killing one elderly White woman and seriously injuring several other people. The bombing was the most dramatic incident in a wave of sabotage that occurred after the Rivonia trial defendants were sentenced to life imprisonment in June. Frederick John Harris, a White teacher, member of the anti-Government African Resistance Movement (ARM) and former chairman of the Non-Racial Olympic Committee, was arrested later the same day and charged with murder. Police discovered a letter written by him to Prime Minister Verwoerd in which he said that Verwoerd either accede to the demands of the ARM or it would be forced to put into operation a plan to kill White South Africans.

At his trial, Harris admitted that he had planted the bomb but claimed he had only meant it as a spectacular demonstration to obtain publicity for the ARM and had never intended it to kill anyone. He said that he had telephoned warnings to both the police and two newspapers and had fully expected the area to be cleared before the explosion took place. He was found guilty of murder and sabotage and sentenced to death by the Pretoria Supreme Court on 6 November 1964. Harris was the first White in 20 years to be condemned to death for a politically motivated crime.

17 November British Prime Minister Harold Wilson announces the imposition of an immediate embargo on arms shipments to South Africa in protest against apartheid. Wilson told the British House of Commons that the decision was 'in line' with UN 'resolutions on this question'.

In answer to a question by former Prime Minister Alec Douglas-Home on whether the arms embargo was 'in effect an unilateral denunciation of the [1955 British–South African] Simonstown Agreement' that permitted Britain's use of the Simonstown naval base near Cape Town, Wilson said the agreement could be abrogated only by mutual consent. South Africa's Prime Minister Verwoerd held that Britain's failure to deliver 16 British Buccaneer jet fighter-bombers in 1965 as scheduled would mean the termination of the base pact.

Wilson clarified the point by saying that all contracts currently entered into would be honoured, including the sale of the 16 planes, but that no new contracts would be undertaken. Verwoerd welcomed this statement saying that now that the issue of the Buccaneers had been settled, immediate action with regard to the Simonstown Agreement had 'clearly been avoided'.

30 November The UN Special Committee on Apartheid, established by a resolution adopted by the Security Council in June, recommends that the only feasible way of forcing South Africa to abandon its racial segregation policies would be to implement complete economic sanctions against the country. The committee also reported that prompt action was required to deal with the country's explosive racial situation.

30 November Prime Minister Verwoerd announces in Parliament that the 90-day detention clause provided for in the 1963 General Law Amendment (Sabotage) Act would be suspended as from 11 January 1965. The clause had earlier, on 30 June, been extended for one year.

The clause had been under intense attack by opposition leaders, churchmen and academics since it was introduced. Over 100 university professors and lecturers had protested against it on 8 June claiming 'it violated the principle that no person should be imprisoned except after due process of law'.

1 9 6 5

1 January The Bantu Laws Amendment Act goes into effect. The new law, the most rigid of the apartheid legislation so far enacted, was acknowledged by the government to be the 'second leg' of its overall plan for separate development. The bill provided the legal framework for stripping Blacks of most of their remaining rights in White areas in return for independence in their own tribal homelands. It made the more than seven million Blacks living outside Bantustans 'temporary dwellers' in White South Africa.

Under the provisions of the bill, the minister of Bantu administration was empowered to establish 'proscribed areas' in which he could limit both total number of Black workers and the number of Blacks employed in any particular industry. He could also ban the further use of Black labour in any geographical area and send surplus Black workers to the Bantustans. It became an offence for a Black to be in a proscribed area for more than 72 hours unless he was born and permanently resided there, continuously worked there for one employer for at least 10 years, lived there lawfully for at least 15 years, or had obtained special permission from the government to be there.

The Opposition had strongly opposed the measure, even taking the unusual step of opposing its first reading. They claimed that the bill would result in an increased number of migratory labourers, seriously disrupt Black family life and create a shiftless mass of Black workers who were 'stateless' in their own country.

11 January The government announces that it is temporarily suspending the provisions of the May 1963 General Law (Amendment) Act. Under provisions of the act, police were authorized to arrest suspects without warrants and repeatedly imprison them for up to 90 days without access to legal advice or visitors and without the courts being able to interfere. Some 73 people being held under the 90-day detention clause at the time of the announcement had to be either promptly tried in court or else released. Justice Minister John Vorster was given leave to reinstate the detention law when he determined it was required.

1 March The UN Special Committee on Apartheid reports on the results of its study, authorized by the Security Council in a June 1964 resolution, into ways to persuade South Africa to ease its apartheid policies. The committee recommended that a total trade embargo, as well as an embargo on petroleum products, arms, ammunition, military vehicles and equipment, be placed on South Africa. It further suggested that: the emigration of technicians and skilled workers to South Africa be ended; communications be interdicted; and political and diplomatic steps, such as the withdrawal of diplomatic recognition, be taken.

1 March The first general elections ever held in Bechuanaland take place under the terms of a constitution agreed to in November 1963. The pro-multiracial Bechuanaland Democratic Party (BDP), headed by Seretse Khama, won 28 of the 31 seats in the legislative assembly. The BDP, while condemning apartheid, said that it realized that Bechuanaland was economically dependent on South Africa and must pursue a policy of 'good neighbourliness'.

South African Prime Minister Hendrik Verwoerd announced on 4 March that the restriction imposed on Khama in 1949, after he had married a White woman, prohibiting him from visiting South Africa had been lifted in October 1964. He explained that this was done 'when it became clear that Bechuanaland had been placed on the road to independence and after I had indicated on behalf of the South African Government that, since this was in accordance with the policy of separate development, the Republic would desire friendly relations with such a neighbour State'.

9 March The South African government announces that White immigrants from other countries in Africa would be eligible to take up South African citizenship after a one-year residency period rather than the normal five years because of 'their knowledge of conditions in Africa and the fact that they had already to a greater or lesser degree adapted themselves to the continent'.

24 March Provincial elections are held and result in a substantial increase in National Party seats and votes in all four provinces. The National Party, which already controlled the provincial councils in the Orange Free State, Transvaal and Cape, doubled its number of seats in the United Party-controlled Natal provincial council from four to eight seats. The liberal Progressive Party did not win a single seat in a White constituency, but gained the two seats reserved for Coloureds in the Cape province assembly in an election held on 10 March. The Nationalist gains had been considerable among English-speaking South Africans.

30 April The British protectorate of Basutoland becomes self-governing. Some 97 years of British rule ended when Paramount Chief Moshoeshoe II swore allegiance to Queen Elizabeth II and assumed the title of king.

The constitution under which Basutoland obtained self-government had been approved on 15 May 1964 and the territory's first general elections were held on 29 April. As a result of the elections, the traditionalist Basutoland National Party (BNP) won a slim victory, gaining 31 of the 60 seats in the Legislative Assembly. The leader of the BNP, Chief Leabua Jonathan, was defeated in his bid for a seat and so could not immediately assume the premiership. He soon won a seat in a by-election and became prime minister.

15 October The prime minister of Basutoland, Chief Leabua Jonathan, announces that he will ask Britain to grant the country independence on 29 April 1966. He explained that the date was chosen because it would be the anniversary of the country's first general election.

The British agreed to 'accept the Prime Minister's statement of intention' regarding independence. Britain said that Basutoland could ask for independence as from 29 April on the condition that either a simple majority of both houses of Parliament requested independence or referendum on the issue resulted in a majority of the population in favour of the move.

11 November The White minority government of Ian Smith declares Rhodesia's independence from Great Britain. The Unilateral Declaration of Independence (UDI) came after British efforts failed to persuade the Rhodesian government to resume their negotiations on a constitutional dispute. Britain had been demanding that a constitution it had agreed with Rhodesia in 1961 be amended to give the Black majority the eventual control of the government.

The independence proclamation, broadcast by Smith, announced the adoption of a new constitution to replace the 1961 one and, like the old charter, provided for the continuation of White minority rule over the country's four million Blacks. Britain condemned UDI as illegal, suspended Rhodesia's constitution and announced the imposition of a series of punitive measures, including economic sanctions, in an effort to regain control of its African colony.

Britain quickly brought the matter before the UN saying that 'the illegal regime based on minority rule is a matter of world concern'. The UN Security Council, meeting in an emergency session on 11 November, adopted a resolution condemning 'the unilateral declaration of independence made by a racist minority in Southern Rhodesia' and called on 'all states not to recognize this illegal racist minority regime in Southern Rhodesia and to refrain from rendering any assistance to that illegal regime'. The General Assembly passed a resolution on the same day calling on Britain to 'take all the necessary steps to put an end to the rebellion by the unlawful authorities in Salisbury' and on its members to end aid in any form to Rhodesia. South Africa and Portugal were the only two countries to vote against the resolutions.

South African Prime Minister Hendrik Verwoerd issued a statement on 11 November announcing that South Africa would not take part in any embargo against Rhodesia. He said that as the matter was a purely domestic issue between Rhodesia and Britain, South Africa could not agree with Britain's actions in involving the UN in the dispute and that South Africa would 'continue its policy of non-intervention', would 'express no views on the arguments put forward by either Britain or Rhodesia in this matter', and would 'continue to maintain normal friendly relations with both countries'.

The leader of the Opposition, Sir de Villiers Graaff, urged the government to recognize the Smith regime in Rhodesia saying that such recognition was 'inevitable'. He expressed 'the hope and wish that the action of our Government will be such that it will indicate the sympathy we feel for them'. He said the futures of the two countries were linked and held that the future of control in southern Africa should be White.

1 9 6 6

3 January The Transkei, the Xhosa Bantustan that was granted self-government in 1963, announces new zoning regulations reserving all or part of 23 White-occupied towns and villages for Black ownership and occupation. Whites were not forced to vacate their premises under the terms of the regulations but, under the new regulations, any property that did become vacant could be sold only to Blacks. Multiracial hospitals in the territory were required to establish separate facilities for the treatment of the various races under the new ordinance.

25 January Prime Minister Hendrik Verwoerd informs Parliament that the government would not prevent South African oil companies from shipping supplies to Rhodesia in defiance of the British oil embargo but would continue its 'non-intervention policy' in relations between Britain and Rhodesia.

Verwoerd's statement was in reply to a demand made by the leader of the Opposition, Sir de Villiers Graaff, that South Africa grant *de facto* recognition to the Rhodesian government. Graaff contended that the 'people of South Africa will never forgive the Prime Minister if he sits idly by while civilized government and stability are destroyed in Rhodesia'. Verwoerd had held that openly supporting the Smith regime in Rhodesia would sour relations with Britain and could, in fact, increase instability in the region. The opposition party's objections to government policy eased off over the year as it became gradually more apparent that South Africa was, in fact, giving Rhodesia a considerable amount of aid.

16 February South Africa is reported to be shipping oil to Rhodesia in defiance of a British embargo imposed on the country after the White minority government of Ian Smith issued its unilateral declaration of independence. According to reports in the Johannesburg newspaper, the *Rand Daily Mail*, South Africa was said to be transporting at least 35,000 gallons (159,110 litres) of oil a day, although the British contended that the figure was much lower. Oil was also reportedly being carried to Rhodesia on the South African railways via Mozambique. The oil was said to be shipped by private individuals with the tacit approval of the South African government.

South Africa's major suppliers of oil agreed on 3 March to limit the sale of oil to South Africa to only 10 per cent more than the amount they sold the country in 1964 in an effort to discourage the transshipment of oil to Rhodesia. The 10 per cent figure was estimated to be the expected increase in oil consumption in South Africa during the coming year. The agreement came as the result of an informal meeting in London between the British Government and representatives of Shell, British Petroleum and Socony Mobil.

Prime Minister Verwoerd warned Britain on 16 April not to exert too much pressure against South Africa to curb what he called its 'normal' trade with Rhodesia. In his reply, British Prime Minister Harold Wilson criticized Verwoerd for South Africa's continued shipment of oil to Rhodesia in defiance of the British embargo and warned that the shipments could result in UN sanctions being imposed on South Africa.

4 March The government announces that it will soon begin construction of a second oil-from-coal plant. The building of the facilities, which were expected to supply 30 per cent of South Africa's demand for oil, were seen by observers as part of the government's intensified drive to attain national self-sufficiency in the face of continued threats of international economic sanctions. Plans were also under way for the construction of a refinery to further decrease the country's dependence on outside assistance in meeting its energy needs.

The government's drive for self-sufficiency was further highlighted in June when it asked all of the country's major oil companies to increase their tank storage capacity from three to six months, with an eventual goal of storing enough oil to meet the country's needs for 12 months. It was also disclosed that the Nationalists were purchasing a fleet of oil tankers and actively engaged in searching for oil reserves within its borders.

On 14 December, a government spokesman claimed that South Africa could withstand being subjected to sanctions for up to three years, while the countries imposing sanctions could only survive without South African gold, uranium and other strategic supplies for two years.

18 March The South African Defence and Aid Fund, which had been established in Britain in 1956, is declared an unlawful organization under the provisions of the 1950 Suppression of Communism Act. The fund had figured prominently in the trial of White lawyer Abram Fischer, whose case was the most publicized of a spate of political trials taking place at this time. It was accused in court of being a channel for funds from Britain to anti-apartheid organizations and activists in South Africa.

31 March General elections are held in South Africa and result in the National Party being returned to power for the fifth successive time. The Nationalists, who obtained the largest parliamentary majority since 1933, won 126 seats in the newly enlarged 166-seat House of Assembly, to the United Party's 39 and the Progressive Party's one. The National Party did well in both urban and rural areas, increased its strength among English-speaking voters, gained seven of the 10 new seats and captured 13 others from the United Party. The Progressive's only member of the former parliament, Mrs Helen Suzman, retained her seat with a small increase in her majority, but the party otherwise fared badly.

The National Party had campaigned on the strength of its 18 years in government and advocated the continued implementation of its apartheid policies and the maintenance of White rule. The opposition United Party based its campaign on the immediate recognition of Ian Smith's Whites-only government in Rhodesia and on its opposition to the development of Bantustans. It argued that the establishment of Bantu homelands would enable the Communists to exert their influence on the independent African states and would, therefore, be a threat to White rule in southern Africa. The Progressive Party fought the campaign on its platform that the privileges and rights of South Africa's citizens should not depend on their colour or race but on their character and ability.

4 June United States Senator Robert F. Kennedy begins an unofficial speaking tour of South Africa at the invitation of the multiracial National Union of South African Students. His requests to meet Prime Minister Verwoerd and other senior government officials were rejected as 'not convenient', but he did hold talks with both Opposition and non-White leaders and drew large and enthusiastic crowds wherever he went in the country. Speaking from Kenya on 14 June, Kennedy claimed that the majority of Black South Africans opposed the implementation of sanctions because they believed that they would also be adversely affected. He returned to the US on 19 June, still denouncing apartheid but adding that it took the US 'such a long time to accomplish what's right that we should keep this in mind in any criticism of South Africa'.

18 July The International Court of Justice, meeting in The Hague, rejects by a vote of 8–7 an Ethiopian–Liberian suit challenging South Africa's right to govern South West Africa. The court ruled that neither Ethiopia nor Liberia had 'established any legal right or interest in the subject matter of this claim . . .' and said that the League of Nations as a whole, which had mandated the territory to South Africa in 1920, was the only body legally entitled to bring South Africa to court over its administration of South West Africa. Both Liberia and Ethiopia had been members of the League, which ceased to exist in 1946. The court held that mandatory states such as South Africa 'were to be agents of the League and not of each and every member of it individually'. By ruling against the two plaintiffs on that issue, the court did not have to decide on their two main contentions: that the League mandate for South West Africa was still in force, with the UN assuming the League's supervisory functions; and that South Africa's apartheid policy, as allegedly introduced into South West Africa, constituted a violation of its legal obligations under the League's mandate system.

Ethiopia and Liberia had filed the suit with the International Court of Justice after South Africa continued to ignore the court's 1950 advisory opinion on the issue. The court had, at that time, found that South Africa was still bound by the League of Nations mandate and that that mandate had been taken over by the UN.

Prime Minister Verwoerd hailed the court's decision in a nationwide radio address on 18 July as a 'major victory for South Africa'. He interpreted the decision as an 'inducement to devote ourselves anew to the guardianship which we accepted in respect of the lesser developed peoples of South Africa and South West Africa'. The largest Black nationalist organization in the territory, the South West African People's Organization (SWAPO), said that decision now left them with no other alternative but 'to rise in arms and bring about our liberation'. The Organization of African Unity issued a statement on 19 July condemning the court's decision saying that the court had 'diminished its prestige and created doubts regarding its integrity'. The US said that the court's prior advisory opinion had not been affected by this decision and that South Africa was still bound, under the League mandate, to accept UN supervision.

6 September Prime Minister Verwoerd is stabbed to death during a parliamentary session in the House of Assembly by Dimitrio Tsafendas. Tsafendas, who was employed as a temporary parliamentary messenger, had reportedly complained that Verwoerd was 'doing too much for Coloured people and not enough for poor Whites'. Finance Minister Theophilus E. Donges was appointed acting prime minister until the ruling National Party could hold a parliamentary caucus on 13 September to elect Verwoerd's successor.

Verwoerd's assassination shocked South Africans and provoked international expressions of dismay. While many, if not most, world leaders strenuously opposed his policies of apartheid, they deplored his death. Some leaders, however, like Singapore Prime Minister Lee Kuan Yew, said: 'If you run regimes like that, this is part of the risk of running them.' Kenyan President Jomo Kenyatta issued a statement saying, 'Perhaps this assassination will act as a timely lesson to Verwoerd's supporters in redeeming their country from many more such deaths.'

On 7 September, Justice Minister John Vorster announced that Verwoerd's assassination appeared 'to be the work of a deranged individual acting independently'. He said that the assassin's 'actions are now being investigated to the finest detail'. Tsafendas was subsequently declared insane by the Cape Town Supreme Court on 20 October and was to be indefinitely detained in prison. He was reported to be unable to 'give a single coherent reason for committing the murder'.

13 September Justice Minister Balthazar Johannes (John) Vorster is unanimously elected prime minister by the 164-member parliamentary caucus of the ruling National Party in Cape Town. The only other candidate for the post, Transport Minister Barend Jacobus Schoeman, withdrew from the race in the interests of party unity. In his acceptance statement, Vorster pledged 'to walk further along the road set by Hendrik Verwoerd'. In an address to the nation on 14 November, he promised to continue South Africa's policy of apartheid, which, he said, was 'not a denial of human dignity' but a means to give 'an opportunity to every individual within his own sphere'.

30 September The British high commission territory of Bechuanaland becomes the independent state of Botswana as President Sir Seretse Khama formally takes control of the government. Sir Seretse, aware that his country's lack of resources and general poverty made it economically dependent on its White-ruled neighbour, was reportedly seeking friendly relations with South Africa in spite of his avowed policy of nonracialism. He was said to have the solid support of Botswana's 3,900 White inhabitants.

4 October Basutoland becomes the second British high commission territory to achieve independence when it officially becomes the Kingdom of Lesotho. Paramount Chief Motlotlehi Moshoeshoe II assumed the rank of king while Prime Minister Chief Leabua Jonathan took up the reins of government. The new country, a constitutional monarchy completely surrounded by South Africa, was entirely dependent on its White neighbour economically. Although Jonathan was bitterly criticized by his more militant countrymen for his policy of *détente* with South Africa, he considered Lesotho's location and economic situation made friendly relations with South Africa imperative. Apparently with this in mind, he had signed an agreement with South African Prime Minister Verwoerd on 2 September that the two countries would not interfere in each other's domestic affairs.

27 October The UN General Assembly terminates South Africa's mandate to administer the territory of South West Africa. In a resolution declaring that 'South Africa has failed to fulfill its obligations in respect of the administration of the mandated territory', the General Assembly declared that 'henceforth South West Africa comes under the direct responsibility of the United Nations'. South Africa was called upon to 'refrain and desist from any action, constitutional, administrative, political or otherwise' that would 'alter the present international status of South West Africa'. Under the provisions of the resolution, a 14-member *ad hoc* committee for South West Africa was established and instructed to decide on practical measures for administration of the territory. The committee was given until April 1967 to report its findings to the Assembly. The move came after the International Court of Justice ruled against an Ethiopian–Liberian suit challenging South Africa's right to govern South West Africa. Following that decision, the majority of the UN Afro-Asian group of nations pushed for the UN to end the mandate.

On 1 November, Prime Minister Vorster declared that the UN resolution on South West Africa was illegal. He announced, 'We will continue to administer the territory as in the past' and added that the UN 'has no power whatsoever to take a decision of the kind it has taken' and that, therefore, his government would take no action on the matter.

16 December The UN General Assembly unanimously votes to impose economic sanctions against Rhodesia. The move comes after British Prime Minister Harold Wilson and the leader of the Rhodesian Whites-only government Ian Smith, during talks which ended on 3 December, failed to agree an end to the rebellion. Britain had earlier rejected Black African calls for an extension of the embargo to South Africa saying that it preferred not to involve a third party in its dispute with its colony and on 13 December opposed a proposed blockade of South Africa.

---

1 9 6 7

---

10 January Lesotho Prime Minister Leab'ua Jonathan arrives in Cape Town for talks with his South African counterpart, John Vorster. His visit made him the first leader of an independent Black African state to visit South Africa. Jonathan was received by the South Africans with full honours and was not subject to any of the usual apartheid restrictions. Observers saw the visit as a major coup for Vorster, who had been making a determined effort to improve South Africa's relations with Black Africa as part of his 'forward-looking' foreign policy.

After a meeting lasting two hours, the two leaders issued a statement expressing their commitment to 'peaceful coexistence on the basis of reality, mutual respect and noninterference in one another's domestic affairs'. Jonathan also said, 'Everyone knows that I have come to ask South Africa to help my economically embarrassed country. We in Lesotho are thankful for the freedom we have already won. We realise that any help which may be given will be meaningful only to the extent that it enables the establishment of a stable and prosperous African continent.' Vorster added, 'On fundamental issues we found ourselves in complete accord, more specifically on the fact that differences in political philosophy are no bar to fruitful cooperation.'

8 March The Defence Amendment Act, which was designed to make military service compulsory for the vast majority of young White men, is first published. The bill was seen as part of the government's attempts to strengthen the defence forces in the face of the international arms embargo. It stipulated that all White 18-year-old men were liable to serve in either the Citizen Force for one year, and then undergo annual training for the next nine years, or in the newly created commando reserve for 60 days, with annual training for the following 19 years. The bill also made it illegal to reveal anything about the defence forces that was 'calculated to alarm or depress the public or prejudice the Government in its foreign relations'. The United Party supported the bill, which easily passed into law.

13 March South Africa signs a major trade agreement with Malawi, one of its first with a Black African country. Observers saw it as part of Prime Minister Vorster's 'forward-looking' foreign policy. Under the terms of the agreement, certain Malawian products, such as tea, cotton waste, some tobacco and essential oils, were allowed to enter South Africa duty free, while all other goods were subjected to most-favoured-nation rates. Malawi's President Hastings Banda attacked the leaders of other Black African states who had criticized Malawi's cooperation with South Africa as 'physical and moral cowards as well as hypocrites' and accused them of trading with South Africa in secret.

21 March The minister of Bantu administration and development, Michael C. Botha, outlines the government's plan for granting self-rule to the Ovamboland territory in South West Africa. According to the plan, the 240,000-strong Ovambo tribe, who make up approximately 45 per cent of the population of South West Africa, would eventually be able to either become fully independent or enter into a partnership with other countries. Ovamboland would be governed by a legislative council made up of elected representatives and traditional leaders, while South Africa would provide the council with the services of specialized civil servants as and where they were needed. Botha said that such plans for self-rule 'also applied to other national units in South West Africa who may wish to adapt their systems of self-government to their particular circumstances'. He added that the final choice for the acceptance of self-rule would remain with the inhabitants of the territories. The plan was in keeping with the recommendations of the 1964 Odendaal commission on the development of South West Africa, which called for the territory to be divided into 10 ethnic homelands.

Although South Africa reported that the leaders of the Ovambos supported the plan, delegates from African countries protested at the UN on 21 March that they saw it as the mere extension of South Africa's Bantustan policy. They, along with Asian representatives to the UN, issued a statement denouncing the South African government as trying 'to create a fiction of self-government' in South West Africa while attempting to break up 'the territory into numerous and non-viable units with a view to covering up South African domination'.

25 April The British high commission territory of Swaziland attains self-government when Prince Makhosini Dlamini is sworn in as prime minister.

Swazi voters went to the polls on 19–20 April and elected the pro-royalist Imbokodvo National Movement to all 24 legislative assembly seats. The victory of Imbokodvo over its main rival, the more militant, pan-African Ngwane National Liberatory Congress, was seen as a major show of support for Swazi King

Sobhuza II and Imbokodvo party leader Dlamini. The opposition had protested the results of the election on the basis that Imbokodvo won only 80 per cent of the total votes but gained all of the assembly seats and demanded that Britain suspend the 'fradulent constitution' and introduce proportional representation.

19 May The UN General Assembly, meeting in a special session, establishes an 11-member UN council for South West Africa to administer the territory until it gains independence, some time before June 1968. The General Assembly had, over South African protests that it was not empowered to do so, terminated South Africa's mandate over the area in October 1966.

The resolution establishing the council, while not explicitly mentioning military enforcement, called for it to be based in South West Africa and 'to take all the necessary measures for the maintenance of law and order . . .'. South Africa was called on 'to facilitate the transfer of the administration . . . of South West Africa to the Council', while the council was instructed to 'proceed to South West Africa' and to oversee the removal of South African administrative personnel and military forces.

South African Prime Minister Vorster said on 24 May that his country 'did not need the services of a United Nations committee to administer South West Africa' and added that his government would neither recognize the council nor enter into discussions with it.

On 28 November, the council reported to the General Assembly that, because of South Africa's refusal to cooperate, it was 'impossible for the Council to discharge effectively all of the functions and responsibilities entrusted to it by the Assembly'.

31 May Charles Swart, South Africa's last governor general and first president, steps down from office. He was supposed to be succeeded by Finance Minister Donges, who had been elected to the presidency on 28 February, but Donges suffered a brain haemorrhage on 11 May and was unable to assume his duties. Former Senate head Jozua Naude was subsequently sworn in as acting president on 1 June.

21 June A new General Laws Amendment Act, more commonly known as the 'Terrorism Act', goes into effect. The act, which had first been published on 27 May, was pushed through Parliament by the government in reaction to recent terrorist acts that had taken place in South West Africa and was made retroactive to 27 June 1962. Justice Minister P.C. Pelsar described the bill as 'a very far reaching measure'.

The act made terrorism, defined as any act committed with the intention of endangering law and order or inciting to or conspiring in the commission of such an act, a separate offence and equated it to treason. Terrorist acts included murder, the possession of arms, ammunition or explosives and the receiving of military training. The act provided for the arbitrary arrest and indefinite detention of suspects, summary trials without a jury and the transfer of the burden of proof from the accuser to the accused. Mass trials of suspects, who had been charged with different offences, were permitted under the terms of the act. Any offence committed by a group of defendants at any particular time could result in all of the defendants being found guilty of individual offences committed by any member or members of the group.

21 July The Black nationalist leader and 1960 Nobel Peace Prize winner, Albert Luthuli, dies in Groutville. Luthuli, who had previously suffered a stroke that had impaired his movement and vision, was hit by a train as he crossed a railway bridge. The deposed Zulu chieftain was arguably South Africa's most prominent Black leader and had been banished to Groutville by the South African government in 1959 for his anti-apartheid activities. Although a militant champion of racial equality, Luthuli was nevertheless regarded as a moderate because of his opposition to violence and his call for cooperation with Whites in the struggle to obtain full rights for Blacks.

7 August In the most important political case taking place at the time, some 37 Blacks go on trial in Pretoria accused of committing acts of terrorism in South West Africa. The men, all members of the nationalist South West African People's Organization (SWAPO), were accused of conspiring to overthrow the South African-run government in the territory by violent means and to replace it with a SWAPO-led government. They also faced charges that, between June 1962 and May 1967, they had committed acts of terrorism including murder, arson, armed robbery, shooting at the police and receiving military training. The accused had all been captured in South West Africa and had been held in detention for periods from 200 to 400 days before the start of their trial.

8 September Prime Minister Vorster announces that Yuri Nikolayevich Loginov had been arrested in Johannesburg as a Soviet spy. The government, which was staunchly anti-Communist, had often claimed that its opponents were in the pay of the Communists but Loginov was the first Soviet ever to be arrested in South Africa for spying. He confessed to working for the Soviet intelligence service in South Africa and in 23 other countries.

Loginov was allegedly in the country to gauge Rhodesia's dependence on South Africa and to find out how South Africa had been cooperating with an unnamed Western country in atomic and rocket research. On 10 October, the Soviet representative to the UN Disarmament Committee, meeting in Geneva, read out an East German statement that accused West Germany of having concluded 'far-reaching agreements with the Republic of South Africa on the production and testing of atomic weapons on South African territory'.

Loginov was released in July 1969 in exchange for 10 West German agents. He reportedly 'sung like a canary' about the names of Soviet agents in 23 Western countries. The exchange was thought to have been part of a secret international weapons deal in which South Africa was expected to 'acquire vital military equipment and goods'.

The episode was a boost to the government. They not only acquired weapons despite the UN arms embargo, but could also point to a real Soviet spy as proof of the Communist threat when clamping down on 'Communist anti-Government protestors'.

10 September Malawi becomes the first Black African state to establish formal diplomatic relations with South Africa, a step which was seen in South Africa as being of immense historical significance.

Malawian President Hastings Banda decided to establish the link with South Africa at legation level in spite of the strong condemnation his decision drew from the Organization of African Unity. He said that diplomatic relations would be established by 1 January 1968 between the two countries and would be fully reciprocal. Malawi's first ambassador would be a White. Banda, however, assured his ruling Malawi Congress Party that South Africa had agreed to receive a Malawian 'of full blood and colour' and that such an envoy would be sent as soon as possible.

3 December A team of South African surgeons, headed by Dr Christian Barnard, performs the world's first heart transplant. The patient, Louis Washkansky, lived for 18 days before succumbing to pneumonia. The operation, which was hailed as a major medical breakthrough, made the South African doctor a hero and provided the South African public with an international scientific first of which they could be collectively proud.

14 December British Prime Minister Harold Wilson announces his government's decision to continue its three-year ban on the sale of arms to South Africa, in conformity with UN resolutions, and reaffirmed his position in parliamentary debates held on 18–19 December. The statements followed speculation in the British press that South Africa was ready to place orders, reportedly worth up to £200 million, for British naval ships and other military equipment.

In a New Year's Eve broadcast, Prime Minister Vorster said that South Africa was not dependent on Britain for its defensive arms requirements, but that he would have to review the Simonstown naval agreement in the new year in light of Britain's refusal to sell it such equipment. That agreement had given Britain access to the strategic Simonstown naval facilities near Cape Town in return for handing the facilities over to South Africa. The South African press, meanwhile, said that if Britain refused the order, it would go to the French who were not abiding by the UN arms resolutions.

On 19 December, the US announced that it was also renewing its ban on sale of arms to South Africa.

<hr>

1 9 6 8

1 January The first Black African diplomat to be accredited to South Africa takes up residence in a 'White' suburb of Cape Town. The arrival of the Malawian diplomat was condemned by conservative (*verkrampte*) members of the ruling National Party, who considered it a weakening of the country's apartheid system.

Prime Minister John Vorster defended his 'forward-looking' foreign policy in August after it came under heavy attack from the *verkramptes*. He contended that establishing diplomatic relations with neighbouring Black states was necessary to ensure that southern Africa remained 'free of Communism' and that it did not, as they claimed, affect South Africa's policy of separate development.

26 January The Pretoria terrorism trial ends with 30 of the original 36 South West African defendants being found guilty of terrorist activities and membership in the banned South West Africa People's Organization (SWAPO). They were sentenced to prison terms ranging from five years to life. Three others, who had testified that several of their co-defendants had received terrorist training abroad, pleaded guilty to violating provisions of the Suppression of Communism Act and received five-year suspended sentences. One defendant was acquitted, one had been acquitted earlier and one had died. On 22 November, the appeals court reduced five of the men's sentences from life to 20 years' imprisonment.

In announcing the verdicts, Judge Joseph Ludorf said that as the punishable acts 'were committed before the (1967) Terrorism Act passed by Parliament' and as 'this is the first trial in which persons are charged with contravention of the Act because of the retrospective effects thereof', 'we have decided not to impose the death penalty in the case of any one of the accused'. He went on to say that 'the accused, because of their level of civilization, became easily misguided dupes of Communist indoctrination' and that they had obtained 'active financial and practical assistance' from the Soviet Union, China and elsewhere.

Former SWAPO Secretary Toivo Herman ja Toivo, while admitting that he had assisted 'those who had taken up arms', claimed it was because 'we believe that South Africa has robbed us of our country'.

29 January The government begins evicting more than 12,000 Blacks from an area near Dundee in northern Natal province that had been reserved for Whites only under the provisions of the 1961 Group Areas Act. A committee, made up of representatives from five church groups, unsuccessfully appealed to the government to postpone the eviction on the grounds that it would cause the Blacks severe hardship. The move was condemned by the international community as an example of one of the worst aspects of the apartheid laws.

19 February South Africa's electoral college, consisting of members from both houses of Parliament, elects Jacobus Johannes Fouche to be South Africa's second president. Fouche took over from acting president Jozua Naude. President-elect Theophilus E. Donges had died on 10 January without ever taking office.

20 February Defence Minister Pieter (P.W.) Botha informs Britain that it 'cannot continue to rely on our benevolent acquiescence in the use of our airfields or Simonstown naval base or any other of our harbour facilities in peace or war, except if we deem it in the interests of South Africa to make them available' if it continues to enforce its embargo on the shipment of arms to South Africa.

In an address to Parliament, Botha said that South Africa had previously viewed the 1955 Simonstown agreement, under which control of the strategically located British royal naval base near Cape Town was transferred to South Africa, and other defence pacts with Britain as necessary for the Western allies to guard the sea lanes around South Africa and to defend southern Africa from aggression.

22 February Parliament passes the Prohibition of Mixed Marriages Amendment Bill. The bill declared that the marriage of a male South Africa citizen and a woman of a different race which had been contracted abroad was invalid in South Africa. It closed a loophole in the original act, which had been passed in 1949 and was considered one of the cornerstones of apartheid. The bill was considered to be in response to the marriage abroad of one of Afrikanerdom's most famous poets, Breyten Breytenbach, to a Vietnamese woman.

23 February The South African and Lesotho governments announce an agreement in principle for the joint construction of a series of power stations and dams. The Oxbow hydroelectric project would provide both countries with electricity and power.

In an address to Lesotho's National Assembly on 26 February, Prime Minister Chief Leabua Jonathan emphasized that the agreement was strictly a business enterprise and did not imply approval of South Africa's racist policies.

26 March The government introduces three bills into the House of Assembly that were designed to strengthen its policy of apartheid.

The Separate Representation of Voters Amendment Bill extended until 1971 the existing terms of office of the Whites elected by Coloureds to represent them in Parliament. The seats, which would not be refilled if they fell vacant before that date, would then be abolished. The Opposition attacked the bill as a further diminution of Coloured rights and as a government move to ensure that those seats did not go to the Opposition, as they traditionally did. The bill passed the House on 3 May and Senate on 20 May.

The Coloured Persons' Representative Council Amendment Bill was designed to provide separate representation for Coloureds, in line with the government's apartheid policies, after the government had removed them from even indirect participation in the White Parliament. It transferred the representation of Coloureds to an expanded Coloured persons representative council, which would be authorized to legislate for Coloureds in such areas as social welfare, education and local government. The council, which had previously served in a purely advisory capacity, would have 40 elected and 20 appointed members to maintain a committee for liaison with Parliament. The bill completed its passage through Parliament on 21 May with support of the Opposition, except for the Progressive Party's Helen Suzman.

The Prohibition of Political Interference Bill was designed to make multiracial political parties illegal. It prohibited the involvement of one racial group in the political affairs of another and barred any political party from receiving financial assistance from abroad. The bill passed Parliament on 21 May. It resulted in the total demise of the Liberal Party and in the Progressive Party becoming a Whites-only organization.

5 April Interior Minister Michael Botha introduces the Development of Self-Government for Native Nations in South West Africa Bill. It provided for the establishment of legislative councils for seven different tribal groups in the territory. The councils were expected to form the bases for the self-governing Bantustans that were to be eventually established in the area.

The opposition United Party opposed the bill on the grounds that the majority of South West Africans lived outside the areas designated for their tribal groups. Opposition leader Sir de Villiers Graaff said the bill would necessitate 'a population movement unrivalled in the history of the world' and said, 'It is utterly preposterous to talk of these groups as nations, or to suggest they are entitled by a process of self-determination to be led to independence. Independence for such little groups can only be a mockery and a delusion.'

8 April South African Finance Minister Nicolaas Diederichs announces that South Africa, the producer of more than two-thirds of the West's total annual gold output, had decided to suspend all gold sales for the 'immediate future'. The ban on sales applied both to foreign central banks at the official exchange rate of $35 an ounce and to the commercial markets, which sold gold at the fluctuating free market price. Diederichs said that 'at present, the reserve bank of South Africa is buying all newly mined gold' and stressed that South Africa reserved its right to sell gold on the free market 'when it became necessary'. He added that the decision about when, where and in what quantity South Africa would sell its gold would be based solely on what was in South Africa's best interests.

South Africa's move was taken in response to a gold crisis that had broken out in March and resulted in a rush of speculative buying. The crisis, described by financial experts as the worst since the Great Depression of the 1930s, was caused by rumours that the US was unable to maintain gold's official $35 price and would be forced to revalue it. To deal temporarily with the crisis, the London Gold Pool, made up of the US and six West European countries, devised a two-tier pricing system. Under the new system, governments would buy gold at the official price while the private market paid a price that fluctuated with supply and demand. Finance Minister Diederichs, however, criticized the new pricing system as a 'gimmick' that could not endure in the long run. He reaffirmed his country's demand for an increase in the official price of gold, which should be effected in an 'orderly manner', but claimed that 'the eyes and ears of certain authorities were simply closed to any case for an increased gold price'.

South Africa's decision not to sell gold caused great confusion in the world financial markets and raised fears of a worsening economic crisis.

17 April South Africa refuses entry into South West Africa to 26 representatives from the UN Council for South West Africa. The move forced the council temporarily to abandon its attempt to establish the UN's authority in the territory. The 11-nation council was established to enforce the 1966 UN resolution rescinding South Africa's mandate over South West Africa, a resolution that South Africa maintained was invalid.

On 7 May, the council reported to the General Assembly that South Africa's defiance of the UN would 'inevitably lead to the outbreak of racial war and violence'. It requested that 'forceful measures' be taken and proposed that the issue be sent to the Security Council, where 'effective measures' could be invoked. Most observers doubted that such measures would be taken, especially as the majority of Western powers opposed them.

7 May The multiracial Liberal Party, founded in 1953 on a platform of universal suffrage and a common electoral roll, disbands in anticipation of the passage of the Prohibition of Political Interference Bill. The party decided to cease to exist rather than to become a Whites-only organization as required under the bill, which was introduced in Parliament on 26 March to make integrated political parties illegal. The Liberals had an estimated 3,000 supporters, half of whom were non-White, at the time of its demise but no representation in Parliament.

Some 400 members of all races attended the party's final meeting, at which party president Alan Paton declared, 'Man was not created to go down on his belly before the state. We refuse to make a god of preservation of racial differences.' The party was supported by prominent people but had never been able to make a significant impact on White South African politics in its own right. Observers, however, believe that one of the main effects the Liberal Party had on the South African political scene was that it weakened the opposition United Party by attracting to it many of the United Party's leading, English-speaking, intellectual members.

The country's only other multiracial party, the Progressive Party, was reported on 7 April to be continuing in existence as an all-White party. Party leader Jan Steytler pledged that the Progressives would 'continue to work for the day when once again there will be freedom of association in South Africa'. The party had one representative in Parliament, Mrs Helen Suzman, who was often a lone voice against the government's apartheid legislation and was internationally recognized as such.

12 June The UN General Assembly passes a resolution proclaiming that 'South West Africa shall henceforth be known as Namibia in accordance with the desires of its people'. The name was given to the territory by the nationalist SWAPO and is derived from the Namib desert that runs along the territory's coast.

9 August Prime Minister Vorster announces that he is reshuffling his Cabinet to make way for younger men. The move was widely interpreted as an attempt to strengthen his *verligte* (enlightened) element of the ruling National Party against the *verkrampte* (ultra-conservative) forces, led by Albert Hertzog. Hertzog, until then the minister of health, was removed from the Cabinet as a result of the reshuffle.

The *verkrampte* section of the party believed that Afrikaners must continue their 'mission' without being contaminated by the liberal attitudes of English-speaking Whites. In their view, liberalism led to Communism.

The *verligte* Afrikaners, while agreeing that apartheid must be strictly pursued inside South Africa, claimed that the country needed to maintain a policy of good relations with the outside world, including friendly Black states in Africa such as Malawi and Botswana. They felt that the National Party should be the party of South African Whites, including the English and Jewish communities, instead of the party of Afrikaner nationalism.

6 September The last British protectorate in South Africa becomes independent. King Sobhuza II received the symbols of Swaziland's sovereignty at an independence ceremony in the new country's capital of Mbabane. The king, who was expected to be Swaziland's dominant political figure, was to govern through the royalist Imbokodvo National Movement (INM). The INM held all 24 seats in the country's first legislative assembly and was led by Prime Minister Prince Makhosini Dlamini.

Observers were optimistic about the new country's future. Despite the fact that much trade and investment was controlled by neighbouring South Africa, Swaziland's economic outlook was promising. It contained the fifth largest asbestos mine in the world as well as an iron mine and exported considerable amounts of timber, rice, sugar and fruit. Over 90 per cent of its population of approximately 400,000 people were Swazi tribesmen, so the threat of intertribal warfare that plagued so many other independent Black African states appeared to be remote.

4 October The International Bank for Reconstruction and Development, more commonly known as the World Bank, and the International Monetary Fund (IMF) end their annual meeting in Washington.

A major issue at the meeting had been how to deal with newly mined South African gold. The representatives were afraid that South Africa's decision to withhold gold unless it could be guaranteed a $35-an-ounce minimum price on the free market as well as on the fixed market would result in wildly fluctuating markets and, since the price was tied to the dollar, could ultimately affect the value of the dollar. A compromise plan was presented in which South Africa could sell the newly mined gold to the IMF and central banks at the official rate of $35 an ounce when the free market price was $35 or lower and when South Africa needed foreign exchange to avert or reduce a balance-of-payments deficit. During normal times, South Africa would be required to sell in the free market and thus prevent the free market price from rising sharply above the official price. South Africa rejected the proposal on 4 October.

17 October In a move seen as a step towards introducing separate development into South West Africa, the minister of Bantu administration and development, Michael Botha, officially opens the Ovamboland legislative council. On 2 October, South Africa had promulgated a constitution for Ovamboland as the first of six Bantustans it planned to establish in South West Africa. At the opening ceremony, Botha told the Ovambos, 'You are now the rulers in your own homeland.' He said, 'This body [the council] is the future parliament of Ovamboland' and added that 'the members of your Executive Council occupy positions which can be compared to those of ministers of state'.

Under Ovamboland's new constitution, the legislative council would consist of not more than 42 members, with six from each of the Ovamboland's seven regions. The executive council was chaired by the chief councillor and had seven members, one member being selected by each of the seven regional authorities.

7 November The UN General Assembly condemns Britain's failure to topple Rhodesia's Whites-only government and passes a resolution urging Britain to use force against the regime of Prime Minister Ian Smith. The resolution called on all member nations to stop any financial dealings they might be conducting with the Rhodesian government. It urged the Security Council to widen the scope of the economic sanctions it had already imposed on Rhodesia and to extend the sanctions to Rhodesia's allies, South Africa and Portugal. The resolution also called for the immediate release of all Black nationalists being detained in Rhodesian prisons and for the expulsion of all South African troops from Rhodesia.

14 November The 72-member Ciskei tribal authority is officially reconstituted as a legislative assembly in preparation for the 1,000-square-mile (2,590-square-kilometre) area in the eastern Cape province becoming a self-governing Bantustan. A six-man executive council, with authority over the local affairs of the area's 750,000 Xhosa tribesmen, was also established. According to Minister of Bantu Administration and Development Michael Botha, the Ciskei civil service would originally be half White and half Black, but it was planned that the Whites would all gradually be replaced by Xhosa.

13 December An Afro-Asian resolution to expel South Africa from the UN Conference on Trade and Development was defeated in the General Assembly. The motion, which had earlier been ruled an 'important question' requiring a two-thirds majority vote for passage, received 11 votes short of the required number. It had been the subject of heated controversy since the UN legal counsel found that it would be unconstitutional for the organization to expel a member state from a group that was open to all UN members. The Afro-Asian group disagreed with this ruling and tabled the resolution. Most Western countries voted against resolution, while most Communist countries abstained.

12 February The South Africa Amendment Bill is passed by Parliament. The bill repealed the provisions of the 1909 act that called for the incorporation into South Africa of Rhodesia and the former British high commission territories, which had since become the independent nations of Swaziland, Botswana and Lesotho. The original South African Act of 1909 had been amended after the country withdrew from the Commonwealth in 1961 and formed the basis of South Africa's constitution. The new amendment was seen as being in recognition of the political fact that South Africa would never obtain its often-stated goal of incorporating the British protectorates into a greater South Africa.

13 March The South West Africa Affairs Bill completes its passage through Parliament. The bill enabled the government to apply any South African laws, including apartheid legislation, in South West Africa and to change any law when it was applied in South West Africa 'as they deem fit'. The bill also provided for the transfer of the certain administrative powers from the South West African administration to the South African government, such as Black education.

The Opposition condemned the Bill, which it said diminished the South West African legislative assembly's power and would reduce South West Africa to the status of a South African province.

2 May South African Defence Minister P.W. Botha announces the development of a ground-to-air missile, which he described as 'the most advanced and effective weapon of its kind'. The French government, which was ignoring the UN ban on arms sales to South Africa, had provided financial help for the development of the missile and a French electronics firm had assisted with its design.

5 May The Public Service Amendment Bill is introduced by the minister of the interior and the police, S.L. Muller. The bill provided for the establishment of a highly autonomous Bureau of State Security (BOSS). It was to be headed by a chief who was directly responsible to a special minister appointed by the President rather than to Parliament and with a budget not subject to the approval of the Treasury. BOSS was empowered to investigate all matters that affected state security. The amendment was opposed by all sections of the legal system, from law students to judges. The leader of the arch-conservative (*verkrampte*) Afrikaners, Albert Hertzog, also fought against the bill, which he feared would be used against the *verkramptes*.

13 May Robert Sobukwe, the founder and former president of the banned Pan-African Congress, is released from the maximum security prison on Robben Island, off Cape Town. He had spent nine years in prison, six of them under a special act of Parliament.

Sobukwe, who organized the anti-pass law demonstrations that culminated in the 1960 Sharpeville massacre, was originally jailed in 1960 for three years. Shortly before his scheduled release in 1963, however, Parliament enacted special legislation which enabled it to detain any political prisoner who was deemed likely to further 'the aim of Communism' for a further 12 months, reviewed annually. The law was known as the 'Sobukwe Clause'. His annual review was due on 30 June.

Sobukwe was released under restrictions. He was prohibited from travelling outside the municipal limits of the city of Kimberley and banned under provisions of the Suppression of Communism Act from teaching or meeting with groups of more than three people.

30 June The General Law Amendment Act, a controversial measure giving BOSS virtually unlimited power over the admission of evidence in court and over news of its activities, goes into effect.

Criticism of the bill, which came from the South African judiciary and press as well as from Parliament, centred on two clauses: Clause 10 prevented newspapers from reporting any BOSS activities that the government deemed might be 'prejudicial to security', and Clause 29 prohibited a person under investigation from testifying on his own behalf if the government felt that such evidence was harmful to state interests.

The justice minister of the Transvaal, Jacobus Marias, protested on 26 June that the judiciary had not been consulted on the provisions of the bill and warned that passage of the bill would seriously infringe upon the independence of the judiciary. The Cape Bar Council, Pretoria Bar Council and Society of Advocates of Natal all denounced the provisions as being 'far beyond what might be regarded as necessary' and described them as having 'invaded the power of the courts'. The bill was also opposed by leading judges.

Prime Minister Vorster said on 9 August that BOSS had no powers to arrest or detain and, on 5 September, announced that a commission of inquiry would be established to both hear any objections to the government's security legislation and to investigate South Africa's security network.

10 July The editor in chief of the *Rand Daily Mail*, Laurence Gandar, and chief reporter Benjamin Pogrund are found guilty of contravening the 1959 Prisons Act. They had been accused of publishing articles in 1965 on conditions in South African prisons, while knowing the information was false or without having made 'reasonable' efforts to verify it. The articles were based on information given to

Pogrund by former inmates and prison officers who charged that prisoners were subjected to brutality, torture and sodomy. They also claimed that one Black prisoner had been beaten to death. Gandar and the newspaper were both fined while Pogrund got a suspended sentence.

Gandar and Pogrund first appeared in court in June 1967 but the trial had to be postponed several times because some of the newspaper's informants were, themselves, being tried for spreading falsehoods about prison conditions. The trial, begun in November 1968 but again adjourned, resumed in February 1969. The defence claimed the issue at stake was freedom of the press, while the prosecution argued that the two men had committed a statutory offence against the provisions of the Prison Act.

14 August The Lebowa territorial authority is officially opened by Michael Botha, the minister of Bantu administration and development. The inauguration of the authority, which was the administrative unit for some one million tribesmen in northern Transvaal, was seen as the first step towards the area's becoming a self-governing Bantustan under South Africa's separate development programme. The move was criticized by the international community as another of South Africa's efforts to carry out its separation of the races.

The Basotho territory authority, in the northeastern part of the Orange Free State, had been inaugurated in April.

16 September Prime Minister Vorster announces that a general election will be held early in 1970, a full year before it was due. The announcement came after the battle between the *verkrampte* and *verligte* branches of the ruling National Party came to a head at a party congress held in Pretoria on 10 September.

The growing feud was seen by most observers to be based on the *verkrampte* opposition to four of Vorster's policies: closer cooperation between English- and Afrikaans-speaking Whites; the immigration of Roman Catholics into South Africa; the admission of diplomats from Black African states; and the granting of permission for a New Zealand rugby team, with some Black Maori members, to tour South Africa in 1970.

The leader of the *verkrampte* faction, Albert Hertzog, claimed that Vorster's policies were not representative of the wishes of true Nationalists. He condemned Vorster's recruitment of English-speaking Whites into the National Party and claimed that only a true Afrikaner Calvinist should lead the country. When Vorster forced votes on resolutions endorsing his policies on immigration, cooperation between English- and Afrikaans-speaking Whites, and cooperation with Black African states, the *verkramptes* debated against the policies but voted for the resolutions. The resolution on integrated sport, however, was vehemently opposed and was voted against. The small size of the rebel vote, however, was seen as unrepresentative of the strong grass-roots support the *verkrampte* faction enjoyed.

When Hertzog tried to force Vorster to expel him from the National Party, the prime minister instead called an early general election. He explained his decision by saying that South Africa could not afford to give the impression of a divided government. The move was seen by most observers as undercutting Hertzog's efforts at becoming a 'martyr' by trying to force Vorster to expel him from the National Party.

19 September A consortium of South African, French, German and Swedish firms sign a contract for the construction of the Cabora Bassa hydroelectric power project in Mozambique. The $315-million dam on the Zambezi River was intended to provide Mozambique, South Africa and Rhodesia with cheap electrical power. The project had first been proposed at a 1967 meeting in Lisbon between the South African and Portuguese governments. Work was scheduled to begin later in 1969 and to be completed in 1974, with an initial output of 1.2 million kilowatts foreseen. The project was being built by Zamco, an international consortium led by South Africa's Anglo-American Corporation with interests from West German, French and Swedish companies, who had been given a provisional contract in 1968 and awarded the final contract on 3 September.

Even before the contract had been awarded, the anti-Government Mozambique Liberation Front (Frelimo) announced on 22 January that it intended 'to paralyze the work on the dam, or to make it more costly than the contractors had calculated'. The dam has been a constant target of sabotage since construction began.

24 September The first elections to fill 40 seats of the newly expanded 60-member Coloured Persons' representative council are held. The government appointed the other 20 members.

The council had been enlarged and transformed into a legislative rather than an advisory body as a result of the 1968 Coloured Persons' Representative Council Bill. The Bill was designed to provide separate representation for Coloureds after the 1968 Separate Representation of Voters Amendment Bill had abolished their indirect representation in the White Parliament. The council's powers were extremely limited. All draft legislation in the areas of its responsibility, such as education, social welfare and pensions, had to be passed by the government's minister of Coloured affairs, and eventually approved by the state president. Frustrated at the council's limited powers, many Coloureds boycotted the elections and only 48 per cent of the electorate participated in the polling. The fiercely anti-apartheid Labour Party won 26 seats, the pro-Government Federal Party won 11, and the more moderately pro-government Republican and National People's Parties each won one seat. One member was elected as an independent but he subsequently joined the Federal Party. The results were said to have surprised the government, who said that the voting showed the Coloureds were 'only children in politics'. To offset the anti-apartheid element, the government appointed 20 pro-Nationalists to the council in October, including 13 candidates who had been defeated in the September elections.

25 September The 11-nation UN Special Committee on Apartheid announces the failure of the UN's economic sanctions against South Africa. The report released by the committee blamed South Africa's four main trading partners – the US, Britain, Japan and West Germany – for the failure, saying that not only had they ignored the boycott, but that trade between South Africa and the four had actually increased since the UN decided to impose sanctions in 1962.

25 October The ultra right-wing Herstigte Nasionale Party (Reformed National Party) is formed by *verkrampte* dissidents from the National Party. The launch of the new party was seen as formalizing the split between the conservative *verkrampte* and moderate *verligte* factions of the ruling party.

The rift between the two groups had been intensifying all year. Conservatives attacked the government and prominent Afrikaner businessmen and academics for their liberal leanings and claimed that Prime Minister Vorster was steering the ruling National Party away from its traditional policies. They attacked the government's attempts to improve relations with English-speaking Whites and neighbouring Black African countries, and claimed that the structure of apartheid was being weakened by the admission of non-White athletes and diplomats into South Africa.

Former Cabinet minister Albert Hertzog, who was named leader of the new party, had been ousted from the National Party on 4 October. He and other disaffected Nationalists called a rally on 8 October to make plans for a party congress and to discuss strategy for the forthcoming general election. Some 2,000 people attended the meeting.

21 November The General Assembly approves a resolution calling attention to the 'urgent necessity' of widening sanctions against the Whites-only regime in Rhodesia and extending them to include South Africa and Portugal. The Assembly reiterated its traditional protest against apartheid and asked the Security Council to consider the use of force against apartheid. It also urged all member states to act to secure the release from detention of political prisoners held for their opposition to apartheid.

30 December The IMF announces that subject to certain conditions it would agree to purchase gold from the South African authorities. The move provided, in effect, a partial 'floor' of $35 an ounce for South Africa's gold production. The decision was taken after extensive negotiations had been conducted between South African and Western financial officials and came 21 months after the 'gold crisis' of March 1968 and the establishment of the two-tier price system for gold. The agreement was greeted with approval by the financial world, which hoped it would have a stabilizing effect on the world money markets.

---

1 9 7 0

30 January Prime Minister Leabua Jonathan of Lesotho declares a state of emergency after violence erupts during the country's first general election since independence. Jonathan's Basutoland National Party was thought to have lost the election, which was held on 27 January, although the counting had not yet been completed. He suspended the constitution and ordered the arrest of Opposition leader Nitsu Mokhehele on charges of incitement to breach the public peace after Mokhehele claimed victory for his Basotho Congress Party. Jonathan seized power on 31 January and ordered the counting of the ballots to be suspended. He annulled the election, suspended Parliament and placed King Moshoeshoe II under house arrest. The king was later exiled to the Netherlands, where he remained until he accepted a government order banning him from participation in politics and was allowed to return home in December. Jonathan continued to rule under the state of emergency regulations.

The main issue in the election had been Lesotho's relations with South Africa, which totally surrounds the country. Jonathan's government had pursued a policy of close political and economic relations with South Africa, while Mokhehele promised to distance Lesotho from its racist neighbour. Jonathan had announced in March that a new constitution was being drafted. Those talks, however, failed in August and he announced on 5 October that Lesotho would 'have a holiday from politics for five years'.

2 February The Bantu Homelands Citizenship Bill is introduced in Parliament. Under the provisions of the bill, all Black South Africans became citizens of the appropriate tribal homeland, regardless of whether they lived there or not. The bill did not immediately apply to either Zulus or Swazis as their homelands had not reached the 'required stage of constitutional development'.

Under the provisions of the bill, Blacks would be considered aliens in South Africa and South Africa would continue to represent them internationally.

The Bantu Homelands Citizenship Bill completed its passage through Parliament on 26 February and was a major step in the South African government's plan to make Black South Africans foreigners in their own country.

27 February The current session of Parliament ends, and with it Coloured voters lose all representation in the national legislature. The Whites elected by Coloured voters to represent them in Parliament had their terms of office expire under the provisions of the 1968 Separate Representation of Voters Amendment Bill and, under that bill, their seats were abolished. It was the end of a process that the National Party had been pursuing since coming to power in 1948, the complete removal of Coloured representation in the all-White assembly.

2 March The Whites-only government of Prime Minister Ian Smith issues a proclamation declaring Rhodesia a republic and severing Rhodesia's last links with Britain. The parliament was dissolved and new elections were scheduled to be held on 10 April under a new republican constitution. Britain described the moved as an illegal act by an illegal government, while most Western nations showed their disapproval by breaking off diplomatic relations with Rhodesia. The only exceptions were South Africa, Portugal and Greece.

On 10 April, White Rhodesians went to the polls in the first elections to be held under the country's new republican constitution. Prime Minister Ian Smith's Rhodesian Front Party won all 50 seats reserved for Whites. Some 16 other seats were reserved for non-Whites.

22 April Whites-only general elections are held in South Africa. They result in Prime Minister John Vorster's ruling National Party being returned to power for the sixth time since 1948 but, for the first time, with a reduced majority. The National Party heavily defeated the extremely right-wing Herstigte Nasionale Party (HNP) in general elections but lost nine seats to the opposition United Party. The result, while a victory for Vorster over his extremist opponents, was seen as the first crack in the hitherto solid support for the National Party.

The National Party won 117, down from 123, seats in the National Assembly, the United Party 47, up from 38, and the Progressive Party retained its one seat.

The HNP entered 80 candidates in the election but failed to gain any seats and polled only 3.56 per cent of the vote. The four former Nationalist Members of Parliament who formed the HNP lost their seats to National Party candidates.

Prime Minister Vorster declared the result as 'a clear mandate' for his government to continue pursuing their apartheid policies. Most observers believed that the participation of the HNP in the campaign forced Vorster to move further to the right than he would normally have done. They pointed to actions such as Vorster's cancelling meetings with the leaders of neighbouring Black states and refusing Black American tennis star Arthur Ashe a visa to visit the country as examples of this hardening of position.

Although the National Party emerged from the pollings as the clear party of power, the election destroyed the myth of Afrikaner unity. The Opposition welcomed the results, calling it a watershed. They claimed that it stopped the recent swing towards the right.

6 May The 1970 population census is conducted. The results showed that the population of South Africa was made up of some 15 million Blacks, four million Whites, two million Coloureds and 600,000 Asians. The number of Blacks had increased 36.3 per cent from the 1960 figures, while the White population went up by only 22.4 per cent. The results also showed that, despite the government's policy of separate development, more Blacks lived outside the homelands than in them. The government contended that the percentage of Blacks in homelands was increasing, while the Opposition claimed it proved the policy was 'in ruins'.

15 May The International Olympic Committee (IOC) officially withdraws its recognition of the South African National Olympic Committee. It prohibited South African athletes from competing in any Olympic Games until its national committee was recognized by the IOC. South Africa was banned from participating in either the 1964 or 1968 games but had been, until this decision, a full member of the IOC. The committee had originally decided to allow racially mixed South African teams to participate in the 1968 games in Mexico City but withdrew its permission after being threatened by a mass boycott from other national squads if South Africa was permitted to participate.

South Africa was the first country to be expelled from the Olympics since the modern games were begun in 1896. The IOC said the expulsion was based on a finding that South Africa had violated the Olympic Charter's Rule One, that 'no discrimination is allowed against any country or person on grounds of race, religion or political affiliation' since South Africa applied its apartheid policies to sport.

19 May Prime Minister Vorster embarks on a historic visit to Malawi, the first visit by a South African head of state to an independent Black African country. After their meetings, which were described as 'amicable', the two leaders stressed their hopes for continued mutual cooperation in spite of their differences in outlook. Vorster told Malawian Prime Minister Hastings Banda, 'We treasure our way of life and we appreciate your way of life and it is in that spirit that we seek cooperation and tender cooperation.'

On 21 May, Vorster continued making history by beginning an 'entirely informal' trip to Rhodesia at the invitation of Prime Minister Ian Smith. He became the first head of state to visit the country since Smith's government unilaterally declared Rhodesian independence in November 1965. The visit was seen as a morale-booster for that country's internationally isolated Whites.

3 June Prime Minister Vorster begins a tour of Europe. The trip was officially described as 'a working visit' and 'strictly private', but most observers saw it as an attempt by Vorster to break down the barriers that the international community had thrown up in recent years to isolate South Africa because of its apartheid policies.

The tour was highly secret and not announced until his arrival in Lisbon. Upon his return to Johannesburg on 18 June, Vorster said that he had made European leaders more aware of the 'dangers of Communist penetration of the Indian Ocean' and that the trip was 'very successful' in proving that South Africa was 'not as isolated as our enemies try to make out'.

11 June The minister of Bantu administration and development, Michael Botha, officially opens the Zulu territorial authority at Nongoma, the capital of Zululand. The authority was headed by Chief Gatsha Buthelezi, who was known to be an outspoken opponent of the Nationalists' racial policies. It was established under the government's separate development plan and was seen as being the first step towards self-government for South Africa's three million Zulus.

6 July British Foreign Minister Sir Alec Douglas-Home announces to Parliament that Britain's new Conservative government is considering ending the country's ban on the sale of arms to South Africa. In discussing the 1955 Simonstown agreement by which Britain is entitled to use the strategic South African naval base in exchange for the sale of arms, he said: 'We certainly dare not limit our vital sea communications. It is in this context of sea routes, particularly the sea routes that carry oil, that the Simonstown agreement falls.' The Labour Party, who had instituted the arms ban while in power, had warned the government on 24 June that any resumption of the sale of arms to South Africa 'would place Britain firmly in the camp of the white racist regime of South Africa, endanger the existence of the Commonwealth and flout the authority of the United Nations'.

On 10 July, South African Defence Minister P.W. Botha called for a complete review of the Simonstown Agreement, saying that 'as the agreement exists today, it apparently can be interpreted by alternative British governments as it suits them'. He had earlier claimed that Britain's Labour government, in instituting an arms embargo against South Africa, had been in violation of the agreement. Reports were that the South African government was taking the same stance in its arms negotiations with the British.

On 20 July, the British government officially announced that it would consider the sale of arms to South Africa. Foreign Secretary Sir Alec Douglas-Home said that as part of the 1955 agreement, Britain handed over to South Africa both the naval base and the responsibility of providing for the defence of the Cape of Good Hope sea routes. He added that Britain, as a consequence of the agreement, should consider providing the South Africans with 'certain limited categories of arms, so long as they are for maritime defence directly related to the security of the sea routes' between the Atlantic and Indian Oceans.

The decision was condemned by the Afro-Asian bloc in the UN. The UN Security Council met on 17 July to discuss a measure to prevent Britain from selling South Africa arms in defiance of the council's arms embargo set in 1963.

The Organization of African Unity (OAU) issued a statement on 22 July calling the British intention of resuming arms sales 'a hostile act against the African governments and peoples'. The presidents of Uganda, Zambia and Tanzania (Milton Obote, Kenneth Kaunda and Julius Nyerere) sent strong protest letters to the British government.

17 July The UN Security Council convenes a special session to examine ways of preventing Britain from selling arms to South Africa in defiance of the council's 1963 arms embargo.

On 23 July, the council passed a resolution tightening its arms embargo against South Africa and condemning violations of the ban. The resolution urged the implementation of the arms ban 'unconditionally and without reservations whatsoever' and called on member states to ban the sale to South Africa of vehicles or equipment for the use of military or paramilitary, of patents or licences for the manufacture of arms, naval vessels or aircraft, and of spare military parts; it also barred training of South Africa's military forces or the cooperation by any member nation with such forces.

20 July South Africa enters the uranium fuel market when Prime Minister Vorster announces that South African scientists have discovered a new process for enriching uranium. The process was expected to produce uranium more cheaply than had previously been possible in the West. Vorster said that the process would be employed in a new plant that would compete with Western markets. The method was reportedly derived from completely new principles and not based on either the British–Dutch–German centrifuge process or the UK diffusion process.

Vorster, in making his announcement, said that the government's 'sole objective in the further development and application of the process is to promote the peaceful application of nuclear energy'. He added that, in view of the fact that South Africa was one of the world's largest uranium-producing countries, it would benefit from being able to market uranium in its much sought-after enriched form. He also announced that the country was about to embark on a nuclear power programme of its own and said that the enriched uranium would be used in power generation and sea water desalinization projects and that South Africa was prepared to have its nuclear activities subjected to safeguards, including inspection.

South Africa's ability to enrich uranium was of major importance since enriched uranium is an essential ingredient in nuclear weapons. Since South Africa became capable of enriching uranium, the international community has suspected that South Africa had a nuclear bomb, a charge South Africa denies.

8 September The third Non-Aligned Summit Conference opens in Lusaka, Zambia, and is attended by more than 50 countries. Delegates passed a resolution condemning arms sales to South Africa and Portugal and criticized Britain for its inability to end the Rhodesian problem.

14 September The trial of 20 Black activists ends with the acquittal of 19 of them. The 20 were originally arrested in 1969 under the provisions of the Suppression of Communism Act on charges of furthering the aims of the banned African National Congress (ANC). Those charges were dropped on 16 February but the group was rearrested on new charges of violating the Prevention of Terrorism Act. Three other Blacks, who had originally been facing the same charges, gave state evidence against the defendants. The only person found guilty, Benjamin Sello Ramotse, was sentenced to 15 years' imprisonment.

The trial had been postponed several times but finally opened in Pretoria on 24 August. The judge found that the defendants, who were accused of planning the violent overthrow of the government, had already been tried on substantially the same charges in 1969 under the Suppression of Communism Act and that since they had been cleared and had those charges dropped, they could not be retried on the same charges under a different act.

The most prominent of the accused was Winnie Mandela, wife of jailed ANC leader Nelson Mandela. Although she was acquitted, she was placed under house arrest on 1 October and banned from attending social, political or instructional gatherings for five years, and confined to her house from dusk to dawn on weekdays and holidays. The other 18 acquitted people were reported on 2 October to have also been put under banning and house arrest orders. The report caused some 1,500 students to rally in Johannesburg in protest. The government later announced that Mrs Mandela was the only one under house arrest and that the others had only been prohibited from attending 'certain gatherings'.

On 9 December, the South African appeals court, its highest court, upheld the Supreme Court decision to acquit 19 blacks from the 1969 trial on charges of subversion and terrorism.

15 September Prime Minister Vorster announces to Parliament that South Africa is prepared to enter into non-aggression pacts with any other African country that wishes to do so. He made it clear, however, that South Africa would fight against 'Communist-inspired terrorism' in any country that asked it for assistance and that it would not only repel any 'large-scale invasion by terrorists' but would pursue the retreating terrorists into the countries from which they came.

14 October Zambian President Kenneth Kaunda begins a tour of Western Europe and the US as the head of an OAU mission to persuade Western nations to withdraw their military and economic support of South Africa and Portugal. He described the question of arms sales to South Africa as 'a question of life and death'. After meeting with Kaunda, French President Georges Pompidou approved a ban on the sale of French arms that could be used to suppress internal uprisings, including helicopters and armoured cars. France was a major supplier of arms to South Africa, but since the 1963 UN ban had protested that it supplied South Africa only with defensive and not offensive arms. Tanzania's President Nyerere warned the UN on 15 October that the continued sale of arms to South Africa would result in African countries turning to the Communists for assistance.

28 October Provincial elections held in South Africa result in the ruling National Party losing seats to the opposition United Party. The Nationalists retained control of the Transvaal, Cape and Orange Free State assemblies, while the United Party increased its majority in Natal, the assembly it traditionally holds. Neither the right-wing Herstigte Nasionale Party (HNP) nor the moderate Progressive Party won any seats.

The election results continued the trend set in the April general election. The United Party ate into the Nationalist majority for the first time since 1948, while the National Party politically eclipsed the breakaway HNP. United Party leader Sir de Villiers Graaff described the results as 'a new trend in the politics of South Africa'. The Government blamed the results on a low turnout, which it claimed was 'detrimental to Nationalist party candidates'.

13 November The Archbishop of Canterbury, Dr Michael Ramsey, begins a 20-day tour of South Africa. He said that the purpose of his trip was to learn about the church's situation in South Africa and added that: 'There is no need for me to discover that apartheid is contrary to the Christian gospel and the dignity of man.' The archbishop's anti-apartheid remarks on this and other occasions during his visit caused him to be attacked by pro-government newspapers.

At the end of his tour, Ramsey said that South Africa was in danger of a violent revolution if the government did not remove the injustices and inhumanities of its White-ruled society. The Afrikaner press called the trip 'a fairly disastrous excursion' and said that Ramsey's 'whole conduct was calculated to hamper promising contact between South Africa and Black Africa'.

15 November The British government makes public a reply from Prime Minister Edward Heath to an earlier letter from the Archbishop of Canterbury, Michael Ramsey, in which he explained the Conservative government's position on arms sales to South Africa. He said that the 'situation affecting the security of the [Cape] sea routes has changed, and for the worse' and said that Britain could not let the Soviet presence go 'unanswered'. He said, 'The best way of ensuring this is to see that the Simonstown Agreement, which gives assurance of valuable support for the Royal Navy in this vital area, remains effective.'

Although the government hinted several more times before the end of the year that it was planning to go ahead with the resumption of arms sales to South Africa, it had not yet made the final decision pending further consultations.

13 January The Polaroid Corporation in the US announces the introduction of a one-year 'experiment' to improve the conditions of its Black employees in South Africa. The move came after Polaroid's Boston headquarters were picketed by employees opposed to the company doing business with racist South Africa. Polaroid called on its South African distributor, Frank & Hirsch Ltd, and its suppliers to 'improve dramatically the salaries and other benefits of their non-White employees' and to 'train non-White employees for important jobs within their companies'. A Polaroid spokesman also announced that the company would finance the education of some 500 Black South African students and said, 'We feel we can continue doing business in South Africa only by opposing the apartheid system. We hope other American companies will join us in this program.' Polaroid had previously said it would stop selling the South African government the photoidentification system reportedly used to make up the passbooks that all Blacks were required to carry. Frank & Hirsch Ltd announced in February that they would increase Black wages by 13–30 per cent by the end of July.

The South African government accused Polaroid of adopting a 'holier than thou' attitude. Opponents to trade with South Africa also criticized the plan, calling it a 'paternalistic act of charity' designed to allow Polaroid to continue doing business in South Africa. South Africa represented 1 per cent of Polaroid's total worldwide sales.

20 January The Anglican dean of Johannesburg, Gonville Aubrey ffrench-Beytagh, is arrested under the provisions of the Terrorism Act. Police say his detention was 'not connected with his political views or his church life, but for reasons connected with his private life'. He was released on bail on 28 January after being charged with planning to incite violence and participation in the activities of the banned Communist Party and African National Congress. New charges against him under the Terrorism Act were announced on 30 June, when he was accused of attending meetings in South Africa in 1968 and 1969 'to bring about political changes in South Africa by violent means' and of participating in a campaign in Britain in 1970 to raise money for guerrillas engaged in activities to overthrow the Portuguese government in Mozambique as a prelude to overthrowing the South African government.

ffrench-Beytagh was convicted on 1 November of plotting to overthrow the government of South Africa and sentenced to five years' imprisonment. His conviction was overturned on 14 April 1972 by the Bloemfontein appeals court, which found that although he was 'intractably opposed to the present Government's policies in relation to what is generally known as apartheid', he had not been on trial for his political views and there was no real proof of his involvement in terrorism. He left the country after his release.

The trial of such a high-ranking member of the church was only one of several moves the government took against the church during the year. Prime Minister John Vorster warned on 17 June that 'certain clergymen ... were planning a second Sharpeville situation' and said that the government would 'act against them with the greatest possible degree of hardness'. Relations between the church and government seriously deteriorated as a result of this policy.

22 January Commonwealth leaders end an often acrimonious nine-day conference in Singapore that was dominated by Britain's plans to resume the sale of arms to South Africa. The meeting concluded after a compromise declaration of principles was agreed to, which, in effect, maintained members' freedom to pursue their own independent activities. The compromise was seen as postponing, not preventing, a possible crisis over the issue of arms sales. It had been feared that failure to reach a compromise could harm the cohesion and viability of the Commonwealth.

The turning point in the conference came on 20 January when officials agreed to create a study group to consider the question of British arms sales to South Africa. Although the agreement officially left Britain free to conclude any arms deal at any time, it broke a deadlock at the conference and prevented an open break between Britain and several African nations. The study group was made up of representatives of Australia, Britain, Canada, India, Jamaica, Kenya, Malaysia and Nigeria. They were to study the question in light of 'factors affecting the security of maritime trade routes in the South Atlantic and Indian oceans, which are of vital importance for a large number of Commonwealth countries'. The group was instructed to study the question further and report to the Commonwealth through the secretary general as soon as possible. Britain agreed to participate on the condition that it retained its right to take action as it considered necessary to give effect to its global defence policy, in which the facilities at Simonstown constituted an important element. The British government stressed that it was bound to honour the Simonstown agreement and said that it had received South African assurance that maritime equipment supplies by Britain will be used only for the purposes stated.

Prime Minister Heath reported to the British parliament on 26 January that under the Simonstown agreement, Britain was only obligated to supply South Africa with 'the equipment and spare parts required to keep operationally efficient' three ships that Britain had previously sold South Africa under the agreement. He added that the ships would be for the sole purpose of protecting the sea routes and promised that Britain would stop the sales if South Africa violated this condition. His statement was seen as a compromise to quieten opposition to the sales. Heath, by omitting mention of any sales of new frigates or aircraft other than helicopters, temporarily limited himself to a minimal programme of replacement arms sales.

3 February The Bantu Homelands Constitution Bill is introduced in Parliament. The bill enabled the government to grant self-government on an equal footing with the Transkei to any Bantustan with a territorial authority that requested semi-autonomy. The government had to consult with the authority involved but did not need parliamentary approval before issuing a simple proclamation of self-government. The bill stipulated that every semi-autonomous territory, while remaining an integral part of South Africa, could have its own flag and national anthem but could not enter into military or diplomatic relations with other nations. The bill reflected government opinion that Bantustans did not have to be economically viable or have their lands consolidated before being granted self-government and that tribal chiefs could request self-rule whenever they felt their areas were prepared for it.

8 February Labour Minister Marais Viljoen announces that Coloured workers will be permitted to work on construction sites in Pretoria and Johannesburg in jobs previously reserved for Whites, although White workers would still be given preference. The measure was necessary because of a shortage of some 4,700 skilled workers and 1,600 apprentices.

The move, a victory of economic reality over strict apartheid policies, met with mixed reactions. The leader of the White building workers' union called it 'shocking', while the director of the builders' association said his organization favoured such a relaxation of the apartheid principles in industry.

18 February Some 20 people are arrested under the Suppression of Terrorism Act. All of the accused were members of the African People's Democratic Union of South Africa or the Non-European Unity Movement. Both groups were legal in South Africa and advocated the establishment of a multiracial franchise.

22 February British Foreign Secretary Sir Alec Douglas Home announces that Britain plans to sell helicopters to South Africa. The announcement came after a British government White Paper found that Britain was 'legally obligated' to provide South Africa with seven Wasp helicopters under the terms of the 1955 Simonstown agreement. South African Defence Minister P.W. Botha said shortly after Douglas-Home's remarks that South Africa 'will accordingly take the necessary steps to place an order' for the helicopters.

Britain's decision was seen both at home and abroad as violating the UN arms embargo against South Africa and of lending support to the racist South African regime. The British defence secretary under the former Labour government, Denis Healey, argued that Britain must only sell South Africa those arms to which it was legally entitled.

25 February The South African police carried out coordinated raids on student and church groups in Johannesburg, Port Elizabeth and Cape Town. The offices of the National Union of South African Students (NUSAS), the University Christian Movement and the South African Council of Churches were all raided. The police contended that the raids were conducted as part of the investigation into the affairs of the Anglican dean of Johannesburg Gonville Aubrey ffrench-Beytagh, who had been arrested on terrorism charges in January. Church leaders protested that the government was persecuting the Church, while NUSAS obtained a court order saying that the raids were illegal because the search warrant used did not empower the police to seize documents. The police protested that the offices searched were 'front organisations of unlawful organisations or are Communist-controlled or inspired'. The materials were returned but reseized under a new search warrant.

3 March Mrs Winnie Mandela, wife of jailed African National Congress leader Nelson Mandela, is sentenced to one year's imprisonment for violating the conditions of the house arrest imposed on her in 1970 but is released pending appeal. Under those terms, she was only allowed to be visited by her doctor and two children. She was accused of allowing her sister, her sister's children and a co-defendant in her 1970 terrorism trial to visit.

22 March Ghanaian Foreign Minister William Ofori-Atta informs his national assembly that he is willing to visit South Africa. The announcement was the first of several during the year that were seen as a victory for South African Prime Minister John Vorster's new 'outward looking' foreign policy. The governments of the Central African Republic, Dahomey, the Ivory Coast, Madagascar, Mali, Niger, Togo and Upper Volta all gave their 'tentative support' to the principle of holding talks with the South Africans.

30 March John Vorster, giving the first press conference ever held by a South African prime minister, says that he would be willing to discuss South Africa's separate development policy with Black African leaders. Observers saw the conference as representing a significant change in South African politics and as emphasizing the government's new willingness to hold external dialogues. Vorster said that press conferences would be held twice a year in the future.

13 April The chief minister of the semi-independent Bantustan of the Transkei, Paramount Chief Kaiser Matanzima, asks the South African government for 'full control of our own affairs' and a larger share of the land surrounding the Transkei that had officially been declared White. Speaking at the Transkei National Independence Party meeting, Matanzima said that he would 'negotiate with the republican government until they accede to our requests'. He warned that race relations would suffer unless the question of land was 'fairly settled'. Matanzima was known as a supporter of the government's apartheid policies.

South African President James Fouche, speaking at the opening of the Transkei legislative assembly on 14 April, indicated the government's refusal of the request. Although he said that the government was preparing to transfer 'certain' police and prison services to the Transkei, he did not indicate that it was prepared to accelerate the speed at which the Transkei was being moved towards independence. Opposition leader Sir de Villiers Graaff warned that the government could lose control of the timetable for the Bantustan's independence.

22 April Prime Minister Vorster announces plans for a new sports policy. The move comes in the aftermath of South Africa's expulsion from the international Olympic movement and from the Davis Cup tennis competition. Vorster said that South Africans of all races would be allowed to compete in international sporting events held in South Africa. He further said that he had no objection to international tennis matches held in the country being open to 'all rated players' regardless of race, or to matches being played between Black or Coloured rugby teams and visiting teams. He added, however, that the new policy represented no change 'on the club, provincial and national levels' and said that he was opposed to multiracial teams representing South Africa abroad, except at the Olympics and possibly the Davis Cup competition.

The moderate Progressive Party's only Member of Parliament, Helen Suzman, called the announcement 'nothing more than camouflage' which was 'an absurd technical manoeuvre to placate overseas sports administrators'. International Olympic Committee President Avery Brundage said on 22 April that South Africa had been expelled from the games because of its ban on interracial competition within the country and that Vorster's comments had been ambiguous on that point. He added that South Africa had 'opened the door a little but probably not enough'.

22 May Two White South African policemen are killed when a land-mine explodes in northeastern Namibia. Seven other people, including two Black trackers, were hurt in the blast. It was believed to be the first time that guerrillas had inflicted fatalities in any area controlled by South Africa. The land-mine was thought to have been set by members of the South West African People's Organization (SWAPO). In a parliamentary statement on 24 May, Police Minister Stephanus Lourens Muller claimed that six sets of footprints had led away from the mine in the direction of Zambia.

8 June Helen Joseph, leading South African author and critic of apartheid, is released from house arrest. She had first been confined in 1962. Those under house arrest are forbidden from meeting with more than one person at a time, are required to report to a police station daily and must remain home alone from

6:30 p.m. until the following morning. The lifting of these restrictions did not include removing her name from a list of people who cannot be quoted in any South African publication.

21 June In what was considered an important advisory opinion, the International Court of Justice rules that South Africa's administration of Namibia is illegal and 'the continued presence of South Africa being illegal, South Africa is under obligation to withdraw its administration from Namibia immediately and thus put an end to its occupation of the Territory'.

The court had been asked by the UN Security Council on 29 July 1970 to give an advisory opinion regarding South Africa's continued administration of South West Africa in defiance of the council's Resolution 276 declaring its presence to be illegal. The court had previously ruled on the question in 1966 when it found that the two countries who had brought the matter before them, Liberia and Ethiopia, had no legal right to question South Africa's role in Namibia even though they were members of the League of Nations and its successor, the UN. The 1966 opinion had not included a ruling on whether apartheid was being practised in the territory. The court also issued a supplementary ruling that UN members were obliged to 'abstain from entering into treaty relations with South Africa in all cases in which the Government of South Africa purports to act on behalf of, or concerning, Namibia'.

The South African government called the court's decision an 'international political vendetta' against South Africa. Prime Minister Vorster vowed that South Africa would continue to administer Namibia and to 'carry out this duty with a view to self-determination for all population groups'. He added that since the original 1966 decision the International Court had been 'packed' with judges hostile to South Africa.

17 August Malawian Prime Minister Hastings Banda begins an official state visit to South Africa, making him the first Black head of state ever to do so. Political commentators saw the trip as the crowning achievement of Prime Minister Vorster's 'outward-looking' foreign policy. The visit came in response to one that Vorster made to Malawi in 1970, which had been his first visit to an independent Black state.

Banda, speaking in the Black township of Soweto, said that: 'I do not like this system of apartheid. But I prefer to talk. If I boycott South Africa, I isolate you, my people, my children.' He also met with Black leaders, including the heads of the self-governing Black homeland areas of Transkei and Zululand, Chiefs Kaiser Matanzima and Gatsha Buthelezi.

26 September The Minister of Coloured affairs, J.J. Loots, announces that the government will gradually turn larger Coloured areas into municipalities under the control of the Coloured Persons' Representative Council.

The announcement followed the publication on 12 August of an official statement on the government's Coloured policy, in which it stated that it would continue its current policy of separate development. The Nationalists had been divided on the issue of the country's two million Coloured people. One faction, strongly backed by academics, wanted Coloureds to be fully integrated into the White community and to enjoy the full rights of citizenship, while the other faction pushed for a total separation of the races.

24 November Britain and Rhodesia sign an agreement to end Britain's constitutional dispute with Rhodesia's White supremacist government. The agreement provided greater political rights for Rhodesian Blacks and was intended to open the way for their eventual assumption of political power. According to British Foreign Secretary Sir Alec Douglas-Home, the agreement was 'fully within the five principles to which the government have constantly adhered' in efforts to reach a settlement, and provided for immediate greater rights for Blacks and moves towards eventual majority rule. The Organization of African Unity opposed it as an 'outright sellout' because it did not move quickly enough to Black rule and advised Black Rhodesians to 'take matters into their own hands'. South Africa approved of the plan, which it said was good for 'the sake of Rhodesia, states in southern Africa and the free world'.

Britain's five principles were: the unhindered move towards full majority rule; guarantees against retrogressive amendments being made to the constitution; the immediate improvement of the Black population's political status; movement being made towards ending racial discrimination; and any settlement of the Rhodesian conflict being acceptable to the Rhodesian people as a whole.

3 December Prince Goodwill is installed as king of the Zulus in ceremonies held in Nongoma, Natal. Chief Gatsha Buthelezi, the government-appointed executive officer of the Zulu territorial authority, later accused the South African government of attempting to oust him by supporting the royalist faction in Zululand politics.

12 January The South African government sends police reinforcements into the Ovambo tribal area in Namibia in an attempt to end the month-long strike of 13,000 miners that has crippled the region's economy. The police described the move as taking 'precautions against unrest'.

The strike was the first in Namibia's history in which Black workers were able to paralyse large segments of the area's economy. The strike, which was accompanied by serious unrest in the Ovamboland Bantustan, began on 12 December at a mass meeting during which Black workers demanded both an end to the contract system and the return of 14 Ovambo workers who had been arrested in early December for breaking their contracts and forcibly taken back to Ovamboland.

Under the contract labour system, which had been in operation for the previous 42 years, the Ovambos were recruited by a private organization, the South West Africa Native Labour Association (SWANLA), to work in government and private industries outside Ovamboland on renewable contracts of 12–18 months. The Ovambos were not permitted to work outside Ovamboland except under this contract system and employers were not allowed to hire Ovambos who were not contract labourers. The migrant workers were, furthermore, not allowed to have their families accompany them to their work places. Wages were extremely low, while the disruption to family life was enormous.

On 20 January, the government agreed with the strikers that it would abolish the SWANLA and make major modifications to the contract labour system. In future, workers would negotiate their terms of employment with a new manpower recruiting body to be run by the Government-appointed Ovambo Executive Council and would be allowed to market their skills for higher rates of pay. Individual contracts would clearly set out salary levels and other job terms and workers would be allowed to change jobs. The majority of the strikers were returning to work by 1 February.

While the strike was in progress, violence in the area had been steadily escalating. In incidents between 28 and 31 January, which observers were not directly relating to the strike, at least 10 people were killed in clashes with the police.

14 January The Davis Cup Nations' Committee announces that it will allow South Africa to compete in the 1972 international tennis competition as a result of changes in the country's political climate. South Africa had been barred from participating in the international tennis championships since 1971 because of its apartheid policies. The committee decided that South Africa would play in the South American sector rather than the European one, as it had in the past, in order to prevent possible demonstrations by some European countries over South Africa's apartheid policies.

2 February The government announces that Blacks with urban residency permits could in future bring their wives from the homelands to live with them. The move was dependent on accommodation being available.

6 March The new UN Secretary General Kurt Waldheim arrives in South Africa on a mission to help determine the future status of Namibia. His visit, at the invitation of the South African government, had been requested by the Securiy Council at a February meeting in Ethiopia.

While in South Africa and Namibia, Waldheim talked with both government and opposition leaders, White and non-White, and said that South Africa's determination not to hand over control of Namibia to the UN did 'not necessarily' make his visit pointless. He said that 'the aim of South Africa is to grant self-determination to Namibia. The aim of the UN is the same. The purpose of my visit is to clarify this situation and see if it provides any basis for further discussions.' Prime Minister John Vorster said of the trip that a 'number of ideas' had been raised and that these would be 'the subject of further discussion'.

On 1 August, the Security Council approved a resolution asking Waldheim to continue his efforts to obtain Namibia's independence from South Africa.

23 March South Africa establishes a new semi-autonomous Bantustan in Namibia's East Caprivi area. At the opening of the first session of the legislative assembly, said the minister for Bantu administration and development, Michael Botha, 'We grant every people in southern Africa the right to its own way of life', but added that 'propaganda will be made which will try to persuade you that the events of today are of no real advantage'.

1 April The names of four of the Bantu homelands are officially changed. Basotho ba Borwa (Southern Sotho) became Bsotho-Qwaqwa; Tswanaland became Bophuthatswana; Machangana became Gazankulu; and Zululand became Kwazulu.

Kwazulu's new constitution came into effect on the same day. Under the terms of its constitution, Kwazulu took the first steps towards achieving self-government by turning its territorial authority into a legislative assembly. In one of its last acts in its old form, the territorial authority had unanimously rejected a draft clause in the constitution requiring each member to take an oath of allegiance to the South African government. They agreed, instead, to pledge to 'honour and respect the State President of the Republic of South Africa as the Paramount Chief'. Under another one of its clauses, the Zulu royal family was barred from exercising executive powers.

Three other homelands had their territorial authorities become legislative authorities, the first step towards attainment of self-government at a later stage. Vendaland also moved further along the road to self-government by replacing its territorial authority with a legislative assembly. The Gazankulu Bantustan became operative on 11 April, when its legislative assembly held its first session. The Bantustan, located in the northern Transvaal, was established as the homeland of the Shangaan tribe.

23 May The British foreign secretary, Sir Alec Douglas-Home, announces that the Pearce Commission, which had been investigating Rhodesian responses to the 1971 Anglo-Rhodesian agreement, had found that the 'people of Rhodesia as a whole do not regard the proposals as acceptable as a basis for independence'. He said that, as a result, Britain would not rescind its economic sanctions against Rhodesia.

1 June Bophuthatswana becomes the first Bantu homeland to gain self-government under the 1971 Bantu Homelands Constitution Act. The Transkei had been self-governing since 1963.

Bophuthatswana was made up of 19 separate areas, five large sections and 14 smaller enclaves, divided from each other by land reserved for Whites, and had a population of about 1.7 million people. The 72-member legislative assembly had 48 nominated members and 24 members who were elected by all citizens eligible to vote, including those not resident in the homeland. The chief minister, who headed the Cabinet, was elected by the legislative assembly and appointed his five ministers.

On 4 October 1972, general elections were held for the 24 elective seats. They resulted in Chief Lucas Mangope's Bophuthatswana National Party winning 20 seats, while the remaining four were won by the Seopesengwe Party. The first session of the newly elected legislative assembly opened on 2 November.

6 June Weeks of student criticism of the government's apartheid policies results in Justice Minister Petrus Perlser's announcement of a month-long ban on student protest marches and outdoor meetings.

The students had been protesting against the government's apartheid policies since the expulsion on 29 April of the graduation speaker at Turfloop, the all-Black university college of the north near Pietermaritzburg, who urged Blacks to 'disassociate themselves from the system breeding such evils and work for the eradication of it'. White students soon joined the anti-apartheid protests and police were brought in to put down protests at the University of Cape Town on 2 June. A rally to affirm the right of peaceful protest at St George's Cathedral ended in violence. On 16 June, Interior Minister Theo Gerdener resigned, reportedly in protest over the use of force against student demonstrations.

30 June The South African government announces that it will retain the link between the rand and the British pound sterling and would allow its currency to float with the pound. Britain had freed the pound from its official price of $2.6057 and allowed it to float on 23 June to a new level determined by supply and demand. By the time of the South African statement, the pound was down to $2.44.

On 25 October the International Monetary Fund announced that it had approved a South African proposal to change the rand's par value in relation to gold from 1.09135 to 1.0455 grams of fine gold per rand. The new value represented a devaluation of 4.2 per cent in terms of gold but a 4 per cent appreciation in terms of the rand's current market exchange rate. The rand had, since June 1972, been pegged to the British pound sterling and had been floating downwards with sterling since June. This parity change, however, meant that the rand was, in effect, being pegged to the US dollar and would be quoted at purchase rates for the dollar instead of the British currency.

In explaining the move, Finance Minister Nicolaas Diederichs said that South Africa's balance of payments position had continued to improve since June and that, by returning to a fixed parity at a reasonable exchange rate, 'the best balance will be achieved between the aims of growth and stability, and South Africa will, in addition, comply in full with its obligations to the world community and promote international monetary stability'. He added that the step had been made possible by the stronger performance of the economy.

1 August Ciskei, with about one million inhabitants, becomes the third Black homeland to be granted self-government. The chief executive councillor of the legislative assembly, Chief Justice J.K.M. Mabandla, became the Ciskei's chief minister, and the heads of the territory's six departments became ministers. The constitution was approved by the legislative assembly in April and the first elections to be held under it were scheduled for 1973.

On 2 August, Mabandla said that it was inevitable that the two Xhosa-speaking areas of the Transkei and Ciskei should eventually be united into a single Xhosa nation. He said that such a Xhosa state would incorporate all White land between the Fish and Kei rivers in the eastern Cape and from the Orange River south to the coast, including the major port of East London.

This theme was taken up on 5 August by the chief minister of the Transkei, Chief Kaiser Matanzima, who said that the semi-autonomous Black homelands should unite to form 'one Black nation'. He said he had returned from a visit to the US 'inspired' with 'a spirit of nationalism and a refusal to accept second-class citizenship' and said he was 'more determined than ever to work toward a consolidation of African-occupied southern Africa'.

The minister for Bantu administration and development, Michael Botha, said on 11 August that Matanzima's proposal was 'ill-judged' and had originated with 'persons in circles here and abroad much more interested in the downfall of the Government than in the progress of the Bantu nations'. He added that if

Black leaders persisted in their demands for more land, they would be to blame if independence was delayed.

2 October Lebowa, the North Sotho homeland near Pietersburg, becomes South Africa's fourth self-governing Black homeland. Of the territory's total citizens about 1.2 million lived inside the homeland, while another million worked outside and earned 88 per cent of the citizens' total income.

30 October The Johannesburg city health department announces that Black doctors will be paid the same as White ones. The move comes after a walk-out by 10 Black doctors in Soweto and meant a rise of 300 per cent in their salaries. Black wages were also increased in the platinum mining and other industries.

---

1 9 7 3

9 January Rhodesia closes its Zambezi River border with Zambia to prevent terrorists based in Zambia from infiltrating the country. The Zambezi was considered the dividing line between the 'White south' and 'Black north', and observers saw the move as the first skirmish in an inevitable battle between Black sub-Saharan nations and the 'White supremacist' nations of southern Africa.

When Rhodesia attempted to reopen the border on 3 February, Zambian President Kenneth Kaunda refused to open the Zambian side of it. The closure had repercussions throughout southern Africa and posed the threat of an escalation of the long-running Zambian–Rhodesian conflict into open warfare. Relations between the two former members of the Federation of Rhodesia and Nyasaland had been strained since the federation disbanded in 1963. They worsened after Rhodesia's unilateral declaration of independence in 1965, and most commentators felt that a confrontation at some point between the two was inevitable.

The border closure apparently caught Prime Minister John Vorster by surprise and severely affected South Africa's profitable trade with Zambia.

17 January The head of the semi-autonomous Black homeland of Kwazulu, Chief Gathsa Buthelezi, refuses to discuss government plans for consolidating Kwazulu into six separate landlocked areas. The issue of land consolidation was a major one with all homeland leaders. Buthelezi demanded that any plans for the future boundaries of Kwazulu include the entire Zululand game reserve and Richards Bay on the Indian Ocean. He said that his government refused to allow itself 'to be used for a facade. While we accept that we are powerless, like all Black people in this country, we cannot accept being used to create the impression that we have scope for negotiations when under these circumstances we have none at all.' He added that he would, however, 'bow to the unilateral decrees of the White minority Government'.

23 January Prime Minister Vorster announces that a multiracial commission would be established to investigate the Coloured community's political, social and economic future. The commission, the first of its kind, was seen as recognition by the government of the increasing Coloured dissatisfaction with the Coloured Persons' Representative Council. The government announced in June that the council would become a totally elected body in 1979.

1 February Venda and Gazankulu are granted self-government under the 1971 Bantu Homelands Constitution Act, bringing to six the total number of semi-autonomous Black homelands. Elections for the legislative assembly were held in: Ciskei on 23 February; Lebowa on 11 April; Venda on 15–16 August; Gazankulu on 16–17 October; and the Transkei on 24 October. In the Ciskei and Lebowa elections, the incumbent chief ministers were defeated while everywhere else they were returned to power.

6 February The first violent incidents occur in the wave of illegal Black strikes hitting Durban. Police charged some 25,000 strikers who demonstrated for a wage increase; 200 strikers were arrested.

The strikes had begun in October 1972 when thousands of Black stevedores demanded more money. The strikes were centred in Natal but in February 1973 they quickly spread to the brick factories and then out to the textile engineering, steel and iron industries. Essential services in Durban, South Africa's third largest city and main seaport, were brought to a standstill.

Labour Minister Marais Viljoen blamed the disturbances on the National Union of South African Students (NUSAS) and the Trade Union Council, saying, 'Agitators see Black unrest as the only remaining means of unseating the Government.' He said that the establishment of Black trade unions would not be allowed. Trade Union Congress secretary Jock Espie warned on 28 January that Black workers 'just can't live on what they are earning' and said that the movement for higher wages was 'gathering a momentum of its own and fast developing into an avalanche'.

The strike of Black municipal workers in Durban ended on 7 February after Mayor Ronald Williams issued an ultimatum that the men either return to work or be discharged.

The strikes, and the international attention given to them, resulted in wage increases for Black employees; the granting of limited powers to strike to Blacks; the decision by some trade unions to operate 'parallel' Black unions; and the introduction of measures to increase Black workers' status and prospects.

27 February Prime Minister Vorster orders the banning of Dr Richard Turner, a lecturer at the University of Natal, and seven present and former leaders of the NUSAS under the provisions of the Suppression of Communism Act. They had been accused of steering the NUSAS in a direction likely to endanger national security. The accusation came in the interim report of a parliamentary commission that was established in 1972 under the chairmanship of A.L. Schlebusch to investigate the Christian Institute, the NUSAS, the South African Institute of Race Relations, the University Christian Movement and any other related or similar bodies. Vorster said he had been obligated to act 'in the interests of the country and of students and of parents who send their children to university'. The eight were prohibited from attending or visiting any educational institutions or gatherings of more than two people and could not publish or be quoted in the press for a period of five years.

3 April Chief Minister Kaiser Matanzima of the Transkei calls for the eventual federation of White and Black states in South Africa. Prime Minister Vorster, in replying on 29 April, said that he did not oppose the federation of Black homelands, even though he found the idea unfeasible, but he would not 'share the sovereignty of the White people'.

12 April Swaziland's King Sobhuza II repeals the country's 1968 independence constitution, disbands all political organizations and parties and assumes complete executive, legislative and judicial powers. The move was approved by the parliament and followed the emergence in 1972 of a parliamentary opposition group. Such a group was permitted under the provisions of the constitution but violated Swazi tradition, which is dominated by royalists. The king insisted that there was no crisis in the country, but said that the old constitution had to be discarded because it contained 'destructive elements' that created a 'foreign spirit of bitterness'.

A royal commission was established in September to draft a new constitution, which would have 'regard to the history, the culture, the way of life of the Swazi people and the need to harmonize these with modern principles of constitutional and international law'.

25 April The government issues a report saying that a total of 61,410 Blacks had been involved in some 160 reported illegal strikes between 1 January and 31 March. The strikes began in Natal and spread to Johannesburg in May and resulted in wage increases for some 700,000 of the country's 6.5 million Black workers. The wages, even after the increases, were still generally below the poverty line.

27 April Land consolidation proposals and adjustments affecting the Gazankulu, Kwazulu, Lebowa, South Ndebele, Swazi and Venda homelands are tabled in Parliament. The plans, which were expected to result in the resettlement of some 363,000 Blacks, were approved on 6 June. Proposals for the consolidation of the Bophuthatswana were announced on 25 May and expected to affect some 120,000 Tswanas. On 11 December, plans for the Transkei and Ciskei, which involved the acquisition of the homelands of Port St Johns and Indwe, were presented.

The chief ministers of several of the 10 Black homelands denounced the proposals, which would designate only 14 per cent of the total land area in South Africa as tribal homelands and would leave the homelands fragmented and unviable. The proposals were said to consolidate some of the scattered enclaves by transferring some 2,800 square miles (7,252 square kilometres) away from the homelands and giving them some 4,300 square miles (11,137 square kilometres) of land reserved for Whites, mostly in Natal and the Transvaal. The leaders also protested over not being consulted in the formulation of the plans, called the concessions limited and objected to their implications. Kwazulu's Chief Gatsha Buthelezi rejected the proposals 'outright' and threatened to stop cooperating with the South African government, while the Transkei's Kaiser Matanzima warned there would be a 'blood-bath' if changes were not made. Boputhatswana Chief Minister Lucas Mangope said that the government's proposals would mean the resettlement of some 250,000–500,000 Tswanas and said they exposed the 'powerlessness' of the homeland governments.

18 May The deputy minister of Bantu administration and education, T.N.H. (Punt) Janson, appears to concede in a speech that urban Blacks would be a permanent feature in South Africa. He said that Black workers 'and their descendants will be in the White areas for many years' and should be made 'as happy as possible'. He promised a new 'charter' to cover the growing number of migrant workers.

This attitude went against the orthodox party dogma. Janson was thus seen as a leading reformer who was trying to increase the Nationalists' sensitivity to racial affairs. He invited suggestions on 28 July on how to humanize the influx control measures and pass laws that regulated Black movement. On 11 September, he indicated that all laws which affected Blacks would be reviewed and simplified in the interests of 'contented and happy communities'. In October, he announced that elected representative councils would be established to work with the 22 Bantu administration boards that controlled the estimated six million Blacks living outside Bantustans. The councils, which were to provide channels for consultation, would be the first official body to represent Blacks outside the Bantustans. The White government board would retain control of final decisions. On 19 November, he told Blacks not to put up with insulting officials and urged them to lodge complaints.

22 May The government introduces the Bantu Labour Relations Regulation Amendment Bill, giving Black workers a limited legal right to strike for the first time in 30 years. The proposal was unexpected and followed a wave of illegal strikes by tens of thousands of Blacks throughout Natal and in the Johannesburg area.

The bill set out the conditions under which Black workers could strike, gave the procedures to be followed in strikes, and listed those categories of employment from which workers were unable to strike, such a essential services. Under one of the bill's clauses, the minister of labour was able to make wage proposals offered by a part of any industry binding on the entire industry. The purpose of that clause was to insure that those employers who raised wages would not be undercut by those who did not.

Under the provisions of the bill, the government-appointed Blacks would be allowed to attend wage negotiation meetings. The general secretary of the Trade Union Congress, who had advocated Black trade union rights, called the bill 'a meaningless sop' and said that 'substituting Government-appointed Africans for White Government officials will make no difference as these people do not really represent African workers'.

28 May Sports Minister Piet Koornhof announces a relaxation of apartheid rules in sports, which would allow multiracial competition at national and international events. Strict apartheid would still be maintained at the local and provincial levels. Koornhof said that the changes should eventually allow South Africa to again participate in international sporting events.

The 1973 South Africa Games, held in Pretoria, had allowed interracial competition in boxing and football and it was announced that a second football tournament in which White, Coloured, Black and Asian teams would compete against each other would be scheduled. The government also decided that Black cricketers on foreign teams would be allowed to play in South Africa. The measures were still not enough to convince New Zealand of South Africa's intentions and a much-anticipated South African Springbok rugby team tour of New Zealand was 'deferred' on 10 April after Prime Minister Norman Kirk put pressure on the New Zealand Rugby Union to withdraw its invitation to the all-White team.

29 June The Verligte (Enlightened) Action Movement is formed. Originally a White political group, it decided in July to open its membership to all races. The movement said its main concern was to improve the country's political situation.

25 July The three-year-old state of emergency is lifted in Lesotho. Chief Leabua Jonathan had imposed emergency restrictions since suspending Parliament following disputed elections in 1970. An interim National Assembly was established on 27 April.

1 August The first elections to the Ovamboland legislative assembly are held amidst general unrest. A boycott called by the South West African People's Organization (SWAPO) was almost universally observed and only 1.6 per cent, or 1,300 of the 50,000 eligible to vote, did so.

The Ovambo Independence Party, a traditional party supporting the South African government's policy of separate development and the division of the country's tribal groups into 'ethnic' homelands, was guaranteed victory after the SWAPO call for a boycott as none of the opposition groups had nominated candidates.

15 August The Trade Union Council of South Africa, a 190,000-member group representing White, Coloured and Indian workers, unanimously voted to set up parallel Black unions in their industries 'in the hope that in time they could become integrated'. The 80,000-member Confederation of Metal and Building Unions had taken a similar step on 2 August.

11 September A wage dispute at the Western Deep Levels gold mine in Carletonville ends in a riot during which police kill 11 Black miners and another is hacked to death by fellow miners. Some 27 other people were injured. The violence had erupted after Black machine operators' demands for wage increases had failed. Pay rises over the past 15 months had resulted in a narrowing salary differential between the skilled machine operators and the unskilled underground drivers, a situation the skilled men did not like. The machine operators had reportedly attacked other workers who refused to join the strike.

A judicial inquiry reported on 25 October that the police were not at fault, but passions were slow to die down. The horror of the incident, which caused an international outcry, overshadowed the extent of all the victories Blacks had won in the industrial sphere that year.

3 October Prime Minister Vorster says that his government would not stand in the way of changes in South Africa's traditional patterns of work. Black advances in wages and labour relations, brought about by the strikes earlier in the year, were paralleled by advances in employment opportunities. They were apparently linked to the government's growing realization that skilled non-White labour was increasingly vital for industry to be manned and for full employment, growth and stability to be maintained.

5 October The UN General Assembly votes to reject South Africa's credentials, reversing the 3 October vote of its credentials committee. The president of the General Assembly ruled that the decision did not affect the South African delegations' right to participate. On 14 December, the Assembly passed a resolution rejecting the South African government's right to represent the South African native peoples and announced that the 'liberation movements' recognized by the Organization of African Unity were the authentic majority representatives. Prime Minister Vorster, meanwhile, declared that South Africa intended to remain in the UN, despite the mounting opposition.

8 November The leaders of the semi-autonomous Black homelands of Bophu-thatswana, Ciskei, Gazankulu, Kwazulu, Lebowa and the Transkei meet in Umtata, the Transkei, to develop a common policy in their demand for more land. The summit meeting, the first of its kind, was seen by observers as an indication that the Black leaders were uniting in their approaches to the government. The leaders agreed upon the formation of a federation as their long-term goal, protested against government financing, adopted resolutions calling for the abolition of influx controls, the establishment of a Black bank, the condemnation of racial discrimination and the consolidation of the homelands into single units.

28 November An Arab oil embargo is imposed on South Africa at a time of general price increases and oil cuts. The embargo accelerated the extension of conservation measures and introduced the possibility of oil rationing in 1974.

11 December The UN Security Council announces that it is suspending talks with South Africa over the future of Namibia. The decision to end Secretary General Kurt Waldheim's contacts with the South Africans over the territory followed reports that Waldheim had failed to obtain from the South African government satisfactory clarifications on its policies to meet UN requirements for the self-determination and eventual independence of Namibia.

16 December Former Interior Minister Theo Gerdener launches the Democratic Party. Gerdener, who resigned from the government because his liberal views clashed with those of other members of the Cabinet, said that the new party would promote the political integration of the White, Coloured and Asian communities, while accepting the policy of establishing self-governing states for the various Black peoples of South Africa.

1 9 7 4

4 January A five-point 'declaration of faith' is signed by the leader of the United Party's Transvaal branch, Harry Schwarz, and Kwazulu leader Chief Gatsha Buthelezi. Although it was signed on Schwarz's initiative and was not supported by any other United Party leader, it was regarded as the highest level of dialogue between Whites and non-Whites in the twentieth century. The declaration, described as a 'blueprint' for the multiracial country's government by consent, called for the eventual establishment of Black–White federation, educational and material opportunities for all races, the planning of future policy by a consultative council comprising representatives from all racial groups, and guarantees of cultural identity and rights of the 'various groups' that made up South Africa.

The declaration was attacked by the party's traditionalist hierarchy, which supported a modified form of apartheid, but was endorsed on 23 January by party leader Sir de Villiers Graaff. The bitter disagreements over the declaration were seen as further proof that the party had split into conservative and reformist factions.

9 January Botswana announces plans to appoint a government labour representative in South Africa. The move was seen as part of a major attempt by the governments of the countries supplying South Africa with its migrant labour force to improve their nationals' terms of employment and to decrease the countries' dependence on wages remitted from South Africa. South Africa's dependence on this migrant labour was highlighted in October 1973 when Michael Botha, the minister of Bantu administration and development, announced that there were 475,387 Black migrant workers from neighbouring countries in South Africa. Of these workers, 148,856 were from Lesotho (with 80,625 employed in the gold mines), 139,714 from Malawi (112,432), 127,198 from Mozambique (88,585), 36,480 from Botswana (22,214), 10,032 from Swaziland, 3,249 from Rhodesia and the rest from elsewhere in Africa.

By the end of June, recruitment from southern Botswana had dropped from 9,665 in the first six months of 1973 to 6,593 for the same period in 1974. Malawi's President Hastings Banda, following the deaths on 4 April of more than 70 Malawian miners in an air crash, unilaterally suspended the recruitment of Malawian labour for South Africa. This led to drawn-out but inconclusive bargaining for improved conditions. By the end of the year, some 45,000 Malawians had returned home from working in South Africa.

22 January Some 10,000 Black textile workers win a wage rise after a brief strike in Durban. It was the first strike in a year that was to see some 57,656 Blacks participate in 374 strikes against 120 organizations and factories. The strikes came despite the fact that some 2,000 liaison and works committees had been set up for Blacks in the hope of avoiding the industrial unrest of the previous year. The strikes began in Durban but spread to Witwatersrand and East London. The strikes, especially in the gold mines, often turned violent and led to some 50 deaths and hundreds of injuries over the years. The violence resulted in a mass exodus of foreign migrant workers from the mines, which caused serious labour shortages in South African industries. This in turn led to industry raising wages and easing petty apartheid restrictions to attract labour.

30 January Johannesburg city council, controlled by the opposition United Party, announces that 'petty apartheid' practices will be dismantled, including racially segregated parks, queues, entrances, libraries and seats. Durban, Cape Town, Pietermaritzburg also took similar steps and the National Party-controlled Krugersdorp town council announced in November it was also moving in the same direction.

The moves were seen as a continuation of a trend that began in 1971 and were largely prompted by labour shortages. Restrictions against non-Whites in public accommodation and labour were lifted. These measures included decisions to allow Black nurses to care for White patients in private hospitals, Blacks to become motor mechanics and traffic policemen and Coloureds to be given greater access to office jobs. In all cases, apartheid laws remained on the books despite the *de facto* changes. It was also announced on 9 December that Blacks would be able to join the South African army for the first time. They were to receive the same pay as Whites and be allowed to carry weapons, but would not be trained as officers.

Prime Minister Vorster was opposed to the policy of easing the minor apartheid regulations and said on 8 February that the government would intervene if these relaxations caused any friction.

6 March Prime Minister Vorster and the leaders of eight Black homelands meet for the first time in what was described as the first official meeting ever convened between Blacks and Whites in South Africa. The talks, said by one Black leader to be 'brutally frank', were called for at the November 1973 homelands leaders meeting in Umtata and centred on the South African government's plan for the separate development of Black homelands and their eventual independence. Vorster agreed to reappraise some issues raised by the Black leaders, including pass law regulations, influx control, taxes and wage inequalities. The major issue of land consolidation was not, however, settled. The leaders of Basotho-Qwaqwa, Bophuthatswana, Ciskei, Gazankulu, Kwazulu, Lebowa, Transkei and Vendaland all attended the meeting.

12 March The Transkei legislative assembly unanimously passes a motion to request the Transkei's complete independence from South Africa within five years. The motion was passed on the provision that Transkei receive all the land promised to them by then and that its independence would not prejudice its claims to other areas. Prime Minister Vorster announced on 1 April that the homeland would be granted its independence within this period.

The Transkei's decision to ask for independence was criticized by the leaders of the Kwazulu and Lebowa homelands, who said that it was in violation of the spirit of the 1973 Umtata meeting at which the homeland leaders had decided to request independence together.

15 March The government, conscious of the need to placate its right wing following concessions to Black workers, enacts two pieces of legislation designed to widen its powers to suppress anti-apartheid groups.

The Affected Organizations Act was introduced on 19 February and enabled the president to ban any organizations that were engaged in politics from obtaining funds from abroad. The bill, which did not define 'politics', also gave the government more sweeping powers to investigate suspected organizations. Heavy penalties could be imposed either for obstructing such investigations or for accepting funding. The act was first applied against the National Union of South African Students on 13 September, and observers felt that trade unions would be the next target.

The Riotous Assemblies Amendment Act empowered the government to ban any private or public gathering of two or more people if it felt that such a gathering threatened law and order. Under the provisions of the act, anyone in the news media who disseminated the speech of any person banned under the act from attending a meeting could be jailed for up to one year. The act was first used to prevent protest meetings against the visit of Paraguayan dictator Alfred Stroessner.

24 April General elections in South Africa result in the ruling National Party being returned to power for the seventh consecutive time, and with an increased majority. The Nationalists gained 122 seats in an enlarged House of Assembly (118 in the previous assembly), for a 75-seat majority. The opposition United Party, which had been rift by internal dissensions, gained 41 (47), while the Progressive Party had a resurgence of support and increased its seats from one to six. On 12 June it won a seventh seat in a by-election. The ultra-right Herstigte Nasionale Party failed to win a seat, as did the new Democratic Party.

Prime Minister Vorster hailed the result as 'a clear indication that the people had once again chosen the policy of separate development'. The liberal Progressive Party had campaigned on a platform of a qualified franchise for all citizens in a multiracial state. Progressive Party leader Colin Eglin, who won a seat for the first time, described the election as a victory for his party's platform and said that 'for the first time, a significant number of White South Africans have shown that they are prepared to come to terms with modern, multiracial South Africa'. Observers believed that the elections were a clear defeat for the opposition United Party, which lost five seats and had been split in pre-election disputes into conservative and reformist factions.

25 April A virtually bloodless military coup overthrows Portugal's civilian government. The coup leaders, a group of young military officers calling themselves the Armed Forces Movement, enjoyed widespread public support. General Antonio de Spinola, the former deputy general staff chief whose dismissal for opposing Premier Marcello Caetano's colonial policies sparked off an unsuccessful coup attempt in March, emerged as the leader of the junta. Caetano had attempted to retain Portugal's colonies by force, while Spinola held that Portugal was incapable of gaining a military victory over the African rebel movements. He was named president in May and his prime minister, Brigadier General Vasco dos Santos Goncalves, was appointed in July. Although the new government immediately recognized the colonies' right to self-determination, Spinola made it clear that 'self-determination should not be confused with independence' and said he preferred to see the territories enter a federal relationship with Portugal. However, the liberation movements in the Portuguese colonies, the Front for the Liberation of Mozambique (Frelimo), the Popular Movement for the Liberation of Angola, the National Front for the

Liberation of Angola and the African Party for the Independence of (Portuguese) Guinea and Cape Verde, all came out in opposition to the federal system of alliance with Portugal and vowed to fight on to obtain independence.

South Africa recognized the new military junta on 28 April. The coup, which brought in a government willing to recognize the Black liberation movements in Portuguese Africa, had a forceful immediate and long-term impact on South Africa. It increased both South Africa's and Rhodesia's sense of isolation and feelings of being the last bastions of White supremacy on the continent. On 14 June, the government replaced police units along the 1,400-mile (2,250 km) border with Angola and Zambia with army troops, fearing the impact of the unrest in the Portuguese colonies of Angola and Mozambique.

29 May Prime Minister Vorster and Rhodesian Prime Minister Ian Smith hold joint talks at which they commit themselves to peaceful coexistence with Black-ruled Mozambique and pledged non-interference in the country's domestic affairs. The pledge was seen as major piece of statecraft by Vorster and as setting the tone for *détente* in southern African following Portugal's withdrawal. A reciprocal pledge came from the new Mozambican leader Joachim Chissano on 12 September.

15 June Black workers get their largest pay rise in South African history. The increases, ranging from 33 to 66 per cent, were seen as the industry's response to the falling numbers of Black miners. By the end of the year, the number of Black miners working underground was 274,000 as compared to 322,000 in 1973. The fall was the result of the strikes and intertribal feuding that had been taking place on the mine fields all year. The hardening of the attitudes of neighbouring Black African countries towards migrant work also resulted in a decrease in the number of their citizens working in South Africa.

15 June The exodus of over 500 Namibians to Angola is reported to have begun. Observers believed the mass move was due to the anticipated democratization in the former Portuguese colony following Portugal's departure. The Namibians illegally crossed the closed Ovamboland border into neighbouring Angola. Among those leaving were many teachers and skilled workers, as well as members of the banned South West African People's Organization (SWAPO). South African officials alleged that the SWAPO members had gone to Angola to receive terrorist training.

10 July The vice president of the South African Atomic Energy Board, Dr Louw Alberts, confirms that South Africa is capable of producing a nuclear bomb and of extracting and enriching uranium. He said, 'We have now a bargaining position equal to that of any Arab country with a lot of oil.' South Africa was known to own about a quarter of the West's known uranium resources.

4 August South Africa's Newspaper Press Union (NPU) proposes the adoption of a strong self-disciplinary code in an attempt to ward off government legislation to curb the press. The newspapers owners and managers agreed to a revised press code, without prior consultation with the South African Society of Journalists, under which the NPU's Press Council could fine any publication up to R10,000 which it found guilty of provoking 'racial incitement' and other offences. Interior

Minister Connie Mulder said on 12 August that if the NPU members observed the new regulations, the government would abandon its plans to impose a strict new press censorship.

On 9 October, however, the government gazetted the Publications Act. The new act replaced the Publications Control Board and established a completely new system of censorship. A major change was that there would be no appeals permitted.

7 September Mario Soares, the Portuguese foreign minister, and Samora Machel, president of Frelimo, officially sign a cease-fire agreement and set a date for Mozambique's independence. Frelimo had been fighting a guerrilla war against Portuguese rule over Mozambique since shortly after its foundation in 1962.

The transitional government was officially installed on 20 September. Frelimo's third in command, Joachim Chissano, was sworn in as prime minister and inherited a country with its economy in ruins. Machel soon announced his plans to turn Mozambique into a people's democracy and 'revolutionary base against imperialism and colonialism in Africa'.

30 September The UN General Assembly refuses to recognize South Africa's credentials for the fifth consecutive year, but the ruling does not unseat the delegation. The Assembly, in an unprecedented resolution, also urged the Security Council to 'review the relationship between the UN and South Africa in the light of the constant violation by South Africa of the principles of the Charter and the Universal Declaration of Human Rights'. The secretary general accepted the credentials on 15 October of the first South African delegation to include non-Whites. On 24 October, the head of the delegation, Roelof F. 'Pik' Botha announced his government's intentions to do 'everything in [its] power to move away from discrimination based on race or color'. Unconvinced by these two gestures, the majority of the Security Council voted on 30 October to expel South Africa from the UN. It was only the veto of the US, Britain and France which prevented the expulsion.

South Africa's participation in the UN was still not guaranteed. On 12 November, in an unprecedented ruling, the president of the UN General Assembly Abdelaziz Boutfeflika suspended South Africa from participating in the remainder of the Assembly's session. He argued that the Assembly's rejection of the South African delegation's credentials in September expressed its 'will' to suspend South Africa. His action, which barred South Africa from voting, making proposals and appealing in the session but did not suspend it from any other UN body, was criticized by the US and several other delegations. South Africa responded to the suspension by recalling its UN ambassador and freezing its $1 million annual contribution to the organization.

7 November South Africa announces a new five-year plan to treble the size of the Simonstown naval base. On 4 November Defence Minister P.W. Botha had offered the base's facilities to 'every country in the free world which is friendly toward us'.

16 November The leader of eight of South Africa's nine Black homelands announce that they will not accept South Africa's timetable for their independence if it means they forfeit their right to a full share of the country's wealth. They specifically refused to become independent until after their land, which was fragmented into as many as 50 separate geographical areas, was consolidated into a viable economic unit and a sound economic infrastructure was developed. Transkei, divided into just two separate areas, was the only Bantustan to maintain its commitment to early independence. It was considered the only Bantustan that could possibly be economically viable.

Prime Minister Vorster responded to the announcement by saying, 'If there are any of you who nourish the hope of one man–one vote in the White Parliament, then you are being misled because it will not happen.' He had, on 5 November, reiterated his goal of independent Black-ruled Bantustans and vowed that 'in White South Africa, the White will rule'.

20 November The Masters and Servants Act and portions of the Bantu Labour Act are repealed in a move seen by many observers as a significant attempt by the government to reduce tensions among Black workers. The repealed laws had made it a criminal offence for workers to breach service contracts or to cause tension between different groups in the population. The government had already initiated moves towards closing the racial wage gap, and gave tax incentives in the Budget to encourage the training of Black workers.

5 December The government announces that a second oil-from-coal complex some ten times larger than the pioneering Sasol plant is to be built over the next six years. The project involved a possible total capital investment of some R3.4 thousand million and required an initial investment of more than R1 thousand million. The announcement was seen as significant in times of escalating fuel costs.

1 9 7 5

5 January Three days of riots break out at the world's largest gold mine, Vaal Reefs, 100 miles (160.9 km) southwest of Johannesburg. The riots resulted in the deaths of eight Black miners. A further 30 were seriously injured. On 6 January, 12,000 of the mine's 21,500 Black workers went on strike.

The disturbances were sparked off by a Lesotho government ruling that 60 per cent of the money earned by Lesotho nationals in South African mines must be kept in Lesotho bank accounts and could not be retrieved until the miners returned home. Another factor was competition between the tribes for jobs within the relatively well paid South African mining industry. The disturbances and strike underscored the importance to the economies of neighbouring Black African states of remittances from migrant workers in South African mines.

The strikes spread to other mines, and after further riots, the Anglo-American Corporation on 15 January dismissed 2,400 striking Lesotho gold miners and began sending them back to Lesotho.

9 February South African Foreign Minister Hilgard Muller flies to Zambia for a day of meetings with Rhodesian nationalists and Black African leaders. The state-owned Zambian television described the visit as 'epoch-making'.

Prime Minister John Vorster continued the diplomatic offensive in Black Africa with a visit to Liberia from 10 to 12 February. Vorster acknowledged that he made the trip only after it was reported in the London *Times* on 17 February. Liberian President William Tolbert said that Vorster told him, 'I would be only too pleased to get South West Africa off our backs', but he stressed that South Africa would not withdraw precipitously.

11 February Ten provincial legislators resign from the opposition United Party to form a new political organization, the Reform Party. All 10 were members of the Transvaal provincial council and belonged to the liberal faction of the United Party. On 19 May, the Reform Party merged with the Progressive Party and produced a joint programme calling for a federal system of self-governing states based on territorial rather than racial divisions. Each state would be free to decide its franchise and electoral system within the framework of a federal constitution.

26 March The annual budget presented by Finance Minister Owen Horwood increases defence spending by 36 per cent to $150 billion. A further 36 per cent was also provided for land purchases in connection with the government's homelands policy and overall government spending was increased by 19.3 per cent.

5 April A plant to enrich uranium for use in the manufacture of atomic power goes into operation at Valindaba, Pretoria. On 7 April Prime Minister Vorster told Parliament that South Africa had an entirely new method of upgrading natural uranium into nuclear fuel.

The enrichment plant raised fears that South Africa intended to develop a nuclear weapon. These fears were heightened when the *Washington Post* reported on 14 April that the US Nuclear Corporation of Oak Ridge, Tennessee, had sold South Africa 97 pounds of highly enriched uranium – the kind used in the construction of atomic bombs. The US Nuclear Regulatory Commission said it had approved the sale after South Africa agreed to safeguards that would prevent the diversion of the uranium towards the production of nuclear weapons.

11 April A special ministerial session of the Organization of African Unity (OAU) adopts the 'Dar es Salaam Declaration on Southern Africa'. Acceptance of the declaration represented a victory for moderate African leaders as it called for a peaceful solution to the problems of southern Africa and approved limited contacts with the South African government. But the declaration also urged the political, economic and cultural isolation of South Africa until it abandoned apartheid.

2 May The South African government reinstates the rights of Blacks to buy the leases on their homes. The policy had been terminated in 1967 by Prime Minister Hendrik Verwoerd with his 'temporary sojourner' policy. The new policy allowed Blacks to buy the 'right of occupation' of homes in segregated Black townships on a 30-year lease and also allowed them to bequeath or sell the houses. Blacks, however, continued to be barred from buying the land on which the houses stood.

5 May The first television transmission takes place in South Africa. Television had been blocked by the government for four years because the ruling National Party regarded it as 'morally corrupting'. The first test transmissions featured scenes from an annual industrial and agricultural exhibition. Regular transmissions in English and Afrikaans did not start until January 1976. The government retained a tight control over the broadcasting authority, the South Africa Broadcasting Corporation, and especially the news programmes.

6 June The US, Britain and France veto a UN Security Council resolution to impose an arms embargo against South Africa because of its failure to withdraw from Namibia. The resolution was jointly proposed by Cameroon, Guyana, Iraq, Mauritania and Tanzania and was supported by China and the Soviet Union. The veto by France, Britain and the US angered many Black African countries who became convinced that the Western countries were more concerned about protecting their commercial and geopolitical interests than the principle of Black majority rule.

16 June The British government officially terminates the 1955 Simonstown agreement, under which it kept a naval mission in the strategic port near Cape Town. Britain's decision to withdraw had been made in 1974. After the formal withdrawal, South African Defence Minister P. W. Botha said that the end of the Simonstown agreement should be seen as a challenge rather than a tragedy.

25 June Mozambique obtains independence from Portugal after 500 years of colonial rule. Samora Machel, installed as the country's first president, declares that he will build 'the first truly Marxist state' in Africa.

The withdrawal of Portugal from Mozambique and the establishment of a left-wing anti-apartheid government in the former colony was a major blow to the South African government since the Portuguese had always insured that the colony would not be used as a base for guerrilla attacks on South Africa. The Portuguese had also performed an important role in allowing oil and other supplies to transit through the Mozambican port of Beira to support Rhodesia in the face of an UN economic boycott. Mozambique was not only an important market for South African goods, but also a popular holiday destination for South Africans.

Machel's government closed the Beira oil pipeline to Rhodesia, thus increasing the pressure on the White minority government of Ian Smith. The closure of the pipeline also meant that more supplies had to be routed through South Africa, leaving it the only link between Rhodesia and the outside world. Machel also initially cut back on trade with South Africa and allowed Mozambique to be used as a base for African National Congress (ANC) guerrillas, effectively ending his country's status as a buffer state between South Africa and a hostile Black Africa.

25 August Prime Minister Vorster and Zambian President Kaunda hold an unprecedented meeting at Victoria Falls, on the Zambezi River border between Rhodesia and Zambia. The two men presided over the opening session of constitutional talks between Rhodesian Black nationalists and the government of Ian Smith. The talks broke down after one day, but the summit had a wider importance in that the acknowledged leader of Whites in southern Africa (Vorster) had cooperated with the acknowledged leader of Blacks in southern Africa (Kaunda) to bring their respective clients together in an attempt to resolve their differences.

1 September A multiracial constitutional conference on the future of Namibia, which had been proposed by the all-White South West African legislative assembly in November 1974, opens at the Turnhalle in the Namibian capital of Windhoek. The conference was attended by some 134 delegates representing the territory's 11 main ethnic groups. The South West African People's Organization (SWAPO) was invited but refused to attend. The talks adjourned on 12 September after passing a resolution calling for the independence of the area as a single entity from South Africa 'as soon as possible, if possible within three years' but resumed in secret session on 10 November.

The UN and the OAU both refused to recognize the conference because of its non-democratic and ethnic basis. South Africa, which had consistently refused to yield the territory to UN control, had become more flexible since events in the former Portuguese colonies of Mozambique and Angola and in Rhodesia and now agreed that the inhabitants of Namibia should be consulted about their future.

21 September South Africa devalues the rand by 17.9 per cent in an attempt to strengthen its balance of payments position and protect the country's gold reserves. The protection package announced by the Ministry of Finance and the South African Reserve Bank also raised bank interest rates to 8.5 per cent and relaxed foreign exchange controls to encourage borrowing from abroad.

23 October Some 500 Cuban troops are reported to be aiding the Marxist guerrilla group, the Popular Movement for the Liberation of Angola (MPLA), in their fight against both the Portuguese colonial forces and other nationalist guerrillas in Angola. By the end of the year, the Cuban presence had swollen to 7,500 and sparked off fears within US President Ford's administration that Angola was on the verge of becoming a Soviet satellite.

10 November Portugal transfers sovereignty of Angola to the Angolan people, a sign that it does not recognize any of the three guerrilla factions as the legitimate government. On 11 November the Marxist MPLA proclaimed its leader, Agostinho Neto, president of the People's Republic of Angola in the Angolan capital of Luanda. The National Union for the Total Independence of Angola (Unita), led by Dr Jonas Savimbi, and Holden Roberto's National Front for the Liberation of Angola (FNLA) jointly form the People's Democratic Republic of Angola hours later in their stronghold 75 miles (120.7 km) north of Luanda.

The confused state of Angola at the time of its independence created both dangers and opportunities for the South African government. It opposed the MPLA because of its pro-Soviet inclinations and because it offered sanctuary to SWAPO guerrillas fighting against South African rule in Namibia. It, therefore, attempted to destabilize the MPLA by supplying covert aid to the opposing Unita forces of Jonas Savimbi in the southern part of Angola and the FNLA forces of

Holden Roberto in the north. At the same time, it positioned itself to intervene militarily in Angola, partly to support Unita and partly to attack SWAPO bases. Even before independence, on 23 October, the MPLA reported that South African troops were marching on the Angolan town of Sa da Bandeira, 150 miles (241.4 km) inside the border with Namibia. On 25 November MPLA announced the capture of Black South African soldiers in a battle in southern Angola.

25 November The MPLA, aided by Cuban troops, launches a counter offensive against Unita and halts Unita's advance against the capital. South African troops are captured during the hostilities, some 600 miles inside Angolan territory, demonstrating their involvement in the actual fighting and causing an outcry throughout South Africa.

26 November Breyten Breytenbach, Afrikaans poet and writer, is sentenced to nine years in prison for conspiracy to overthrow the government. Breytenbach, who had been living in exile in Paris, was arrested on 1 August when he illegally entered South Africa on a French passport. He unexpectedly pleaded guilty to the charge of conspiracy to overthrow the government and 11 other illegal acts under the Terrorism and Suppression of Communism Acts.

27 November Defence Minister P.W. Botha appeals for Western help in preventing Soviets from gaining a foothold in Angola. He also admitted to supporting Unita and FNLA forces. On 31 December, Prime Minister Vorster added his voice to that of Botha's when he warned that 'only a bigger Western involvement, not only in the diplomatic but all other fields' could keep Angola from being 'hounded into the Communist fold'.

The South African government was reluctant to launch a full-scale attack on the MPLA government in Angola without the full support of the US and possibly Britain. Without US support, it faced the possibility of Soviet intervention, defeat and increased Soviet influence in the region. US intervention would ensure victory and a close long-term relationship with the premier Western power.

16 December US President Gerald Ford expresses his 'serious concern' over the involvement of the Soviet Union and Cuba in Angola and appealed for 'discussion in Congress of the geopolitical significance of the part of Africa to the United States and the West', although he opposed sending US military advisers or combat troops to southern Africa. It was reported that the Unita and FNLA forces had received $25 million in covert US military aid in the previous three months. But the Senate blocked any serious US involvement on 19 December by passing a resolution prohibiting, without specific Congressional authorization, covert military assistance for any party in the Angolan conflict.

The South Africans, who had been encouraged by positive noises from Ford and Secretary of State Henry Kissinger, had advanced further into Angola and on the same day as the Senate resolution the MPLA displayed four South African soldiers captured more than 400 miles (643.6 km) north of the Angolan border with Namibia. On 17 December Defence Minister P.W. Botha signalled a long-term South African commitment in Angola when he announced a three-month requirement for reservists in the border regions with Angola and Namibia.

25 December William Schaufele, the newly appointed US assistant secretary of state for Africa, begins a tour of Africa in attempt to convince African nations not to recognize the MPLA at the New Year meeting of the OAU. Ugandan President Idi Amin, chairman of the OAU, said at the outset of Schaufele's trip, 'We should not let ourselves be brainwashed by the Western powers that the presence of Soviet technicians in Angola is an indication that the Soviet Union wants to colonise Africa.'

29 December The British *Financial Times* reports that South African troops launched a major offensive 400 miles (643.6 km) inside Angola which cleared a large portion of southern Angola of MPLA forces. On 30 December, the MPLA claimed it had killed a 'large number' of South African troops during a battle for the town of Cela, 400 miles (643.6 km) north of the Namibian border. The South African government remained close-mouthed about the details of its involvement in Angola, admitting only that three South African soldiers had been killed in Angola, but refusing to say where or how.

1 9 7 6

16 January Chief Gatsha Buthelezi emerges as the undisputed political leader of the Zulu people after putting down a challenge by Zulu King Goodwill Zwelithini.

Inkatha, a national cultural liberation movement, was modelled on the original Inkatha organization founded in 1928 by Goodwill's grandfather King Solomon and reactivated in March 1975 by Chief Buthelezi, who became its president. Buthelezi ensured that his power would remain unchallenged by passing a resolution at the Inkatha meeting opposing the foundation of political parties while the Zulus were 'still in chains', and by obtaining the King's agreement to refrain from involvement in politics or from committing any political action.

On 14 March, Chief Buthelezi went on to make an important call for majority rule and rejected the government's policy of separate development and of creating independent Black homelands.

11 February The Organization of African Unity (OAU) officially recognizes the government established by the Popular Movement for the Liberation of Angola (MPLA) under President Agostinho Neto and admits the People's Republic of Angola as its forty-seventh member state. An extraordinary summit meeting held in January to discuss the issue ended in deadlock, with delegates almost equally divided between those who wanted to recognize the MPLA and those who wanted to establish a coalition government made up of the three nationalist groups fighting for power. Sierra Leone's recognition of the MPLA government on 29 January finally tipped the scales in its favour.

Portugal, the former colonial power who had granted independence to the people of Angola as a whole in November 1975 rather than hand over the reins of power to any one group, recognized the MPLA government on 22 February.

12 March The South African government announces that it is withdrawing all South African troops from Angola, except those guarding the hydroelectric projects on the Cunene River border with Namibia. Those troops were also withdrawn on 27 March after the Angolan liberation group, the MPLA, agreed to observe the Angolan–Namibian border and to guarantee the safety of both the Cunene River projects and their staff. The agreement was made through the good offices of the Soviets and British and after the intervention of the UN secretary general.

South Africa had been under a great deal of international pressure to withdraw the troops after it became clear that they had been involved in the actual fighting in Angola. The South African government had previously insisted that the troops were only involved in guarding the Namibian border with Angola. The South Africans believed that the pressure to withdraw showed that they were alone in their attempt to counteract Soviet authority in Africa. The Cuban troops, who had been brought in to assist the MPLA's battle for control of the country, remained in Angola after the South African troops withdrew.

The South African withdrawal followed a US House of Representatives decision on 27 January to reject President Gerald Ford's request for a $28 million military aid package to the anti-Marxist guerrilla groups fighting the MPLA, the National Movement for the Total Liberation of Angola and the National Front for the Liberation of Angola. The vote came despite Ford's warning that it was opening the door for Angola to become a Soviet sphere of influence in southern Africa.

On 31 March, the UN Security Council censured South African aggression against Angola and called on the South African government to compensate the People's Republic of Angola. The US and other Western countries abstained on the resolution because it did not also condemn the intervention in Angola of other countries, most notably the Soviet Union and Cuba.

31 March Finance Minister Owen Horwood presents South Africa's 1976–7 budget to Parliament. The record $9.1 thousand million budget included $1.6 thousand million for defence, which represented a 42 per cent increase over the previous budget. Horwood said that political developments in southern Africa meant that South Africa had to increase its efforts in defence.

18 April Prime Minister John Vorster arrives in Israel at the beginning of a five-day visit. The visit ended with the two countries signing a sweeping economic, scientific and industrial cooperation pact. The visit, described in South Africa as an important event, was condemned by the Organization of African Unity (OAU) and the Arab League. The Soviet government's newspaper, *Pravda*, said the visit reflected 'the racist–Zionist alliance against African and Arab liberation movements'.

On 31 October, South Africa was reported to have agreed to sell coal to Israel so Israel could lessen its dependence on Arab oil.

19 May The South African government announces plans to establish a 1,000-mile (1,609-km) long buffer zone along the Namibian border with Angola to limit forays by Black nationalists into Namibia. The decision to create a half-mile no man's land followed a pledge by Angola in April that it would try to guarantee the integrity of the border that was crossed by members of the Namibian independence movement, the South West African People's Organization (SWAPO), on a regular basis.

7 June Parliament begins debating a controversial bill under which the some three million members of the Xhosa tribe would lose their South African citizenship when the Transkei homeland became independent on 26 October. Under the provisions of the bill, all Xhosa would automatically become citizens of the independent Transkei regardless of where they were born or lived and would thus forfeit their South African nationality. At the centre of the debate was the future of some 1.3 million Xhosa who lived and worked outside the Transkei in South Africa. The bill meant that they would be stripped of the citizenship of the country in which they were born and lived and given citizenship of a place they had very likely never even seen. The Transkei's draft constitution handled the problem by giving all Xhosa the opportunity to apply for Transkeian citizenship after independence, while the South African bill made them all automatic citizens.

The chief minister of the Transkei, Chief Kaiser Matanzima, denounced the South African government's plan, saying he would not let the Transkei become the dumping ground for 'stateless Blacks'. When the controversial bill was published by the government on 26 May, the opposition United Party unexpectedly joined forces with the reformist Progressive Party to oppose it. Opposition leader Sir de Villiers Graaff said his party's opposition was based on the fact that the bill 'deprived great numbers of citizens' of their citizenship without their consent.

16 June The worst racial violence in South African history to date breaks out in the Black township of Soweto. The trouble began as protest by 10,000 schoolchildren against a government regulation requiring the use of Afrikaans as the language of instruction in Black schools, but it quickly escalated into a riot. The police opened fire on the demonstrating students in the heavily populated township outside Johannesburg and set off a wave of violent demonstrations that spread throughout the country. The violence, which continued sporadically until February 1977, spread out from Soweto to Black townships in Pretoria and other towns in the Transvaal. By 11 August, the unrest spread to the Cape peninsula where arson, looting and violence broke out in the Black townships of Langa and Guguletu.

Large numbers of Coloureds participated for the first time in anti-apartheid protests, especially Coloured students at the University of the Western Cape and schoolchildren who wanted to express their solidarity with the Blacks, as the disturbances spread to Cape Town. The culmination of their activity was a two-day strike. Many observers believed that the Coloureds became actively involved in the rioting partly because of the heavy-handed actions of the riot police. They were accused of indiscriminately beating up Coloured students and recklessly using firearms. By September the situation in some places was described as chaotic and many of the schools, especially in the Black areas, were virtually empty.

By the end of the year, some 500 people had died as a result of the disturbances, including many children. Most of the dead had been shot by riot police. Schools, offices, shops and other buildings in Black areas throughout the country were destroyed in arson attacks. Although the disturbances had begun with the specific language issue in schools, they rapidly took on a wider anti-apartheid character and were harshly put down by the riot police. Winnie Mandela, wife of the jailed African National Congress leader Nelson Mandela, said that 'the language issue is merely the spark that lit the resentment that is building up among Black people'.

The government responded to the unrest by blaming Communist agitators, 'Black Power' activists and organized subversives, and said that the outbreaks of violence were caused by organized agitation and intimidation and had not developed spontaneously. It did, however, concede to some of the Blacks' grievances and announced that concessions would be made. These conciliatory measures included revoking, on 6 July, the controversial law that had sparked off the rioting, that required the use of Afrikaans in township schools. The revised regulations permitted the principals of Black schools to select either of the two official languages of South Africa, English or Afrikaans, for courses not taught in the African tongue. The choice would require government approval, which was described as a formality. The government also promised to pass the long-delayed legislation to enable Blacks to own property in the townships, to improve the quality of Black education and to grant Blacks municipal self-government in the Black urban townships.

18 June The government rejects the Theron Commission's report that had advised that changes be made in the social and political status of the country's 2.4 million Coloureds. The 18-member government-appointed commission, which had taken three years to complete its study into conditions in the Coloured community, recommended that Coloureds be once again given direct representation in Parliament. They had had such representation until 1971, when government legislation transferred responsibility for them to an expanded Coloured Persons' Representative Council. The commission also called for the repeal of the Prohibition of the Mixed Marriages Act and the section of the Immorality Act prohibiting sexual relations between Whites and non-Whites.

In replying to the report, the government said that it believed that its policy of 'parallel development', apartheid as applied to the Coloured community, had 'over the past quarter of a century been beneficial to the Coloured people themselves and to the republic as a whole'. For this reason, the government said that it could not 'in any way commit itself to standpoints which would return the republic to a situation of political exploitation and conflicting group interests'.

The publishing of the Theron Commission report was seen in South Africa as an event of major domestic political importance. It had been expected that the government would make major concessions to the Coloureds as a result of this study. When its recommendations were rejected, the Coloureds were extremely disappointed and angry. Some observers described the government's actions as having 'crushed the Coloured community's hopes for a new deal'.

24 June Prime Minister Vorster meets US Secretary of State Henry Kissinger in Switzerland. It is the first highest-level meeting between US and South African representatives since the Second World War. The talks were seen in South Africa as a major diplomatic achievement for the country and as a step closer towards ending the international ostracism of South Africa. Kissinger, however, emphasized that he was not meeting Vorster 'to make concessions or to lend approval to the system of Government. I am meeting to see if South Africa is willing to contribute to a moderate and peaceful evolution of events in southern Africa.' Americans saw his trip as part of a US initiative to lessen the influence of Communism in other parts of southern Africa after having failed to do so in the Angolan conflict.

This meeting led to South Africa being involved in further discussions on the problems of southern Africa, including a second meeting between Vorster and Kissinger that was held in Switzerland on 4 September. After that meeting, it was announced that Kissinger would conduct shuttle diplomacy in southern Africa to negotiate with Black African leaders on South Africa and Rhodesia, while Vorster held meetings with Rhodesian Prime Minister Ian Smith. Kissinger eventually met Smith in Pretoria in September and put to him proposals on the establishment of an interim government in Rhodesia leading to majority rule. The most significant result of the Vorster–Kissinger–Smith talks was the 24 September announcement that the Rhodesian government had accepted the Kissinger proposals for Black majority government coupled with guarantees for White minority rights. Although negotiations continued for some time after the announcement, the talks, and Vorster's contributions to them, were seen as foreshadowing the end of Rhodesia's 14-year constitutional dispute.

18 August The Turnhalle constitutional conference on the future of Namibia being held in Windhoek announces that it has set 21 December 1978 as the date for full independence for Namibia. The conference, which opened in November 1975, proposed the creation of an interim government that would prepare a constitutional basis for the transfer of power to a permanent government when full independence was declared. The proposal was immediately criticized by the UN, Black African leaders and the US for failing to comply with a UN resolution that demanded the withdrawal of South African troops from the territory by 31 August and the carrying out of elections under UN supervision. The conference was attacked for failing to include representatives from SWAPO, who had refused to participate.

South Africa would not accept UN supervision over Namibia but became more flexible in its position on the territory's future after the events in Rhodesia, Angola and Mozambique and eventually agreed to the demand that the inhabitants of Namibia should be given the opportunity to freely express their views on the issue. This change in policy resulted in a dialogue with the territory's ethnic groups and eventually culminated in the constitutional talks being held at the Turnhalle between the representatives of all the ethnic groups in Namibia.

The conference also announced that Namibia should be a unitary state, a point which the South African government's delegates initially resisted, and that an interim government be established to govern the area as soon as a draft constitution had been agreed. These proposals were approved by South Africa but rejected by the UN, SWAPO and the OAU, which contended that SWAPO was entitled to foreign military aid in its attempts to liberate Namibia. In December, the UN Committee on the Ending of Colonialism came out in support of the guerrilla war in Namibia.

24 September Rhodesian Prime Minister Ian Smith accepts British proposals for Black majority rule in Rhodesia as presented by US Secretary of State Henry Kissinger.

The proposals were first set out by British Prime Minister James Callaghan on 22 March and were endorsed by the US on 2 August. They provided for: the attainment of majority rule within two years; the immediate formation of an interim government by representatives of the current Rhodesian government and Black leaders to govern until majority rule was attained; an end of economic sanctions against Rhodesia; and the end of guerrilla activities upon the formation of the interim government.

Smith's acceptance of the plan met with varied responses. It was welcomed by both the US and Britain, who called it 'a victory for realism and common sense'. The leaders of the 'front line states' (so called because they bordered on South Africa or Rhodesia), however, met in Zambia on 29 September to criticize the plan, saying it meant the 'legalizing' of the White Rhodesian power structure. The leaders of Rhodesia's Blacks called the plan 'seriously flawed' and said it was open to abuse by Smith.

26 October The Transkei becomes the first Black homeland to be granted independence under South Africa's policy of separate development. Its independence meant that all three million members of the Xhosa tribe, regardless of where they were born or living, automatically lost their South African nationality and became citizens of the Transkei.

Transkei's statehood was seen by the rest of the world as the logical extension of South Africa's apartheid policies and was not recognized by any country other than South Africa.

On 11 November, the Transkei government ordered all South African police to leave its territory in an apparent assertion of its independence. The move did not, however, convince any of the sceptics about the legitimacy of the Transkei's independence.

17 November The leaders of the three main White opposition parties, the United Party, the Progressive Reform Party and the Democratic Party, meet in Johannesburg in an attempt to form a united opposition front in Parliament. It was the first meeting of a steering committee that was expected to eventually unite the three parties. A spokesman for the committee said that an agreement had been reached at the meeting on the basic issues of power sharing with Blacks in a federal system and on eliminating discrimination.

19 November Leading South African businessmen, concerned at the depressed state of the South African economy, announce the formation of a fund to improve the living conditions of the country's urban Blacks. It would be directed by 15 executives, from diverse political backgrounds, and would provide money for home ownership and educational and recreational facilities. Leading businessmen and National Party members in recent months had begun to call for the introduction of concrete reforms. They blamed the government's apartheid policies for the national and international loss of confidence suffered by South Africa and pressed for the abolition of the racial restrictions.

29 November The leader of the Kwazulu homeland, Chief Gatsha Buthelezi, announces the formation of the Black United Front, a political party aimed at moderate middle-class Blacks and church leaders. The chief, known as a vocal opponent of both apartheid and the recent Black student violence, said that the

Front was not 'anti-White but pro-South African, Black and White'. He said it called for the end of restrictions on Black movement within South Africa, the creation of a multiracial political system, the integration of the country's educational system and the abandonment of separate development under which Blacks were deprived of their South African citizenship and given political rights only in separate tribal areas.

15 December The South African Institute of Race Relations announces that some 433 people were in detention as a result of the widespread arrests made under the security laws after the township violence erupted earlier in the year. Of them, 102 were being held under the provisions of the Internal Security Act and were not facing specific charges and some 56 were schoolchildren. Some 114 people had been banned. On 31 December Department of Justice officials said that all those detained under the Internal Security Act had been released.

15 December In the most important of the political trials held that year, some nine members of the South African Students' Organization and the Black People's Convention, described as 'black consciousness' organizations, were found guilty under the Suppression of Terrorism Act of conspiring to endanger and endangering the maintenance of law and order. The 15-month trial was one of the longest in South African history.

The two other trials of international importance that year involved Cape Town and Johannesburg journalists. A reporter for the *Cape Times* and *Rand Daily Mail* was convicted of producing and distributing 'highly subversive and inflammatory pamphlets', while a *Cape Argus* journalist, his wife and a university lecturer were convicted on similar charges.

---

1 9 7 7

---

3 January The South African Defence Department releases an official account of South Africa's involvement in Angolan civil war. According to the report, the South African troops joined forces with the pro-Western National Union for the Total Independence of Angola (Unita) and the National Front for the Liberation of Angola to fight the Soviet and Cuban-backed Popular Movement for the Liberation of Angola (MPLA). It was the first time South Africa officially admitted joining forces with the pro-Western Angolan factions.

At the height of its involvement, South Africa had some 2,000 troops in Angola, compared to an estimated 13,000 Cuban soldiers. The US Department of Defence reported that South Africa and its allies controlled most of the Angolan coast at one point and could easily have taken the rest of the country. Unita leader Jonas Savimbi, however, wanted to reach a settlement with the MPLA, and South Africa agreed to a cease-fire until the Organization of African Unity (OAU) had negotiated a political settlement for the country. The OAU failed to reach an agreement and, by increasing its military aid to the Cuban and MPLA troops, forced the South Africans to withdraw. The country fell to the MPLA, which formed a government in Luanda.

5 January Black schools reopen in Soweto amid continued but diminishing student boycotts. On 10 January, firebombs exploded in Black schools in the Langa and Nyanga townships outside Cape Town despite government efforts to ensure the peaceful reopening of schools after more than six months of boycotts and violence. Sporadic school boycotts and unrest continued in the Black urban townships throughout the year. A major new development was that urban terrorism was beginning to threaten White safety. Bombs exploded in a crowded Johannesburg shopping mall in the White downtown area (24 November), at the police station in Germiston (6 December) and outside the railway station in Benoni. Although no one was hurt in any of the blasts, tensions and fears ran high. To counter this terrorism and anti-apartheid protests, the South African security police stepped up the number of detentions they made under security laws. An estimated 778 people had been held by police by November.

1 March The Reverend Leon Sullivan, a director of the General Motors Corporation, announces that 12 major US corporations had adopted a six-point programme of principles to promote racial equality in their South African plants. The points, known as the Sullivan Principles, were: the establishment of equal and fair employment practices; the integration of all company facilities; equal pay for equal or comparable work; an increase in the number of Black employees holding managerial positions; the development of training programmes for non-White workers; and the improvement in education, health facilities, housing and transportation for employees.

The companies who adopted the Sullivan Principles were: American Cyanamid Co., Burroughs Corp., Caltex Petroleum Co., Citicorp, Ford Motor Co., General Motors, IBM, International Harvester Co., 3M Co., Mobil Oil Corp., Otis Elevator Co. and Union Carbide Corp.

7 April Prime Minister John Vorster meets with the ambassadors of the US, Britain, France, West Germany and France to discuss the future of Namibia, which South Africa had administered in defiance of a UN resolution passed in 1966 terminating its mandate. At the Cape Town meeting, Vorster rejected their joint plan for South African withdrawal from Namibia and for the holding of UN-supervised elections. South Africa had earlier agreed to grant Namibian independence at the end of 1978 under a constitution dividing power along racial lines. Meanwhile, debate was under way in the Namibian capital of Windhoek on a constitutional conference to form an interim government, without the participation or support of the Black nationalist South West African Peoples' Organization (SWAPO). The five Western nations tried to convince Vorster to reach a compromise that would persuade the UN Security Council to stop the debate calling for an arms and trade embargo. Vorster said after the meeting that he welcomed discussion 'with any government' on the Namibian question but stressed that the Namibian people must approve of any independence plan. On 29 April, Vorster reported that some progress was being made in the efforts to find a compromise plan for the future of Namibia.

Despite worsening relations with the US, South Africa continued to support the five Western nations in their efforts to negotiate settlements in Rhodesia and Namibia. On 10 June, South Africa formally agreed to discontinue its plans to establish an ethnically based interim government in Namibia and to accept a transitional government that would include SWAPO representatives. It also accepted the holding of UN-sponsored elections in Namibia and announced the appointment of an administrator to govern until the election of a constituent assembly. On 1 September, the South African-appointed administrator general for Namibia, Justice Marthinus T. Steyn, assumed his duties, with SWAPO approval, in what was seen as the first step of a Western-sponsored independence plan for the territory. Among his first actions was abolishing the law prohibiting mixed marriages.

It became obvious in November and December, however, that they had reached a major stumbling-block in preparing for Namibian independence. SWAPO refused to participate in elections until South African troops had withdrawn from Namibia, while South Africa refused to remove its troops until SWAPO stopped the guerrilla war it had been conducting from bases in Angola.

18 May Prime Minister Vorster meets US Vice President Walter Mondale in Vienna. The meeting was later seen as marking the beginning of rapidly souring relations between the two countries. It was obvious after the talks ended that they had been heated on the subject of apartheid. After this meeting, South African Cabinet members began to make speeches that were more pointedly anti-US in tone. South Africa continued its rapid move, first seen in Vorster's New Year speech in January, away from the West and towards an isolationist stand. The US's controversial ambassador to the UN, Andrew Young, visited South Africa in May amid signs of worsening relations between the two countries but his visit was marked by moderation and a spirit of conciliation which surprised the South Africans.

Contacts between South African officials and Western diplomats on the issue of Rhodesia continued throughout the year. Andrew Young and British Foreign Secretary David Owen conducted shuttle diplomacy to try to find a solution. They met South African Prime Minister Vorster in Pretoria on 29 August.

15 June Four days of rioting to mark the first anniversary of the 16 June 1976 Soweto riots result in the deaths of eleven Blacks and one White. More than 30 other Blacks were injured and some 300 arrested in demonstrations commemorating the uprising in 1976 that led to more than seven months of violent upheaval.

28 June The opposition United Party, which was founded in 1934 and had held power from 1934 to 1948, votes to dissolve itself and to establish a new political party to seek moderate changes in the country's political structure. On 29 June, the former United Party and the small Democratic Party merged into the New Republic Party. Six former United Party Members of Parliament refused to join the new group, saying that its stand on race reform was 'wishy-washy'. Instead, the six began talks with the liberal Progressive Reform Party on the possibility of forming a union.

7 July Foreign Minister Roelof 'Pik' Botha and Agricultural Minister Hendrick Schoeman, in what was seen as a major departure from government policy, call for the repeal of two laws that made interracial sexual relations illegal. The two laws, the Immorality Act and the Mixed Marriages Act, were considered the basis of apartheid legislation but both men described them as 'not necessary for our survival'.

26 July The *Washington Post* reports the formation of the Soweto Committee of 10. The group was founded by former members of the advisory Soweto Urban Bantu Council, which had collapsed in June after the majority of its members resigned under pressure from the militant Students' Representative Council (SRC). The new group was made up of Black professionals and businessmen who wanted to represent the township's 1.2 million people in their relations with the South African government. The Committee of 10, which was thought to cooperate closely with the powerful SRC, had compiled a series of proposals by which Black residents would be responsible for the administration of Soweto's police, educational systems, local elections and municipal services. The committee also proposed making Soweto's governing Black council, and eventually other Black township councils also, equivalent to an autonomous South African (White) city council and to make it directly responsible to Parliament.

5 August In a speech seen as confirming the deterioration in South African–US relations, Prime Minister Vorster denounces US policy towards South Africa and appeals to the American people to reject President Jimmy Carter's approach to the problems in southern Africa. He warned that America's African policy would result in 'chaos and anarchy in South Africa' and that 'the end result . . . will be exactly the same as if [South Africa] were subverted by Marxists'.

20 August Prime Minister Vorster proposes a reorganization of the government to give more power to Asians and Coloureds. According to his plans to reform the constitution, two new parliaments would be established, one for Asians and one for Coloureds, in addition to the existing White parliament. The proposals were seen as a major admission that the government realized the Coloured and Asian communities could no longer be left out of the process of government. The plans, however, had no provisions for urban Blacks, who were only to be given political rights in the homelands. Although it was thought that the announcement of the reorganization signalled the beginning of a modest reform, the exclusion of Blacks reemphasized the government's policy that reforms would only take place within the policy of separate development.

23 August Prime Minister Vorster denies that South Africa is developing nuclear weapons. His first public statement on the issue came in response to a formal French warning on 22 August that there would be 'serious consequences' for South Africa if it staged a nuclear-weapons test. The warning followed an accusation by the Soviet Union that South Africa was 'nearing completion' of an atomic bomb and had built a nuclear testing site in the Kalahari Desert. The Soviets reportedly informed the US of this and the two countries cooperated in pressurizing South Africa to abandon the test. On 20 August, the US announced that it had formally asked South Africa if it intended to test a nuclear weapon and that South Africa had assured them that 'they do not have and do not intend to develop nuclear explosive devices for any purpose, either peaceful or as a weapon', a claim Vorster later denied. The US also said it was trying to convince the South Africans to put its nuclear reactors under the safeguards established by the Nuclear Nonproliferation Treaty, which South Africa had not signed.

5 September Two anti-apartheid opposition groups merge to form the Progressive Federal Party (PFP). The PFP had 18 seats in the 171-seat parliament and was made up of the 12 members of the liberal Progressive Reform Party and the six former members of the opposition United Party who had left that organization because they wanted to take a firmer stand against apartheid than the one taken by the United Party.

12 September Black Consciousness Movement leader Stephen Biko, a charismatic 30-year-old thought by many to be a future national leader, dies while in police detention. He was known as a moderate and highly respected leader and was considered a hero by many of the younger generation of Black township dwellers. Biko was at first reported to have died as the result of a hunger strike but it later emerged that he had succumbed to brain injuries suffered during a 'scuffle' in his cell.

Biko had been arrested on 18 August 1977 in Grahamstown for writing inflammatory pamphlets and inciting unrest among the Blacks of Port Elizabeth. He was held in prison in Port Elizabeth and kept naked, supposedly to prevent him from hanging himself with his clothing. It later emerged that during interrogation Biko had hit his head. Police say it happened during their attempts to subdue him after he became violent. After the incident, he was examined by a doctor who signed a certificate stating that he had exhibited 'no evidence of abnormal pathology', in spite of the fact that Biko was weak, suffered loss of appetite, had slurred speech and was hyperventilating – all signs of brain damage. Biko was transferred to Pretoria for treatment in a prison hospital on 12 September. He made the 750-mile (1,206.8-km) journey on the floor of a police vehicle and died in a Pretoria jail cell, not in hospital. He never received treatment for brain injuries.

International outcry followed as well as demands for an investigation. The official inquest found that he had died of extensive head injuries, obtained some eight days prior to his death. Those injuries had affected his circulation and caused kidney failure. The inquest into his death exonerated the police, saying, 'The available evidence does not prove that the death was brought about by any act or omission involving or amounting to an offence on the part of any person.' The US denounced the ruling saying they found it shocking. Reactions inside South Africa ranged from Justice Minister James Kruger saying that Biko's death 'leaves me cold' to some 10,000 Blacks and diplomats from 13 Western countries attending his funeral on 25 September. Biko's death led to a renewed wave of violence in the Black urban townships, especially in his home area of the Eastern Cape.

19 October In the most sweeping curbs in 20 years, the South African government bans some 18 anti-apartheid organizations, shuts down two major Black newspapers and bans or arrests some 50 people. The government said that the crackdown was aimed at countering a threat to 'the maintainence of law and order' which the proscribed organizations had posed. The Black People's Convention, the South African Students' Organization and other Black Consciousness organizations were all officially named as prohibited organizations, while their leaders were banned or detained in a series of pre-dawn raids staged by the police. The ecumenical Christian Institute was also proscribed and its leaders, Reverend Beyers Naude and Reverend Theo Kotze, were placed under banning orders. The Chairman of the Soweto Committee of 10 Nthato Motlana, who had been campaigning for self-government for Black communities, was arrested.

The greatest shocks to liberal opinion, both domestically and internationally, were thought to be the banning of Donald Woods, the editor of the *East London Daily Dispatch* and a well-known White campaigner against apartheid, and the closure of the moderate Black newspaper, *The World*, and its sister publication, *The Weekend World*. The editor of the two papers, Percy Qoboza, was among those detained. Those three events were seen by observers as directly threatening the freedom of the press and a warning of a like fate for newspapers that sympathized with Black aspirations. Woods, confined under his banning order to East London, escaped to Lesotho in December.

The international reaction to the detentions and bannings was both harsh and prolonged. On 4 November, the UN Security Council unanimously passed a resolution to impose a mandatory embargo on the shipment of arms to South Africa. It was the first time that a member nation was the subject of UN sanctions, as the only other country under UN sanctions, Rhodesia, was not a member. By the end of the year, South Africa was isolated as never before.

22 November The Polaroid Corporation announces that it is ending sales to South Africa after discovering that its distributor, Frank & Hirsch Ltd, had been supplying the South African government with cameras and film in violation of a 1971 agreement. Polaroid said that its products were used by the government to produce the photographs used in the passbooks that every Black over the age of 16 was required by law to carry.

Polaroid was the first US company to withdraw from the South African market in protest against apartheid. The company did not, however, lose a large amount of money by ending its sales to South Africa since its total annual sales in the country amounted to less than $4 million.

Few other US corporations, however, were expected to follow Polaroid's lead. On 23 November, the 130 member firms of the US Chamber of Commerce's Johannesburg chapter defended their presence in South Africa claiming that they provided Blacks with better job opportunities and higher living standards than they would otherwise enjoy.

On 4 December, the *New York Times* reported that some 350 US firms had business dealings with South Africa, with a total of $1.7 thousand million in direct investment there. This represented only 1.2 per cent of US foreign investment but 17 per cent of South Africa's total foreign investment.

24 November Rhodesian Prime Minister Ian Smith announces that his government will accept the principle of one man, one vote and Black majority rule. He had previously refused to negotiate on the basis of universal suffrage because he felt such a system would not provide adequate guarantees of security for the White minority. The announcement comes amid an intensification of the guerrilla war and after the apparent failure of joint British–US efforts to reach a political settlement to the country's problems.

30 November White South Africa goes to the polls in a general election that results in an overwhelming victory for the ruling National Party. Prime Minister Vorster, whose government won substantial support from the country's English-speaking Whites, claimed the victory was a mandate for the continuance of his apartheid policies.

Vorster said that he had held the snap election a year and a half early, and at the height of international uproar against South Africa, to demonstrate South Africa's rejection of international interference in its domestic affairs. His National Party won a total of 134 seats in the 165-seat Parliament, increased its majority by 18 seats and won 65 per cent of the popular vote. The liberal PFP emerged from the election with 17 seats to become the country's official Opposition party. It replaced the United Party, which had disbanded in June after 29 years as the Opposition. The PFP, which was founded in September, did well in the Cape Peninsula, a traditionally liberal area, and in Johannesburg's well-off suburbs, but it did not do very well anywhere else. The moderate New Republic Party won 10 seats, while the right-wing South Africa Party won three.

5 December Bophuthatswana becomes the second independent Black tribal homeland under South Africa's separate development programme. The new country was not recognized by any other nation except South Africa and the equally unrecognized first independent homeland of the Transkei.

Bophuthatswana's 16,000 square miles (41,400 square km) of territory was separated into six unconnected areas scattered across north central South Africa. It was considered to be potentially rich, with more than half of South Africa's deposits of platinum, but it was totally economically dependent upon South Africa. The South Africans were, in fact, furnishing over 70 per cent of the country's first yearly budget of $83 million.

Upon independence, Bophuthatswana became the homeland of some 2.5 million members of the Tswana tribe, some 1.4 million of whom worked and lived in South Africa. They automatically became Bophuthatswanan citizens and lost their South African citizenship under the provisions of the homelands policy. To protest against this policy, less than 13 per cent of the eligible voters participated in the September 1976 elections for an independent parliament. Chief Lucas Mangope, tribal Tswana leader and first president of the new country, won almost all the legislative seats.

1 9 7 8

1 February The worst scandal in South African history erupts when Auditor General F.G. Barrie presents to Parliament his report on the Department of Information. The report claimed that unnamed Information Department officials had been making unauthorized expenditures for the previous three years and criticized those officials for their frequent, expensive and unnecessary trips abroad. The report alleged that up to $460,000 had been spent on attracting favourable publicity for South Africa, without the Treasury or Parliament's knowledge. Before it was over, the scandal overshadowed all other events in South Africa and caused the resignation of John Vorster, first as prime minister and then as president, the resignation of a probable prime minister, 'Connie' Mulder, and the disgrace of the man who came up with the idea to improve South Africa's image abroad, Information Secretary Eschel Rhoodie. His plan was to set up a secret fund to finance the waging of 'psychological and propaganda warfare' to influence the 'opinion-formers and decision-takers' in the four targeted countries of the US, Britain, West Germany and France into forming favourable opinions of South Africa and to dispel the country's negative image abroad. The Information scandal also led to the emergence of Defence Minister P.W. Botha, a member of the *verligte* (enlightened) wing of the National Party, as prime minister. The scandal and Botha's attempts to contain it, however, caused great internal tensions in the ruling party.

3 March Rhodesian Prime Minister Ian Smith, Bishop Abel Muzorewa, Reverend Ndabaningi Sithole and Chief Jeremiah Chirau sign an internal settlement agreement that is intended to transfer power to the country's Black majority by 31 December 1978. The agreement was said to have paved the way for the establishment of a transitional government that would supervise the elections for a new Rhodesian parliament and the enactment of the country's new constitution. Under the agreement, Smith would retain the title of prime minister, while the chairmanship of the council of state would rotate among all four leaders. On 29 September, however, Smith announced that the elections for the new parliament would have to be delayed 'for purely mechanical reasons', thus virtually ruling out the handing over of power to the country's Black majority by the 31 December deadline.

The four visited Pretoria on 15 November for their first talks with P.W. Botha since he became prime minister. Botha reportedly warned them not to delay further a vote on majority rule, saying he would not support the Rhodesian interim government if the elections were put off past April 1979.

The Salisbury Agreement was dismissed outside Rhodesia as unacceptable and illegal. The UN rejected it on 14 March, as had the Organization of African Unity. The principal critic of the agreement was the Patriotic Front. The Front was an unstable alliance of the two main guerrilla movements operating outside Rhodesia, Joshua Nkomo's Zimbabwean African People's Union and the Marxist Zimbabwean African National Union led by Robert Mugabe. The Front boycotted the talks in Salisbury, which led to the agreement, and said it would not recognize the internal agreement. The US and Britain held that any settlement that did not include the Patriotic Front would not be acceptable to the people of Rhodesia as a whole, and continued their efforts throughout the year to reach a separate agreement with it.

14 March The South African Black Alliance (SABA) is formed by the (Black) Inkatha Movement, the (Coloured) Labour Party and the (Asian) Reform Party. The alliance, the country's first non-White multiracial political party, pressed for the abolition of apartheid and the adoption of a new, nonracial constitution for South Africa. It sought to change the South African system of government by presenting a 'united front' against the current political and social order and coordinating the actions of other anti-apartheid organizations, such as the liberal White groups. The Natal-based Zulu organization, Inkatha, was thought to be the main driving force behind the establishment of the alliance. SABA was led by Inkatha's head, Chief Gatsha Buthelezi.

25 April Prime Minister Vorster announces that his government will accept a Western-sponsored plan for independence of Namibia. The plan had been drawn up by the five Western members of the UN Security Council that made up the 'Western Five' contact group on Namibia: Britain, Canada, France, West Germany and the US.

Under the terms of the plan, Vorster agreed to the holding of a cease-fire in the continuing guerrilla war that was taking place in the northern section of Namibia, the holding of UN-supervised elections and the phased withdrawal of South African troops from the territory. The plan, although basically the same as earlier ones presented by the contact group, differed from the others in that it detailed the duties of the special UN representative who would govern the area during elections along with the South African administrator general. It called for South Africa to begin withdrawing its troops as soon as the UN approved the plan, with the exception of 1,500 men who would be stationed in two bases in the north of Namibia until the constituent assembly elections had been held and would be withdrawn completely after the election results were officially declared. The plan left the subject of Walvis Bay, Namibia's only deep-water port over which South Africa refused to relinquish its claim, to be decided by an independent Namibian government and South Africa. After obtaining South Africa's approval, the contact group concentrated on securing the agreement of the South West African People's Organization (SWAPO) to the plan. SWAPO released some additional demands on 28 April, but the Western Five said they were confident they could get SWAPO agreement at their next meeting.

The future of the talks, however, was thrown into doubt when South African troops conducted a cross-border raid into Angola on 4 May, destroying SWAPO guerrilla bases and killing a considerable number of people, including women and children. South Africa said the 'limited military action' had been staged in response to a recent rise in the number of guerrilla attacks carried out in Namibia from bases in Angola. As a result of the raid, SWAPO broke off the negotiations on the Western plan and continued its guerrilla activity in Namibia.

30 April The Azanian People's Organization (Azapo) is founded to press for the abolition of apartheid and the establishment of a nonracial society. Azania was the Black nationalists' name for South Africa. Like the other new multiracial party formed that year, the Black Alliance, the Azapo membership was open to all non-Whites and was committed to peaceful change but, unlike the alliance, it rejected cooperation with the White government. Two of Azapo's leaders were detained by police on 5 May but later released.

8 May Prime Minister Vorster publicly addresses the issue of the 'Information scandal' when he accepts full responsibility for allocating the secret funds to the Information Department. He confirmed that, since 1972, the funds had been authorized by the government without the knowledge of Parliament or the Treasury, and administered by the Ministry of Information, which oversaw the Department of Information. Much of the money was taken from the Defence Department's enormous budget. Vorster claimed that the money was used to fight 'the psychological and propaganda onslaught against the Republic', but added that he abhorred the irregular way that some of the funds had been spent and announced that an investigation would be opened to determine if the secret government funds had been misused.

11 June SWAPO, a guerrilla organization fighting for the independence of Namibia, announces it will resume talks with the five-nation Western contact group that was attempting to negotiate a Namibian settlement with SWAPO and the South African government.

The announcement came at the end of a two-day meeting between SWAPO leaders and representatives of Angola, Botswana, Mozambique, Tanzania and Zambia. Observers believed that SWAPO's decision to resume negotiations was the result of the contact group's intensive behind-the-scenes diplomatic efforts and strong pressure from the front line presidents.

On 20 June, however, the South African government announced that it was unilaterally moving ahead with its plans to stage constituent assembly elections in Namibia by beginning voter registration.

15 June Prime Minister Vorster announces the abolition of the Department of Information. He also announced that Information Secretary Eschel Rhoodie, who had headed the agency, had resigned and that the Department's legitimate functions would be transferred to other ministries.

27 July The UN Security Council overwhelmingly approves the plan of the five Western members of the council for the independence of Namibia and passes a resolution that it should be put into operation as soon as possible. The two-part plan called for the a UN peace-keeping force to monitor the cease-fire and elections and for Namibia's only deep water port, Walvis Bay, to be part of an independent Namibia.

The Walvis Bay resolution caused a dispute since South Africa had refused to give up its claim to the port. South African Foreign Minister Roelof 'Pik' Botha said the resolution might cause South Africa to reconsider its acceptance of the Namibian agreement. He added, however, that South Africa was still committed to discussing the future status of the port with an independent Namibia, as was spelt out in the original agreement it had reached with the contact group in April. Despite the problem over Walvis Bay, the UN described the Namibian settlement as a triumph for Western diplomacy.

6 August Martti Ahtisaari, United Nations Secretary General Kurt Waldheim's special representative for Namibia, arrives in the Namibian capital of Windhoek to discuss the territory's transition to independence. The South African government had agreed to Ahtisaari's visit as part of the Security Council's plan for Namibian independence, but reserved its decision on whether to accept that plan until after receiving his report. Prime Minister Vorster had accepted the plan in April but withdrew that acceptance as a result of the Security Council's July adoption of a resolution declaring Walvis Bay part of an independent Namibia, in spite of earlier agreeing that the issue would be decided between the Namibian and South African governments after Namibia's independence.

Ahtisaari met the South African-appointed Administrator General Justice M.T. Steyn for talks on drawing up a schedule for the implementation of the contact group's independence plan, but he was unable to get the two sides to agree on a structure for the transition of power. He also failed to get South Africa to discontinue its voter registration drive or to abandon its insistence on 31 December 1978 as the date for independence.

Meanwhile, on 30 August, Waldheim released the details of the UN's programme for implementing the Western plan for Namibian independence. The plan called for the deployment of a 7,500-strong UN task force, making it the largest UN operation of this nature since the UN intervention in the Congo in the 1960s. The following day, however, Pik Botha informed the UN that South Africa objected to the size of the task force, agreeing to only a maximum of 5,000 troops. South Africa also rejected the UN's discarding of the agreed date for both elections and independence.

20 September John Vorster, South African prime minister since 1966, shocks the nation by announcing his resignation from the post on the grounds of ill health. He let it be known, however, that he was available to fill the largely ceremonial position created by the death of state president Nicolaas Diederichs on 21 August. Parliament overwhelmingly elected Vorster president on 29 September, thus constitutionally removing him from the political fallout caused by the 'Information scandal' and ensuring he would not participate in the continuing controversy it had caused.

28 September Defence Minister P.W. Botha is elected by a National Party caucus to succeed John Vorster as prime minister. He was a member of the *verligte* (enlightened) branch of the party and was known to be committed to the introduction of a new constitution that would give Coloureds and Asians a greater say in the running of the country. Immediately upon his election, Botha said that he would work to improve relations among the races but ruled out any possibility of totally abandoning apartheid. It was, however, expected as he took office that the conservative segment in the party would limit his freedom of action in introducing reforms.

16 October In what is seen as a last-minute attempt to save the Namibian peace plan, the group of five Western foreign ministers fly to Pretoria for talks with South African officials aimed at avoiding the complete breakdown of the Namibian negotiations. The trip had become necessary after former Prime Minister Vorster unexpectedly announced his government's rejection of the UN plan for the territory's independence on 20 September, along with his resignation from the premiership.

The Security Council, on 29 September, voted to give South Africa until 23 October to either accept the plan or face the prospect of having further economic sanctions imposed against it. The South African Cabinet insisted on 3 October that it had not rejected the plan and that the Namibian elections, which it had unilaterally rescheduled for December, would not bar any future negotiations with the UN.

At the meetings, the contact group failed to get South Africa to abandon its plans to hold the constituent assembly elections. It did reach a compromise on the size and national composition of the UN peace-keeping force for Namibia and on the role of the South African-appointed administrator general for Namibia, whose authority the UN had previously refused to acknowledge. South Africa also agreed to reopen talks with the UN's special representative for Namibia, Maarti

Ahtisaari, on the implementation of the Waldheim report released in August. South Africa insisted on going ahead with its elections but, on 19 October, Prime Minister P.W. Botha accepted that UN-sponsored elections would be 'the verdict of the people of South West Africa'. The South Africans promised to do everything they could to persuade Namibia's newly elected constituent assembly to cooperate in holding the second, UN-sponsored, elections. South Africa also indicated that its troops would be withdrawn from the territory only when hostilities had completely ended. It still insisted on setting a firm date for the UN elections, which were to be held whether the violence had ended or not and, thus, whether South African troops were still in the country or not.

29 October A further scandal involving the disbanded Department of Information erupts when the South African press reveals that some of the department's funds had been used to finance the launching and running of a pro-government English-language newspaper.

The *Sunday Express*, a weekly English-language newspaper based in Johannesburg, reported that the government had contributed almost $14 million to the creation of the *Citizen* in 1976 in an attempt to compete against the anti-government views voiced by most of the country's English-language publications.

The *Express*'s allegations were followed on 30 October by a report in South Africa's most influential English-language newspaper, the *Rand Daily Mail*, that another $15 million of Department of Information money had 'disappeared' into private corporate hands.

2 November Justice Anton Mostert releases information gathered from his one-man judicial inquiry into exchange regulations, ordered when the information scandal first broke out in June, despite Prime Minister Botha's request that he keep the findings of his inquiry secret. The information suggested that officials of the Department of Information had committed certain irregularities. It indicated that the department had loaned South African millionaire Louis Luyt some $6.9 million to finance the purchase of the powerful South African Associated Newspapers (SAAN), which published the anti-government *Rand Daily Mail*, *Sunday Express* and other English-language opposition papers. Mostert alleged that when Luyt's bid for SAAN failed, the department loaned him on favourable terms the $13.8 million he needed to launch the pro-government English-language newspaper, the *Citizen*. The money was given on the strict understanding that Information Secretary Eschel Rhoodie maintain full editorial control.

Mostert's report implicated former Information Minister 'Connie' Mulder and led to his resignation from the Cabinet on 7 November and as leader of the Transvaal wing of the ruling National Party on 11 November. Former Prime Minister Vorster, former head of the Department of Information Eschel Rhoodie and General Hendrik van den Bergh, head of the Bureau of State Security, were all also implicated.

Botha wound up the Mostert commission on 7 November and dismissed Mostert for having made his findings public. Amid opposition objections that he was engaging in a cover-up by silencing Mostert, Botha then appointed a commission of inquiry into the Information scandal which was headed by Justice Rudolf Erasmus of the Cape province Supreme Court.

25 November Andries Treurnicht, known as a hardline supporter of the government's apartheid policies, is elected to head the powerful Transvaal wing of the ruling National Party. Treurnicht thus became the country's second most powerful man, after the prime minister, since the Transvaal representatives commanded the largest block of seats in parliament. Observers believed that the conservative Treurnicht's leadership might influence the Transvaal members of parliament to block Botha's reforms.

Treurnicht replaced former leader Connie Mulder, who resigned as result of the Information scandal, by beating the moderate candidates favoured by Prime Minister Botha. Many believed that his victory resulted from the fact that a considerable number of conservative members of the National Party were angered by Botha's forcing Mulder to resign. They apparently felt that there was nothing wrong with using public funds to finance pro-government projects and felt that Mulder, Information Secretary Eschel Rhoodie and General van den Bergh had been made the government's scapegoats.

4 December White voters in Namibia go to the polls to elect a constituent assembly in controversial elections that were boycotted by the Black opposition parties. They were also opposed by the UN, who feared South Africa would attempt to impose an 'internal solution' on the Namibian problem that would not take into account the nationalist SWAPO. The moderate, multiracial Democratic Turnhalle Alliance won 41 of the 50 seats in the assembly and received some 82 per cent of the vote. The results of the election were announced on 15 December. Immediately upon election, the alliance indicated that it was willing to cooperate with UN-sponsored elections.

On 12 December, SWAPO leader Sam Nujoma called on Pretoria to organize 'free and fair' elections in Namibia under UN supervision, in which he said SWAPO would participate. He added that if the South Africans refused, SWAPO would begin a 'protracted armed struggle' against the South African-sponsored government in Namibia.

5 December The three-member commission into the Information scandal, led by Judge Rudolf Erasmus, reports that officials of the disbanded Department of Information had misappropriated public funds and were engaged in illicit practices. The commission's findings confirmed what had already been known but actually added little to it.

The commission charged Information Secretary Eschel Rhoodie and his brother Deneys, deputy head of the department, with financial misconduct; it was recommended that criminal charges be pressed against them. Their passports were revoked but Eschel Rhoodie had already left South Africa. It also criticized former Information Minister Connie Mulder, who had been forced out of politics as result of earlier revelations, for 'serious irregularities' and incompetence in an attempt to cover up the scandal. General Hendrik van den Bergh, head of the South African security police, was similarly charged.

The commission did not level charges against either President Vorster or Prime Minister Botha, who was defence minister during the time that the money was being siphoned off the defence budget to finance the Department of Information's secret operations. To find Vorster innocent, the commission had to totally ignore the testimony of Rhoodie, Mulder and van den Bergh, all of whom repeatedly stated that Vorster had been involved from the beginning and had received regular reports on the secret projects' progress.

22 December The South African government agrees to a UN plan for the independence of Namibia and to the deployment of a UN peace-keeping force in the territory until after the UN-sponsored elections.

South Africa had agreed to the plan in April but withdrew its support in September after a dispute over the size of the UN force. Pretoria told Secretary General Kurt Waldheim that it accepted figures of 1,500 South African soldiers and 7,500 UN troops to supervise the transition to independence. The peacekeepers were scheduled to arrive in Namibia in early 1979 and the UN-sponsored elections would be held seven month later.

Waldheim for his part agreed to the South Africans' demand that the guerrilla war being waged by the nationalist SWAPO completely end before it carried out the UN's proposals. He announced that both sides had agreed to a comprehensive ceasefire and said that he wanted the elections to be held no later than 30 September 1979. The year thus ended with the talks continuing.

5 March The South African government formally rejects a UN-sponsored cease-fire plan for Namibia. The following day, South Africa carried out a major raid against South West African People's Organization (SWAPO) guerrilla bases in Angola. South Africa said that it rejected the plan, which had been scheduled to come into effect the following week, because it would allow SWAPO guerrillas based in Namibia to be armed during the proposed election for the independence government and because it did not provide for UN monitoring of SWAPO bases in Angola and Zambia. The South Africans said that without monitoring of such bases, SWAPO could infiltrate Namibia from those bases and either influence the elections or forcefully take over the new government.

2 April The commission headed by Judge Rudolf Erasmus issues its report on the alleged misuse of public funds by the defunct Department of Information. The commission concluded that the then prime minister and current president, John Vorster, had not concealed any knowledge of the Department's irregular activities from Parliament, and cleared his Cabinet of any wrong-doings. The report contradicted the statements made to the commission by the two men most closely linked to the scandal, Information Minister Connie Mulder and his subordinate, Eschel Rhoodie, both of whom contended that Vorster had been informed of and given his approval to the department's plans to buy the US newspaper, the *Washington Star*, and to finance the pro-government South African newspaper, the *Citizen*.

Mulder was ousted from the ruling National party on 6 April for his refusal to retract his accusations against Vorster. He had earlier been warned by the party to either publicly endorse the Erasmus commission's report or face expulsion, but he had refused to accept sole responsibility for the scandal.

17 April Four days of polling begins in Rhodesia in the first one man, one vote elections in the breakaway British colony's history. The elections were held under the transitional government's constitution, published on 2 January, passed by Parliament on 20 January and approved in a Whites-only referendum on 30 January. It provided for a 100-seat House of Assembly, of which 28 seats were to be reserved for Whites for 10 years after independence. Under the terms of the constitution, the country would in future be called Zimbabwe Rhodesia. It had been expected that the name would simply be Zimbabwe, the nationalists' choice, but Rhodesia was apparently added to boost White morale.

When the results were announced on 24 April, Bishop Abel Muzorewa was set to become Zimbabwe Rhodesia's first Black leader, with his United African National Council winning 51 seats. Some 63.97 per cent of the Black electorate participated in the vote. Muzorewa's main rival, Reverend Ndabaningi Sithole and his Zimbabwe African National Union won 12 seats. He charged that the election was filled with 'grave irregularities' but did not formally repudiate the vote. Although some international observers called the vote 'free and fair', others held that the results were unacceptable as the election had been conducted under the provisions of a constitution that had been approved only by Whites.

Non-Blacks voted on 10 April for 20 of the 28 seats reserved for them, while the candidates for the remaining eight seats were chosen by former Prime Minister Ian Smith's Rhodesian Front at a later date. The guerrilla Patriotic Front, led by Robert Mugabe and Joshua Nkomo, refused to take part in the elections. It vowed to continue its seven-year guerrilla war, which it did with mounting ferocity.

1 May A government-appointed commission of businessmen, labour leaders and advisers issues the report of its inquiry into the country's labour conditions and calls for sweeping changes in racial laws as applied to the job market. The 14-member commission was headed by the prime minister's adviser, Nicolaas Wiehahn. It recommended the official recognition of Black trade unions, enabling them to hold collective bargaining with employers and to strike, and for an end to the enforcement of apartheid legislation on the shop floor. Prime Minister P.W. Botha, while rejecting a recommendation to extend labour rights to South Africa's Black migrant work force, accepted 'in principle' all of the commission's other recommendations and, on 2 May, Labour Minister Stephanus Botha announced that the government was removing most of the restrictions on Black employment, including the ban on Black trade unions.

8 May The government releases a report by a former economic adviser to the prime minister, Pieter Riekert, that calls for the removal of some restrictions on the country's Black population. The report, which tried to make the management of apartheid more efficient, recommended that those aspects of the system that were time consuming and difficult to administer be abolished but that the system itself be retained. The report proposed lifting both the curfew imposed on Black urban residents and the three-day limit to cities by Blacks without urban residency permits. It supported the basic internal passport system itself since it prevented the free migration to the cities of rural Blacks. The report also recommended that Black urban migration be more closely tied to job requirements and the availability of housing. It recommended that the wives of Black workers be issued with residence permits and proposed that White employers be penalized for hiring Blacks without employment permits. At present, only the Blacks were at fault in those situations.

Economic Affairs Minister J. Christiaan Heunis announced on 8 May that the government accepted most of the Riekert report's recommendations.

1 June The new state of Zimbabwe Rhodesia formally comes into being as the country's new constitution, derived on the basis of the internal settlement agreement, comes into effect. The installation of the new Black government of Prime Minister Bishop Abel Muzorewa ends some 89 years of White rule.

Muzorewa had taken the oath of office as prime minister on 29 May and announced his 17-member Cabinet the following day. To no one's surprise, former Prime Minister Ian Smith found a seat in the Cabinet, but was unexpectedly named minister without portfolio. Observers saw that as a sign of his greatly reduced power.

On 22 May, the new Conservative government in Britain announced that it would send a permanent representative to Zimbabwe Rhodesia in order to maintain 'the closest possible contact' with the new Black government. The British said they would move slowly on the question of recognizing the new government so as to avoid a total break in diplomatic relations with the rest of Black Africa, who were denying the new country recognition because of their belief that the elections were rigged.

4 June The final report of the Erasmus commission inquiry into the Information scandal results in the resignation of President John Vorster. The report criticized Vorster's judgement as prime minister in relation to the actions of the Department of Information and said that he must take some of the responsibility for the Department's irregular activities. The final report revised one issued in April that had cleared him of any wrong-doing. It said that Vorster 'knew everything about the basic financial arrangements for the department's funds' and added that 'because he did not reveal irregularities that came to his attention, concealed them from the Cabinet and delayed taking purposeful steps to put an end to this wrong state of affairs, he is jointly responsible for the fact that the irregularities continued'. The commission, however, cleared both Prime Minister P.W. Botha and Finance Minister Owen Horwood of complicity in the scandal saying they had 'inherited' it from Vorster.

Despite the present government's complete exoneration, the scandal and Vorster's resignation badly affected the Afrikaner community. Vorster, since he became prime minister in 1966, had come to personify the Afrikaner values of moral correctness and determination to many Afrikaners. The discovery that members of his government had misused official funds and that he had lied about his involvement in a scheme to make foreign bribes was seen by observers as having eroded Afrikaner self-confidence.

1 August The Commonwealth heads of government meeting opens in the Zambian capital of Lusaka. The leaders adopted a nine-point plan worked out by Britain, Australia, Jamaica, Nigerian, Tanzania and Zambia. The plan was designed to obtain genuine Black majority rule by holding free and fair elections supervised by Britain. They also established a framework to hold an all-party constitutional conference in London in September. The aim of the conference would be to reach an internationally acceptable agreement by 15 November for a cease-fire and an interim administration in preparation for the new elections.

1 August Prime Minister Botha names Gerrit Viljoen as the new administrator general of Namibia to replace Marthinus Steyn. Observers believed that the change came as a result of conservative White anger against what they saw as Steyn's liberal tendencies. Viljoen, by contrast, was reported to be the head of the powerful Afrikaner secret society, the Broederbond. While supporting the basic tenets of apartheid, Viljoen reportedly agreed that some concessions would have to be made to urban Blacks. Botha reportedly hoped that Viljoen's Broederbond connection and conservative image would win back the support of disaffected conservative Whites, while at the same time Viljoen would implement enough reforms so that South Africa's plans for Namibia would have some acceptance among Blacks and the international community.

5 August Prime Minister Botha opens the annual meeting of the Natal branch of the National Party in Durban. He used the occasion to announce a 12-point plan which he said would ensure the country's security and progress. He rejected both the demands of the left wing of the party for one man, one vote and the right wing's insistence on total separation of the races under White domination. Botha, instead, insisted that he stood for the recognition of the rights of all groups in the country and a division of power. Among his points were: the acceptance of a multinational society and the existence of minority groups; the abolition of all unnecessary discriminatory measures; the creation of a constellation of South African states; and the promotion of a free enterprise system.

31 August Prime Minister Botha becomes the first South African leader to visit the Black township of Soweto. His visit to the area that was home to more than 1.5 million Blacks was largely ignored by Soweto's residents. He was, however, warmly received by some 5,000 residents to whom he said that 'this is not just a courtesy call. This is one of the highlights of my career.' He said that his presence and that of his Cabinet colleagues was 'proof that we are prepared to open our hearts to you'.

The visit was part of a series of symbolic gestures which, while not being accompanied by any concrete new policy proposals, was seen as proof of Botha's desire to reform the apartheid system.

10 September Zimbabwe Rhodesian Prime Minister Bishop Abel Muzorewa, Patriotic Front leaders Robert Mugabe and Joshua Nkomo and Rhodesian Front leader Ian Smith meet under British auspices at Lancaster House in London for an all-party constitutional conference. British Foreign Secretary Lord Carrington chaired the meetings.

An agreement was reached on the independence constitution and cease-fire by early December, allowing Britain to proceed with appointing Lord Soames as governor. His arrival in Salisbury on 12 December was seen as marking the end of its 15-year rebellion against the Crown. His assumption of his duties as governor came only after Britain had first obtained the agreement of the Patriotic Front and the Rhodesian government on a cease-fire to end the seven-year guerrilla war.

13 September The South African government formally declares the Black homeland of Venda independent as part of its policy of separate development.

South Africa and the other two nominally independent homelands of the Transkei and Bophuthatswana are the only countries to recognize Venda's independence. The move automatically deprived South Africa's 500,000 Venda tribesmen of their South African citizenship and made them citizens of the new homeland.

Venda was made up of some 2,500 square miles (6,475 square km) of land, in two sections, in northeastern Transvaal. Two-thirds of its adult men lived or worked in South Africa and the remittance of their salaries made up 77 per cent of the new country's gross national produce. South Africa was to provide some $36.3 million of Venda's $43.6 million 1979 budget.

Observers saw Prime Minister Botha's continuation of the separate development policy as proof that his reform policies were designed to create an urban Black middle class to protect South Africa against Black revolutionary tendencies and that those policies would be carried out at the expense of 'poor and unemployed Black masses who did not qualify for permanent urban residence and employment and would be thrust away out of sight in the impoverished and overcrowded rural reserve areas'.

22 September A US reconnaissance satellite picks up traces of a nuclear explosion off the southern coast of South Africa. The US, in releasing a report on the occurrence on 25 October, said that it did not know who was responsible for the explosion, but suspicion immediately centred on South Africa. The South African government, who had been believed to be preparing for a nuclear test as early as 1977, denied any knowledge of or responsibility for the explosion but refused to either confirm or deny that it had the ability to detonate an atomic blast.

The pattern of the twin flashes of light picked up by the Vela surveillance satellite indicated a nuclear explosion, but scientists maintained that they could also have be caused by a natural phenomenon. The US had to admit on 26 October that it was 'not clear that there has been a nuclear detonation'. US monitoring equipment deployed to the area after the incident failed to detect any corroborating evidence, such as atmospheric radiation, of a nuclear test.

25 September Labour Minister Stephanus Botha makes a major concession to Black workers when he announces that all Blacks, including those who are officially resident in the homelands, will be able to join trade unions at their work places.

Parliament had passed legislation in May that gave urban Blacks limited collective bargaining rights while prohibiting migrant workers from being unionized. The country's unofficial Black unions had refused to apply for official recognition under the provisions of the law because of its exclusion of migrant workers. As a result of prolonged criticism from both Whites and Blacks, Botha decided to allow migrant workers to unionize. Under the new rules, only Blacks from other African countries were excluded from the Black unions.

The labour legislation still prohibited multiracial unions, while White unions were still permitted to negotiate the closed-shop contracts that effectively excluded Blacks from certain jobs.

8 October Former Information Secretary Eschel Rhoodie, who had been at the centre of the Information scandal, is jailed for six years for embezzlement of government funds. Rhoodie had fled South Africa in November 1978 after being charged with misusing the government's secret propaganda funds and was arrested in France in July 1979. He was extradited in August, despite the fact that no formal extradition treaty existed between France and South Africa, after a French court rejected his defence that the charges against him were political in nature. He was later granted bail pending an appeal.

8 November A Johannesburg by-election results in the ruling National Party losing a parliamentary seat for the first time since 1970. The loss of the seat did not hurt the party's massive majority in Parliament but was seen as a sign of conservative White discontent with Botha's reformist policies.

Botha insisted that the result would not affect his attempts to reform the country's racial legislation, but he told representatives of the Coloured Representative Council the following day that 'One man, one vote in this country is out. That is never.'

12 November A UN-sponsored conference on Namibia opens in Geneva after several months of stalemate in the peace negotiations. In a bid to block the impasse, the UN proposed a plan for the establishment of a demilitarized zone on both sides of the Angolan–Namibian border. The zone was intended to prevent the infiltration of Namibia by SWAPO forces from their bases in Angola and Zambia during the election campaign. The conference ended on 16 November with all sides agreeing to the plan except South Africa. The South Africa government did, however, promise to study the proposal and on 5 December agreed to it in principle while presenting several detailed objections.

21 November The South African subsidiary of the Ford Motor Company rules that 700 of their workers had effectively resigned as a result of their third walkout in four weeks. The company's problems with its Black workforce had started in early November when it dismissed Black employee Thozamile Botha for unauthorized absences. His co-workers at the plant in Port Elizabeth contended that he was fired because of his political activities as leader of Port Elizabeth's Black Civic Organization and not for his attendance record. His dismissal sparked off a wave of unrest in the eastern Cape which observers said was caused by political activists. Blacks staged three days of strikes to demand Botha's reinstatement. When the company agreed to their demand, White workers struck saying that the company was showing favouritism to Blacks. The Blacks then began a series of strikes to demand the firing of a White foreman for making racist remarks about Blacks. As a result of this action, the company decided that the Blacks were no longer its employees but that they would be permitted to reapply for their old jobs. The situation had returned to normal by early December, with many workers seeking reemployment at their old companies.

21 December A peace treaty to end the seven-year guerrilla war in Zimbabwe Rhodesia is signed at London's Lancaster House by Robert Mugabe and Joshua Nkomo for the Patriotic Front and Prime Minister Bishop Abel Muzorewa for the government. The Lancaster House agreement was signed seven years to the day that the guerrilla war, which claimed over 20,000 lives, started. Under the terms of the cease-fire, all troops movements across the country's borders were to stop by midnight on 21 December, while the truce would formally go into effect on 27 December. The governor of Zimbabwe Rhodesia, Lord Soames, granted an amnesty to all Patriotic Front guerrillas and nationalist exiles and declared the Front a legal party.

In recognition of the achievement, the UN Security Council voted at the same time to lift the trade sanctions which had been imposed against the country in 1966, while the front line African states of Angola, Botswana, Mozambique, Tanzania and Zambia declared on 23 December that they had ended their economic boycott of the country, permitting the opening of its borders with Botswana, Zambia and Mozambique. A 1,300-man Commonwealth peace-keeping force began to take up its monitoring positions on 23 December to oversee the assembling of both government troops and guerrillas, as stipulated in the cease-fire.

---

1 9 8 0

18 January Worldwide gold prices jump to an all-time record price of $835 an ounce. South Africa and the world's other main gold producer, the Soviet Union, were the main beneficiaries of the metal's meteoric rise in price. The buoyancy in gold and the resulting rise in stock market prices caused an economic boom in South Africa. The price of gold throughout the year averaged more than $600, which was double the 1979 figure. Meanwhile, the value of the daily trading on the Johannesburg stock exchange was over R3 million, which was more than an entire week's figures of less than a year previously.

The boom was also aided by the belief among investors that the political situation in South Africa was not putting their investments at risk. As a result of the boom, Finance Minister Owen Horwood was able to introduce a budget on 26 March that made major cuts in income taxes while increasing pensions, subsidies and special funds for Blacks. The result was a country enjoying unprecedented prosperity, while political tensions continued to simmer.

Critics of Prime Minister P.W. Botha's slowness in introducing concrete reforms to South Africa's racial legislation complained that the country's enviable economic condition should have enabled him to proceed with his social advances. They contended that instead of moving forward, his reforms appeared to falter in the face of intense right-wing opposition.

4 March The results of Zimbabwe's first one-man, one-vote elections are announced. The Zimbabwe African National Union-Patriotic Front took 57 of the 80 seats reserved for Blacks in the new 100-seat parliament and Governor Lord Soames asked its leader, Robert Mugabe, to form the new government. The Zimbabwe African Peoples Union (ZAPU) party of Mugabe's former guerrilla colleague, Joshua Nkomo, won 20 seats and the United African National Council, led by the prime minister of the transitional Zimbabwe Rhodesian government Bishop Abel Muzorewa, won three. In the separate White vote, held on 14 February, former Prime Minister Ian Smith's Rhodesia Front captured all 20 seats reserved for Whites. The elections had been held under British supervision and were observed by an 11-nation Commonwealth team as well as independent electoral observers. All observer groups declared that the elections, conducted under difficult circumstances, were 'free, fair, secret and without undue intimidation'. Some 94 per cent of the Black electorate had participated in the voting.

Mugabe was formally appointed prime minister on 11 March after submitting his list of ministerial appointments to Lord Soames. He described his 22-member Cabinet as an attempt to reassure, reconcile and unify all Zimbabweans. It included two Whites and four members of his main rival, ZAPU. ZAPU leader Joshua Nkomo turned down Mugabe's offer of the largely ceremonial position of president and became home affairs minister. Mugabe went out of his way to reassure Whites that their interests would be taken into account by his government, saying: 'We will insure that there is a place for everybody in this country.' Although an avowed Marxist, Mugabe went on to add that as the country's economic structure was based on capitalism, 'whatever ideas we have must build on that'. His promise of moderation was also extended to his South African neighbour, of which he said: 'The reality is that we have to coexist with them', and he added, 'We should pledge ourselves ... to noninterference in South African affairs and they to noninterference in our affairs.' But by 1 September South African–Zimbabwean relations had deteriorated to such an extent that Mugabe severed diplomatic ties.

7 March A public disagreement between Prime Minister Botha and Minister of Public Works Andries Treurnicht over Botha's reformist policies breaks out when Botha criticizes Treurnicht for a speech he gave protesting the participation of a Coloured team in a national schools rugby festival. Botha's public condemnation of Treurnicht led observers to report that Botha was trying to oust the right-wing Treurnicht from the Cabinet. Treurnicht emerged, however, from a Cabinet meeting on 11 March and a parliamentary caucus meeting on 12 March still in the Cabinet. Observers saw Botha's inability to get rid of Treurnicht as an indication that the party's right wing was still powerful and as a warning that Botha would not be able to introduce any reforms without encountering stiff opposition.

17 April The independent nation of Zimbabwe officially comes into being at midnight when Britain's Prince Charles formally hands over the new country's charter of independence to the Reverend Canaan Banana. Banana was then sworn in as president and Robert Mugabe took the oath of office as prime minister. The independence ceremonies marked Zimbabwe's return to the international community after 14 years of political and economic isolation caused by its illegal unilateral declaration of independence from Britain.

22 April Demonstrations staged by Coloured schoolchildren in Cape Town, Durban and Johannesburg to challenge the government's unequal spending on White and non-White education are broken up by police using tear gas. Thousands of other students join in the protests over the next several weeks and boycott classes. The action was seen as proof that the alienation of the country's young Coloureds and Blacks, which most observers dated to the 1976 Soweto riots, was intensifying. Students staged boycotts, demonstrations and marches, particularly in the Eastern Cape and Cape peninsula. By the end of the year some 768 people had been arrested and detained without trial as a result of the students' activities. The Coloured students returned to the classrooms only after Prime Minister Botha announced on 5 May that he considered their complaints 'justifiable' and promised to undertake an examination of the country's policies on educational spending, but sporadic protests continued.

8 May Prime Minister Botha accepts the recommendations of the Schlebusch commission, which issued its interim report the previous day, to abolish the Senate and create a 60-member multiracial president's council to advise the president on major political, economic and community issues. The council was to be made up of Whites, Coloureds and Asians, while Blacks were to be represented in a separate council. The decision to exclude Blacks adhered to the traditional Nationalist policy of separate development by which Blacks had political rights only in the homelands.

On 2 October, Botha announced the names of 54 people who would serve on the commission, the first multiracial body established since the National Party came to power in 1948. Only 15 non-Whites agreed to become commissioners as a result of a boycott protesting the exclusion of Blacks The opposition Progressive Federal Party refused to participate for the same reason. Botha had to abandon his original plan to establish a separate Black council after Black leaders, including Zulu leader Chief Gatsha Buthelezi, voiced their strong opposition to it.

The all-party commission, established in 1979 under the leadership of Justice and Interior Minister A.L. Schlebusch, had been given the task of studying ways to change the South African constitution. Observers saw Botha's commitment to changing the constitution as one of the most important political initiatives of his administration.

12 May The South African government informs the UN that, although it is still interested in granting Namibia independence, it requires more assurances that the South West African People's Organization (SWAPO) guerrillas will abide by the terms of any agreement worked out between the UN and South Africa. Foreign Minister Roelof 'Pik' Botha told UN Secretary General Kurt Waldheim that South Africa was sceptical of the UN's commitment to impartial elections and cited UN Security Council Resolution 435, which described SWAPO as the 'sole and authentic representative of the people of Namibia', as proof of their partiality towards the guerrilla group. Resolution 435, which also provided for UN-supervised elections for Namibia, had previously been approved by both South Africa and SWAPO. Although most of the major sticking points to a settlement had been resolved during the course of the protracted negotiations, mutual mistrust and suspicion between the South Africans and SWAPO delayed the implementation of the resolution.

Observers also believed that South Africa was intentionally slowing the pace of the UN talks so it could strengthen the Namibian constituent assembly that it had established in the territory in the hope that the assembly could eventually win general public support. Towards that end, Pik Botha announced on 1 May that the government would proceed with its plans to give the assembly legislative powers.

1 June Storage tanks at the South African Oil, Coal and Gas Corporation synthetic fuel plant at Sasolburg, near Johannesburg, are bombed as the culmination of two weeks of anti-government demonstrations by South Africa's non-White communities. Oliver Tambo, leader of the banned African National Congress, claimed that his organization had been responsible for the blast, which caused considerable damage. The bombing was one of several violent attacks the banned organization carried out during the year. The sabotage, and the student boycotts and industrial action that preceded it, led Prime Minister Botha to warn that his government would crack down on all sources of discontent.

7 June South African air and ground troops mount their largest conventional assault since the Second World War when they raid SWAPO guerrilla bases deep within Angola. More than 350 guerrillas were believed to have been killed in 'Operation Smokeshell', along with 17 South African soldiers. The South African casulties were believed to be the highest ever suffered in any single operation of the 14-year guerrilla war.

SWAPO leader Sam Nujoma said after the raid that his organization might reverse its earlier decision to endorse the UN plan. Representatives from the UN Western Five contact group, the US, Britain, Canada, France and West Germany, persevered and on 24 November announced that South Africa had provisionally agreed to a March 1981 start for the cease-fire, as long as it was preceded by a conference of all parties participating in the Namibian peace process. It was agreed that such a conference would be held in Geneva in early 1981 to discuss the implementation of Resolution 435.

16 June Two months of Coloured unrest, sparked off by a student boycott in April to protest inferior educational standards, culminates in three days of clashes between Coloureds and the police in Elsie's River, outside Cape Town. The fighting was the worst outbreak of violence since the 1976 Soweto riots. At least 30 people were killed and some 175 injured after police abandoned an earlier policy of restraint and began firing into the crowds.

The riots had started earlier in the week as Coloureds tried to commemorate the 1976 Soweto unrest despite government bans on all commemorative and political meetings. The demonstrators ignored the ban and on 16 June began a two-day work boycott to mark the Soweto anniversary. Soon police cars were stoned and shops were looted and set alight. Reverend Allan Hendrickse, the leader of the Coloureds' main political organization, the Labour Party, blamed the riots on the Coloureds' lack of a political platform.

26 August Prime Minister Botha conducts a major reshuffle of his Cabinet. The move was seen by observers as an attempt to bring people known to be personally loyal to him into Cabinet while at the same time curbing the power of his extreme right-wing opponents. Botha loyalists General Magnus Malan and Gerrit Viljoen were given the defence and national (White) education portfolios respectively, while apartheid hardliner Marius Steyn was removed as minister of Coloured relations.

To consolidate his position, Botha also replaced the conservative head of the South African Broadcasting Corporation, Piet Meyer, with one of his supporters, Wynand Moulton. He also placed his protégés into key positions on the board of governors of the corporation and gave his supporters vital positions in the civil service. Observers saw his actions as attempts to ensure that he had the support of the country's press and civil service so that he could prepare himself for any future confrontation with Afrikaner hardliners.

3 September The National Party wins a by-election in Simonstown that had been expected to go to the Progressive Federal Party's candidate. Observers interpreted the results as a sign that South Africa's English-speaking population supported Prime Minister Botha's reformist measures.

The by-election victory came the day after Botha delivered a strong attack against the party's right-wing hardliners. His speech was made at the Transvaal National Party congress, the stronghold of his main conservative opponent Andries Treurnicht. Many observers believed the speech, coming as it did after Treurnicht's pro-apartheid one, was intended to demonstrate to the English-speaking electorate that Botha's reforms were practical and acceptable to mainline Nationalists.

27 November All 71 journalists striking against Johannesburg's only Black daily newspaper, the *Post*, are fired. The Argus Company, which owned the paper, was the country's largest English-speaking newspaper group and was, ironically, known for its support of Black causes and liberal view. Black journalists went out on sympathy strikes at at least nine other Argus newspapers and one news agency. Over 130 members of the Black journalists' union, the Media Workers Association of South Africa (MWASA), joined the strike. This represented almost every Black journalist in the country. Three leaders of the MWASA were banned by the government, which effectively silenced them as journalists.

The strikes took place as government pressures on the English-language press were intensifying, causing great anxiety about the freedom of the press. Many people both in and out of the media feared that the government would use its power to ban opponents in order to silence criticism in the press. Botha's establishment of a commission of inquiry into the media also caused many journalists to fear the creation of a legal system of press control.

14 January The UN-sponsored conference on Namibia ends in the outright failure of the parties to agree on a way of implementing UN Resolution 435.

South Africa alleged that the UN Western Five contact group of the US, Britain, Canada, France and West Germany would be biased towards the South West African People's Organization (SWAPO) during the proposed election campaign. It demanded that the UN withdraw its 1973 recognition of SWAPO as 'the sole authentic' representative of the Namibian people and end its financial contributions to the guerrilla group. The UN agreed on condition that South Africa set a date for the proposed elections. South Africa refused, saying an election was premature. SWAPO condemned the South Africans for their 'manifest intransigence and prevarications' and demanded UN sanctions be placed against them.

Observers believed that South Africa's delaying tactics were due to their belief that the Republican administration due to take office in the US later that month would listen more sympathetically to their views. South Africa apparently also wanted to give the Democratic Turnhalle Alliance more time to gain popular support in Namibia prior to the elections, fearing a SWAPO victory would lead to an increased Soviet presence in the region.

30 January South African forces launch a major raid into neigbouring Mozambique, destroying three guerrilla bases of the banned African National Congress (ANC) in the capital of Maputo. It was the first South African raid ever conducted in Mozambique. Some 13 people were believed to have been killed, including one South African. The chief of the South African defence forces, General Constand Viljoen, said that Maputo had been the target of the attack because the ANC used it as a 'springboard for terrorism against South Africa'. He warned that South Africa would continue pursuing ANC terrorists across national borders. The attack was internationally condemned as an invasion of sovereign territory and as an example of South Africa's attempts to destabilize the governments of its Black neighbours.

The ANC continued to step up its campaign of urban terrorism and sabotage throughout the year. Such incidents increased some 200 per cent by the end of June.

2 February South Africa's most influential businessman, Harry Oppenheimer, publicly attacks Prime Minister P.W. Botha's 'total strategy' as a threat to the country's parliamentary system. Oppenheimer, chairman of De Beers Consolidated Mines and the Anglo-American Corporation, said that Botha believed a 'total onslaught' was being waged against South Africa from external and internal Marxism, Western pressure, rising Black nationalism and arch conservatives within the National Party, and that this belief could prevent him from carrying out promised reforms in time. He said that if substantial progress was not quickly made towards genuine political power sharing and social justice, the country was headed towards armed revolution.

Botha, sensing the disquiet that was affecting the business community, called a conference of business leaders. The businessmen had been pressing for changes in the conditions of their non-White work force for some time. They felt that more contented workers were less likely to strike and that a calmer domestic scene would attract more foreign investors.

3 February The multiracial President's Council is formally inaugurated. The largely advisory council was the first mixed-race body to be established since the Nationalists came to power in 1948. It comprised government-appointed White, Coloured and Asian members and was designed to advise the president on constitutional reforms. The council was divided into five committees, dealing with constitutional, economic, science, planning and community matters. It replaced the ceremonial upper house of the South African parliament, the Senate, which was abolished on 1 January.

Critics opposed the exclusion of Blacks from membership of the council and, for that reason, the opposition Progressive Federal Party as well as the main Coloured and Indian parties refused to participate in its workings.

One of the first recommendations the council made was the restoration of Pageview and District Six in Cape Town to the Indian and Coloured communities respectively. The areas had been rezoned for White occupation several years previously and the inhabitants were forcefully removed, causing great resentment. It had been widely expected that such concessions would be given to the non-White communities as symbols of reconciliation and there was, therefore, considerable disappointment when Botha rejected the council's recommendation. The rejection confirmed that Botha had no intention of changing the cornerstones of the apartheid legislation, such as the Immorality Act and the Group Areas Act. More ominously, many observers believed it indicated that he was unwilling to change the system at all.

31 March Finance Minister Owen Horwood presents South Africa with an annual budget that is markedly different from the 1980 version. The spectacular economic boom of the previous year appeared to be at an end. The price of gold, which averaged $600 an ounce in 1980, had fallen to $400 an ounce, resulting in sharply decreased revenues and a wider deficit than expected. At the same time, the defence budget was increased by 30 per cent, reflecting South African anxieties about its isolated position as a White enclave in an increasingly Black southern Africa.

By the end of the year, the economic decline showed every sign of continuing. Gold had dropped below the $400-an-ounce price and the value of the national currency, the rand, followed it down, losing 23 per cent of its value against the US dollar in the course of the year. Inflation, running at 15 per cent, was the worst since the 1920s, but analysts reported that the economy was still fundamentally sound and they did not expect a major recession.

29 April White South Africa goes to the polls. The National Party is returned to power but with a reduced majority. The ruling Nationalists won 131 seats in the 165-seat parliament, a loss of six from the previous parliament. The main opposition group, the liberal Progressive Federal Party (PFP), won 26 seats, for a gain of nine, and the largely Natal-based New Republic Party took eight seats, down two. The extreme right-wing Herstigte Nasionale Party (HNP) again failed to capture any seats but increased its share of the vote from 4 per cent in 1977 to a surprising 13 per cent.

Prime Minister Botha reportedly was shocked by the results of the election. His party, in addition to suffering a loss of seats to the PFP, lost a substantial number of votes to the HNP. That loss was more worrying because the HNP, formed in 1969 by a splinter group from the National Party that opposed the National Party's relatively moderate apartheid policies, was attempting to capture the conservative Afrikaner vote that traditionally belonged to the Nationalists. The HNP had won support across a broad spectrum of Afrikaner voters and analysts predicted that a further small swing to the right would result in that party actually capturing seats from the National Party.

Botha was caught between wanting to avoid a split in the Afrikaner movement and continuing with his promised reforms. The National Party was split between reformist and conservative factions, which made it vulnerable to attack from the HNP. Botha had to choose between continuing with his reforms and risking a complete split within his party or slowing down or stopping the reforms and risking a backlash of non-White anger. He chose the latter option.

15 May Foreign Minister Roelof 'Pik' Botha arrives in the US for talks with US officials on the stalled Namibian peace process. His visit came as a result of intense diplomatic manoeuvring by US officials, involving visits to both South Africa and the front line states. The new administration made a settlement of the Namibian problem one of their main foreign policy objectives. South Africa's apparent belief that the new US administration would be easier to deal with appeared to be correct as Ronald Reagan adopted a less confrontational approach than his predecessor, Jimmy Carter.

According to a leaked State Department document, the US would attempt to end South Africa's international isolation if South Africa cooperated in attaining an acceptable independence settlement for Namibia. The new administration linked a Namibian settlement with the need for a greater emphasis being placed on South Africa's 'major concerns', such as the withdrawal of Cuban troops from Angola and the guaranteeing of constitutional rights for Namibia's Whites. The Reagan administration's critics attacked this new approach, saying the South Africans would not respond to it and would never soften their position on Namibian elections unless their Democratic Turnhalle Alliance was assured of winning. The linkage between the withdrawal of Cuban forces from Angola and Namibian independence was to become of major significance. Many observers saw it as a South African delaying tactic that caused the talks to drag on for several more years and condemned the US for its role in supporting it.

19 August Some 1,500 illegal squatters are forcibly removed from a camp outside Cape Town to their independent homeland of the Transkei. The deportations were possible under a South African law that allowed the government to summarily deport without a hearing all illegal 'alien' immigrants. Under the separate development policy, all members of a tribe became citizens of their appropriate homeland once it became independent and they automatically lost their South African citizenship, regardless of where they were born or lived. The squatters were predominately the wives and children of Black migrant workers from the Transkei, who had illegally come to Cape Town to join their husbands and fathers.

24 August South African forces launch a 'limited' invasion of Angola in pursuit of SWAPO guerrillas based in the country. The Angolan government accused the South Africans of having carried out a major incursion into Angolan territory in order to establish a no-man's land along the Angolan–Namibian border. It claimed that such a buffer zone would be handed over to the South African-backed Angolan guerrilla group, the National Union for the Total Independence of Angola (Unita), and would make SWAPO raids into Namibia from Angola less possible. Angola went on to claim that some 45,000 South African troops were involved in attacks up to 80 miles (128.7 km) into Angolan territory. The South Africans dismissed the figures as 'totally laughable' and said their mission was to pursue SWAPO guerrillas and destroy SWAPO bases.

The action came after the signing on 4 February of an Angolan–Cuban accord that said, 'The withdrawal of Cuban forces stationed in Angola will be carried out once every eventuality of acts of aggression or armed invasion ceases to occur.' Observers believed that the raids undermined the US argument that the Cuban troop presence in Angola was not needed for the country's security, as the Angolan government had always insisted.

26 October The Western Five contact group on Namibia – the US, Britain,

Canada, France and West Germany – present new proposals in an attempt to break the impasse in the independence talks. The new plan was a variation on a previous Western proposal and UN Resolution 435 for a cease-fire and elections. Under the new proposals, the constitution had to be approved by two-thirds of the assembly, which had to be composed of representatives from all of Namibia's significant racial and ethnic groups. The plan was intended to ease South African fears that SWAPO could immediately dominate a post-election Namibia.

Reactions to the plans were a mixture of the positive and the cautious. South Africa expressed fears that the UN would be unable to adequately monitor any elections. The South African-backed Democratic Turnhalle Alliance, the major political group in Namibia, was positive but wanted 'guarantees' that the plan could be enforced, while SWAPO supporters said it opened the door to 'a just solution'.

The year ended with the talks apparently back on track but no closer to setting a date for the proposed cease-fire, elections or independence day.

27 November Some 14 Black trade union activists are arrested in pre-dawn raids across South Africa under provisions of the Suppression of Communism Act. Observers believed that the raids had been part of the government's efforts to uncover links between legal Black trade unions and the banned ANC. Consultants in the labour field had been warning the government that the labour movement would become increasingly more politicized if Blacks were not allowed other political outlets.

The Black trade union movement was, to date, the only sector of Black life to benefit from Prime Minister Botha's promised reforms. Black trade unionists were using their positions to become involved in more overtly political areas. The government attempted to counteract this trend by requiring all Black unions to register, so they could be closely monitored. Many of the unions, however, refused. Employers tended to negotiate with the non-registered unions believing that they were more representative of the views of the Black workers.

2 December South Africa frees 39 of the 44 mercenaries who had hijacked an Air India plane to South Africa on 26 November after being involved in a failed coup attempt against the government of President Rene France in the Seychelles. The release of the mercenaries was strongly protested both nationally and internationally and led to the belief that the South African government had been involved in the coup attempt as part of its plan to destabilize Black African nations. Their release came after requests from President France that all of the mercenaries be extradited to the Seychelles. The remaining five mercenaries, including leader Colonel 'Mad Mike' Hoare, also received exceptionally lenient treatment. They were released on bail after being charged with the less serious crime of kidnapping, which carried no minimum jail sentence, instead of with hijacking, which carried a minimum penalty of five years.

1 9 8 2

5 February The secretary of the predominately non-White African Food and Canning Workers Union in the Transvaal, Neil Aggett, becomes the first White to die in police custody. Aggett, a doctor detained under the South African security laws since November 1981 for his union activities and alleged support of the banned African National Congress (ANC), was found hanged in his Johannesburg jail cell. The government claimed his death was a suicide. Aggett's relatives and colleagues strongly contested the police version and organized a national work stoppage to protest the treatment of political prisoners. Aggett's death came only days after a judicial commission recommended the implementation of a series of safeguards to protect the well-being of detainees.

The controversy increased when Black activist Ernest Moabi Dipale died in detention on 8 August. The minister of police and prisons, Louis Le Grange, stated the following day, 'You won't get much information if you keep a detainee in a five-star hotel or with his friend.' He contended that 'only six, seven or eight of these cases died from some form of assault'. This was the first official admission that police were to blame for any of the deaths.

The police were officially cleared of responsibility for Aggett's death on 21 December after an inquest. Several witnesses told the inquest of the physical and psychological torture they endured while in detention. The magistrate, however, ruled that responsibility for Aggett's death probably, but not 'beyond a reasonable doubt', lay with his fellow political prisoner and friend Auret van Heerden. The ruling was condemned by Aggett's family, supporters and the union movement.

15 February The South African-sponsored Democratic Turnhalle Alliance (DTA) in Namibia suffers a crippling blow when the party representing the majority Ovambo tribesmen, the National Democratic Party (NDP), withdraws from the coalition. The split came as a result of the friction between the White leader of the DTA, Dirk Mudge, and the Black leader, the NDP's Peter Kalangula. The DTA was hurt by its perceived links with South Africa and suffered a loss of support throughout the year. The decline of the DTA was seen as being matched by an increase in support for the Namibian guerrilla group, the South West African People's Organization (SWAPO).

3 March The ruling National Party of Prime Minister P.W. Botha expels 16 arch-conservative members for failing to support Botha's reformist racial policies. The split, which had been threatened since shortly after Botha took office in 1978, came as a result of Botha's proposals to introduce a form of power sharing with South Africa's Coloured and Asian communities and was led by Cabinet ministers Andries Treurnicht and Ferdinand Hartzenberg.

On 24 February, some 22 right-wing Nationalists expressed their total opposition to any relaxation of a Whites-only Parliament by refusing to support a motion expressing confidence in Botha. The revolt was seen by most observers as the most significant development in the politics of White South Africa since the Nationalists first came to power in 1948. An emergency party meeting, convened on 27 February to discuss the crisis, gave Botha an overwhelming vote of confidence. The prime minister then gave Treurnicht and Hartzenberg until 3 March to reconsider their position on racial reform or face expulsion from the party. The two men resigned their ministerial posts on 2 March and, on the following day, were expelled from the National Party along with 14 of their supporters.

The split, which still left the National Party with overwhelming support in Parliament, was seen as important because it caused Botha to again slow down on his reform policies and dedicate his time to maintaining Afrikaner unity and power.

9 March A multiracial commission established by the government of the Black Kwazulu homeland and headed by Zulu leader Chief Gathsa Buthelezi issues its report on multiracial power sharing in Natal province. The commission recommended the merger of the province's White administration with the Black Kwazulu government. It argued that unless substantial progress was made towards power sharing, which meant abandoning plans to turn Kwazulu into an independent Black homeland, the province would suffer as Blacks came to believe that violence was their only option for obtaining power. The report, drafted by academics and signed by prominent businessmen, was approved by the liberal opposition party, the Progressive Federal Party (PFP). It was however, immediately rejected by the government, whose approval was necessary if any of the commission's proposals were to be implemented.

Chief Buthelezi continued throughout the year to vigorously oppose government plans to grant independence to his Kwazulu homeland. He rejected the government's separate development programme, under which the Transkei, Bophuthatswana, Ciskei and Venda had all become nominally independent nations while remaining totally dependent on South Africa, and demanded that the Zulus be given full political rights in South Africa.

20 March Former Minister of State Administration and Statistics Andries Treurnicht officially launches the right-wing Conservative Party of South Africa. Treurnicht, as leader of the new party, reasserted his belief in South Africa's traditional apartheid policy and urged his some 7,000 supporters not to allow Botha to 'dilute' apartheid.

The Conservative Party announced its 15-point policy plan, which was, as widely expected, based on a strictly defined system of a separation of the races. Treurnicht stressed that his party opposed any form of power sharing or attempts at political integration, mixed government, or moves towards establishing a unitary state.

The first test of strength for the conservative movement came in an 18 August 1982 Transvaal provincial council by-election in Germiston. While the National Party retained the seat, its total vote was substantially reduced and the Nationalists received fewer votes than the combined total gained by the Conservative Party and the other right-wing Afrikaner party, the Herstigte Nasionale Party (HNP). Although the National Party easily defeated the two right-wing parties in by-elections in Walvis Bay and the Orange Free State constituency of Parys on 4 November, many analysts believed that an electoral pact between the CPSA and HNP could pose the first serious threat to the National Party's reign since 1948.

12 May The President's Council, an appointed body established by Prime Minister Botha in 1981 to advise the government on constitutional reforms, presents its plans for power sharing to the Cabinet. According to the proposals, Coloureds and Indians would be allowed to participate in the running of local, regional and central government bodies but Blacks would still be excluded because of their 'cultural differences, relative numbers, conflicting interests and divergent political objectives'.

The council recommended the creation of an executive president with almost unlimited powers who would serve a seven-year term of office. The president would appoint a multiracial Cabinet, which would answer directly to him and not to Parliament. A single parliament would be established with a separate chamber for Whites, Coloureds and Asians. All of the racial groups were to elect their own representatives and would pass legislation for their own racial communities. The three chambers would have joint legal responsibility for issues of 'common concern'. The National Party unanimously accepted the plans at a special federal congress on 31 July.

The proposals were attacked from both ends of the political spectrum. The right-wing Conservative Party called them 'the end of White self-determination' in the country, while the liberal PFP condemned the exclusion of Blacks. Other observers, however, argued that the plans, as flawed as they were, still provided for Asian and Coloured Cabinet ministers for the first time.

30 June Chief Gatsha Buthelezi, leader of the Zulu tribal homeland, wins a major political battle when the Natal Supreme Court overrules the government's plan to transfer some 3,000 square miles (7,770 square km) of Kwazulu to neighbouring Swaziland. The transfer would have resulted in almost one million Zulus losing their South African citizenship.

Swaziland had been willing to accept the Ingwavuma section of Kwazulu and the ethnic Swazi homeland of Kangwane in the eastern Transvaal when the South African government announced its intention earlier in the month to cede both areas to its neighbour. The plan met with powerful opposition, led by Buthelezi, and was abandoned after the court's ruling.

1 July Rioting begins at four gold mines near Johannesburg as some 75,000 Black miners become engaged in the most widespread unrest in the mining industry since before the Nationalists came to power in 1948. The riots, over a lower than expected wage increase, resulted in 10 Black deaths before it ended on 6 July.

Strikes virtually closed down the motor industry in the eastern Cape when over 10,000 Black and Coloured workers at the Ford, General Motors and Volkswagen auto plants took industrial action on 15 July to demand higher wages.

The industrial unrest resulted from the general downturn in the economy which led to lower wage increases while inflation hit 16 per cent. Unemployment among Blacks rose sharply as the recession took hold and figures varied from the official 450,000 to the unofficial three million. The country's financial difficulties were exacerbated by the sharp fall in the price of its prime export, gold, which fell from over $800 an ounce in 1981 to around $300 an ounce at some points in 1982. The fall in gold revenue had a serious result on South Africa's balance of payments position. It also resulted in South Africa requesting a $1.1 thousand million loan from the International Monetary Fund (IMF), its first request for such a loan in six years. The loan was granted in November, despite a UN General Assembly resolution asking the IMF to reject the request.

6 July The five Western members of the UN Security Council (the 'Western Five' contact group on Namibia – the US, Britain, Canada, France and West Germany) begin a series of meetings with representatives from Angola, Botswana, Mozambique, Nigeria, Tanzania, Zambia, Zimbabwe and the Namibian guerrilla group, SWAPO, at UN headquarters in New York to discuss Namibian independence. South Africa was not represented at the talks because of the Black African nations' refusal to deal directly with the South African government.

On the same day that the talks opened, the South African government demanded that Cuba withdraw its estimated 15,000–20,000 troops from Angola as a prerequisite to Namibian independence, arguing that the Cuban military presence would impede the UN-sponsored free and fair elections. Angola and Cuba opposed the linkage saying that the Cuban troops were a defence against South Africa's illegal raids across the Namibian border into Angola in pursuit of SWAPO guerrillas. Angola had, however, previously said that it would no longer need the Cubans as protection against South Africa once the proposed UN peace-keeping force was in place in Namibia, and Cuba had promised its troops would leave when requested to do so by Angola. The US was in favour of the linkage.

The Western Five continued its efforts throughout the year to have all sides in the dispute agree a formula for a cease-fire and free elections.

27 July Some 42 White mercenaries are convicted in a Pietermaritzburg court of air piracy following their involvement in the failed November 1981 coup attempt in the Seychelles. The mercenaries, led by the legendary Colonel Michael 'Mad Mike' Hoare, had used a hijacked Air India plane to make their escape from the Seychelles to Durban. They were sentenced to terms of six months to 10 years, while another mercenary was acquitted. Five other mercenaries, on trial in the Seychelles, were convicted of treason. Four were sentenced to death and the fifth to life imprisonment.

Hoare sparked off a controversy when he alleged that the South African government had sponsored the coup attempt, a charge the government vehemently denied. Suspicions against South Africa had been rife when it originally decided in December 1981 to release 40 of the mercenaries without charge and to charge five others with the relatively minor crime of kidnapping. That decision, seen as a violation of The Hague convention against hijacking, had been widely condemned both at home and abroad and had led to calls for the suspension of South African Airways' foreign landing rights. The government reversed its decision in January and formally indicted the men on 18 January.

The suspected role that South Africa had played in the coup was seen as confirmation that the government was engaged in a covert policy aimed at destabilizing the governments of its Black neighbours. Prime Minister Robert Mugabe of Zimbabwe publicly accused South Africa of attempting to destabilize his administration. His claim appeared to have been supported when Zimbabwean troops killed three South African soldiers during a raid on Zimbabwean territory in August. The South African government, while admitting that the men belong to the South African Defence Force, denied that the raid had been officially sanctioned. Many observers also believed that South Africa was secretly supporting the Mozambique National Resistance (MNR) guerrillas in Mozambique. The MNR, as part of their campaign to overthrow the Mozambican government in Maputo, were bombing oil pipelines and rail lines. Their activities also destabilized the economies of both Malawi and Zimbabwe. In Angola, the South African government was financing the National Union for the Total Independence of Angola rebels of Jonas Savimbi in their fight against the Marxist government. South Africa was also accused of financing a rebel group in Lesotho. Observers saw South Africa's policy of destabilization as increasingly aggressive and aimed at maintaining its economic and political control of southern Africa.

21 October Barbara Horgan becomes the first White woman in the history of South Africa to be found guilty of treason and is sentenced to 10 years' imprisonment. Horgan had been charged with membership in the banned ANC. She admitted belonging to the ANC but rejected the government's claim that such membership constituted treasonous activity since she had never engaged in hostile acts or violence against the state. The Rand Supreme Court in Johannesburg disagreed and sentenced her to an extraordinarily long sentence.

9 December South African troops launch a pre-dawn raid on the suspected headquarters of the banned ANC in the Lesotho capital of Maseru. Some 42 people were killed, including 12 civilians with no ANC connections. South Africa blamed the deaths of seven women and children on the ANC, saying that the terrorist organization had 'deliberately located its headquarters in civilian houses throughout the residential suburbs of Maseru' to discourage South African retaliation. The Lesotho government strongly denied that the dead had been ANC supporters, calling them South African refugees, and said that Lesotho did not allow terrorists to use it as a base for their activities.

19 December A series of four explosions destroys the Koeberg nuclear power station, the country's first nuclear power plant. The banned ANC which had been conducting a low-intensity campaign of sabotage against the government throughout the year, claimed responsibility for the attack, saying it was 'a salute to our fallen heroes' in Lesotho. Although the government disclosed few details of the bombings, it was thought that one of the plant's two nuclear reactors had been damaged. Officials were forced to admit on 21 December that the opening of the plant, scheduled for 1983, would have to be delayed. The bombing was seen as a major coup for the ANC.

1 9 8 3

4 January The Labour Party, a multiracial party with a predominately Coloured membership, becomes the only major anti-apartheid group to express its willingness to participate in the new constitutional system when it votes to endorse the government's controversial proposals to establish a tricameral Parliament. The plans called for the setting up of separate legislative chambers for White, Coloured and Asian representatives but would exclude the participation of the country's Black majority.

The Labour Party's decision to participate in the restructured parliament caused a serious break with the Black Alliance, an umbrella organization established in 1978 to oppose apartheid. Labour Party leader Allan Hendrickse maintained that in spite of the fact that the constitution was seriously flawed by its exclusion of Blacks, the Labour Party could use the Coloured chamber as a platform to campaign for Black political rights. He said: 'South Africa is in the process of reform. We are going to be part of that process. We are going to be sitting there, forcing the pace.'

19 January South Africa dissolves the Namibian national assembly and reimposes direct rule on the territory after five years of semi-autonomous government. The move followed the resignation earlier in the day of the Namibian Council of Ministers, the territory's highest governing organ, and its chairman, Dirk Mudge. Their resignation was 'in protest against the humiliating way' in which the Namibian government had been treated by the South Africans.

Negotiations continued throughout the year in an apparently futile attempt to establish first a cease-fire and then the elections. France, one of the five Western contact nations that had been conducting the negotiations, became disillusioned with the absence of progress in the talks and announced that it was suspending its efforts. Meanwhile, South Africa, with US support, continued to insist that it would not agree to the implementation of UN Resolution 435 calling for a cease-fire and the holding of free and fair elections until the removal of 'intimidating' Cuban troops from neighbouring Angola. The Angolan government contended that the Cubans would not leave Angola until the South African-backed rebel group, the National Union for the Total Independence of Angola had ceased to be a threat to it.

27 January The nine member nations of the Southern African Development Coordination Conference meet in Lesotho to discuss methods of decreasing their economic dependence on South Africa. The member states – Angola, Botswana, Lesotho, Malawi, Mozambique, Swaziland, Tanzania, Zambia and Zimbabwe – accused South Africa of conducting a policy of destabilization against them. The Conference states accused South Africa of conducting this campaign in order to force its member states to end their aid to the banned African National Congress (ANC) and to stop providing ANC guerrillas with bases from which to launch attacks in South Africa. They also believed that South Africa was attempting to maintain an economically dominant position in the region. Botswana's Finance Minister Peter Mmusi summed the mood up by saying: 'It is not much use to develop ports and pipelines, roads and railways, and then watch in silence as they are blown up.'

18 March The worst drought of the century is reported to be hitting southern Africa for the second successive year. South Africa and Namibia were among those countries seriously affected, as were Botswana, Lesotho, Mozambique, Swaziland, Zambia and Zimbabwe. Most of the countries were receiving only 25–50 per cent of their normal rainfall. Crop failures were followed by major stock losses and starvation in some areas. South Africa, normally a major exporter of corn, had to begin importing grain. Corn prices escalated, making it difficult for poorer people to afford and raising the country's inflation rate. Summer rains helped ease the situation somewhat but drought conditions continued unabated in many sections of the country.

The economy, already in a recession, suffered an estimated loss of R1 thousand million in foreign exchange because of the drought's effects on its agricultural exports. Unemployment was estimated at between 500,000 and three million.

20 May A car bomb explodes outside the Pretoria headquarters of the South African Air Force in what was thought to be the largest-scale terrrorist attack ever conducted in South Africa. The banned ANC claimed responsibility for the blast, which killed 19 people, including Blacks, and injured over 200 others. Most of the casualties were civilian pedestrians. The bomb was a major departure from the usual ANC tactics of sabotaging military targets or making symbolic attacks on empty government buildings rather than engaging in terrorist activity that was likely to involve civilians. Observers feared that the bombing heralded the beginning of a deadly shift in the ANC's campaign against the government. ANC leader Oliver Tambo confirmed those fears when, on 21 May, he said that his group's attacks would be taking a new direction. He added: 'Never again are our people going to be doing all the bleeding.'

In condemning the attack, Defence Minister Magnus Malan warned that the government would continue its policy of making retaliatory cross-border raids into countries that harboured ANC guerrillas.

23 May The South Africa Defence Force launches a major raid against ANC 'terrorist camps' in Maputo, Mozambique, in retaliation for the Pretoria car bomb. Reports differed as to the number of casualties and amount of destruction caused by the air strike. The Mozambican government claimed five people were killed, including women and children, and a further 40 injured in attacks on private homes and a jam factory. The South Africans insisted that 64 people, primarily ANC terrorists, were killed with 44 more injured in the reprisal raid on six ANC targets, including an anti-aircraft missile base. The South Africans later admitted that a jam factory had been hit in error.

29 June The banning order against Black activist Winnie Mandela, wife of jailed ANC leader Nelson Mandela, is renewed for a further five years. The ban, the sixth imposed against her in the past 21 years, prohibited her from belonging to any organization, attending any gathering of more than two people, or having anything she said or wrote published.

2 August The United Democratic Front, an extra-parliamentary umbrella organization composed of more than 550 affiliated trade union, community, religious, sports and other organizations, is formed at a meeting attended by some 7,000 people to coordinate resistance to the proposed constitutional changes on power sharing. The new multiracial grouping, officially open to 'democrats of all races', was described as the largest anti-apartheid movement since the banning of the ANC in 1960 and was thought to represent over one million people. Its campaign against the reforms gained significant support from the Black, Asian and Coloured communities, but had little affect on the outcome of the Whites-only referendum, held in November, on the adoption of the constitutional changes.

The Front was regarded by the government, and others, as the internal wing of the ANC and was said by them to share the ANC's 'philosophy and objectives'. The organization was led by Albertina Sisulu, wife of the jailed ANC leader Walter Sisulu, the son of a former ANC leader, Archie Gumede, and Oscar

Npetha. It had among its supporters jailed ANC leader Nelson Mandela, White anti-apartheid campaigners Helen Joseph and Beyers Naude, charismatic Coloured leader Reverend Allan Boesak and the South African Council of Sports leader Hassan Howa.

The National Forum was also formed during this period to rally opposition to the constitutional reforms but, unlike the UDF, restricted its membership to non-Whites. The new group was fully committed to the principles of Black Consciousness, a tradition made famous by Steve Biko and the founder of the Pan-African Congress, Robert Sobukwe.

2 November Prime Minister P.W. Botha's controversial constitutional reforms are approved in a national, Whites-only referendum. The result of the vote, in which over 75 per cent of the eligible Whites participated, was seen as a resounding victory for Botha. He had staked his political career on obtaining public support for his plan to grant limited legislative powers to South Africa's Coloured and Asian communities, while maintaining the exclusion of the Black majority from power.

Most observers had expected the proposals to be approved, but the two-thirds margin of victory surprised even Botha's ardent supporters. His opponents had fought a bitter campaign against the reforms ever since they had been formally introduced in Parliament in May, with both ends of the political spectrum urging voters to reject the proposals. The ultra-right Conservative Party and Herstigte Nasionale Party had protested on the grounds that any reform in the country's apartheid system would eventually and inevitably lead to the end of White domination. The liberal opposition party, the Progressive Federal Party, called the proposals a 'sham' and condemned them for failing to address the country's main problem, which was the lack of political rights for its 21 million Blacks.

The country's Coloured and Asian communities were divided over the plan, with the predominately Coloured Labour Party supporting the proposals while prominent Indian leaders rejected them. Opposition stemmed not only from the belief that any reforms which excluded Blacks were certain to fail but also from the fact that under the provisions of the new constitution Coloureds and Indians would play a subservient role to Whites and would, therefore, be unable to make any significant changes without White approval.

The new constitution provided for the establishment of a tricameral legislature, with separate chambers for White, Coloured and Asian representatives. The members of each chamber would be elected by the racial group they represented and each chamber would have responsibility for legislation affecting their own group, such as housing, welfare, education, health and local government. Areas of 'common concern', such as foreign affairs and defence, would be considered by committees composed of representatives from all three chambers. Whites would comprise the largest chamber, and would decide all the major issues, such as the election of the state president.

The other main feature of the constitution was that it replaced the office of prime minister with a strong executive presidency. The president would appoint a multiracial cabinet, which would be directly responsible to him and not to Parliament. The president would also control the President's Council, previously an advisory body, which would replace the Senate as the upper house of the legislature and would be empowered to resolve disputes among the three legislative chambers.

25 November A series of local Black elections start under new legislation granting local councils some administrative authority in the Black townships. The elections, which continued until 7 December, were largely boycotted by Blacks in protest at their exclusion from the new tricameral parliament. The poor voter turnout was seen as a defeat for the government of Prime Minister Botha, which had changed the role of the councils from purely advisory to having some authority as a concession to Blacks for their exclusion from national government.

29 December The former commander of the strategic Simonstown naval dockyard, Commodore Dieter Gerhardt, and his wife, Ruth, are convicted of spying for the Soviet Union after a closed trial lasting 45 days. Gerhardt admitted that he had spied for the Soviets for over 20 years but maintained that he had been a double agent working for Western intelligence. He was sentenced on 31 December to life imprisonment, while his wife was sentenced to 10 years in prison.

16 February South African and Angolan officials sign an agreement in Lusaka, Zambia, for the establishment of a joint monitoring commission to supervise the withdrawal of South African troops from Angola. The South Africans agreed to withdraw in return for an Angolan agreement to stop nationalist guerrillas from the South West African People's Organization (SWAPO) infiltrating Namibia from their bases in Angola. The agreement was the result of intensive diplomatic manoeuvring by the US, led by Assistant Secretary of State for African Affairs Chester Crocker.

The South Africans had invaded 200 miles (321.8 km) into southern Angola in December 1983 in pursuit of SWAPO guerrillas. The operation was described as the most formidable invasion of Angola in recent years and involved up to 10,000 troops. The South Africans claimed the action was aimed at disrupting SWAPO's preparations for its annual incursion into Namibia. Observers felt that it was also designed to force the Angolan government to the negotiating table.

The South African forces began disengaging from Angola on 31 January and were expected to totally withdraw from Namibia according to a timetable drawn up by the monitoring commission. It was hoped that the agreement reached by the two sides would allow the UN-sponsored talks to proceed on a cease-fire and eventual elections prior to Namibian independence. The commission began its work on 1 March, and by 3 May the South African forces had withdrawn to within 25 miles (40 km) of the Angolan–Namibian border. The South African government refused to proceed with the withdrawal, however, claiming that the Angolan government was incapable of preventing SWAPO incursions into

Namibia. The South Africans were still in Angola by the end of the year, and the peace talks once again appeared to be stalled.

16 March South African Prime Minister P.W. Botha and his Mozambican counterpart, President Samora Machel, sign a historic non-aggression pact at Nkomati, on the South African–Mozambican border. The pact, known as the Nkomatic Accord, was designed to end the persistent hostilities between the two countries and had been reached after intensive diplomatic activity, encouraged by the US, Britain and Mozambique's former colonial power, Portugal.

Under the provisions of the treaty, the first of its kind between South Africa and a Black African nation, the two countries promised to prohibit the use of their territory for the organization, basing or transporting through of armed groups hostile to the other nation and to desist from aiding or supporting any such insurgency. Machel, while recognizing the 'great and even antagonistic' differences between the two countries' political, economic and social systems, said that the two were 'indissolubly linked by geography and proximity'. Botha called the agreement 'mutually beneficial'. The main losers from the accord were expected to be the banned African National Congress (ANC) which had been using Mozambique as a base to launch attacks against South Africa, and the Mozambique National Resistance (MNR), a South-African sponsored guerrilla group attempting to overthrow Machel's Marxist government.

As a result of the Nkomati Accord the level of ANC terrorist acts dropped noticeably over the remainder of the year. South Africa, however, was seen as not abiding by its promise to end its support of the MNR. The number of terrorist attacks launched by the MNR became greater and more accurate after the accord was signed and observers felt that the accord had failed to live up to expectations as a method of ensuring peace in the region.

29 May Prime Minister Botha begins an official tour of western Europe in an effort to ease South Africa's international isolation. The eight-nation trip, the first overseas mission by a South African head of state in some 20 years, was hailed in South Africa as a diplomatic breakthrough. Observers felt that Botha's reformist policies had gone some of the way towards ensuring him a warmer reception than he might otherwise have experienced, but believed that he still had to listen to some 'quite candid' remarks against South Africa's racial policies. He conferred with the heads of government in Portugal, Switzerland, Britain, West Germany, Belgium, France, Italy, and Austria and held talks with the Pope at the Vatican.

15 July Violence breaks out in the Black township of Tumahole in the Orange Free State as more than 1,000 young people demonstrate against rises in rent and the sale tax. The demonstrations sparked off another outbreak of the periodic Black violence that had been hitting the country since just before the Nationalists came to power in 1948 and was, as had been frequently happening, led by schoolchildren and young university students. The unrest, which continued on and off all year, for the first time involved attacks against local Black authorities who were seen as cooperating with the White authorities. Such leaders were branded as turncoats and several were murdered. The violence mainly centred on the Johannesburg area, but some disturbances also occurred in Cape Town. In an unusual move, the government began deploying the military to help the police quell the violence. The use of such troops was severely condemned both domestically and internationally by critics who maintained that it created a civil war situation.

25 July The South African government, represented by its Namibian administrator-general, and representatives from the guerrilla group SWAPO hold their first direct talks on a cease-fire. The talks, held in Cape Verde, broke down after South Africa refused to guarantee that a cease-fire would lead to the eventual independence of Namibia. Many observers believed that the disagreement was part of a South African strategy to delay peace talks until it had established an internal political grouping in Namibia that could successfully contest any elections in which SWAPO participated.

14 August Police destroy hundreds of makeshift shelters and arrest at least 50 people at Black squatter camps outside Cape Town. The move was part of the government's efforts to evict Blacks who did not have permission to live in the region.

On 2 October, the minister of cooperation, development and education, Gerrit Viljoen, announced that the illegal Blacks in the Cape Town area, estimated at between 70,000 and 100,000, would be relocated to a new settlement near Cape Town called Khayelitsha. The Black township had originally been set aside for legal Black residents. Viljoen stressed that the transferred Blacks would still be considered law breakers, but said that the housing would be better than in the largest of the illegal settlements, Crossroads, and that they could also be 'better controlled' at Khayelitsha. The announcement caused widespread unease in the squatter camps, somewhat eased by a further announcement that such moves would be voluntary. The government did make it clear, however, that it had not backed down from its intention to remove all the squatter camps the following year. Meanwhile, new arrivals to the squatter camps came on a daily basis from the poor rural homeland areas, looking for employment or to be reunited with husbands and fathers in defiance of the country's pass law system.

22 August The first-ever elections to the Coloured chamber of the country's new tricameral parliament are held. Voting for the Indian chamber took place on 28 August. Both elections were hit by large-scale voter boycotts and participation was estimated at between 18 and 30 per cent of the electorate.

Over 170 people were arrested prior to and during the Coloured elections and more were detained during the Indian vote. The government blamed the low turnout on 'voter intimidation' but said that the turnout had been high enough to consider the results a mandate. Political observers, however, questioned the legitimacy of the new legislative body.

The multiracial Labour Party, with a majority of Coloured members, won 76 of the 80 seats in the (Coloured) House of Representatives. The National People's Party won 18 of the 40 seats in the (Indian) House of Delegates, with the Solidarity Party capturing 17 seats and independents taking the remaining five seats.

Meanwhile, more than 625,000 Black students boycotted classes from 22 August in protest against the elections. The protest was accompanied by violence, and several schools were burned while local officials' homes and cars were destroyed.

5 September The retiring prime minister, P.W. Botha, is elected South Africa's first executive president under the country's new constitution. He was elected unopposed by a 86-member electoral college, drawn from members of the new tricameral parliament. Botha's election had been somewhat guaranteed since the White chamber, controlled by his National Party, had contributed 50 members to the electoral college to the Coloured's 23 and Indian's 13.

The new position of executive president was an extremely powerful one, combining the duties of the prime minister and the old-styled ceremonial presidency. The executive president had complete control over the Cabinet, which reported directly to him and not to the parliament, and over the President's Council, a body which had replaced the Senate as the upper house of the legislature.

13 September Six Black and Indian dissidents take refuge in the British consulate in Durban to avoid being arrested for their parts in organizing the boycott of the August elections to the new Coloured and Indian parliamentary chambers. Britain allowed the six to remain in the consulate because, under South African law, they faced imprisonment without having formal charges made against them. The consulate was legally a part of Britain and, therefore, out of South Africa's jurisdiction. Britain's decision strained relations between the two countries and South Africa retaliated by refusing a British request to extradite four South Africans wanted on arms smuggling charges.

Three of the six left the consulate on 3 October and were immediately arrested. They were formally charged with treason on 10 December, the same day that the government lifted the detention orders against them and the three dissidents still in the British consulate. The British responded by saying: 'The situation has now changed and we expect the three to leave the consulate immediately.' They left on 12 December.

15 September President P.W. Botha announces his new Cabinet, the first in South African history to include non-White members. Reverend Allan Hendrickse, leader of the (Coloured) Labour Party, and Amichand Rajbansi, leader of the (Indian) National People's Party, were both designated ministers without portfolio. Hendrickse was named chairman of the Ministers' Council of Coloured Affairs, while Rajbansi became chairman of the Ministers' Council for Indian Affairs. The new Cabinet had little credibility outside the White community because of its exclusion of Blacks, but it was still hoped by many that it would act as the catalyst for further reforms.

3 October The Mozambican government and the rebel MNR group that was dedicated to overthrowing it announce a cease-fire agreement. The agreement resulted from South African-sponsored talks held in Pretoria between the two sides. Observers attributed South Africa's role in the talks as an attempt to salvage the Nkomati Accord reached between South Africa and Mozambique in March.

The agreement already showed signs of breaking down on the day it was announced and both sides said they expected further fighting. Further talks were held on 8 October on how and when to implement the agreement but these talks ended on 11 October, apparently without definitive progress being made. Although all parties to the negotiations insisted that the peace process would continue, the talks broke down in November after the MNR claimed that the South African mediators were biased in favour of the Mozambican government.

16 October Bishop Desmond Tutu, the Black Anglican head of the South African Council of Churches, is awarded the Nobel Peace Prize for his role as 'a unifying figure in the campaign to resolve the problem of apartheid in South Africa'. Tutu, a proponent of non-violence but also an ANC supporter, was the second South African to receive the award. The former head of the banned ANC, Albert Luthuli, won the prize in 1960 for his civil disobedience campaign against South Africa's system of apartheid.

The Norwegian Nobel Committee, who makes the award, said that the selection of Bishop Tutu 'should be seen as a renewed recognition of the courage and heroism shown by Black South Africans in their use of peaceful methods in the struggle against apartheid'. Observers believed that the international prestige and publicity attached to the Nobel Peace Prize would make it more difficult for the South African government to act against the outspoken Tutu or the Council of Churches.

Tutu, who had been in New York when the announcement was made, returned to South Africa where he immediately began speaking out against the oppression of the country's Black majority. He also attacked US President Ronald Reagan for his policy of 'quiet diplomacy', or 'constructive engagement', in which the US government desisted from publicly criticizing South Africa while privately applying pressure for change.

5 November South Africa's two major Black trade unions, the Federation of South African Trade Unions and the Council of Unions of South Africa, join forces with the multiracial alliance, the United Democratic Front, to launch a major strike against government policies affecting non-Whites. The strike represented the first cooperative effort between Black unions and a political group. It was coordinated by an *ad hoc* Transvaal Regional Stayaway Committee and was accompanied by a significant outbreak of violence. Strikers demanded the resignations of Black township officials and protested against the detention of political prisoners as well as rent and bus fare increases and the sales tax.

The government reacted to the protests by detaining many of the strike leaders and, as it had on several recent occasions, deployed the military to help contain it. The South African business community condemned the detentions, saying that they were harming labour relations and urged the Government to either try the detainees or release them.

1 9 8 5

21 March South African policemen open fire on a funeral procession in the Black township of Langa, outside Uitenhage, killing 21 people and injuring dozens more. The casualties, which occurred on the twenty-fifth anniversary of the Sharpeville massacre, were the highest in a single act of racial violence since Sharpeville itself. The police version of the incident was that they had fired on a mob of Blacks who were marching on White Uitenhage brandishing sticks and throwing petrol bombs and rocks. Most observers discounted this story and accepted the Black version that the police opened fire, without warning, on unarmed Black mourners.

The original funeral procession was for some of the 15 Black activists who had been killed by the police in racial unrest the previous week. Township violence, which had started in September 1984 as a protest against Black exclusion from political participation under the provisions of the new constitution, continued throughout 1985. A deadly aspect of the violence was the emergence of a campaign to assassinate Black 'collaborators', those Blacks seen as cooperating with the apartheid government. After the Uitenhage killings, most observers described the violence as 'endemic' and Blacks were being killed on a daily basis, either by the police or by each other. Black councillors and policeman, their relatives and friends were among the most common victims of the Black on Black 'vengeance' killings.

By the end of the year, it was reported by *The Times* (of London) that some 965 people had been killed in the period from 1 September 1984 to 10 December 1985. Almost all of the violence had occurred in Black townships and all but a few of the victims were non-White. Approximately half of the total number of deaths were caused by the police, while the other half were the result of the assassinations of Black 'collaborators' and feuding between Black factions.

18 April President P.W. Botha announces that the South African government will unilaterally establish a 'transitional government' in Namibia. All legislative powers and executive authority were turned over to the newly established Multi-Party Conference. The South African-appointed administrator-general retained considerable constitutional powers, while the South African government remained in control of foreign and defence issues. The Conference, seen as the predecessor to the transitional government, was a coalition made up of six Namibian political parties but excluding the leading Namibian guerrilla group, the South West African People's Organization (SWAPO). SWAPO refused to participate in the transitional government, calling it a South African puppet. The UN five-nation contact group, comprising the US, Britain, Canada, France and West Germany, condemned the move as a further obstacle in the path of finding a negotiated settlement to the future of Namibia. The new government, installed on 17 July for a two-year term of office, was also condemned by the UN.

22 May Angola announces that two South African commandos had been killed and a third wounded during a raid on the Angolan oil enclave of Cabinda. The oil fields in Cabinda, a small northern enclave separated from the rest of Angola by a thin strip of Zairean territory, provided the country with some 80–90 per cent of its foreign exchange. South Africa admitted that it had infiltrated its troops into the area but claimed that they had been on a reconnaissance mission aimed at gathering information on SWAPO bases and not raiding the oil fields. The disclosure embarrassed the South Africans, who had announced on 17 April that they had withdrawn their troops from southern Angola in order to establish a dialogue with the Angolan government that could result in the withdrawal of Cuban troops from the region.

14 June Commandos from the South African Defence Forces carry out a pre-dawn raid on African National Congress (ANC) targets in the Botswana capital of Gaborone. Sixteen people were killed in the raid, including women and one child. The South Africans justified the raid by saying that South African warnings to Botswana to expel ANC terrorists had been ignored. The South Africans charged that since they signed the Nkomati non-aggression pact with Mozambique, the ANC had relocated its bases in Botswana and used them to carry out terrorist attacks inside South Africa. It claimed that 36 people had been killed in the previous 12 months in attacks conducted by ANC guerrillas based in Botswana. Botswanan President Quett Nasire denied the allegations and called the attack 'a bloodcurdling act of murder of defenceless civilians'.

The raid was internationally condemned as a violation of sovereign boundaries. The US recalled its ambassador amid rumours that US–South African relations were at their lowest point since the Reagan administration began its policy of 'constructive engagement'.

10 July The US House of Representatives votes to end the ban on US military aid to the pro-Western rebel groups in Angola. The Senate had voted on 11 June to repeal the Clark Amendment, which had been enacted in 1976 to stop the Central Intelligence Agency (CIA) from providing support for the National Union for the Total Independence of Angola (Unita). The US legislators said that the move to repeal the amendment was meant to free the president so he could make foreign policy decisions 'without unnecessary congressional restrictions', but that it did not necessarily signify that there were plans to resume aid to Unita.

The congressional debates over the repeal of the Clark Amendment highlighted the divisions within the US government over aid to Unita. The Pentagon and CIA favoured financing Unita, while the State Department urged finding a diplomatic solution to the Angolan problem. Meanwhile, right-wing Republicans were pushing to give the Angolan 'freedom fighters' some $27 million in 'non-lethal' aid to be followed by a like amount for military equiptment. President Ronald Reagan went on record saying that he was in favour of giving Unita covert, rather than overt, aid, while his critics warned that any aid to Unita would result in the US publicly aligning itself with Unita's other main supporter, South Africa.

20 July President Botha introduces an indefinite state of emergency to combat the increasing racial violence that has erupted in many of South Africa's Black townships. The decree affected 36 magisterial districts around Port Elizabeth in the eastern Cape province and around Johannesburg. Under the terms of the state of emergency, the first since the aftermath of the Sharpeville massacre in 1960, the police were granted sweeping powers of arrest, detention, search and seizure. Most civil liberties were abrogated. Emergency regulations were extended to cover Cape Town and the surrounding areas on 25 October.

Within the first few days of the emergency, some 792 people, mostly Blacks, had been detained under the new regulations. The opposition leader Frederick van Zyl Slabbert called the emergency 'a devastating comment' on the Botha government and its promised reforms.

The state of emergency was condemned by the UN, which called for limited, voluntary economic sanctions against South Africa. The European Community also condemned the events in South Africa, and France announced that it would immediately suspend all new investments in the country. The US while condemning apartheid, refused to publicly condemn the South African government. It did, however, indicate that 'quiet pressure' was being put on it to end the emergency.

5 August Sixteen Black and Asian members of the United Democratic Front (UDF), South Africa's main anti-apartheid coalition, go on trial in Pietermaritzburg on charges of treason. The trial was described as the largest treason trial since that of ANC leaders Nelson Mandela and Walter Sisulu in 1964. The 16, eight of whom had been arrested in 1984 and eight in February 1985, represented most of the top leadership of the multiracial organization. Although the UDF claimed to be non-violent, the government considered it a front for the banned ANC, which espoused the overthrow of the government by force. Charges were dropped against 12 of the defendants on 9 December after the prosecution admitted that legal errors had been made in the preparation of the case. The case against the other four continued.

6 August Four days of rioting breaks out in the Black townships around Durban, resulting in some 52 deaths. Zulu tribesmen battled with Indians, other Blacks and the police before the unrest could be contained. It was the worst outbreak of violence since the wave of township unrest began in September 1984. Relations between Blacks and Indians had always been uneasy but worsened after the introduction of the tricameral parliament in 1983 that included Indians but not Blacks. The fighting occurred in an area previously unaffected by the country's state of emergency and was seen by most observers as an indication that the violence was spreading despite the emergency regulations in force.

On 8 August, the violence spread to the Cape province as police clashed with a multiracial crowd of some 1,000 students, who had been marching on the official residence of President Botha to protest the state of emergency. On 28 August, demonstrators also tried to march on Pollsmoor prison, where ANC leader Nelson Mandela was being held. The march ended in a riot when police attacked the demonstrators with whips. Three days of fighting between marchers and police ensued, resulting in the deaths of 28 people.

15 August President Botha delivers a major policy speech in Durban in which he rules out making significant concessions to the country's Black population. Many observers had expected Botha to use the long-awaited speech to announce major reforms in South Africa's racial policies, but reformist hopes were dashed when Botha instead rejected demands by both South African Blacks and foreign critics that apartheid be abandoned. The speech was described as a 'public relations disaster' in that Botha came across as defiant and a victim of the traditional Afrikaner community's 'laager mentality' of retreating into itself to repel outsiders. Anti-apartheid activists in South Africa expressed deep disappointment with the speech, saying, 'He had a golden opportunity, but the hopes were dashed.'

1 September Finance Minister Barend du Plessis announces the imposition of a four-month freeze on all foreign loan principal repayments, but says that interest payments will still be met during the moratorium. Foreign investment in South Africa was also to be frozen. The moves were necessary to protect South Africa's financial position as foreign banks, concerned about the country's stability in the light of the growing racial violence, refused to rollover loans that were coming due. The banks' refusal to extend credit caused the value of the rand to fall and led the governor of the South African Central Bank to undertake an emergency mission to the Western financial capitals to secure alternate sources of finance. He blamed South Africa's debt crisis on 'two or three' US banks for intimating 'that their exposure to South Africa was too large'. He claimed that their motives for such a statement were political rather than economic. Swiss banker Fritz Leutwiler acted as the mediator between the South African government and its 28 main foreign creditors to negotiate a rescheduling of the South African debt. The two sides held their first face-to-face meeting on rescheduling the debt on 23 October but little progress was made either then or in the following weeks. Leutwiler said on 13 November that the South African government would have to move a long way towards instituting political reforms for the talks to succeed but by December he told the South Africans that he thought the talks would eventually result in a rescheduling plan. Most observers believed, however, that the country's political climate had to be significantly improved for investors to accept that South Africa was seriously addressing its racial problems and, on 10 December, the South Africans were forced to extend the moratorium until 31 March.

Prominent South African businessmen, reportedly shocked by the sudden financial crisis, urged President Botha to negotiate with Black leaders. Business leaders went on to meet the leaders of the banned ANC in Zambia to discuss ways of easing the unrest in South Africa. The meeting was publicly condemned by Botha and strained relations between the government and the business community.

16 September South African defence forces pursue SWAPO guerrillas into Angola for the second time in three months. The South Africans described the raid as a preemptive strike against SWAPO to prevent it from launching an expected new campaign of attacks in Namibia.

On 20 September, South African Defence Minister Magnus Malan officially acknowledged for the first time that South Africa was supporting Unita.

30 September President Botha outlines his government's agenda for racial change. He said that the government was willing to restore citizenship to the country's eight million Blacks who had been deprived of it under the homeland policy but made no move towards granting them political rights.

Observers believed that the statement, in which he dropped the rhetoric of apartheid, was the result of White unease over the level and duration of violence that had been gripping South Africa for the past year. The government had apparently begun to believe that the use of force against the Black unrest was increasing instead of decreasing tensions and prolonging the violence.

Botha's announcement was meant to show that the Government was in favour of negotiating a settlement to the situation. Observers added that it was unlikely that such a compromise between the White minority government and Black nationalism could be achieved since Botha was rejecting negotiations with the ANC as long as that group followed its policy of violence, while the ANC refused to negotiate with the government while it was a banned group with its leadership in jail or exile. Opposition leader Frederick van Zyl Slabbert attempted to break the impasse by meeting ANC leaders in Zambia in October. Van Zyl Slabbert urged the government to recognize the ANC and allow it to play a role in the political process.

2 November The government accuses the press of being a 'catalyst' in sparking off the continuing township violence and imposes the most sweeping media curbs in recent South African history. The new regulations, made under the provisions of the state of emergency, severely restricted newspaper, television and radio coverage of racial unrest by both domestic and foreign journalists. As a result of the ban, all pictoral coverage of the unrest ended and reports of the situation in the townships became vague.

29 November Delegates from 36 Black unions meet in Durban to launch a radical new labour federation, the Congress of South African Trade Unions. The congress, representing half a million Black workers, was the largest trade organization of its kind in South Africa. The congress issued a policy statement on 1 December in which it called for the lifting of the state of emergency, resignation of President Botha, abolition of the pass laws and disinvestment of US and British companies of their South African holdings. The National Union of Mineworkers was seen as the major force behind the new federation, which most observers believed would soon outshadow the more politically moderate Trade Union Council of South Africa.

20 December The Lesotho Liberation Army, a rebel group allegedly financed by South Africa, claims responsibility for conducting a raid on two houses in the Lesotho capital of Maseru. Nine people, identified as members of the ANC, were killed in the attack. South Africa denied involvement in the raid while warning its neighbours against harbouring insurgents.

23 December Six Whites, including three children, are killed in a bomb explosion at a shopping centre in the Natal seaside town of Amanzimtoti. The government blamed the bombing on the banned ANC and alleged that ANC guerrillas were deliberately attacking 'soft' targets.

ANC President Oliver Tambo had announced at a June meeting in Zambia of the ANC leadership that the organization would increase its attacks against the government even at the risk of many more civilian casualties and said it was becoming increasingly more difficult 'to distinguish between soft and hard targets'.

1 9 8 6

20 January The prime minister of Lesotho, Chief Leabua Jonathan, is overthrown in a military coup. The move came after South Africa closed its border with landlocked Lesotho and imposed an economic blockade on the country in protest at Jonathan's allowing the banned ANC to operate from bases in Lesotho. The blockade was lifted minutes after ANC members began being flown out of the country. The replacement of Jonathan, an ANC supporter, with a more pro-Pretoria government was seen as a major setback for the ANC.

The ANC was also ousted from Botswana after South African pressure was brought to bear on the Botswanan government. The government of Mozambique, in keeping with its non-aggression pact with South Africa, continued to make conditions uncomfortable for the ANC based in the country, while Swaziland also signed a non-aggression pact with its White neighbour. Despite these setbacks, however, observers believed that the ANC was still flourishing. During 1985, it was credited with some 200 attacks within South Africa, which represented a 400 per cent rise in the number of violent incidents over 1984 figures. Some observers, however, contended that much of the violence was not carried out by the ANC but rather done in its name by Black township activists.

31 January President P.W. Botha officially opens South Africa's new parliamentary session. In a conciliatory speech that was nevertheless short on concrete proposals for reforms, Botha offered Blacks a limited, advisory role in government for the first time. He said that by participating in the proposed national council, they could play a part in shaping constitutional policy.

During his speech, Botha insisted that the country had 'outgrown the outdated colonial system of paternalism as well as the outdated concept of apartheid'. He promised to end the hated pass laws and suggested that jailed ANC leader Nelson Mandela might be released on 'humanitarian grounds'. Mandela's freedom would be in exchange for the release of a South African soldier, Captain Wynand du Toit, captured during a raid on the Angolan oil fields in Cabinda in May 1985 and two Soviet dissidents, Andrei Sakharov and Anatoly Shcharansky.

7 February The leader of the Opposition, Frederick van Zyl Slabbert, resigns from both Parliament and his position as the head of the Progressive Federal Party (PFP). Van Zyl Slabbert, a liberal Afrikaner, called President Botha's reforms 'not good enough – a false start'. His departure, which came at a time when Botha was trying to convince the country that his reform programme was still on track, was seen as part of a trend among liberal Whites to join non-Whites in opposition outside the parliamentary system because of a growing conviction that the government was not serious about implementing real racial reforms. He was replaced by Colin Eglin as leader of the PFP and the Opposition.

15 February Six days of violence erupts in the Black township of Alexandria, near Johannesburg, and leaves over 20 people dead. Among the victims were Blacks who had been accused of 'collaboration' with the Government and killed by other Blacks. The 'necklace' was the common method of killing collaborators.

It involved placing a petrol-soaked tyre around the victim's neck and setting it alight.

4 March President Botha announces that South Africa is willing to begin implementation of the 1978 UN Resolution 435 on 6 August, providing a 'satisfactory timetable' has been negotiated for the withdrawal of Cuban troops from Angola. It was the first time that the South Africans had proposed a firm date for the implementation of the resolution, which provided for the withdrawal of South African troops from Namibia, the holding of UN-sponsored elections and the eventual independence of the territory. It soon became apparent that there was no such timetable being negotiated and the 6 August deadline passed without any progress being made towards achieving Namibian independence. US Assistant Secretary of State for African Affairs Chester Crocker continued throughout the year to attempt to achieve a negotiated settlement of the Namibian problem, but South African and US insistence on linking Namibian independence with a Cuban withdrawal from Angola impeded the peace process.

7 March President Botha lifts the state of emergency that has been in effect in some districts since July 1985 and releases the remaining 329 people still in custody under the emergency regulations. During the period the regulations were in effect, nearly 8,000 people had been detained and some 750 killed.

Botha said that he was lifting the regulations because the level of violence in the Black townships had lessened. Observers, however, contended that the Black violence was showing no sign of abating. They believed Botha was ending the emergency in reaction to the demands of Western governments and bankers that he begin negotiations with non-White leaders. The West welcomed the move, while Blacks remained sceptical.

21 April President Botha announces that the hated pass laws, under which the movement of Blacks was severely controlled, were to be repealed and that those in prison for violating the laws would be released. Legislation was introduced to replace the pass laws with a system for 'orderly urbanization', under which Blacks could theoretically move to urban areas if they could find housing and jobs. Squatting would still be prohibited and the legislation would not apply to the citizens of the nominally independent Black homelands. Botha warned that the government would not allow 'chaotic growth of cities and towns' and insisted that Black mobility would be dependent on housing. The reforms, which were called the most significant package of racial reforms yet offered to the Blacks, only affected laws governing where Blacks could live and work and did not extend to offering them any increased political rights.

18 May The South African defence force launches a combined air and land attack on the capitals of three neighbouring Commonwealth countries, Botswana, Zambia and Zimbabwe. The attack was supposedly against ANC strongholds in Gaborone, Lusaka and Harare but none of the dead were members of the ANC or even South Africans. The leaders of the three attacked countries condemned the raids as unprovoked acts of aggression and denied that their countries were being used as ANC bases. Western governments joined in the condemnation saying that the three countries had been cooperating with South Africa to reduce the level of cross-border violence.

The lack of evidence that the locations attacked had been ANC bases led to Western speculation that the real purpose of the raids was to slow down the work of the Eminent Persons Group (EPG), which had been launched by the Commonwealth in mid-February to seek a peaceful solution to the racial problems in South Africa in lieu of imposing sanctions on the country. The South African government had been seen to be cooperating with the EPG and there was some optimism that the group was making significant progress towards establishing a truce. The raids occurred the same day that the group returned from Gaborone, where they had been conferring with ANC leaders. Observers believed that South Africa felt the EPG mission was going ahead too quickly and that the raids were a way of slowing down their work.

The raids marked a major turning point in the course of the Botha government. After this point, Botha apparently abandoned his attempts to change the apartheid system and began to crack down on opponents. Observers believed that the change came about as a result of domestic pressure on Botha to avoid a split within Afrikanerdom. The failure of the EPG to secure peace in the region, to obtain the release of jailed leader Nelson Mandela or to secure the legalization of the ANC strengthened the anti-apartheid lobbies in the Commonwealth, European Community and US.

18 May A major wave of violence breaks out at the Crossroads squatter settlement near Cape Town. Some 70 people were killed in the fighting that lasted until 28 May and then flared again from 9 to 11 June. More than 50,000 were made homeless in the violence, as right-wing Black vigilantes reportedly attacked sections of the camp that housed anti-apartheid radicals. Government opponents claimed that the vigilantes had been sponsored by the police, who used the violence to suppress opposition and to bring about the forced removals of squatters to the new township of Khayelitsha, about 10 miles (16.1 km) away from Crossroads.

12 June In the face of increasing Black violence, the government imposes a nationwide state of emergency. The security forces were given virtually unlimited powers and severe restrictions were reimposed on the media. Botha said the measures were necessary because the security of the country was at risk from the planned violence that was sweeping it. He contended that the scale of the fighting had increased so dramatically since the last emergency measures were removed in March that the country's ordinary laws were inadequate. In announcing the state of emergency, Botha said that the stricter security measures would 'bring criticism and punitive measures from the outside world' but added that 'the world must take note and never forget that we are not a nation of weaklings'.

Some 1,000 people, mainly Black, Coloured and Asian anti-apartheid activists, were detained on the first day that the decree went into operation. Security Forces were empowered to do whatever they felt necessary to prevent public disorder and were guaranteed freedom from prosecution for any acts they committed. Suspects could be detained without charges and could be denied access to their lawyers or family. Minister of Law and Order Louis Le Grange was empowered to ban all unauthorized television, radio and photographic coverage of the unrest, prohibit the publishing of any 'subversive' statements and ban outright any newspaper or magazine that he felt was a threat to public peace. On 18 August the government released the names of some 8,500 people detained under the emergency regulations, the majority of whom were members of the anti-apartheid umbrella organization, the United Democratic Front. The opposition PFP and the anti-apartheid women's group, Black Sash, protested against the number of children, some as young as 12, that were being held in detention under the emergency regulations.

The imposition of a state of emergency was condemned by the international community as a 'serious mistake'. It gave new impetus to the call for the imposition of economic sanctions against South Africa.

12 June The Commonwealth's EPG releases the report of its six-month attempt to mediate in the racial conflict in South Africa. The EPG urged that wide-ranging sanctions be imposed on the South Africans as 'the last opportunity to avert what could be the worst bloodbath since the Second World War'. The group's leaders, former Australian Prime Minister Malcolm Fraser and former Nigerian leader General Olusegun Obasanjo, warned that unless sanctions were imposed, the result could eventually be the emergence of a 'radical' Black regime most likely aligned to the Soviet Union. Among the measures they wanted immediately adopted were a ban on the importation of South African agricultural products and coal, which formed a large proportion of South Africa's exports, and the suspension of all air links to and from South Africa. They warned Britain, which had consistently resisted imposing sanctions, that it risked a serious breach in the Commonwealth if it did not lift its opposition to the measures.

16 June The tenth anniversary of the Soweto uprising is marked by a one-day strike of Black workers. An estimated 70 per cent of the Black workforce participated in the stay-away. The banned ANC claimed the strike was 'perhaps the greatest national strike in the history of South Africa', while the government insisted that it had foiled an ANC plot to use the occasion to launch a 'massive, popular and multipronged offensive'. The government's restrictions on the press prevented the coverage of any incidents that occurred over the anniversary period, but unofficial reports indicated that the level of Black violence remained high despite the emergency regulations.

26 August Government efforts to break a rent boycott in Soweto result in rioting in which some 20 Blacks are killed and 100 wounded. It was the worst outbreak of violence involving the security forces since the Uitenhage shootings in March 1985.

Some 300,000 families in over 35 districts reportedly participated in the boycotts against the relatively high rents charged for government-owned Black housing. The rents were the main source of funding for the government-appointed Black township councils, and the government was reportedly losing some $500,000 a day in revenue. The councils were despised by most Blacks as apartheid institutions, and the boycott was seen as both an economic and political protest. Rent increases in September 1984 had been one of the main causes of the wave of the violence which had continued intermittently ever since.

2 October The US imposes economic sanctions on South Africa as the Senate votes 78–21 in favour of overriding President Ronald Reagan's veto of the sanctions legislation. The House of Representatives had voted 313–83 on 29 September to impose sanctions. The vote was seen as the biggest foreign policy defeat of Reagan's presidency. The US imposition of sanctions was a major blow to the South African government. Observers felt they had become inevitable after the 18 May raids into neighbouring states and the imposition of a state of emergency led to massive anti-South African demonstrations in the US and to an increase in calls for disinvestment and sanctions.

The sanctions were the most stringent yet imposed by any of South Africa's major trading partners. They included bans on the importation of South African agricultural products, iron and steel and on new US loans to and investments in South Africa. It was estimated that the bans would amount to some $350 million of South Africa's annual $2.2 thousand million worth of exports to the US.

The sanctions were far stricter than those imposed by the European Community on 16 September. The Community voted to ban the importation of South African iron, steel and gold coins and to prohibit new investment in the country. These sanctions were weaker than had been threatened because of British and German opposition to harsher measures. The sanctions came after an unsuccessful mission to South Africa on behalf of the Community by British Foreign Secretary Sir Geoffrey Howe. Black leaders in South Africa were not impressed by the European Community sanctions, calling them 'lukewarm'. They did not include bans on South African agricultural products or coal, both of which made up a large percentage of the South African exports to the European Community and which could have been extremely damaging to South Africa. The final package of sanctions was expected to affect only 5 per cent of South Africa's large export trade to the European Community.

The sanctions, although not harsh in themselves, did cause South African businessmen to suffer a further lose of confidence and led to a 'siege economy' in South Africa.

19 October Mozambican President Samore Machel is killed as his plane crashes just inside the South African border. Machel, who led Mozambique to independence from Portugal in 1975, was one of the key figures in the conflict between the Black states of southern Africa and White-ruled South Africa. South Africa was blamed for the crash, which happened less than a mile (1.6 km) from the border with Mozambique. Some witnesses claimed that the plane had been shot down. South Africa strenuously denied the charges.

11 December The South African government tightens the nation-wide state of emergency in the face of what President Botha calls a 'revolutionary onslaught'. The measures included an almost total blackout of news coverage of the unrest and a ban on most of the remaining forms of political opposition in South Africa. The new measures closed most of the loopholes in the original decree and made it practically impossible to report or comment on the actions of either the defence forces or the police.

1 9 8 7

4 January Reverend Allan Hendrickse, leader of the major party in the Coloured chamber of the House of Assembly and a member of President P.W. Botha's Cabinet, swims on a Whites-only beach in Port Elizabeth to highlight the intense resentment that the Coloured Community felt towards the Group Areas Act. The gesture enraged Botha, who demanded and received an apology. Relations between the two men deteriorated to such an extent that observers felt the tricameral parliament was in danger of collapse. Hendrickse eventually resigned from the Cabinet on 24 August after continuing arguments about the Group Areas Act, which Botha refused to dismantle but agreed to amend. After this clash the previously compliant Coloured legislative chamber began to play an increasingly militant role.

30 January Denis Worrall, considered one of South Africa's most effective overseas spokesmen, resigns his position as ambassador to Britain. The resignation was seen as a blow to the government, coming as it did from a man who was previously one of Botha's main supporters. Worrall was reportedly angered by, among other things, the government's 1986 raids on Botswana, Zambia and Zimbabwe which scuttled the Commonwealth peace initiative.

On 14 February Worrall confirmed that he would contest the upcoming general election as an independent candidate in the constituency of Chris Heunis, minister for constitutional development and planning. Heunis was seen by many as a likely successor to Botha. Worrall described himself as standing politically between the Nationalists and the liberal Progressive Federal Party (PFP).

Worrall's resignation came soon after the announcement by prominent National Party Member of Parliament Wynand Malan that he would contest the general election as an independent. Worrall and Malan announced that they would form a new independent political movement and would enter into a loose alliance with the PFP to contest the elections.

10 February An official US advisory committee, appointed by the Reagan administration in 1985 to study the US's South African policy, announces that 'constructive engagement' has failed and that a new policy is urgently required. It recommended that the US impose economic sanctions against South Africa, attempt to improve its relations with South African Blacks and facilitate 'good-faith negotiations' between the White and non-White communities.

US–South African relations deteriorated further during the year. On 3 June, Reverend Leon Sullivan, an influential Black American campaigner against apartheid, urged the complete corporate pullout of US firms from South Africa within the following nine months. Sullivan had developed a series of fair labour guidelines in 1977 for the treatment of Black workers at US-owned companies in South Africa, which became known as the Sullivan Principles and were voluntarily adopted by the majority of US companies operating in the country. Sullivan praised the record of the principles, which he said gave Black workers more rights than they had had in the previous 300 years, but announced that because of the government's 'intransigence' he would have to abandon his attempts to encourage gradual reform and lend his support to the disinvestment campaign.

That campaign won another major victory when Congress passed legislation in December that would make US firms in South Africa liable for double taxation. It was thought that the new law would give US companies further incentive to pull out of South Africa.

22 April A strike by Black railway workers, begun on 11 March, breaks out into the worst violence seen in South Africa since the state of emergency was declared in 1986. Clashes with the police, which left at least six strikers dead, followed the mass firings of some 16,000 workers. It was believed to be the largest mass dismissal in the country's history.

The strike against the state-owned South African Transport Services (SATS), the country's largest employer, was declared illegal by the government since it affected a 'strategic industry'. The strike action was seen as a direct challenge to the government by the increasingly militant Black trade union movement.

Before the strike ended on 5 June, some 11 workers had died, more than 60 trains were destroyed or damaged in firebomb attacks and the state-owned SATS was believed to have lost millions of dollars in passenger and freight revenue. The SATS were forced to rehire the striking workers in what was seen as a major victory for the previously unrecognized South African Railway and Harbour Workers Union, which had organized the action.

6 May Elections to the House of Assembly show a marked shift to the political right by White voters. The National Party was returned to power with a slightly increased majority. However, Andries Treurnicht's right-wing Conservative Party made a remarkably strong showing, winning several seats from the Nationalists and becoming the country's official Opposition. The main loser in the election was the liberal PFP, which lost eight of its previous 27 seats, and its electoral ally, the New Republic Party, which lost four of its five seats. Three candidates ran highly publicized races as independents lying half-way between the National Party and PFP on the political spectrum, but only former Nationalist Member of Parliament Wynand Malan won a seat. Denis Worrall, the former ambassador to Britain, narrowly lost to Chris Heunis, the minister for constitutional development. Heunis's close win, by a mere 39 votes, damaged his chances of succeeding President Botha; Education Minister F.W. de Klerk emerged as the most likely successor.

President Botha greeted the results as a 'clear mandate on the question of security and on our reform policy'. Liberal Whites and the non-White communities were bitterly disappointed by the shift to the right. PFP leader Colin Eglin said it was 'frightening' that in future parliamentary debates 'the leader of the opposition would be attacking the Government for being too liberal'. The leader of the ANC, Oliver Tambo, said the vote 'blew the whistle for the ANC to intensify the armed struggle', an opinion shared by both Archbishop Desmond Tutu and moderate Black leader Chief Gatsha Buthelezi.

The National Party won 123 seats, up six, with a reduced share of the total vote. The Conservative won 22, up five, but captured 26.4 per cent of the total vote, while the PFP won 19 seats, down from 27.

11 May Kaiser Matanzima is ousted as prime minister of the Transkei by his brother, George, after allegations of corruption. He is banished to a remote village in the Black homeland. The territory, which had been ruled by the Matanzima family since its 'independence' in 1976, had been the scene of continuing unrest in recent years. George Matanzima was himself relieved of the premiership on 24 September when the military ousted eight of his senior Cabinet ministers from office. The new leader, Major General Bantu Holomisa, assumed power after accusing the government of still more corruption and imposed martial law.

The unrest in the Transkei was a source of embarrassment to the South African government, which supplied the area with 80 per cent of its funds and was the only country to recognize its independence.

10 June President Botha extends the country's year-old state of emergency for a further 12 months. Botha contended that the 'background of violence and unrest' which led to the original decree being imposed still existed and accused the banned ANC of playing 'a cardinal role in the underground terror network in South and southern Africa'.

Observers agreed with the government's contention that the state of emergency had succeeded in enforcing calm in the Black townships and in quashing the influence of the multiracial, anti-apartheid United Democratic Front (UDF). They believed that the result was that the focus of Black resistance had, at least in the short term, shifted from local township unrest to armed ANC attacks and from the UDF to the increasingly militant Black trade union movement.

9 July A group of some 60 Afrikaner dissidents, led by former PFP leader Frederick van Zyl Slabbert, begin an historic series of discussions with the leaders of the banned ANC in Dakar, Senegal. The talks ended with the issuance of the Dakar Declaration, in which they expressed the desire to find a peaceful solution to the problems in South Africa and for the end of apartheid and the introduction of a multiracial, democratic system.

News of the talks, which the participants had hoped to keep secret, were leaked and resulted in a right-wing outcry against them. The participants were branded as 'political terrorists' and there were calls for them to be tried for treason. President Botha, while not commenting publicly, was known to be furious about the meeting and his government officially warned van Zyl Slabbert and the others that it would not permit any further discussions with the ANC.

14 July US Assistant Secretary of State for African Affairs Chester Crocker visits the Zambian capital of Lusaka for another round of negotiations on Namibian independence and the withdrawal of Cuban troops from Angola. He emerged from the meetings calling them 'a waste of time'.

The talks came after a March announcement by Sam Nujoma, the leader of the main Namibian guerrilla group, that the South West African People's Organization (SWAPO) was willing to conduct negotiations on the future of Namibia with the South African government without prior conditions. SWAPO had previously insisted that all talks be held in accordance with the 1978 UN Resolution 435. Nujoma insisted, however, that he would never negotiate with the 'puppet' government that had been put into power in Namibia by the South Africans. The South Africans continued to link Namibian independence with the Cuban withdrawal from Angola and, although paying lip service to the implementation of Resolution 435, acted as if it was an obsolete concept that no longer applied to the situation in southern Africa.

Crocker held a further series of fruitless talks in Lusaka in September after Cuba and Angola issued a joint statement on 4 August promising to adopt a 'more flexible' negotiating position.

28 August The government imposes new and sweeping curbs on the already heavily censored media. Under the new regulations, the government could ban or censor any newspaper it deemed to be responsible for inciting unrest. In announcing the measures on 17 August, Botha had accused the media, both domestic and foreign, of presenting the world with a distorted picture of his policies and vowed to curb left-wing newspapers that 'unashamedly support leftist and revolutionary groups'.

Under the new regulations, the government could caution any publication that it was exceeding the permitted limits and, if the warning was ignored, could take action to close the publication without recourse to the courts. Any organization printing even neutral accounts of the banned ANC or other Black nationalist groups was warned. By the end of December, most of the outspoken anti-apartheid organs had been issued with final cautions and were then facing either government censorship or summary closure. Since the government had not proceeded past the warning stage, observers concluded that the purpose of the legislation was to ensure self-censorship and a compliant press.

9 August The (Black) National Union of Mineworkers (NUM) begins a three-week strike in pursuit of a 30 per cent wage rise. More than 250,000 miners were believed to have participated in the action, which affected 16 of the country's 44 gold and coal mines. Some 11 miners died, 300 were injured and 400 arrested before the NUM was forced to accept the Chamber of Mines' original offer of a 15–23 per cent rise on 30 August, in the face of the mass firings of strikers. The victory was costly, however, with the mines suffering an estimated $125–225 million in production losses. The NUM claimed that it had learned valuable lessons during the strike and that 'this strike was a dress rehearsal for further action'.

13 October Leaders of the moderate Inkatha movement and the radical UDF formally sign a truce to end the fighting between the two Black political groups. The truce, however, was broken almost immediately and the fighting, described as intra-Black civil war, continued.

Inkatha, a largely Zulu organization run by Chief Gatsha Buthelezi, and the UDF, a multiracial umbrella group of some 700 anti-apartheid associations, were involved in a bloody feud in Natal province. Since the beginning of the year, some 175 people had died as a result of the fighting. Most of the victims, some as young as 12 years old, were killed in the Black townships around Pietermaritzburg and Durban and were members of the UDF and its ally, the Congress of South African Trade Unions.

Observers believed that the fighting, which started in 1985, had been caused by Inkatha in an attempt to ensure that its power base among the Zulus was not eroded by the more radical UDF. The police were seen to be favouring Inkatha and the UDF claimed the government did nothing to end the 'Black-on-Black' violence because it was trying to reduce the UDF's power while strengthening Whites' belief that a Black-ruled government would disintegrate into violence and chaos.

5 November The former chairman of the banned ANC, 77-year-old Govan Mbeki, is freed after 23 years in prison. The release of Mbeki, who had been jailed for treason with ANC leader Nelson Mandela and six others after the famous 'Rivonia trial' of 1964, was seen as preliminary to the release of Mandela himself and gave rise to the hope that President Botha was seriously considering negotiating with the ANC. Those hopes were soon dashed when the security police imposed such restrictions on Mbeki that he was effectively banned from participating in politics.

11 November The South African government admits for the first time that its troops are actively involved in the fighting in the Angolan civil war. South Africa had previously claimed that its support of the rebel National Union for the Total Independence of Angola (Unita) was limited to supplying logistical aid and arms in its fight against the Marxist Popular Movement for the Liberation of Angola (MPLA) government. The South Africans now claimed that the direct involvement of their troops was necessary to prevent Unita, and its leader Jonas Savimbi, from being overwhelmed by the Soviet and Cuban troops supporting the MPLA. Their ultimate goal was reportedly the formation of an Unita–MPLA coalition government. Savimbi, however, denied that the recent Unita successes had been the result of the South Africans' intervention.

The UN Security Council, meeting in an emergency session on 25 November, unanimously voted to demand that South Africa withdraw its forces. The South African Defence Force leader announced on 5 December that his troops were being withdrawn following 'the successful completion of certain tasks in the interest of South Africa', but the withdrawal of the estimated 2,500–7,000 soldiers had not been completed by the end of the year.

28 January A further round of talks on the withdrawal of Cuban troops from Angola and the independence of Namibia in terms of the 1978 UN Resolution 435 opens in the Zambian capital of Lusaka. One of the driving forces behind the talks, US Assistant Secretary of State for African Affairs Chester Crocker, was joined for the first time by a senior official from the Cuban government. At the end of the talks, the US announced that the Angolan and Cuban sides had, also for the first time, agreed to the eventual withdrawal of the some 40,000 Cuban troops currently stationed in Angola. The US greeted the agreement in principle as 'an important step'.

10 February South African troops crush a military coup in the Black homeland of Bophuthatswana that had earlier in the day ousted President Lucas Mangope. Responding to a call for assistance from Bophuthatswana's 'legitimate' government, South African soldiers and anti-terrorist police rescued Mangope and other senior ministers being held by dissident officers of the Bophuthatswana Defence Force and routed the rebels.

Observers noted that the South African government's response to the attempted overthrow of Mangope was in marked contrast to the 1987 coup in the Transkei. In both incidents, Black military officers overthrew governments that they charged with corruption. In the Transkei, however, the South African government failed to protest the coup and later officially recognized the new government. Their quick action in crushing the Bophuthatswanan rebels renewed suspicions that the South Africans had actually instigated the Transkei coup.

South African President P.W. Botha immediately visited Bophuthatswana to show his support for Mangope's restored government. In a remark that commentators called revealing, Botha announced, 'We are back in control.' He quickly amended it to 'the President of Bophuthatswana is in full control'.

24 February The South African government bans the anti-apartheid umbrella organization, the United Democratic Front (UDF), and 17 other predominantly Black extra-parliamentary opposition groups from participating in politics. Severe restrictions were also imposed upon the Congress of South African Trade Unions (Cosatu), the country's largest trade union federation, which prevented it from carrying on any political activities. The move was bitterly opposed by South African church leaders, who moved to fill the vacuum the restrictions had created. Anglican Archbishop Desmond Tutu, Roman Catholic Archbishop Stephen Naidoo, World Alliance of Reformed Churches president Allan Boesak and some 100 other clergymen were briefly arrested on 29 February in Cape Town while attempting to present a petition to Parliament in protest against the curbs. On 6 March, the churchmen launched the Committee for the Defence of Democracy to take up the work of the banned organizations but the new group was also banned.

17 March A powerful car bomb explodes outside the Krugersdorp Magistrates Court killing three people and injuring 22. The bombing was seen as part of an intensified ANC campaign during which major bombing incidents occurred almost weekly. The attacks decreased in frequency later in the year and it became apparent that there was a split within the ANC between those who wanted to aim their attacks at hard targets with strategic significance, avoiding civilian casualties if possible, and those who aimed to attack soft targets and cause civilian deaths.

26 May Afrikaner liberals and representatives of the banned ANC meet in West Germany in the face of opposition from the South African government. The two sides had originally met in July 1987 for discussions on how to achieve a nonracial South Africa; they published constitutional guidelines, including a Bill of Rights, that were intended to calm White fears about future Black participation in the Government.

13 July US Assistant Secretary of State for African Affairs Chester Crocker announces that the participants in the four-power talks on implementing UN Resolution 435 to bring about Namibian independence had reached a tentative agreement on 'the principles for a peaceful settlement in southwestern Africa'. Delegates from the US, South Africa, Angola and Cuba were meeting in New York, after earlier rounds of the talks had been held in London and Cairo.

5 August Zach J. de Beer becomes leader of the liberal Progressive Federal Party, replacing Colin Eglin. De Beer continued his predecessor's attempts to unite the PFP with the two other main liberal political groups, the National Democratic Party of Wynand Malan and the Independence movement of the former ambassador to Britain, Denis Worrall, into a single liberal party that could attempt to offset the influence that the extreme right-wing Conservative Party was exerting on the government.

8 August South Africa, Angola and Cuba announce that they have reached a cease-fire agreement in the Angolan and Namibian conflicts. The agreement had been negotiated during a series of four-power meetings held in London, Cairo and Geneva with the US, under the chairmanship of US Assistant Secretary of State for African Affairs Chester Crocker. Under the terms of the agreement, South Africa would withdraw all of its troops from Angola by 1 September, at which time Angola and Cuba would present a timetable for the withdrawal of the Cuban troops.

The first of November 1988 was set as the target date for the implementation of UN Resolution 435, which called for South Africa's withdrawal from Namibia and the holding of UN-supervised elections leading to Namibia's independence. The elections were envisaged for July 1989, by which time South Africa was to have completed its phased withdrawal from Namibia and the UN would have deployed a peace-keeping force. The 1 November date was considered unlikely by most observers and, after further negotiations, it was decided that 1 April 1989 would be a more likely time to begin implementing the UN resolution.

The main sticking point to the agreement was that it had been reached without the participation of the main guerrilla groups operating in the area: the South West African People's Organization (SWAPO) and the South African and US-sponsored National Union for the Total Independence of Angola (Unita) in Angola. The exact withdrawal schedule of the Cuban troops was also left undecided, with South Africa wanting the Cubans out within 12 months, while Cuba favoured a four-year withdrawal programme.

31 August The Johannesburg headquarters of the South African Council of Churches, which also housed the offices of the women's anti-apartheid Black Sash organization and other liberal groups, are destroyed in a bomb attack. It followed the 1987 bombing of the country's largest trade federation, Cosatu, and preceded the fire-bombing of the South African Catholic Bishops' Conference in Pretoria.

2 September The South African government withdraws controversial legislation designed to strengthen the Group Areas Act, one of the cornerstones of apartheid legislation which provided for racially segregrated residential and recreational areas, and to provide severe new penalties for those who violated the act. The backdown came in the face of united Coloured and Indian opposition to the bill in the Coloured and Indian chambers of the tricameral legisláture, which was led by the leader of the (Coloured) Labour Party, Reverend Allan Hendrickse. Hendrickse blocked the government's legislative programme whenever possible, making government difficult for the Nationalists, and threatened to do so until the Botha administration completely repealed the hated Group Areas Act.

12 September President Botha holds talks with Mozambican President Joachim Chissano during his first visit to a Black African country. Over the next several weeks, he also visited Malawi, Zaire and the Ivory Coast as part of his efforts to end South Africa's isolation in Africa. Observers believed that the visits and contacts with the outside world, together with the progress being made in the Angolan–Namibian talks, demonstrated that South Africa was slowly beginning to emerge from its political isolation.

26 October Simultaneous elections to separate White, Black, Coloured and Indian local municipal councils are held for the first time throughout South Africa. The government portrayed the elections as the next step in the process of democraticizing South Africa, a claim rejected by most Blacks who had responded to a call from Archbishop Desmond Tutu to boycott the proceedings. Even the official figure of 25 per cent Black participation was disappointing for the government, who had hoped to use the elections to show that they were democratically circumventing Black revolutionaries. Botha had been hoping for a reasonable Black voter turnout to institute his plans for Blacks to participate in a national advisory council which would negotiate constitutional reforms. The plan to use local government as a base on which to build first regional and then national governments was seen by observers as having got off to an extremely bad start, with the local community denying it legitimacy by refusing to participate in the scheme.

In the White elections, the right-wing Conservative Party participated in national municipal elections for the first time. Ita captured 67 of the 110 contested councils in the Transvaal, but generally did less well than expected. The results were interpreted as an indication that the Conservative threat to the National Party was not as great as had been thought.

The election results eased the government's preoccupation with catering for conservative White voters and freed it to pursue slightly more reformist policies.

18 November The trial of the 'Delmas 22', one of the longest political trial in South African history, ends with four Black nationalists being convicted of treason. Seven other defendants were convicted of terrorist offences and eight were acquitted. Three other defendants in the case, which had begun in the town of Delmas in January 1986, had been acquitted in November 1986.

The defendants, all leading members of the UDF, the anti-apartheid umbrella organization, had been accused of treason and subversion for organizing rent strikes and demonstrations that the prosecution claimed caused an atmosphere of violence to be created in an industrial area of the Transvaal in September 1984. The judge, in summing up the case, accepted the government's contention that the UDF was, in fact, the above-ground wing of the banned ANC.

The convictions were condemned as a 'deplorable' misuse of the country's judicial system and were seen as placing further limits on Black South Africans' ability to protest against apartheid.

23 November President Botha reprieves the 'Sharpeville Six', who had been awaiting execution in Pretoria amid international appeals for clemency. The five men and one woman had been sentenced to death after a controversial ruling found that they had had 'a common purpose' with the mob that had murdered a Black councillor in Sharpeville in 1984. They were not, however, convicted of having actually killed him themselves. The commutation of the sentences to between 18 and 25 years in prison was seen by observers as a sign that the Botha government felt it had more freedom of movement in dealing with Black nationalists since beating the Conservative Party in the recent local municipal elections. This and other concessions to international demands was expected to prevent further economic sanctions from being imposed against South Africa.

7 December Jailed ANC leader Nelson Mandela, who had been in a Cape Town clinic recovering from an attack of tuberculosis, is moved to a half-way house in the western Cape province instead of being returned to prison. The move was interpreted as the first step towards Mandela's eventual freedom. It was seen as the government's recognition of the fact that it could not risk the political fallout of Mandela dying in prison and as a concession to the West in order to avoid the imposition of further economic sanctions against the country.

The move followed the release on 26 November of two other aging Black nationalists on 'medical–humanitarian grounds', Pan-African Congress founder and leader Zephania Mothopeng and ANC leader Harry Gwala. Although observers saw the developments as a positive sign of the government's willingness to make some concessions to the country's non-White communities and the West, they did not interpret them as the government's willingness to begin actual negotiations with the ANC on the future of South Africa.

13 December Representatives of the South African, Angolan and Cuban governments meet in the Congolese capital of Brazzaville to sign the Brazzaville Protocol. The agreement provided for Namibian independence and the withdrawal of Cuban forces from Angola. It set 1 April 1989 as the beginning of the transitional period for Namibian independence, while the phased withdrawal of Cuba's 50,000 troops would begin around the same time and be concluded by July 1991.

The accord was the result of a period of intensive diplomatic negotiations that had begun in London in May. UN-supervised elections were scheduled to be held by 1 November 1989, by which time half of the 50,000 Cuban troops in Angola were expected to have already left the country, while the other half moved north of the 13th parallel. The South Africans were expected to withdraw all but 1,500 of its 60,000-man force within a week of the elections.

SWAPO, the nationalist guerrilla group with whom the South Africans had been fighting for more than 20 years, were expected to sweep the elections.

The foreign ministers of South Africa, Angola and Cuba meet under US auspices at the UN headquarters in New York on 22 December to formally sign two accords providing for the independence of Namibia and the total withdrawal of Cuban forces from Angola. The two issues had been linked by the South Africans, who refused to agree to independence for the territory it had administered since the First World War until after the Cubans withdrew from neighbouring Angola. The accords marked the first major US diplomatic victory in Africa in recent years and was largely result of the efforts put in over an eight-year period by Assistant Secretary of State Chester Crocker. The Soviet Union was also credited with playing a role behind the scenes in pushing Angola and Cuba towards reaching an agreement.

1 9 8 9

10 January Cuban troops begin their withdrawal from Angola under the provisions of the UN peace plan for Namibia. According to the terms of the agreement, signed by South Africa, Cuba and Angola on 22 December 1988, all 50,000 Cubans stationed in the country were scheduled to depart by July 1991.

Cuban troops first arrived in Angola in 1975 to assist the Marxist Popular Movement for the Liberation of Angola maintain its grasp on government despite the efforts of South African-backed guerrilla groups to oust it. South Africa had made the Cuban withdrawal from Angola a prerequisite for Namibian independence.

Angolan President Jose Eduardo dos Santos thanked the Cubans in an emotional farewell ceremony, saying, 'You have fulfilled your mission with honour and glory, and your contribution to our country is unforgettable and indestructible.' It was estimated that over 2,000 Cuban soldiers died in Angola.

2 February President P.W. Botha unexpectedly resigns as leader of the National Party after suffering a mild stroke on 18 January. Education Minister Frederik W. de Klerk won the election to succeed Botha by a mere eight votes, but then quickly went on to consolidate his position. Although Botha retained his post as president, and Constitutional Affairs Minister Chris Heunis was appointed acting president, it was widely expected that de Klerk would also succeed Botha as the country's next president in time to lead the party into the general election due to be held within the year. De Klerk beat Heunis, Foreign Minister Roelof 'Pik' Botha and Finance Minister Barend du Plessis in the leadership battle. He had been known as a conservative, but quickly aligned himself with those attempting to reform the country's apartheid system. Unlike Botha and Botha's preferred successor, Heunis, de Klerk did not have a security or military background and relations between Botha and de Klerk soon deteriorated.

On 2 March, Botha precipitated a National Party crisis when he announced that he intended to resume his duties as president instead of stepping down gracefully in de Klerk's favour as expected. His refusal to give way led to confusion over who formulated policy since, for the first time in history, the head of government was not also the head of the ruling party. The party found this situation unacceptable and both its progressive and conservative branches united against Botha's autocratic style of government in favour of de Klerk's more conciliatory manner. Botha grudgingly resigned on 14 August after a final bitter struggle with both de Klerk and his own Cabinet and de Klerk was sworn in as president the following day.

16 February Winnie Mandela is formally denounced and disowned by the United Democratic Front (UDF) for having 'abused the trust' of the nation's Black community. The UDF, an umbrella organization of South Africa's main anti-apartheid groups, was widely believed to the above-ground wing of the African National Congress (ANC). The unprecedented action against the wife of jailed ANC leader Nelson Mandela and a woman who had previously been seen as the 'Mother of the Nation' came after she and the Mandela United Football Club, a band militant of bodyguards, were implicated in the death of a young Soweto boy, 'Stompie' Moeketsi Seipei.

Mrs Mandela's popularity had, in recent years, been slowly declining as other Black leaders criticized her 'imperious' behaviour. Her 30-strong 'supporters' football club' was accused of creating a 'reign of terror' in Soweto. The murder of the 14-year-old boy was seen as the final straw.

1 April The UN-sponsored cease-fire officially comes into effect in Namibia as the first step towards the territory's transition to independence. Fighting erupted almost immediately, when the South Africans detected up to 1,200 armed South West African People's Organization (SWAPO) guerrillas infiltrating the territory from Angola in clear violation of the cease-fire agreement. The South African security forces immediately took advantage of the situation and hunted down the guerrillas, killing over 250 of them and injuring hundreds others. It was among the bloodiest fighting in the entire 25-year civil war. The UN was put in the uncomfortable position of having to side with the South Africans and gave them permission to bring in reinforcements. UN investigators maintained that the invasion was apparently 'not hostile', but had to agree that the South Africans had scrupulously adhered to the cease-fire arrangements, while SWAPO clearly had not. A SWAPO spokesman described the situation by saying, 'Our people are being butchered under the United Nations flag.'

8 April The Progressive Party, led by Zach J. de Beer, Wynand Malan's National Democratic Movement and the Independent Party of former ambassador to Britain Denis Worrall formally merge to form the Democratic Party. De Beer was elected on 10 April to head the new party, which from its inception held 20 seats in the 178-seat parliament.

The merger followed months of negotiations between the three White liberal parties. The new organization advocated the repeal of all apartheid legislation and the adoption of a universal franchise. Former Progressive Federal Party leader Frederick van Zyl Slabbert and William, the brother of new National Party leader F.W. de Klerk, were named as special advisers to the new political body.

12 May National Party leader de Klerk makes his first major policy speech since becoming head of the country's ruling party in February. While promising to continue to pursue social and constitutional reforms, he emphatically ruled out the possibility of Black majority rule.

5 July President Botha holds an historic meeting with jailed ANC leader Nelson Mandela at his official presidential residence in Cape Town. South Africans of all races were shocked when news of the secret 'courtesy visit' was released several days later and speculation was high that one of the world's most famous political prisoners was about to be released. The South African authorities were quick to stress, however, that the visit did not involve a discussion of policy issues and was not expected to lead to further negotiations.

Political analysts speculated that the meeting was the result of the bitter rivalry between Botha and his expected successor, National Party leader F.W. de Klerk. Many expected Botha to release Mandela to both ensure his place in history and to deny de Klerk the opportunity.

2 August Anti-apartheid activists launch a national defiance campaign in the run-up to the September national elections. The campaign of civil disobedience was conducted in defiance of the three-year-old state of emergency regulations restricting dissident activity. The campaign was organized by the Mass Democratic Movement (MDM), a loose coalition of anti-apartheid groups including the United Democratic Front (UDF) and the the mass labour organization Congress of South African Trade Unions. MDM leaders said that the campaign had grown out of the realization that the street demonstrations and violence of previous years had not worked and that the new, peaceful campaign was designed to attract wide support both at home and abroad. Non-White volunteers defied the apartheid laws and risked arrest by presenting themselves at Whites-only hospitals and beaches. Most demonstrations passed off peacefully, but there were some violent incidents. The campaign was supported by Archbishop Desmond Tutu and other church leaders as well as by the Black labour movement.

The campaign culminated in the 'Big March', in which a multiracial crowd of some 35,000 people held a protest march in September in Cape Town against heavy-handed police tactics. The march, led by Tutu and other church and civil leaders, passed off peacefully after President de Klerk decided to allow the protest to go ahead. Observers saw the march as a turning point, establishing a pattern of non-violent demonstrations which was followed throughout the country. They also saw it as a major indication that the new president was reining in the security establishment that had been so powerful under his predecessor.

21 August The Organization of African Unity, meeting in the Zimbabwean capital, adopts the Harare Declaration. The document was drawn up by the ANC and was the most detailed blueprint for talks with the White South African government that the guerrilla group had ever submitted. The declaration called for the establishment of a nonracial, multi-party democracy, a mixed economy and an entrenched Bill of Rights, all of which were long-held ANC goals. While backing 'the armed and other forms of struggle', the document emphasized the chance of negotiating with the government rather than fighting it. Observers believed that its relatively positive tone and its call for talks was a significant development.

6 September The National Party retains control of South Africa as a result of the general elections but loses support to both the left-wing Democratic Party and the right-wing Conservative Party. The recent internal squabbling in the ruling National Party between then President Botha and National Party leader de Klerk had been expected to cost the party votes, but the decline in support was greater than expected. The Conservative Party retained its role as official Opposition but also fared less well than expected, while the performance of the new Democratic Party surprised most observers. President de Klerk nevertheless declared the results of the election a mandate for his party's policy of gradually reforming the apartheid system.

The National Party suffered its largest setback since coming to power in 1948, gaining only 93 seats, down from 123 in the previous parliament. The Conservatives won 39 seats, a gain from its previous 22. Two of those seats were in constituencies outside the Transvaal for the first time, but the party failed to make the expected inroads in key urban seats. The Democratic Party won 33 seats, up from 21, and gained support from liberal Afrikaners. The voter turnout in the elections to the Coloured and Indian chambers of the tricameral legislature was very low after anti-apartheid groups called for an electoral boycott.

De Klerk was officially elected to a five-year term of office as president on 14 September by South Africa's electoral college and was sworn in on 20 September. Calling himself the leader of all South Africans, 'not only those represented in Parliament', de Klerk announced that his goal was that 'all South Africans, in a just and equitable manner, become part of the decision-making processes of South Africa'. He promised to pursue a policy of domestic and regional reconciliation, to stop South Africa's efforts to destabilize the governments of its Black neighbours, to decrease the power of the state security system and to ease the burden on the economy by reducing state spending.

11 October President de Klerk holds his first meeting with key non-White leaders since taking office when he confers with three leading clerics. Anglican Archbishop Desmond Tutu, president of the World Alliance of Reformed Churches Reverend Allan Boesak and General Secretary of the South African Council of Churches Reverend Frank Chican joined de Klerk for 'talks about talks'. The churchmen presented a list of six demands that they insisted the South African government meet before the anti-apartheid movement would agree to hold substantive talks and to drop its call for international sanctions. They called for the end of the national state of emergency, the legalization of banned organizations, the release of all detainees being held without trial and of all remaining political prisoners, reprieves for those being held under a death sentence and an end to restrictions on political activity.

15 October Eight ageing Black nationalist leaders are unconditionally freed from jail in what observers see as a preliminary move towards the release of Black nationalist leader Nelson Mandela. ANC leader Walter Sisulu and four of the others had been in prison since being convicted of sabotage and treason at the famous 'Rivonia trial' in 1964 and given life sentences along with Mandela. The anti-apartheid umbrella organization, the UDF, hailed the releases as a 'massive victory' for both the South African people and the international sanctions campaign. A huge rally was held in Soweto, with government permission, to greet the men. The gathering was seen as being the first ANC rally in South Africa in over 25 years.

7 November Namibians go to the polls in the territory's first nonracial elections. The UN-sponsored balloting was for the 72-seat constituent assembly that would draft Namibia's independence constitution. Voting was extremely heavy, with over 97 per cent of the electorate participating.

The results of the voting, which lasted until 11 November, were announced on 14 November. The guerrilla group that had waged war for Namibia's independence for over 25 years, SWAPO, emerged the winner as expected, but did not obtain the two-thirds majority it would have needed to enable it to draft the country's constitution itself. SWAPO won 41 seats, with 57.3 per cent of the vote. The South African-backed Democratic Turnhalle Alliance won 21 seats and 28.5 per cent of the ballots cast, while several smaller parties won the remaining ten seats.

SWAPO leader Sam Nujoma, who was expected to be Namibia's first president, announced that his group would cooperate with its political rivals in formulating Namibia's constitution, saying, 'we have no intentions of imposing our views on anyone.' He said, 'We offer a hand of friendship to the Whites and invite them to stay and live with us in an independent Namibia.'

16 November President de Klerk announces that all South African beaches will immediately be open for use by people of all races. He also said that the Separate Amenities Act, authorizing the segregation of public facilities, would soon be abolished. The moves were seen as being largely symbolic since 'petty apartheid' legislation had not rigorously been enforced for the past several years and Johannesburg had formally integrated its public facilities in September.

On 24 November, the government announced that the Group Areas Act, long considered one of the cornerstones of apartheid legislation, would not apply in four 'free settlement areas' that were to be established. The members of all racial groups were to be able to live legally in the integrated areas, the only such places in the entire country. Critics called the measures 'a damp squib' and demanded that the Group Areas Act be completely abolished.

21 November Namibia's constituent assembly meets to begin drafting the country's constitution. The final document, which was agreed in principle on 20 December and scheduled to be presented on 12 January 1990, was worked out in an extremely cordial atmosphere and represented a true compromise between the proposals put forward by SWAPO and Namibia's other main political group, the Democratic Turnhalle Alliance. It provided for a Bill of Rights, and established a multi-party democracy with an executive presidency, an independent judiciary and a bicameral parliament elected on a basis of proportional representation. Agreement on the constitution was of crucial importance for keeping to the UN's agreed schedule for granting the territory its independence.

SWAPO leader Sam Nujoma announced his 16-member provisional Cabinet on 21 December. In what observers saw as a major gesture of conciliation, he offered positions in the Cabinet to the territory's other six political parties.

28 November President de Klerk begins the process of reducing the influence of the security establishment he inherited from his predecessor, P.W. Botha, when he announces that the National Security Management System (NSMS) is to be dismantled. The NSMS was an extremely powerful organization that was seen as the *de facto* government in many of the areas in which it operated. It was established in 1986 by Botha under state of emergency regulations designed to crush dissent in the Black townships and gave the military and police extraordinary powers over civilian officials, especially in the Black communities. The NSMS operated through a complicated network of regional and local committees that were comprised in part by civil servants, but led by what became known as the 'securocrats': police, intelligence and army officers. De Klerk said the organization was to be replaced with coordinating committees that would meet on an informal basis as needed.

De Klerk also promised to reduce the power of the NSMS's national counterpart, the State Security Council. The council, headed by Botha and made up of key Cabinet ministers and senior military, police and intelligence officials, was seen as being more powerful in the conduct of national affairs than the Cabinet. De Klerk downgraded the council to a cabinet committee, and significantly scaled down its role.

13 December President de Klerk meets jailed ANC leader Nelson Mandela at his official residence in Cape Town. The two men reportedly discussed South Africa's political future and the possibility of negotiations being held between the government and ANC over Black–White power sharing. The meeting started new rumours about Mandela's imminent release and helped contribute to what observers were calling the 'climate of hope' that was taking over South Africa.

20 December Police announce that more people have died in the Black-on-Black factional fighting that was taking place on a regular basis, especially in the Black townships near Durban and Pietermaritzburg in Natal province. Over the past three years, some 2,500 Blacks had died in the violence between the conservative Zulu movement Inkatha, headed by Chief Gatsha Buthelezi, and the more radical supporters of the UDF.

1 9 9 0

15 January African National Congress (ANC) Secretary General Walter Sisulu and other senior members of the ANC arrive in Lusaka, Zambia for talks with the ANC's leadership. After six days of talks the ANC released a statement reaffirming its readiness to start peaceful negotiations with the South African government.

The gathering brought together the released Black nationalist prisoners with their exiled comrades for the first time in over 25 years. The six-day meeting was at times stormy and contentious and highlighted the differences between the militant younger generation and the moderate older generation recently released from prison. The moderates, however, won support for the position that the militants in the ANC military wing (Spear of the Nation) should follow party discipline and not do anything which would damage the political leadership's negotiating strategy.

25 January The first detailed political statement from Nelson Mandela in 26 years is published inside South Africa. The 5,000-word memorandum was published by *South*, a left-wing Cape Town weekly newspaper; the statement outlined Mandela's strategy for talks between the ANC and the South African government.

The statement appealed to the South African government to talk to the Black opposition in order to save the country 'from civil strife and ruin'. Mandela said that his task was 'to bring the country's two major political bodies to the negotiating table'.

Most of the document consisted of a detailed rebuttal by Mandela of what he said were Pretoria's three main reasons for not talking to the ANC. He said the ANC would not renounce the armed struggle before negotiations began, would not break its alliance with the South African Communist Party and would not compromise on the issue of Black majority rule.

In a brief statement issued separately, Mandela also publicly supported the ANC policy of nationalizing key sectors of the South African economy, including the banks and mines. He wrote: 'A change or modification of our views in this regard is inconceivable.'

31 January Namibia's newly elected constituent assembly unanimously agrees on 21 March as independence day for the territory. The date was 11 days ahead of the 1 April target set by the UN which was supervising Namibia's passage to independence.

The South West African People's Organization (SWAPO) also agreed to drop its proposal for a constitutional provision that would allow preventive detention in the new nation.

2 February President F.W. de Klerk announces that his government is lifting its 30-year ban on the ANC and promises that Nelson Mandela will soon be freed. In a landmark speech to the opening session of Parliament, de Klerk also announced the legalization of the South African Communist Party and the Pan-Africanist Congress and the lifting of restrictions on 33 other opposition groups and 374 individual activists; the release of all nonviolent political prisoners; an end to most news censorship and a suspension of executions. De Klerk said: 'The season of violence is over. The time for reconstruction and reconciliation has arrived.'

De Klerk's speech was warmly applauded by Black leaders. Archbishop Desmond Tutu described it as 'incredible' and the Reverend Allan Boesak said: 'If he had given us more we would not have known what to do with it.' ANC officials praised the speech for going 'a long way towards creating a climate conducive to negotiations'. But it added that the ANC was 'gravely concerned' about the continuance of the state of emergency; urged the immediate release of Mandela and asked the international community not to 'do anything to lessen the isolation of the apartheid regime'.

Conservative Whites were outraged by de Klerk's speech. Andries Treurnicht, leader of the Conservative Party, called for an immediate election to test the acceptance of the reforms with the White electorate. Several Conservative Members of Parliament said that the mood of their supporters was 'ugly' and 'potentially violent'.

US President George Bush said he was 'very encouraged' and added that he would consider asking Congress to ease sanctions against South Africa if de Klerk followed through on his promises. British Prime Minister Margaret Thatcher hailed de Klerk's moves as 'bold and courageous' and said that they demonstrated that her opposition to sanctions had paid off.

10 February President de Klerk announces that ANC Deputy President Nelson Mandela will be unconditionally released on the following day.

In his statement, de Klerk said: 'I call upon Mr Mandela and all other interested parties to make their contribution toward a positive climate for negotiations. The eyes of the world are presently focused on all South Africans. All of us now have an opportunity and the responsibility to prove that we are capable of a peaceful process in creating a new South Africa.' In a response to a follow-up question, de Klerk described Mandela as 'a friendly man . . . He's an elderly man. He's a dignified man. And he's an interesting man.'

11 February ANC Deputy President Nelson Mandela is freed – clearing the way for negotiations to end apartheid in South Africa.

Nelson Mandela left Victor Verster Prison outside Cape Town after more than 27 years in jail. He walked out of the prison gates holding hands with his wife Winnie and immediately flashed a Black power salute. Thousands of journalists were on site to cover his release which was broadcast live by satellite around the world.

His release was greated with an explosion of celebration among South Africa's Blacks. His first public announcement came from the balcony of Cape Town's city hall and was more militant than most Whites expected. 'We have waited too long for our freedom,' he declared. 'Now is the time to intensify the struggle on all fronts. To relax our efforts now would be a mistake which generations to come will not be able to forgive.'

Mandela spent his first night of freedom in the home of Archbishop Desmond Tutu and gave a press conference the following day in which he was at pains to reassure the White community. 'Whites are fellow South Africans and we want them to feel safe,' said Mandela and he added: 'We appreciate the contributions they have made to the development in this country.' Mandela also indicated that the ANC would discuss White demands for 'structural guarantees' to ensure that the ANC's demand for one man, one vote would not lead to Black domination.

Mandela arrived at his home in Soweto the following day where he addressed a cheering crowd of 100,000 in Soweto Football Stadium. This time his speech concentrated on the social needs of the Black community. He called on the young to return to school, for the crime levels in the Black townships to drop, for the 'mindless violence' of intertribal killings to stop.

Also on 13 February, Gerrit Viljoen, the minister for constitutional development and planning and a close associate of President de Klerk, said that he expected South Africa's Black community to participate in the country's next general election.

The release of Nelson Mandela was applauded around the world. Church bells rang in Britain and the US. President George Bush telephoned President de Klerk and Mandela and invited them both to visit Washington.

BIOGRAPHIES

Biko, Stephen
Born 1948 – died 12 September 1977
Stephen Biko, the founder of the Black Consciousness movement, was born in the eastern Cape province. He attended local schools before going on to the University of Durban-Westville, the only medical school in South Africa that admitted Black students, where he was regarded by teachers and students alike as a charismatic man with exceptional leadership qualities.

Biko became involved in politics while at university and established the all-Black South African Students' Organization and the Black People's Convention. The Black Consciousness movement, which sought to imbue Black youth with the concept of Black dignity and self-reliance, emerged from those groups and the several others that were influenced by them. Biko felt that Blacks had to be proud of themselves and their heritage for the liberation struggle to succeed and urged Blacks to stand on their own two feet.

Biko's activities inevitably brought him into conflict with the South African security forces and he was arrested on several occasions but never convicted of a crime. In 1973, Biko was placed under a banning order and restricted to his home town of King Williamstown. The ban was still in effect when he was arrested on 18 August 1977 in Grahamstown for inciting unrest and writing inflammatory pamphlets. Police originally blamed his death on 12 September on the results of a hunger strike they claimed he had undertaken but it later emerged that he had died of extensive head injuries. The official inquest into his death exonerated the police but the inquest findings were rejected both at home and abroad.

Biko was considered an 'extraordinary man' even by the South African government officials who were prosecuting him. His intellect, courage and devotion to the Black cause made him a hero to Black youths and the natural successor to Nelson Mandela and Robert Sobukwe. Many observers believed that his early death deprived South Africa of a future national leader.

Boesak, Allan
Born 23 February 1946
Reverend Allan Boesak, clergyman and prominent anti-apartheid campaigner, was born into a Coloured family in the northeastern Cape. After studying for the priesthood at the Bellville theological seminary in Cape Town, he was ordained as a minister in the Coloured branch of the Dutch Reformed Church in 1968.

In 1981, he was elected chairman of the Alliance of Black Reformed Churches in Southern Africa, a group that rejects the theological arguments used to support apartheid. The following year, Boesak was elected president of the World Alliance of Reformed Churches representing over 70 million people from some 150 different denominations. He became a patron of the United Democratic Front, a political umbrella group of anti-apartheid organizations that many observers believed was a front for the banned African National Congress. He was briefly detained in 1985 on subversion charges after attempting to lead a march to Pollsmoor Prison outside Cape Town to demand the release of Nelson Mandela, leader of the African National Congress, and he was later held for advocating the withdrawal of foreign investment as a means of pressurizing the South African government to change its apartheid policies.

Along with the Anglican Archbishop Desmond Tutu and the Roman Catholic Archbishop Stephen Naidoo, Boesak moved to fill the void created by the government's 1988 crackdown on opposition groups. The three clerics launched a new anti-apartheid organization, the Committee for the Defence of Democracy (CDD), in March 1988 to take up the work of the banned United Democratic Front, only to have the CDD also effectively banned. In a defiant church service shortly after the crackdown, Boesak warned the apartheid South African regime that 'no government can challenge the living God and survive'.

Botha, Pieter Willem ('P.W.')
Born 12 January 1916
P.W. Botha was born into an Afrikaner farm family in the Paul Roux district of the Orange Free State. He attended local schools before going on to study law at the University College of the Orange Free State.

In 1936, Botha was recruited by Daniel F. Malan as an organizer for the Purified National Party in the Cape, where he worked his way up the party hierarchy. He entered Parliament in the Nationalist win of 1948 and was appointed Cape secretary of the National Party the same year. Botha was a staunch supporter of Hendrik Verwoerd, the man known as the architect of apartheid, and was appointed deputy minister of the interior in Verwoerd's government in 1958. He entered the Cabinet in 1961 when he became the minister of community development and Coloured affairs. His rise continued under Verwoerd's successor, Balthazar (John) Vorster, and in 1966 he became minister of defence as well as assuming the powerful position as leader of the National Party in the Cape. He used his position as Defence Minister to transform South Africa's armed forces into a formidable and efficient fighting unit and to cultivate his image as a 'hawk'.

Botha became prime minister in 1978 following Vorster's retirement after the Information scandal, while retaining the defence portfolio. Despite his tough-man reputation, he was considered to be a member of the *'verligte'* (enlightened) branch of the National Party and was known to be committed to the introduction of a new constitution that would give Coloureds and Asians a greater say in the running of the country. Immediately upon his election, Botha said that he would work to improve relations among the races but ruled out any possibility of totally abandoning apartheid. In an early speech, he told Whites they must 'adapt or die'. Observers believed that it was during his 12 years as defence minister that Botha became convinced by his military advisers that some domestic reforms were needed if Whites were to maintain their position in South Africa. They described him not as a reformer but as a 'reformulator' who wanted to change apartheid in order to contain domestic and international forces that were demanding an end to it altogether.

His mildly reformist policies alienated the conservatives in his own party, however, who considered him a turncoat. In 1982, some 16 right-wing dissidents were expelled from the National Party for refusing to support Prime Minister Botha's proposals for power-sharing with Coloureds and Asians and, led by former Minister of State Administration and Statistics Andries Treurnicht, went on to form the Conservative Party. Botha pushed ahead with his plan to give Coloureds and Indians a limited role in government and in 1984 a new constitution establishing a tricameral parliament was implemented. As a result of the new constitution, Botha became South Africa's last prime minister and first executive state president. The exclusion of Blacks from the new power-sharing arrangement, and Botha's back-pedalling on promised reforms in order to appease his party's right wing, led to unprecedented levels of Black unrest. In 1985, he was forced to introduce a national state of emergency in order to contain the violence, much of which was focused on Blacks who were seen as 'collaborating' with the government.

In January 1989, Botha suffered a mild stroke and unexpectedly resigned as leader of the National Party the following month while retaining his position as president. Education Minister Frederik W. de Klerk was chosen to succeed Botha as party leader and it was widely expected that Botha would resign in his favour in time to lead the party into the next general election. Botha, however, precipitated a National Party crisis in March when he announced that he intended to resume his duties as president instead of stepping down gracefully in de Klerk's favour. His refusal to give way led to confusion over who formulated policy since, for the first time in history, the head of government was not also the head of the ruling party. The party found this situation unacceptable and both its progressive and conservative branches united against Botha's autocratic style of government in favour of de Klerk's more conciliatory manner. Botha grudgingly resigned on 14 August after a final bitter struggle with both de Klerk and his own cabinet, and de Klerk was sworn in as president the following day.

Botha, Roelof Frederick ('Pik')
Born 27 April 1932

Pik Botha, South Africa's long-time foreign minister, was educated at local schools in Potchefstroom before going on to the University of Pretoria. He joined his country's diplomatic service in 1953 and held several diplomatic positions in Europe from 1956 to 1966. He was a legal adviser to the Department of Foreign Affairs from 1966 to 1968 and he served as head of the South West African and UN sections from 1968 to 1970.

Botha entered politics as a member of parliament in 1970 and, apart from a posting as ambassador to the UN from 1974 to 1977 and to the US from 1975 to 1977, has been in Parliament ever since. He has served as minister of foreign affairs since 1977 and, following the outbreak of the 'Information scandal', concurrently held the Information portfolio from 1980 to 1986. In 1989 he ran for the leadership of the National Party when President P.W. Botha (no relation) suffered a stroke, but he was defeated by F.W. de Klerk.

Botha, who is on the *'verligte'* (enlightened) wing of the National Party, is considered both a widely respected diplomat and an astute politician.

Buthelezi, Gatsha
Born 27 August 1928

Gatsha Buthelezi was born into the royal family of the powerful Zulu nation and is a direct descendant of the bloodthirsty nineteenth-century Zulu King Shaka. His father was the chief of the Buthelezi tribe, a major constituent of the Zulu nation and the traditional chief advisers to the Zulu king.

While studying at South Africa's Fort Hare University, Buthelezi became involved in the African National Congress (ANC) and in his final year was expelled because of his political activities. This resulted in Buthelezi being warned by the

South African authorities that he faced being blocked from assuming his post as hereditary chief of the Buthelezi tribe unless he mended his ways.

Buthelezi reacted by joining the Department of Native Administration as a clerk for two years. The tactic worked. He became acting chief of the Buthelezi tribe in 1953. This early action has been used by Buthelezi's critics as evidence of his willingness to work with the White politicians in Pretoria, and to compromise his principles for the sake of personal political gain.

Buthelezi, however, refused to accept Pretoria's homelands policy for Kwazulu after he was elected chief executive officer of the Kwazulu territory in 1970. Throughout the 1970s there were reports that the South African government was attempting to remove him from his power base. But in 1975, Buthelezi managed to strengthen that base by forming Inkatha as a 'national liberation movement' based within South Africa.

At the time, Buthelezi appeared to have the tacit support of the exiled ANC. But after a meeting with the ANC leadership in London in 1979, Buthelezi and Inkatha were attacked as 'an instrument of the oppressor'.

The break with the ANC damaged Buthelezi's standing with other tribes in South Africa, most notably the Xhosa and the Tswana tribes, although his standing with the powerful Zulus remained undimmed. During the 1980s, Buthelezi emerged as the leading Black moderate within South Africa and the favourite of the White financial community. He was an outspoken critic of both sanctions and the policy of disinvestment, claiming that they did more harm than good to the Black community of South Africa.

In the latter part of the 1980s, the continuing drop in support for Buthelezi among non-Zulus led to increased violence between Zulus and other tribes. This reached a crescendo after the release of Nelson Mandela in February 1990. The two men had politely corresponded during Mandela's imprisonment but after his release Mandela and Buthelezi emerged as the two rival contenders for the support of the Black community of South Africa.

Crocker, Chester
Born 29 October 1941

Dr Chester Crocker, the man credited with being the driving force behind the 1990 Namibian peace agreement, was educated at Ohio State University and Johns Hopkins University in the US. He worked as a journalist, a staff officer at the National Security Council and an academic before becoming the US assistant secretary of state for African affairs in 1981. He made the settlement of the Namibian problem one of the Reagan administration's main foreign policy goals.

Crocker devised the policy of 'constructive engagement' in which the US refrained from publicly attacking South Africa while privately pressurizing them to change. His acceptance of the South African demand that their withdrawal from Namibia be linked with a Cuban pull-out from Angola appeared to observers as an outgrowth of that policy.

Although constructive engagement proved a failure when Congress overturned Reagan's veto and imposed sanctions on South Africa, the demand for a linkage paid off. After a series of talks that constantly appeared to be on the verge of breaking down, representatives from South Africa, Cuba, Angola and the South West African People's Organization finally signed an agreement in December 1988 that led to the withdrawal of both Cuban and South African troops from Namibia, the holding of UN-sponsored elections in November 1989 and Namibian independence in April 1990. Crocker, who had been consistently attacked by conservatives as an apologist for African terrorists and by most African leaders and the White left as a friend of South Africa, was seen as the man responsible for the US's greatest foreign policy success in Africa in recent years.

Daidoo, Yusuf
Born 1909 – died 19 September 1983
Dr Yusuf Daidoo was born in the Transvaal of Indian parentage; he became involved in politics after returning from medical school in Edinburgh.

A dedicated Communist, Daidoo worked on behalf of South Africa's Indian community and went on to become the president of the South African Indian Congress. His protests against discrimination led him into clashes with the authorities even before the architects of apartheid came to power in 1948. After the Nationalists took office, his activities broadened to include campaigning against policies discriminatory to all non-Whites.

Daidoo soon became a named person under the Suppression of Communism Act and was jailed for six months in 1952 for breaking the ban that prohibited him from addressing meetings. Daidoo went into exile in Britain in 1960, where he became a member of the African National Congress (ANC) after that organization allowed non-Blacks to join in 1969. At the time of his death, Daidoo was a member of the ANC's politicomilitary council and chairman of the South African Communist Party.

De Klerk, Frederik Willem ('F.W.')
Born 18 March 1936
President F.W. de Klerk was born into a political family in the Transvaal. His father, Senator Jan de Klerk, was a member of the Verwoerd cabinet and his brother Willem ('Wimpy') is a leading Afrikaner dissident on the political left. F.W. was educated at local schools in Krugersdorp before going on to Potchefstroom University.

De Klerk began his career as a lawyer in 1962 and worked in a law practice before entering Parliament in 1972. He joined the cabinet in 1978 as minister of posts and telecommunications and later became minister of mining, minerals and energy, public works and social welfare, the interior and finally education minister.

De Klerk was named leader of the National Party in the Transvaal after his predecessor, Andries Treurnicht, left the Nationalists to form the Conservative Party in 1982. De Klerk beat the liberal finance minister, Barend du Plessis, by a mere eight votes in the battle to succeed President P.W. Botha as National Party leader when Botha unexpectedly resigned from the position in February 1989, while retaining the presidency. It was widely expected that he would also succeed Botha as the country's next president in time to lead the party into the next general election but Botha precipitated a National Party crisis when he announced that he intended to resume his duties as president instead of stepping down gracefully in de Klerk's favour as expected.

Botha's refusal to give way led to a bitter feud between the two men. The party found this situation unacceptable and both its progressive and conservative branches united against Botha's autocratic style of government in favour of de Klerk's more conciliatory manner. Botha grudgingly resigned on 14 August after a final bitter struggle with both de Klerk and his own Cabinet, and de Klerk was sworn in as president the following day.

In coming to power de Klerk was known as a conservative, but he quickly aligned himself with those attempting to reform the country's apartheid system. His releasing from prison of Nelson Mandela and other African National Congress (ANC) leaders, his unbanning of the ANC and his opening negotiations with Blacks on the future of South Africa increased the pace of change in the country and created an atmosphere of unprecedented optimism. But at the end of 1990 he faced the problem of uncontrolled Black factional fighting between the ANC and supporters of Chief Gatsha Buthelezi's Inkatha movement.

Havenga, Nicolaas Christiaan
Born 1893 – died 13 March 1957

Nicolaas Havenga was first elected to the South African Parliament in 1915 as a member of the newly formed National Party. In 1924 he was appointed to the post of minister of finance by Prime Minister J.B.M. Hertzog. He supported Hertzog's decision to go into a coalition with Jan Christiaan Smuts in 1934 and remained at the Ministry of Finance until 1939 when Smuts and Hertzog split over the issue of whether or not to actively support Britain during the Second World War.

Havenga temporarily retired from politics after the collapse of the Hertzog government but soon returned as the leader of the newly formed Afrikaner Party. In March 1947 Havenga and Daniel Malan, leader of the Reunited National Party, reached an electoral agreement 'to bring together those who belong together'. Havenga's main aim in joining forces with Malan was to topple Smuts, whom he had come to regard as a traitor to the cause of Afrikanerdom.

The 1948 election gave the Reunited National Party 70 seats while Smuts could still command the support of 74 parliamentarians. Havenga's Afrikaner Party, however, won nine seats, giving Malan a majority and Havenga a key position as the holder of the balance of power. Havenga insisted upon, and received, the finance portfolio. Three years later, the Afrikaner Party and the Reunited National Party merged and returned to the old name of the National Party.

Havenga was always regarded as a moderate within the ranks of Afrikanerdom. In the late 1940s he insisted that the Coloured voters could not be removed from the common electoral roll without the consent of two-thirds of both houses of parliament. His stand on this issue played a major part in keeping the Coloured voters on the voters' list until 1956. Havenga, however, supported the basic tenets of apartheid and as finance minister he increased government spending by 300 per cent to finance the government's strict segregationist policies.

Following Malan's retirement from politics in 1954, Havenga was regarded as his most likely successor. But he was strongly opposed by the right-wing National Party members from the Transvaal who feared that Havenga and his Cape province supporters would attempt to dilute the strict apartheid policies. Disillusioned by party in-fighting, Havenga withdrew his name from consideration 'in the interests of party unity' and announced 'the end of a long public career'. Havenga's capitulation led to the election of the extreme right-winger Hendrik Verwoerd and a major shift in the party's power base from the Cape to the Transvaal. Havenga retired to his business interests and died three years later.

BIOGRAPHIES

Hendrickse, Allan
Born 22 October 1927
Allan Hendrickse was born in the eastern Cape, the son of two schoolteachers. After attending Fort Hare University he was ordained a minister of the Uitenhage Congregational Church of Southern Africa.

While at university, Hendrickse became involved in anti-apartheid politics as a member of the Labour Party. This eventually led to his paying the inevitable price of being detained and restricted under security legislation.

From 1951 until 1969, Hendrickse was a teacher as well as minister and in 1969 was elected to the Coloured Persons' Representative Council. In 1972 he was elected head of the United Congregational Church of Southern Africa. In 1978 he was elected leader of the Labour Party.

Hendrickse's election as leader of the Labour Party (the primary political vehicle of South Africa's Coloured community) coincided with the election of P.W. Botha's election as leader of the National Party and prime minister. Botha set out to try to restructure the constitution to give the Indian and Coloured communities a stake in a political system which would continue to be controlled by the Whites. The result was the introduction of a tricameral parliament with separate chambers for the White, Coloured and Indian communities and an executive president elected by the White chamber.

Hendrickse at first refused to have anything do with Botha's constitutional proposals but Botha persuaded him that he was genuine in his desire to get rid of apartheid. Hendrickse reluctantly agreed to participate and was promptly branded as an 'Uncle Tom' by anti-apartheid activists. Hendrickse himself explained that he was joining 'the system' to dismantle apartheid.

The subsequent 1984 elections were boycotted by 70 per cent of the Coloured electorate and 90 per cent of the Indian voters. But Hendrickse's Labour Party won 76 of the 80 seats in the Coloured chamber and Hendrickse was appointed minister without portfolio.

Hendrickse quickly discovered that he was virtually powerless when Botha refused to consider his public demands that the Group Areas Act be scrapped. In January 1987 Hendrickse hit the headlines when he challenged the apartheid regulations by going swimming along a Whites-only beach in Cape Town. An infuriated Botha forced an apology out of Hendrickse whose political influence was substantially weakened as a result. Hendrickse resigned from the cabinet at the end of the year, but this failed to revive his political fortunes.

Jansen, Ernest George
Born 7 August 1881 – died 25 November 1959
Ernest Jansen received his early education on the family farm near Dundee. He later studied law and was admitted to the bar in 1906.

Jansen took an early and active interest in the politics of his native Natal and was a founding member of the National Party in 1914. He first entered the South African parliament in 1921 and was named speaker of the House of Assembly in 1924. Before the Second World War, Jansen held the posts of speaker and minister of native affairs. He was minister of defence from 1943 to 1947.

Jansen was a leading member of the Afrikaner cultural movement and during the 1930s was the chairman of the group that inaugurated the Voortrekker movement. He also wrote several books on the Voortrekkers. After the 1948 elections, Jansen was named minister for native affairs and helped to frame some of the early apartheid legislation.

He was appointed to the ceremonial post of governor-general in January 1952 and held that position until his death.

Luthuli, Albert
Born 1898 – died 21 July 1967

Albert Luthuli was born in Rhodesia, the nephew of a Zulu chieftain. He returned to Natal, South Africa at the age of ten to live with his uncle and was educated as a teacher at American mission schools and became one of South Africa's first Black teachers.

In 1936, Luthuli was elected chief of the Groutville Zulu in succession to his uncle and left teaching to concentrate on his duties as chief. It was not until 1945, however, that Luthuli became actively involved in Black nationalist politics when he joined the African National Congress (ANC). In 1948, after the electoral victory of the National Party, he was elected president of the Natal branch of the ANC.

Luthuli quickly became the Black community's leading exponent of non-violent opposition to apartheid and organized non-violent rallies and demonstrations in protest against government policies. Luthuli's non-violent approach posed an even greater threat to apartheid policies than violence because it made it difficult for the government to use the force of the law to imprison and silence Luthuli.

In 1952, the government ordered him to resign from the ANC or face the loss of his chieftainship. Luthuli refused to obey. He was removed from his chieftainship, but the action badly backfired on the government. Luthuli continued to be widely referred to as 'chief'; he was elected to the post of president general of the ANC and his activities were brought to the attention of the international community.

At the end of 1956, Luthuli was the leading figure among 155 people who were arrested and charged with high treason. The trial became a major international political event and ended with Luthuli's release and further increased international stature. Two years later, in an attempt to restrain Luthuli's political activities, the government confined him to Groutville and banned him from political gatherings.

After the Sharpeville massacre in March 1960, Luthuli led the campaign against the pass laws and was arrested after he publicly burned his own passbook. Shortly afterwards, the government banned the ANC.

In 1961, Luthuli became the first African to receive the Nobel Peace Prize, awarded for his non-violent struggle against apartheid. He was granted a South African passport to receive the award in Oslo but was forbidden to prolong his stay or to make a requested visit to the US. In his acceptance address, Luthuli denounced South Africa as a country where 'the cult of race supremacy and of White superiority is worshiped like a god' and 'the ghost of slavery lingers on to this day in the form of forced labour'.

Back in South Africa, Luthuli was again confined to his Groutville home. He concentrated on writing his memoirs and trying to steer the ANC from the increasingly violent course that it pursued following the government's 1960 banning of the organization. Luthuli died on 21 July 1967 when, following a stroke that had impaired his movement and vision, he was struck by a train as he crossed a railway bridge near his home.

Malan, Daniel F.
Born 22 May 1874 – died 7 February 1959
Daniel Malan was born in the British Cape colony and educated at Stellenbosch University and then the University of Utrecht, in The Netherlands, where he received his Doctorate of Divinity in 1905.

Malan returned to South Africa as a clergyman in the Dutch Reformed Church. The church was a major repository of Afrikaner nationalism and Malan became an ardent supporter of the Afrikaner cause. He left the pulpit in 1915 to edit the Afrikaner newspaper *Die Burger* and in 1918 was elected to the South African parliament.

In 1924, Malan was named minister of the interior in the government of J.B.M. Hertzog. He used the post to win official recognition for the Afrikaans language and to establish South African nationality. In 1934, Malan left the government to form the Purified Nationalist Party after Hertzog's National Party merged with Jan Smuts's South African Party. But in 1939, Hertzog and Malan again joined forces, to form the Reunited National Party; the following year, Malan emerged as the party leader and the unofficial leader of South Africa's Afrikaner community.

On 26 May 1948, Malan's Reunited National Party won a surprise victory over Smuts. Malan began laying the foundations for apartheid, the government's foreign policy and the structures which helped to ensure that the National Party remained in power for over 40 years.

In 1949 Malan's government introduced the Mixed Marriages Act; in July 1950 the Group Areas Act, another cornerstone of apartheid, became law. Malan, however, was blocked by the courts in his efforts to disenfranchise the Coloured voters and it was not until after his retirement from active politics that the Coloureds were struck off the common electoral roll.

In foreign policy, Malan laid the foundations for South Africa's long-running dispute over Namibia (South West Africa) when he announced on 9 July 1948 that South West Africa would be incorporated into the Union of South Africa and be represented in the South African parliament.

Malan, an ardent republican, also clashed regularly with Britain and the Commonwealth, and argued in vain for the incorporation into South Africa of the British protectorates of Basutoland (Lesotho), Bechuanaland (Botswana) and Swaziland.

Malan resigned from politics on 30 November 1954 at the age of 80. He spent the next four and a half years writing about his political life and principles.

Mandela, Nelson
Born 19 July 1918
Nelson Mandela was born in the eastern Cape into the royal family of the Tembu, a Xhosa-speaking tribe. He left home and gave up his hereditary chieftainship to avoid an arranged marriage.

Mandela was expelled from one college for leading a strike with Oliver Tambo, but eventually obtained a law degree from the University of South Africa. Along with Tambo and Walter Sisulu, he established South Africa's first Black law firm. In 1944 the three men formed the African National Congress (ANC) Youth League.

Mandela quickly established himself as one of the leading firebrands of the ANC. He was first arrested in 1956 on charges of high treason. After his release in 1960, Mandela abandoned the non-violent principles of ANC President Albert Luthuli and went underground to form the ANC's military wing, Umkhonto we Sizwe or Spear of the Nation. He became a wanted man and the press dubbed him the 'Black Pimpernel' because of the disguises he used to avoid the police for 18 months.

Mandela was arrested again on 5 August 1962 and sentenced to five years' imprisonment. While in prison, police raided an ANC safe house in the Johannesburg suburb of Rivonia. In the raid, they claimed to have uncovered plans for a Communist–ANC plot to overthrow the government. Mandela was put on trial again with seven of his comrades and they were convicted of sabotage and treason and sentenced to life imprisonment. At his trial, Mandela won worldwide fame with his five-hour speech from the dock in which he delivered a carefully reasoned argument against the apartheid system and refused to accept the jurisdiction of the court on the grounds that it served a political system which denied him representation.

Mandela spent the next 18 years in the harsh conditions of the maximum security prison on Robben Island and became a leading symbol of South African oppression. There were repeated calls for his release from governments around the world and the ANC made it clear that there could be no discussions with the government until Mandela was released. In 1982 he was transferred to Pollsmoor Prison near Cape Town and the government began a series of secret negotiations with him during which they offered Mandela his freedom in return for a public renunciation of violence.

In August 1988, Mandela was hospitalized for tuberculosis and the South African government began to fear that his death while in detention would spark off a spiral of violence which it could not control. A group of *verligte* (enlightened) members of the National Party pressed President P.W. Botha to release Mandela. Botha met with Mandela in July 1989 but refused to release the ANC deputy president until he had publicly renounced violence.

The position of Mandela caused increased tensions within the National Party. In September 1989, de Klerk succeeded Botha as prime minister and in December he met Mandela. Finally on 11 February 1990, Mandela was released after 27 years in prison. In his first speech after his release, Mandela made it clear that he had not renounced violence as a condition of his freedom.

Shortly after his release Mandela left South Africa for a world tour. On his return he and de Klerk soon started negotiations on a new constitution. In the course of these talks Mandela agreed to drop the ANC's commitment to armed struggle. But by the end of 1990 the greatest threat to Mandela's dream of Black majority rule appeared not to be coming from the National Party but from an increasingly bloody intertribal fighting within South Africa's Black community.

Matanzima, Chief Kaiser
Born 1918

Chief Matanzima, the first president of the Republic of the Transkei, was educated at the Lovedale Missionary Institute in the Transkei and Fort Hare University College. He obtained his law degree in 1939 and became installed as a chief of the Amahale clan of Tembus in 1940. He resigned the chieftainship in 1944 in order to become an articled clerk, and won the Cape Law Society's prize in 1948 when he passed his examinations for admission to the bar.

Matanzima resumed his duties as chief and became a member of the Transkei territorial authority in 1956, becoming its head in 1961. In his role as chairman of the authority's recess committee, Matanzima participated in the drafting of Transkei's constitution for self-government. The Transkei Self-Government Bill, which provided for the Transkei to become the first semi-autonomous Black homeland, was passed in May 1963 and Matanzima was elected its first chief minister in November. He became prime minister when the territory was granted its nominal independence in 1976, an independence that is only recognized by South Africa and the other Black homelands.

After several years of continuing unrest, Chief Matanzima was ousted from power in May 1987 by his brother George amid allegations of corruption. He was banished to a remote village. George Matanzima was himself relieved of the premiership in September when the military ousted eight of his senior cabinet ministers from office. Matanzima was in South Africa at the time of the coup, reportedly on 'sick leave', following implications that he, also, had been involved in corruption. A third coup ocurred soon after and the military was installed in power. Observers firmly believed that the South African government had engineered the coups to remove the Matanzimas in an attempt to stabilize the political situation in the Transkei. Although the South Africans denied the charge, they were quick to recognize the new military government.

Although Chief Matanzima was a firm supporter of apartheid, he strongly opposed the South African government's measures to make all Xhosa automatically citizens of the Transkei when it became independent in 1976, saying he did not want the Transkei to become a 'dumping ground for stateless Blacks'. He also fought with the South Africans for more land, arguing that it was necessary if the Transkei was to become a viable state. Nevertheless, he was constantly and bitterly attacked for selling out to the South African apartheid system and he was branded a collaborator by more radical Blacks.

Mulder, Cornelius Petrus ('Connie')
Born 5 June 1925 – died 12 January 1988
Connie Mulder was born in the Transvaal and attended local schools in Warmbaths before going on to Potchefstroom University. He began his career in teaching before taking a doctorate in Afrikaans at the Witwatersrand University.

Mulder started his political career while still a teacher, serving on the Randfontein city council and twice being elected mayor. Mulder entered Parliament in 1958 and began his rise to the top of the National Party. He became assistant information officer in 1966 under Prime Minister Hendrik Verwoerd and chief information officer in Balthazar (John) Vorster's government the following year. He served as immigration minister, minister of social welfare and pensions, interior minister and information minister, using these last two positions to project himself on to the centre stage of South African politics.

Mulder was interior minister when rioting broke out in Soweto in 1976 and spread to other Black and Coloured townships, while as information minister he used his position to paint a favourable picture of the South African government abroad. He finally went on to become minister of plural relations.

Mulder was one of the country's most powerful and well-respected politicians. He was generally considered to be a future prime minister when his career was suddenly shattered in 1978 by revelations that he had authorized the secret funding of a pro-apartheid propaganda campaign. The Information scandal, known as 'Muldergate', exploded when it became known that as information minister Mulder had authorized the Department of Information, under information secretary Eschel Rhoodie, to secretly spend millions of dollars to finance the pro-government newspaper, the *Citizen*, and to buy favourable media exposure abroad to defend South Africa's apartheid policies.

It became the worst scandal in the country's history and, before it was over, 'Muldergate' overshadowed all other events in South Africa and caused the resignation of John Vorster, first as prime minister and then as president. Mulder strongly defended his actions but was forced to resign first as a minister, then as leader of the Transvaal National Party and eventually from Parliament itself. He was in the political wilderness for the next nine years until he won a seat as a member of the ultra-right-wing Conservative Party in 1987. His long-awaited 'revenge' speech, in which he said he would implicate Prime Minister P.W. Botha and other ministers for their roles in the Information scandal, was never delivered as his health quickly deteriorated.

Nujoma, Sam Daniel
Born 12 May 1929
Sam Nujoma, first president of Namibia, was educated at local mission schools in Windhoek, the capital of what was then South African-administered South West Africa. He worked on the state railways as a labourer and unionist until 1957, when he left to become a municipal clerk in Windhoek.

Along with Herman Toivo ja Toivo, Nujoma founded the Ovamboland People's Organization in April 1959, later changing its name to the South West African People's Organization (SWAPO) in order to broaden its base beyond the majority Ovambo tribe. He was arrested for his nationalist activities in December of that year and fled into exile in 1960 to continue his fight for Namibian independence. Nujoma established SWAPO's provisional headquarters in Dar es Salaam, Tanzania, in 1961. He returned to Windhoek in March 1966 but was formally detained and deported from the territory. Following the August 1966 decision by the International Court of Justice to reject SWAPO's complaint about South Africa's continued administration of Namibia, Nujoma committed SWAPO to an armed struggle against South African rule. He became the commander in chief of the People's Liberation Army of Namibian, SWAPO's armed wing, but did not actively fight in the bush war himself.

Observers saw Nujoma's main achievement as providing SWAPO with a unifying force through his tireless international lobbying. He became internationally prominent in 1973 when SWAPO was granted observer status at the UN recognizing it as 'the sole and authentic representative' of the Namibian people.

Following the signing of the Namibian peace accord with South Africa, Angola and Cuba in December 1988, Nujoma returned to Namibia in September 1989 and was cheered by thousands of supporters as he knelt down and kissed the tarmac. He led SWAPO to victory in the November elections and became president upon its independence on 21 March 1990. After almost a quarter of a century of bush warfare, Nujoma told his compatriots: 'As of today, we are masters of this pastoral land of our ancestors. The destiny of this country is now in our hands.'

BIOGRAPHIES

Paton, Alan
Born 11 January 1903 – died 12 April 1988
Alan Paton, who focused international attention on the plight of South African Blacks when his *Cry, the Beloved Country* was published in 1948, was the son of Scottish immigrants. He gained a degree in teaching at Natal University and began his career as the principal of the Diepkloof Reformatory for delinquent African children in 1938.

Paton went on to become an active opponent of the South African government's apartheid policies and became president of the multiracial Liberal Party from 1960 until it was outlawed in 1968 following a government act banning non-segregated political parties. He was also considered an economic liberal and was a strong opponent of sanctions. He argued that: 'Sanctioneers think they can punish people into the world of righteousness. They cannot, and that was one of the first lessons I learned at the reformatory.'

His views on sanctions and his refusal to support the use of force against the government led to Paton being rejected by many radical anti-apartheid campaigners in his later years. For most of the world, however, the harshness of the apartheid system will forever be brought to life by his masterpiece novel.

Sisulu, Walter
Born 1912
Walter Sisulu, reportedly the son of a White road-building foreman, was born in the Transkei and began his career as a miner. He joined the African National Congress (ANC) in 1940 and, along with Nelson Mandela and Oliver Tambo, came to be seen as one of the driving forces behind the organization. He became its secretary general in 1949 and is described as 'the outstanding thinker and organizer behind the scenes'.

He organized the 1952 defiance campaign against apartheid and was sentenced under the provisions of the Suppression of Communism Act to nine months' imprisonment, suspended for two years, for those activities. He was one of the 156 anti-apartheid activists arrested in 1956 on treason charges, along with fellow ANC leaders Mandela, Tambo and Albert Luthuli, but he was acquitted in March 1961 after one of the longest-running trials in South African history. He was then convicted in 1963 of inciting Black workers to strike in May 1961 and for furthering the aims of the ANC, which had been banned in 1960. He was sentenced to six years' imprisonment but was released pending appeal.

Sisulu was arrested in July 1963 with Mandela and other opponents of the government at a house in the Johannesburg suburb of Rivonia. He was sentenced to life imprisonment at the famous Rivonia treason trial in 1964 for plotting revolution and sabotage. His release from prison on 15 October 1989, along with seven other prominent political prisoners, was seen by observers as a sign that Mandela's release was imminent.

Sisulu became a father-figure to the other political prisoners detained in the harsh conditions of Robben Island and is noted by them for his warmth, wisdom, integrity and refusal to compromise. His wife, Albertina, is herself a leading anti-apartheid activist and is the head of the United Democratic Front and the Federation of South African Women.

Slovo, Joe
Born 1926

Joe Slovo was the son of Lithuanian Jewish parents who immigrated to South Africa when he was nine years old. He was forced to leave school and seek work at the age of 11, but after serving with the Army during the Second World War, he took advantage of special education grants to attend university. Slovo graduated with top honours and a law degree.

While in university, Slovo became involved in Communist Party politics and met his wife, the writer and journalist Ruth First. The couple quickly became the two leading White anti-apartheid campaigners within South Africa, and primary targets of government security operations.

After the Communist Party was banned by the Suppression of Communism Act, First and Slovo stayed with the party as it went underground and helped to maintain the party's close links with the African National Congress. Government banning orders prohibiting them from writing or speaking on political issues or participating in political meetings were placed on both Slovo and First. Slovo, however, continued to work secretly and helped to write the 1955 Freedom Charter and became secretary general of the South African Communist Party.

Slovo was a founder member of the ANC's military wing Umkhonto we Sizwe (Spear of the Nation) and along with Nelson Mandela, Walter Sisulu and others participated in the ANC military planning sessions at the farmhouse in the Johannesburg suburb of Rivonia. He was abroad when the farmhouse was raided in 1963 by the South African security police. First was arrested a month later but was released and also fled abroad.

Slovo took on the task of organizing a terrorist campaign from abroad. Through Slovo, the ANC developed close links with the Soviet bloc which provided the ANC with weapons and training. First concentrated on writing anti-apartheid books and articles.

After Mozambican independence in 1975, Slovo and and his wife moved to Mozambique where Slovo was able to set up terrorist bases from which to launch raids into South Africa. He also became research director of a Marxist think tank at Eduardo Mondlane University. In 1982, Ruth First was killed by a parcel bomb. Two years later, Slovo was expelled by the Mozambican government after Maputo signed the Nkomati non-aggression pact with South Africa.

It was not until February 1990 that South African President F.W. de Klerk lifted the ban on Slovo and he was allowed to return to South Africa. Later that month he was reunited with Mandela.

Smith, Ian
Born 8 April 1919

Ian Smith was born in Rhodesia and educated at Rhodes University in Grahamstown, South Africa. During the Second World War he distinguished himself as a fighter pilot with the Royal Air Force.

After the war, Smith returned to Rhodesia to finish his education and work on the family farm. He entered Rhodesian politics and was elected to the Southern Rhodesian Assembly in 1948. In 1961, Smith founded the Rhodesian Front after government moves to grant greater political representation to the country's Black majority.

Smith was elected prime minister in 1962 after an election in which he promised continued White minority rule and independence from Britain. But the British government refused to grant independence until a constitution guaranteeing political representation to the country's Black majority was accepted. Smith then unilaterally declared independence from Britain in November 1965.

The British responded with a UN-imposed embargo on the sale of all goods to Rhodesia. But the South Africans regarded Smith's government as a buffer against spreading African nationalism and kept him economically and politically afloat by breaking the sanctions and supplying economic and military aid to help fight the Black nationalist guerrillas led by Robert Mugabe and Joshua Nkomo in the Patriotic Front.

But the fall of Portuguese colonial rule in Angola and Mozambique led to the increased isolation of Rhodesia and in 1979, after the Conservative British government of Margaret Thatcher refused to support Smith, he was forced to seek a negotiated solution. In the subsequent constitutional negotiations in London, Smith was forced to accept the principle of Black majority rule.

After elections in 1980, Robert Mugabe succeeded Smith as prime minister and Britain granted independence to Rhodesia which then changed its name to Zimbabwe. Smith remained in Parliament but gradually slipped into obscurity.

Smuts, Jan Christiaan
Born 24 May 1870 – died 11 September 1950
Smuts was born into a prominent Dutch Afrikaner family. After graduating from Victoria College (now the University of Stellenbosch) in 1890, he went on to Cambridge where he read law. He qualified as a London barrister but decided to return to South Africa in 1895.

By the age of 28, Smuts was state attorney for the Transvaal. After the Boer War broke out in 1899, Smuts sided with his Afrikaner heritage and was given an independent command. He quickly emerged as one of the Boers' most effective guerrilla leaders.

At the end of the war, Smuts became a key member of the Boer delegation, drafting first the peace negotiations and then the political structure of postwar South Africa. He was a leading member of the first postwar government of the Union of South Africa.

When the First World War broke out, Smuts played a major role in supporting Britain. In 1917 he went to London to attend an imperial conference and was appointed Britain's minister of air by British Prime Minister Lloyd George. After the war, Smuts helped to create the League of Nations.

In 1920, Smuts succeeded Louis Botha as prime minister of South Africa but was voted out of office in 1925. He returned to power in 1933 in a coalition with J.B.M. Hertzog. The two men split over the issue of supporting Britain during the Second World War. Smuts won with a narrow parliamentary majority of 13.

During the Second World War, Smuts was regularly consulted by British Prime Minister Winston Churchill and sent South African forces to Egypt to help prevent a German–Italian takeover of North Africa. In 1945, he represented South Africa at the San Francisco conference at which the charter of the UN was drafted.

Smuts's United Party was defeated by the National Party in the historic general election of 26 May 1948. Smuts himself lost his seat at Standerton and had to be returned in a by-election in order to lead the opposition. The reasons for Smuts's defeat were manifold. He firmly believed that the future for the Afrikaner community lay in a close association with Britain through the Commonwealth. Many Afrikaners, however, retained bitter memories of the Boer

War; they resented British cultural imperialism and despised Smuts as a 'traitor' to his heritage.

By the end of the war, however, fear of the growing political influence of the non-White population was replacing the traditional dislike of Britain among the Afrikaners. Smuts did not favour Black majority rule, but his traditional approach was one of accommodation and discussion. In 1946, his government passed the Indian Representation Act which extended indirect parliamentary representation to South Africa's Indian community. Smuts also extended unemployment benefits to Blacks and a *de facto* recognition to Black trade unions.

The National Party effectively argued that the Indians, Coloureds and Blacks were not citizens of South Africa and that Smuts's actions were the thin end of a wedge that would eventually lead to the Afrikaner nation being submerged by Black majority rule. Neither Smuts nor his United Party ever recovered from their 1948 defeat.

Sobukwe, Robert
Born 1925 – died 27 February 1978

The founder of the Pan African Congress (PAC), Sobukwe, the son of a poor Xhosa woodcutter, was educated first at mission schools and then at Fort Hare University. He began his career as a school teacher in the Transvaal and went on to become the director of native education. He was dismissed from his position in 1952 for participating in a campaign of civil disobedience.

In 1958, Sobukwe broke away from the African National Congress (ANC) to form the PAC, accusing the ANC of being too slow and conservative in its attempts to achieve Black equality. The emergence of the PAC, with its policy of restricting membership to Blacks, caused a split which still persists within the Black liberation movement. Sobukwe was accused by many of being an anti-White racist, a charge he denied, saying that Blacks had to prove to themselves and the world that they could stand on their own two feet. He argued that in order to gain both self-respect and the respect of others, they must 'liberate' themselves and not wait to be liberated by non-Blacks. He said that after apartheid had been destroyed by Blacks, the new society would be open to people of all races.

Sobukwe regarded the pass laws as the keystone of the apartheid system and organized mass demonstrations to protest against them. Police opened fire at one such demonstration in the Black township of Sharpeville on 21 March 1960 when protesters presented themselves at the police station without their passbooks and defied the authorities to arrest them. Some 61 people were killed and Sobukwe was arrested on charges of incitement. He was imprisoned for three years under the provisions of the Suppression of Communism Act. He was held for a further six years under an amendment to the act, later known as the 'Sobukwe Clause', which empowered the government to detain for an indefinite period anyone serving a sentence for sabotage or a similar crime after the expiration of their sentence. He was released from prison on Robben Island in 1969 and immediately placed under a banning order that restricted him to living in Kimberley in the northern Cape. He spent his final years practicing law in Kimberley, a profession for which he qualified while in prison.

Sobukwe was described as a deeply religious man and a brilliant intellectual. He was credited by many observers as having inspired the Black Consciousness movement that was developed in the 1970s by Steve Biko.

Strydom, Johannes Gerhardus
Born 14 July 1893 – died 24 August 1958

Johannes Strydom was educated at Stellenbosch University before first joining his father on the family farm and then moving into the civil service. Soon afterwards he studied law at Pretoria University and started a successful Transvaal practice.

Strydom quickly became involved in Afrikaner politics. He joined J.B.M. Hertzog's National Party and in 1929 he was elected the Member of Parliament for Waterberg in the Transvaal.

In 1934 Hertzog's National Party merged with Jan Christiaan Smuts's South Africa Party. Strydom was among the ardent Afrikaner nationalists to leave the National Party and support Daniel Malan's new Purified National Party. Strydom played a major role in winning Malan support both within Parliament and among the electorate at large. After the 1948 election victory, Strydom was rewarded with the post of minister of lands and irrigation. His campaigning style and ardent support for apartheid policies earned Strydom the nickname of 'Lion of Waterberg'.

In December 1954, Malan resigned as leader of the National Party and prime minister. He was succeeded by Strydom whose election was seen as a victory for the right-wing Transvaal faction of the party over the more liberal Cape province members.

One of the major problems faced by Strydom was implementing the long-standing policy of removing South Africa's Coloured voters from the common electoral roll. Malan's government had attempted to do this for several years but had been blocked by the courts and the failure of the National Party to achieve a two-thirds majority in both houses of parliament. But after the 1955 election, the National Party achieved the necessary two-thirds support and Strydom succeeded in removing the Coloured voters from the common electoral roll on to their own voters' list.

Suzman, Helen
Born 7 November 1917

Mrs Helen Suzman, one of South Africa's most prominent liberal parliamentarians, was born in the Transvaal, the daughter of Jewish immigrants from Lithuania. She was educated at the Parktown Convent in Johannesburg and the University of Witwatersrand. Suzman was a lecturer in economic history at Witwatersrand from 1944 until 1952 and entered Parliament the following year as a member of the United Party. She joined the group of liberal dissidents who broke away from the party in 1961 to form the Progressive Party (later the Progressive Reform Party and the Progressive Federal Party (PFP)) and was its only member to win a seat in Parliament in the 1961, 1966 and 1970 elections.

Suzman was known as a fearless champion of the civil rights cause in South Africa and was one of the country's few internationally respected White politicians. She consistently opposed calls for economic sanctions against South Africa as a method of pressuring the government into abandoning its apartheid policies, rejecting the political argument that anyone who opposes apartheid must embrace sanctions. This view has led to a cooling of her relations with some Blacks in recent years but she is still greatly admired and respected by most. She resigned from politics in May 1989 after the PFP was disbanded and replaced by the Democratic Party, an organization she is not thought to support because of its willingness to accept some of the concepts of the ruling National Party.

Tambo, Oliver
Born 1917

Oliver Tambo, president of the African National Congress (ANC), was born in the Transkei. He was educated at local Anglican missionary schools before going on to Fort Hare University. He began his career as a teacher and lawyer and joined the ANC in 1944. Along with Nelson Mandela and Walter Sisulu, he became the dominant force in the organization.

Tambo was first elected to the ANC executive in 1949 and has retained his position on it ever since. He was banned in 1954 for two years for his anti-apartheid activities and was among the 154 government opponents arrested in 1956 on treason charges. He was released in 1957 and appointed deputy president of the ANC the following year. Tambo fled South Africa a week after the 1960 Sharpeville massacre and established the ANC's external wing, with its main centres in Botswana, Mozambique, Swaziland and Zambia. He became acting president of the ANC in 1967 after the death of Albert Luthuli and has been president since 1977.

Treurnicht, Andries
Born 19 February 1921

After attending the University of Stellenbosch and the University of Cape Town, Andries Treurnicht was ordained a minister in the Dutch Reformed Church in 1946 and worked in the church until 1960 when he became editor of first *Kerkbode* and then the *Hoofstad* from 1967 to 1971.

Treurnicht was first elected a member of the South African parliament in 1971. In 1976, Treurnicht joined the cabinet as minister for education and training. Successive cabinet posts were: the ministry of plural relations and development, the ministry of public works, statistics and tourism and the ministry for state administration and statistics.

In 1978, 'Connie' Mulder was forced to resign the leadership of the powerful Transvaal branch of the National Party as a result of the Information scandal. The newly elected National Party leader P.W. Botha supported moderate Stephanus Botha for the leadership of the Transvaal branch, but the Transvaal right-wingers voted overwhelmingly for Treurnicht who had established a reputation as a hardline supporter of apartheid. This effectively elevated Treurnicht to the number two position in the National Party and the arch-conservative became the main obstacle to Botha's reformist policies.

Within the cabinet, Botha and Treurnicht clashed regularly but it was not until March 1980 that the rift became public after Treurnicht made a speech protesting the participation of a Coloured team in a national schools rugby festival. At the time, Treurnicht was nearly removed from the cabinet, but protests from the right wing kept him in.

The final rift came in March 1982 when Treurnicht was expelled from the party for his failure to support Botha's proposals to share power with the Coloured and Indian communities. Shortly afterwards Treurnicht officially launched the Conservative Party and was elected its leader. Treurnicht immediately urged his supporters not to allow Botha to 'dilute' apartheid.

Out of the party, Treurnicht continued to act as a political brake on Botha as the Conservative Party took support away from the National Party's traditional Afrikaner base. Treurnicht and the Conservatives reached the peak of their power in the May 1987 general election when they won several seats from the Nationalists to emerge with 22 seats and become the official opposition. In September 1989, Treurnicht's party increased its representation to 39 seats but was reckoned to have run out of steam as it failed to make inroads into important urban areas.

Tutu, Desmond
Born 7 October 1931
Desmond Tutu was born in Klerksdorp, on the West Rand, the son of a school teacher of the Xhosa tribe and a domestic servant from the Tswana tribe. After attending the University of South Africa, Tutu went first to St Peter's Theological College in Rosettenville and then to King's College at the University of London.

Upon his return to South Africa in 1954, Tutu taught in schools for a few years before becoming an Anglican parish priest in 1960. In 1967 he was appointed to a post as lecturer at theological seminary, and then from 1970 to 1971 he was a university lecturer.

From the early 1950s, Tutu was active in opposing apartheid and in working towards turning the Anglican church in South Africa into an anti-apartheid organization. From 1972 to 1975 he was associate director of the education fund of the anti-apartheid World Council of Churches. This was followed by the post of dean of Johannesburg from 1975 to 1976 and then bishop of Lesotho from 1977 to 1978.

In 1979, Tutu was elected secretary general of the South African Council of Churches, which claims to represent some 13 million Christians – most of them Black. In this position, he became increasingly critical of government policies and a more visible figure in the anti-apartheid movement. In 1983, Tutu's campaigning activities led the government to appoint a judicial commission to investigate the activities of the Council of Churches.

But the investigation was cut short in 1984 by Tutu's appointment as bishop of Johannesburg and, later that year, he became the second Black African to receive the Nobel Peace Prize. The Nobel committee said that the award 'should be seen as a renewed recognition of the courage and heroism shown by black South Africans in their use of peaceful methods in the struggle against apartheid'.

Tutu's flair for showmanship, his strident rejection of capitalism and support for sanctions made him controversial both at home and abroad. He became one of the most prominent anti-apartheid Black leaders at large in South Africa and in 1986 was named archbishop. He led a number of delegations to P.W. Botha to protest against the declaration of the state of emergency. When Nelson Mandela was released from prison on 11 February 1990 he spent his first night of freedom in Tutu's Cape Town home.

Verwoerd, Hendrik
Born 8 September 1901 – died 6 September 1966
Verwoerd was born to Dutch parents who emigrated to South Africa when he was three months old. He attended the University of Stellenbosch and in 1927 was appointed professor of applied psychology.

In 1937, Verwoerd started to become active in politics when he was appointed editor of the newly launched Afrikaner nationalist newspaper *Die Transvaler*, which became the principal organ of the National Party. Before the Second World War, Verwoerd sympathized with Nazi Germany and during the war he actively campaigned for a policy of neutrality.

Verwoerd came to be regarded as one of the chief intellectual forces behind the National Party and its developing apartheid policies. After the 1948 National Party election landslide, Verwoerd was appointed a senator and in 1950 was named minister for native affairs. In this position he was responsible for framing most of the major apartheid legislation including the Mixed Marriages Act and the Group Areas Act.

In 1958, Verwoerd was elected to the House of Assembly. In September 1958 he was named leader of the National Party and prime minister following the death of Johannes Gerhardus Strydom. Verwoerd was described at the time of his election as a committed republican and the government's 'most rigid and forceful practitioner of apartheid'.

As prime minister, Verwoerd pushed through the Promotion of Bantu Self-Government Act of 1959 which resettled the Blacks in the Bantu homelands. His increasingly heavy-handed approach to the Black population led to an increasing number of riots which culminated in the Sharpeville massacre in March 1960.

Verwoerd considered one of his greatest achievements to be the severing of South Africa's ties with the British crown and the establishment of a republic on 31 May 1961. The same year, South Africa left the Commonwealth.

Two attempts were made on Verwoerd's life. Verwoerd survived the first attempt, on 9 April 1960, when anti-apartheid campaigner David Pratt shot him twice in the head. Verwoerd died after the second attempt when he was stabbed during a session of the House of Assembly by temporary parliamentary messenger Dimitrio Tsafendas.

Vorster, Balthazar Johannes (John)
Born 13 December 1919 – died 10 September 1983

John Vorster was born in Cape province and after attending the University of Stellenbosch entered practice as a lawyer. Before and during the Second World War, Vorster openly backed Nazi Germany and was a founding member of the Fascist and anti-British Ox-wagon Guard. In 1942 Vorster was interned for his anti-British activities.

Vorster's wartime activities kept him out of active National Party politics until 1953 when he was elected to the House of Assembly as a right-wing member of the party. In 1958 Vorster played a key role in securing the prime ministership for Hendrik Verwoerd, the architect of apartheid; for this, Vorster was rewarded with the post of deputy minister for education, arts and science.

After the Sharpeville massacre Vorster was named minister of justice. Under the Sabotage Act of 1962 he was given wide-ranging powers of arrest and detention and used them extensively to crack down on opponents of apartheid. Opposition leader Sir de Villiers Graaff described Vorster as 'the main inquisitor, lord chief justice and lord high executioner'. Vorster was minister of justice when Nelson Mandela was sentenced to prison.

Following the assassination of Hendrik Verwoerd in September 1966, Vorster was elected leader of the National Party and prime minister. In his acceptance speech, Vorster promised 'to walk further along the road set by Hendrik Verwoerd'. Vorster went on to claim that apartheid was 'not a denial of human dignity' but a means to give 'an opportunity to every individual within his own sphere'.

Vorster at first continued the isolationist foreign policies of his predecessors, refusing to move on the issue of South Africa's plans to incorporate Namibia into South Africa. He also supported the minority White government of Ian Smith in Rhodesia and South Africa became the major conduit for goods breaking the UN-imposed embargo of Rhodesia.

But changing international circumstances also forced changes in Vorster's policies. The 1975 collapse of Portuguese rule in Mozambique and Angola and the establishment of hostile Black governments in those countries had the single biggest impact. Vorster at first tried to use force to topple the government in Angola but when he failed to win US support he was compelled to withdraw and pursue a policy of *détente*. In August 1975 he held an historic meeting with Zambian President Kenneth Kaunda at Victoria Falls. Vorster's *détente* policy, however, made no further progress.

International repercussions also forced Vorster to relax some of the restrictions of apartheid, although the main pillars remained firmly in place. In an attempt to win more public support, Vorster's information minister, 'Connie' Mulder, secretly funded the establishment of a pro-government newspaper and attempted to buy the *Washington Star*. The resultant Information scandal, also known as 'Muldergate', led to the resignation of Mulder. In September 1978 Vorster resigned as prime minister on 'health grounds' and was appointed to the then largely ceremonial post of president. But in June 1979 he was forced to resign when it was revealed that he had known about the misuse of the Information scandal funds.

BIBLIOGRAPHY

Adam, Heribert and Hermann Biliomee, *The Rise and Crisis of Afrikaner Power* (David Philip, Cape Town, 1979).

Annual Register, The, *Annual Surveys 1948–1990* (Longman, Harlow).

Arnold, Millard, ed. *Testimony of Steve Biko* (Maurice Temple Smith, London, 1978).

Ballinger, Margaret, *From Union to Apartheid* (Bailey Bros and Swinfen, Folkestone, 1969).

Benson, Mary, *South Africa: The Struggle for a Birthright* (Penguin, London, 1966).

Biko, Steve, *I Write What I Like* (Harper and Row, San Francisco, 1978).

Brooks, Alan and Brickhill, Jeremy, *Whirlwind before the Storm: The Origins and Development of the Uprising in Soweto and the Rest of South Africa from June to December 1976* (International Defence and Aid Fund, London, 1980).

Bunting, Brian, *The Rise of the South African Reich* (Penguin, London, 1964).

Buthelezi, Gatsha, *Power is Ours* (Books in Focus, New York, 1979).

Butler, Jeffrey, Rothberg, R.I. and Adams, John, *The Black Homelands of South Africa* (University of California Press, Berkeley, 1977).

Carter, Gwendolen M., *The Politics of Inequality: South Africa since 1948* (Praeger, New York, 1958).

Carter, Gwendolen M. and O'Mears, Patrick, *South Africa: The Continuing Crisis* (Indiana University Press, Bloomington, 1979).

Davenport, T.R.H., *South Africa – A Modern History* (Macmillan, South Africa, 1977).

Davidson, Basil, Slovo, Joe and Wilkinson, Anthony, *South Africa: The New Politics of Revolution* (Penguin, London, 1976).

Facts On File Yearbooks 1948–1990 (Facts On File, New York).

First, Ruth, Steele, Jonathan and Gurney, Christabel, *The South African Connection* (Temple Smith, London, 1972).

Gann, L.H. and Duignan, Peter, *Why South Africa will Survive* (Croom Helm, London, 1981).

Harrison, David, *The White Tribe of Africa: South Africa in Perspective* (BBC Publications, London, 1981).

Hellmann, Ellen and Lever, Henry, *Conflict and Progress (Fifty Years of Race Relations in South Africa)* (Macmillan, South Africa, 1979).

Hepple, Alex, *South Africa: A Political and Economic History* (Pall Mall Press, London, 1966).

Hirson, Baruch, *Year of Fire, Year of Ash: The Soweto Revolt: Roots of a Revolution?* (Zed Press, London, 1979).

Horrell, Muriel, *Laws Affecting Race Relations in South Africa; Annual 1948–1976* (South African Institute of Race Relations, Johannesburg, 1978).

International Defence and Aid Fund, *Apartheid: The Facts* (London, 1983).

International Defence and Aid Fund, *Namibia: The Facts* (London, 1989).

Johnson, R.W., *How Long will South Africa Survive?* (Macmillan Press, London, 1977).

Kane-Berman, John, *Soweto, Black Revolt, White Reaction* (Ravan Press, Johannesburg, 1978).

BIBLIOGRAPHY

Keesing's Contemporary Archives, Annual Surveys 1948–1990 (Longman, Harlow).

Kenney, Henry, *Architect of Apartheid* (Jonathan Ball, Johannesburg, 1979).

Knightly, Philip, *The First Casualty* (Andre Deutsch, London, 1975).

Lapchick, Richard, *The Politics of Race and International Sport: The Case of South Africa* (Greenwood Press, Westport, Connecticut, 1975).

Laurence, Patrick, *South Africa's Politics of Partition: The Transkei* (Ravan Press, Johannesburg, 1976).

Mandela, Nelson, *The Struggle is My Life* (International Defence and Aid Fund Publications, London, 1990).

Marquard, Leo, *The Peoples and Policies of South Africa* (Oxford University Press, Oxford, 1969).

Matshoba, Mtutuzeli, *Call Me Not a Man* (Ravan Press, Johannesburg, 1979).

Meer, Fatima, *Higher Than Hope* (Hamish Hamilton, London, 1988).

Meli, Francis, *South Africa belongs to Us* (James Curry, London, 1988).

Official Yearbook of the Republic of South Africa, 15th edition 1989–90 (South African Bureau of Information, Pretoria, 1990).

Price, Robert and Rosberg, Carl, eds. *The Apartheid Regime: Political Power and Racial Domination* (University of California, Institute of International Studies, Berkeley, 1980).

Report of the Study Commission on US Policy Toward Southern Africa, *South Africa: Time Running Out* (University of California Press, Berkeley, 1981).

Rogers, Barbara, *Divide and Rule: South Africa's Bantustans* (International Defence and Aid Fund, London, 1976).

Rosenthal, Eric, *Encyclopaedia of South Africa* (Frederick Warne, London, 1973).

St Jorre, John de, *A House Divided: South Africa's Uncertain Future* (Carnegie Endowment for International Peace, New York, 1977).

Sachs, E.S., *The Anatomy of Apartheid* (Collets, London, 1965).

Serfontein, J.H.P., *Brotherhood of Power* (Rex Collings, London, 1979).

Stultz, Newell, M., *Transkei's Half Loaf: Race Separatism in South Africa* (Yale University Press, New Haven, 1979).

Temkin, Ben, *Gatsha Buthelezi – Zulu Statesman* (Purnell, Cape Town, 1976).

Thompson, Leonard and Wilson, Monica, eds. *The Oxford History of South Africa*, 2 volumes, (Oxford University Press, New York 1969, 1971).

Wilkins, Ivor and Strydom, Hans, *The Super-Afrikaners* (Jonathan Ball, Johannesburg, 1978).

Woods, Donald, *Biko* (Paddington Press, London, 1978).

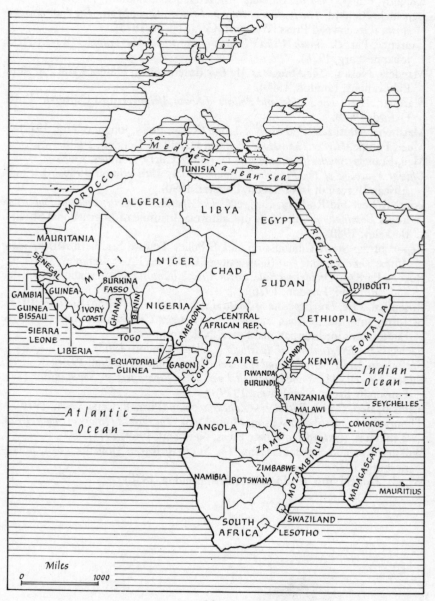

Africa

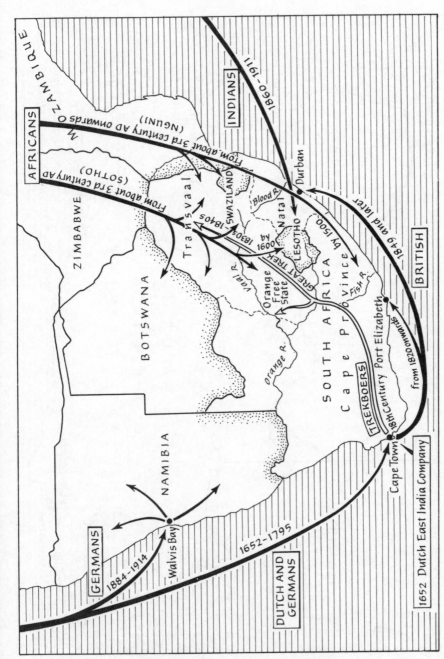

Movements of people into South Africa

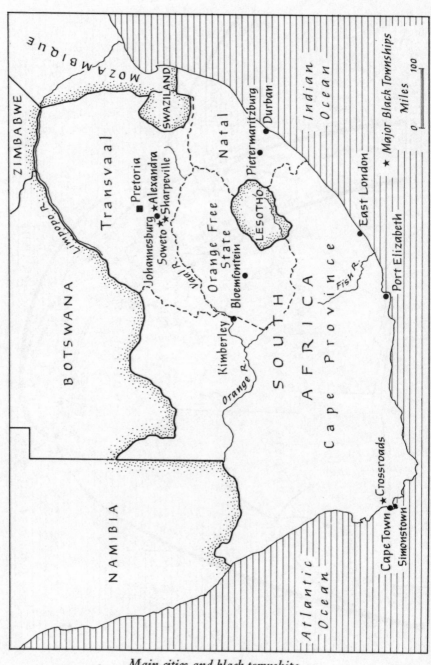

Main cities and black townships

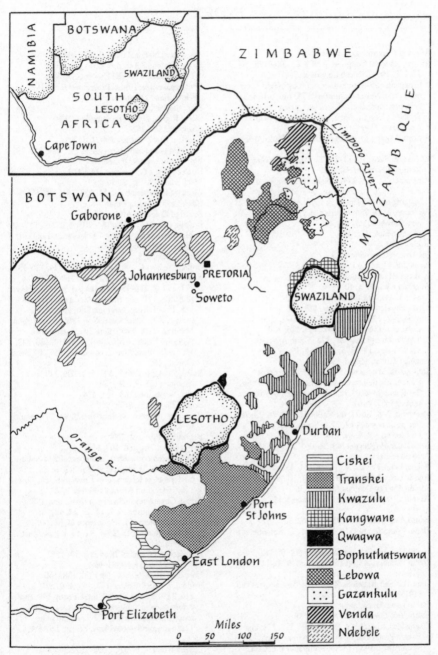

The homelands

INDEX

INDEX

INDEX